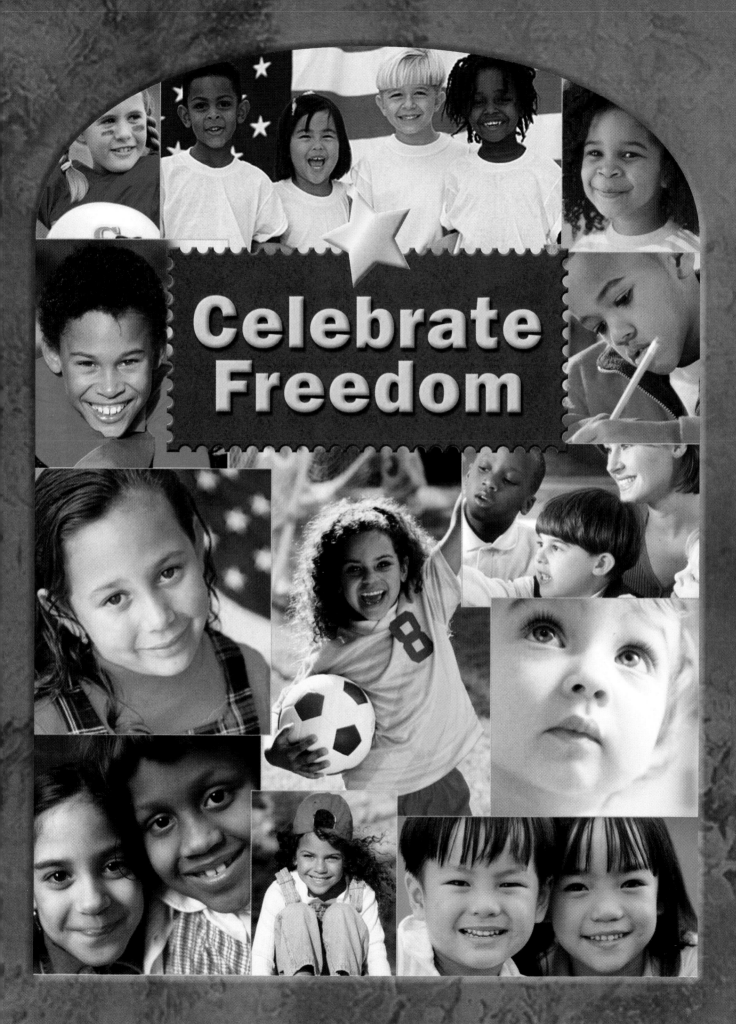

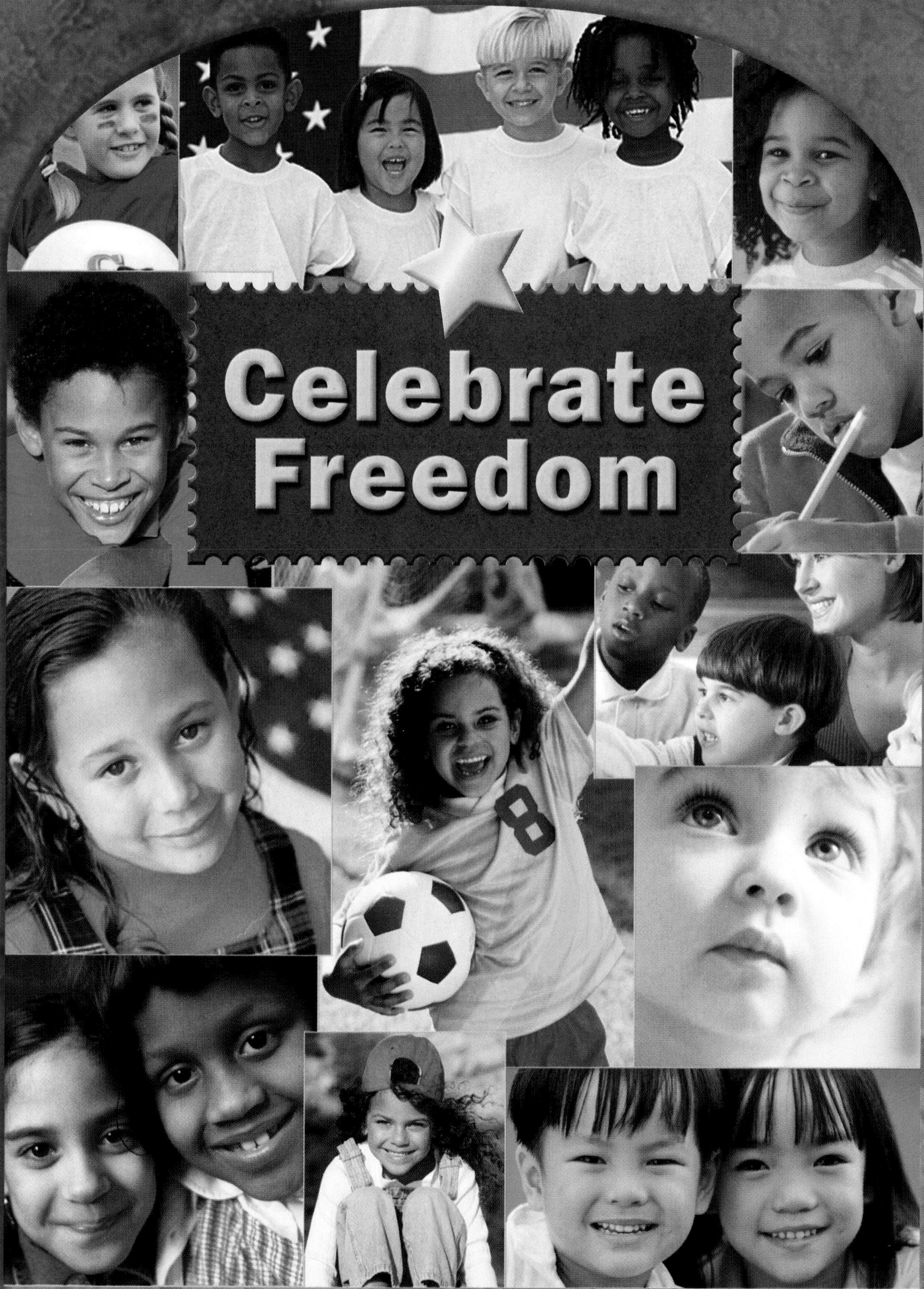
Celebrate
Freedom

Celebrate Freedom

Our country has three important documents. These are the Declaration of Independence, the Constitution, and the Bill of Rights. Words from these documents have been changed here to help you understand them.

Declaration of Independence, 1776

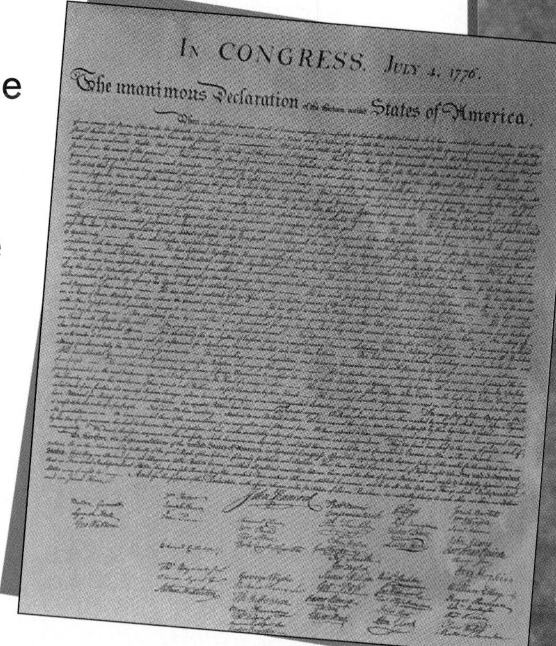

In CONGRESS, July 4, 1776.

The unanimous Declaration of the thirteen united States of America.

We want to change our government. We think it is important to explain our reasons for separating from England. The king does not treat us fairly. Americans believe that all people have rights. We are all free and equal. Everyone has the right to life, freedom, and happiness. We believe that a good government should care for its people.

- **What should a good government do for its people?**

Constitution of the United States of America, 1789

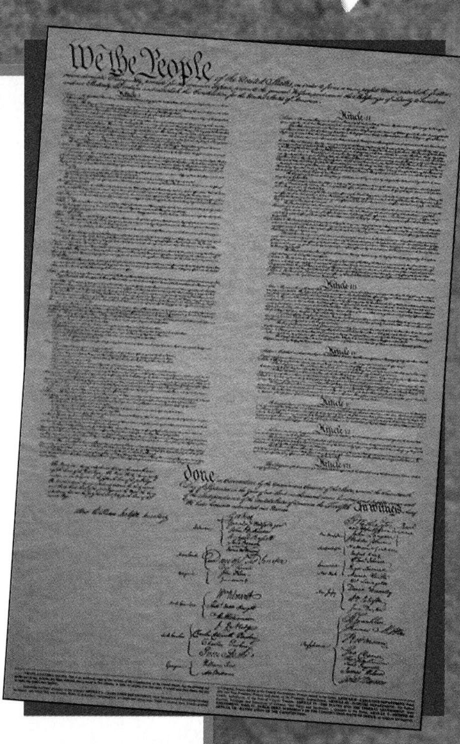

We the People

We the people of the United States want to form a better nation. We want to establish justice and peace. We want to protect and help our people. We want to be a free country. These are our laws. This is how our government will work.

- **What is one thing the Constitution says the people want?**

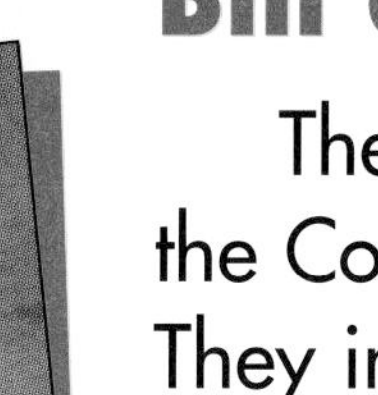

Bill of Rights, 1791

The first ten Amendments (additions) to the Constitution are called the Bill of Rights. They include:

- Freedom of religion
- Freedom of speech
- Freedom of the press
- Freedom to gather and discuss government

- **What is the Bill of Rights?**

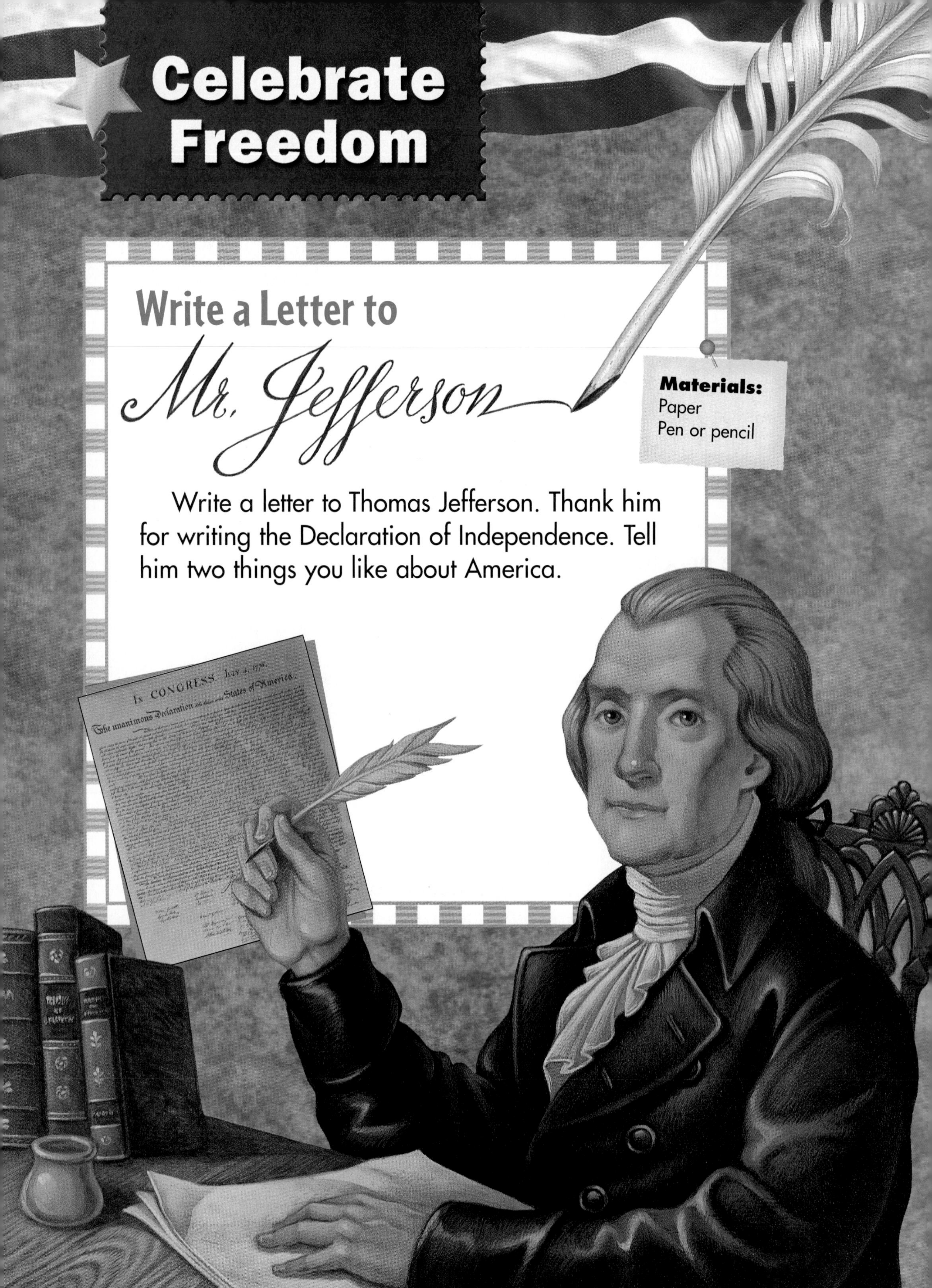

Celebrate Freedom

Write a Letter to Mr. Jefferson

Materials:
Paper
Pen or pencil

Write a letter to Thomas Jefferson. Thank him for writing the Declaration of Independence. Tell him two things you like about America.

Materials:
Construction paper
Markers
Yarn or ribbon

Make a Constitutional Scroll

The Constitution of the United States lists the laws of our country. Laws protect us and make sure that we are fair and do not hurt each other.

Make a list of rules for your school. It will be your constitution. Try to make your rules fair for everyone. Make one rule to keep students safe. Write other rules that would make your school a better place.

Begin your constitution: *"We the students of (Your School Name), in order to make a better, safer, and happier school, list the following rules:"*

Write the school constitution on construction paper. Roll it up. Find a colorful ribbon or piece of yarn to tie it with.

School Constitution
We the students of P.S. 22, in order to make a better, safer, and happier school, list the following rules:
1 Raise your hand before talking in class.
2 Do not run in halls.
3 More class trips.

Celebrate Freedom

Plan a News Show

Materials:
Paper
Markers
Desk
Chairs

"Freedom of the Press" is one of the freedoms in the Bill of Rights. This means that reporters can give the news without the government telling them what to say. It is important for people to have good information. That way, they will be able to make good choices about their lives and government.

Divide into groups and plan a TV news show about things happening in the school or community. Have each group write a paragraph describing an event. Take turns reading your reports to the class.

The Pledge of Allegiance

I pledge allegiance to the flag of the United States of America, and to the Republic for which it stands, one Nation under God, indivisible, with liberty and justice for all.

The National Anthem

Oh, say, can you see, by the dawn's early light,
What so proudly we hailed at the twilight's last gleaming?
Whose broad stripes and bright stars, thro' the perilous fight,
O'er the ramparts we watched, were so gallantly streaming.
And the rockets' red glare, the bombs bursting in air,
Gave proof through the night that our flag was still there.
Oh, say, does that star-spangled banner yet wave
O'er the land of the free and the home of the brave?

History

Working for Freedom

Many Americans have made sacrifices to help our country stay free. Some have even given their lives for our country. Others have worked to protect freedom and equality for all of us.

Elizabeth Cady Stanton

Suffragist

"It is the duty of the women of this country to [gain the right to vote]."

Stanton wrote these words at the first Women's Rights Convention, which met July 19, 1848 in Seneca Falls, New York.

Nathan Hale

American soldier in the Revolutionary War

"I only regret that I have but one life to lose for my country."

In 1776, Americans fought a war to gain freedom from England. Twenty-one-year-old Nathan Hale said these words to the British soldiers who had taken him prisoner. Even when he knew he would be killed, Nathan was proud to fight for his country.

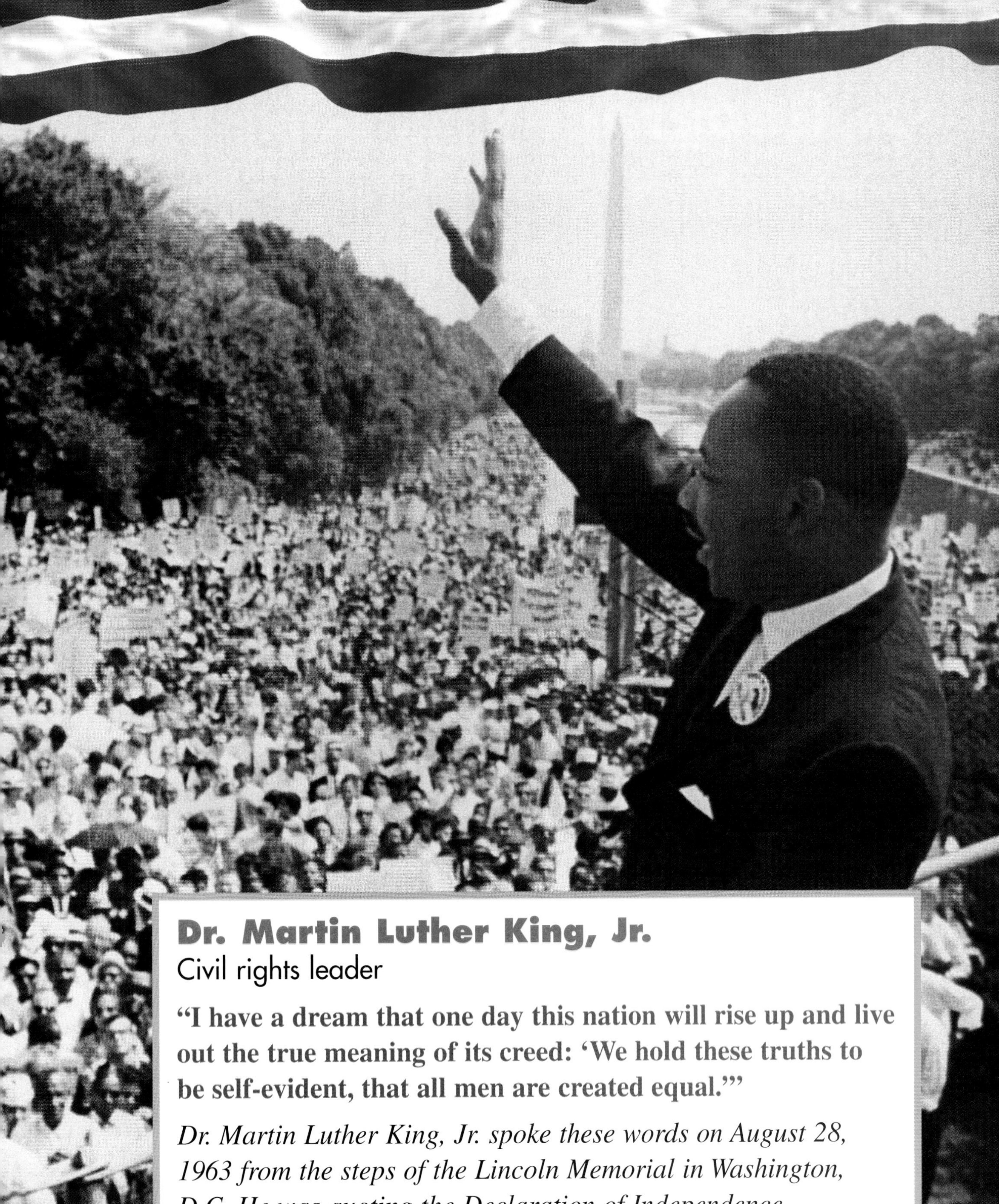

Dr. Martin Luther King, Jr.

Civil rights leader

"I have a dream that one day this nation will rise up and live out the true meaning of its creed: 'We hold these truths to be self-evident, that all men are created equal.'"

Dr. Martin Luther King, Jr. spoke these words on August 28, 1963 from the steps of the Lincoln Memorial in Washington, D.C. He was quoting the Declaration of Independence.

Geography

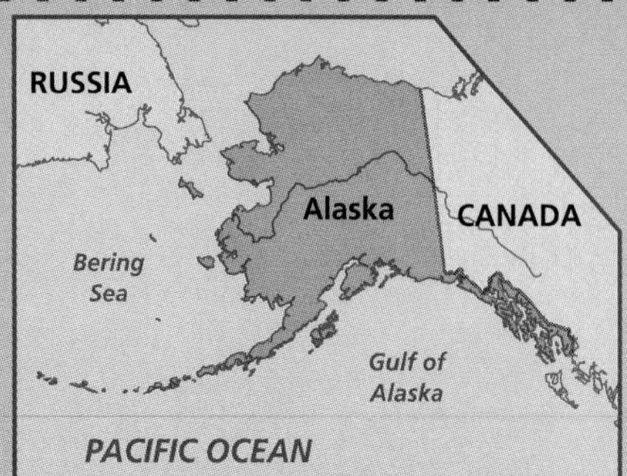

America's Parks

Some United States communities have places that are special to all Americans. These places are called national parks. National parks preserve, or care for, places that are special to America.

What are national parks?

Mount Rushmore

Golden Gate Bridge

PACIFIC OCEAN

MEXICO

Statue of Liberty
Washington Monument
Gateway Arch
Carlsbad Caverns National Park
CANADA
North Dakota
South Dakota
ebraska
Kansas
Oklahoma
Texas
Minnesota
Iowa
Missouri
Arkansas
Louisiana
Wisconsin
Illinois
Michigan
Indiana
Ohio
Kentucky
Tennessee
Mississippi
Alabama
Georgia
Florida
South Carolina
North Carolina
Virginia
West Virginia
Maryland
Delaware
New Jersey
Pennsylvania
New York
Connecticut
Rhode Island
Massachusetts
Vermont
New Hampshire
Maine
Lake Superior
Lake Michigan
Lake Huron
Lake Ontario
Lake Erie
Missouri River
Ohio River
Mississippi River
Brazos River
Grande
ATLANTIC OCEAN
All

Economics

Businesses Making Cents

American businesses produce many different goods and services. Jobs in our communities are based on businesses. Some communities are known for the type of work that many people do there.

 **What do businesses do?**

Shipping, New Orleans, Louisiana

Oil Refining, Houston, Texas

Cheese making, Wisconsin

Film making, Hollywood, California

Government

Community Government

A local government solves problems in a city or a town. The leader of most local governments is the mayor. The local government makes sure the community has the services it needs. Some services are police and fire protection, garbage pickup, and health services.

Who usually leads community government?

Citizenship

Helping People

The Red Cross is an organization that helps communities during hard times. When an earthquake or flood affects a community, workers from the Red Cross arrive quickly. They provide shelter for those left homeless. They collect clothing and food for people. The Red Cross also collects blood for hospitals.

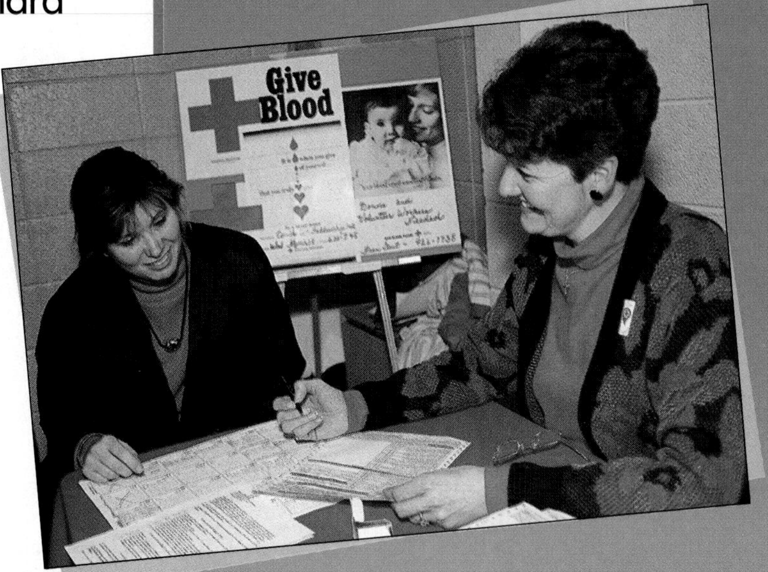

What is the Red Cross?

Red Cross volunteers

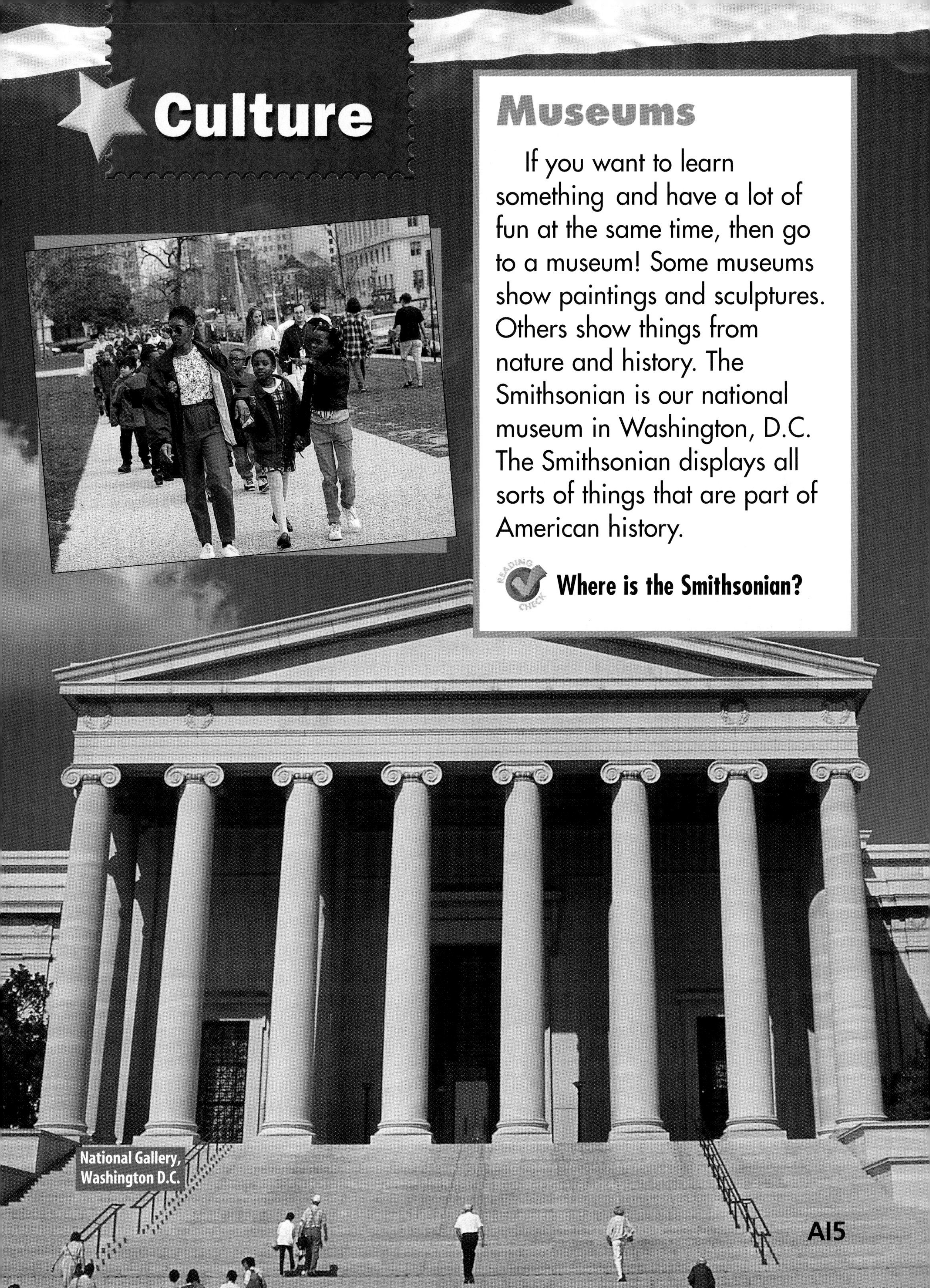

Culture

Museums

If you want to learn something and have a lot of fun at the same time, then go to a museum! Some museums show paintings and sculptures. Others show things from nature and history. The Smithsonian is our national museum in Washington, D.C. The Smithsonian displays all sorts of things that are part of American history.

READING CHECK **Where is the Smithsonian?**

Science, Technology, and Society

Inventions Change Our Communities

There is a saying, "Necessity is the mother of invention." This means that people make things to meet their needs. Inventions make our lives easier or more fun. Think about what your life would be like without things like refrigerators, cars, or electric light. Believe it or not, none of these inventions was widely used only 100 years ago.

What are inventions?

Macmillan/McGraw-Hill

Our Communities

McGraw Hill

NATIONAL GEOGRAPHIC

BEING A GOOD CITIZEN

In this textbook you will meet special people and learn many important things. The stories you read will help you understand some important words that define what it means to be a good citizen. These words are listed below. They help us understand how to be better citizens in our home, neighborhood, school, community, country, and world.

★**COURAGE**★
being brave in the face of difficulty

★**FREEDOM**★
making choices and holding beliefs of one's own

★**HONESTY**★
telling the truth

★**JUSTICE**★
working toward fair treatment for everyone

★**LEADERSHIP**★
showing good behavior worth following through example

★**LOYALTY**★
showing support for people and one's country

★**RESPECT**★
treating others as you would like to be treated

★**RESPONSIBILITY**★
being worthy of trust

About the Cover: A colorful hot-air balloon soars above an image of the town of Camden, Maine.

Macmillan/McGraw-Hill

Our Communities

James A. Banks

Richard G. Boehm

Kevin P. Colleary

Gloria Contreras

A. Lin Goodwin

Mary A. McFarland

Walter C. Parker

Mc
Graw
Hill
Macmillan
McGraw-Hill
New York

PROGRAM AUTHORS

Dr. James A. Banks
Russell F. Stark University Professor and Director of the Center for Multicultural Education
University of Washington
Seattle, Washington

Dr. Richard G. Boehm
Jesse H. Jones Distinguished Chair in Geographic Education
Director, The Gilbert M. Grosvenor Center for Geographic Education
Southwest Texas State University
San Marcos, Texas

Dr. Kevin P. Colleary
Curriculum and Teaching Department
Hunter College
City University of New York
New York, New York

Dr. Gloria Contreras
Professor of Education
University of North Texas
Denton, Texas

Dr. A. Lin Goodwin
Associate Professor of Education
Department of Curriculum and Teaching
Teachers College
Columbia University
New York, New York

Dr. Mary A. McFarland
Social Studies, Education Consultant, K–12,
St. Louis, Missouri

Dr. Walter C. Parker
Professor of Education and Chair of Social Studies Education
University of Washington
Seattle, Washington

Washington, D.C.

HISTORIANS/SCHOLARS

Dr. Joyce Appleby
Professor of History
University of California, Los Angeles
Los Angeles, California

Dr. Alan Brinkley
Professor of American History
Columbia University
New York, New York

Dr. Nancy Cott
Stanley Woodward Professor of History and American Studies
Yale University
New Haven, Connecticut

Dr. James McPherson
George Henry Davis Professor of American History
Princeton University
Princeton, New Jersey

Dr. Donald A. Ritchie
Associate Historian of the United States Senate Historical Office
Washington, D.C.

Dr. John L. Esposito
Professor of Religion and International Affairs, and Director of the Center for Christian-Muslim Understanding
Georgetown University
Washington, D.C.

PROGRAM CONSULTANTS

Betty Ruth Baker, M.Ed.
Assistant Professor of Curriculum and Instruction
Early Childhood Specialist
School of Education
Baylor University
Waco, Texas

Dr. Randolph B. Campbell
Regents' Professor of History
University of North Texas
Denton, Texas

Dr. Steven Cobb
Director, Center for Economic Education
Chair, Department of Economics
University of North Texas
Denton, Texas

Frank de Varona, Ed.S.
Visiting Associate Professor
Florida International University
Miami, Florida

READING INSTRUCTION CONSULTANTS

M. Frankie Dungan, M.Ed.
Reading/Language Arts Consultant, K–6
Mansfield, Texas

Antonio A. Fierro
Program Director for the Texas Reading Initiative, Region 19
El Paso, Texas

Carol Ritchey, M.Ed.
Reading Specialist
Tarver Rendon Elementary School
Burleson, Texas

Dr. William H. Rupley
Professor of Reading Education
Distinguished Research Fellow
Department of Teaching, Learning and Culture
College of Education
Texas A&M University
College Station, Texas

GRADE LEVEL CONSULTANTS

Taber Akin
Third Grade Teacher
Richfield Intermediate School
Richfield, Minnesota

Linda Carleton
Coordinator of Elementary Science, Health, and Social Studies
Wichita Public Schools
Wichita, Kansas

Barb Ceresia
Third Grade Teacher
Wyman Elementary School
St. Louis, Missouri

Virginia Grace
Instructional Coordinator
Cole Elementary School
St. Louis Public Schools
St. Louis, Missouri

Monica Nelson
Third Grade Teacher
Richfield Intermediate School
Richfield, Minnesota

Lacy Prince
Computer Lab Teacher
Pleasantville Elementary School
Houston, Texas

Dell Rodriguez
Third Grade Teacher
Spring Shadows Elementary
Houston, Texas

Avon Ruffin
K–12 Social Studies Instructional Specialist
Winston-Salem/Forsyth County Schools
Winston-Salem, North Carolina

Beth Rustenhaven
Gifted Specialist for Grades K–3
John Garner Elementary School
Grand Prairie, Texas

Dr. Christine Yeh
Child Psychologist
Columbia University
New York, New York

CONTRIBUTING WRITERS

Dinah Zike
Comfort, Texas

Karen C. Baicker
Maplewood, New Jersey

June Lee
New York, New York

Marlyn Mangus
Goodland, Kansas

Linda Scher
Raleigh, North Carolina

RFB&D
learning through listening

Students with print disabilities may be eligible to obtain an accessible, audio version of the pupil edition of this textbook. Please call Recording for the Blind & Dyslexic at 1-800-221-4792 for complete information.

Acknowledgments

The publisher gratefully acknowledges permission to reprint the following copyrighted material:

From **The Town That Moved** by Mary Jane Finsand, pictures by Reg Sandland. Copyright © 1983 by Carolrhoda Books, Inc. Used by permission. From "This Land Is Your Land." Words and Music by Woody Guthrie. Copyright © 1940, (Renewed 1956), (Renewed 1970), Ludlow Music, Inc., New York, New York. Used by permission.

(continued on page R52)

Macmillan/McGraw-Hill

A Division of The ***McGraw·Hill*** *Companies*

Published by Macmillan/McGraw-Hill, of McGraw-Hill Education, a division of The McGraw-Hill Companies, Inc., Two Penn Plaza, New York, New York 10121.

Printed in the United States of America

ISBN 0-02-149264-6

5 6 7 8 9 058/043 06 05 04 03

Contents

NATIONAL GEOGRAPHIC

Unit 5

REFERENCE SECTION

FEATURES

Skills Lessons

Citizenship

Literature

Biographies

Primary Sources

CHARTS, GRAPHS, & DIAGRAMS

TIME LINES

MAPS

Social Studies Handbook

The Social Studies Strands are a way of thinking about Social Studies. Social Studies is the study of people and the world we live in. One way to think about Social Studies is to break it into parts. We call these parts the strands.

The pie chart on the next page shows the eight strands of Social Studies. Each strand teaches us something about the world. As you read your textbook, think about how the Social Studies strands work together to help you understand our world.

The Eight Strands of Social Studies

Economics

Wants and needs, goods and services. Basic human needs are met in a variety of ways.

Citizenship

Rights, responsibilities, pride and hope. Our beliefs and principles help make up our national identity.

Culture

Holidays, traditions, and stories. We learn about ourselves and our families through the customs we share and celebrate.

Geography

Location, place, maps, and more. People and environments surround us and are ever changing.

Science, Technology, and Society

Inventions, computers, and ideas. Technology has changed how people live together in the world.

Social Studies Skills

Many special skills are needed to better understand the world around you.

History

Time and chronology, years and dates. Historical figures and ordinary people help shape our lives.

Government

People work to make the laws that influence our lives. People work with citizens to govern.

Thinking About Reading

Your Social Studies book gives information about people, the communities in which they live, and their governments. Learning *how* to read your book will help you better understand the information that is presented. Below you will find some helpful ways to become an effective Social Studies reader.

Preview → Ask → Read → Review

How to Preview, Ask, Read, and Review:

1. **Preview the lesson.** Read the title, the headings, and the words that are highlighted. Look at the pictures and maps, and read their captions. Think about what you know about the topic. Form an idea of what the lesson is about.
2. **Ask yourself questions before you read.** You might ask, "What new information will I learn in this lesson?"
3. **Read and reread.** Read the lesson carefully. Reread any sentences that do not make sense to you. Look up the meanings of any words you do not know.
4. **Review, or think about, what you have read.** Did you find the answers to your questions?

Preview.
As I look over the page, the title tells me this lesson will be about communication by wire. The highlighted words tell me important people or terms to learn.

Ask yourself questions.
I ask myself, "What will I learn about communication?"

Read and reread.
I carefully read the sentences. I will look up the meaning of *codes*.

Review.
I think about the answer to my question.

Communication by Wire

Samuel Morse was one of the early inventors of the machine called the **telegraph**. The telegraph used special codes to send messages long distances over wires. In 1844 Morse had workers run a wire from Washington, D.C., to Baltimore, Maryland. He then sat in the Capitol building and tapped out the very first telegraph message.

By 1861 telegraph wires ran across the country. People could now get news from faraway places in minutes.

Before long another invention changed how people communicated. In 1876 **Alexander Graham Bell** built a working telephone. People could now speak to each other directly from faraway places.

Use Visuals

An important way to understand what you read is to use **visuals**. Visuals are the pictures, maps, charts, and graphs that you see in your book.

Tip!

★ When looking at graphs, maps, or charts, read the key to find out the meanings of special symbols.

★ Look for objects in the picture that may give more information.

How to Use Visuals

Look closely at the visual. Then ask yourself the following questions:

- What does the picture, map, chart, or graph show?
- How does it help me understand what I have read?
- How does it add to the information I have read?
- What information does the caption or label provide?

Study the picture below. It shows how robots are used to make automobiles. Then read the caption.

Look at the number of robots and how they are being used.

Robots do many jobs on assembly lines, including welding.

The caption tells us that robots work on assembly lines.

Study the picture below. Then copy the diagram on a separate sheet of paper. Think about the information in the picture and caption. Then complete the diagram to tell more about the picture.

A dogsled race is run down a main street in Anchorage, Alaska.

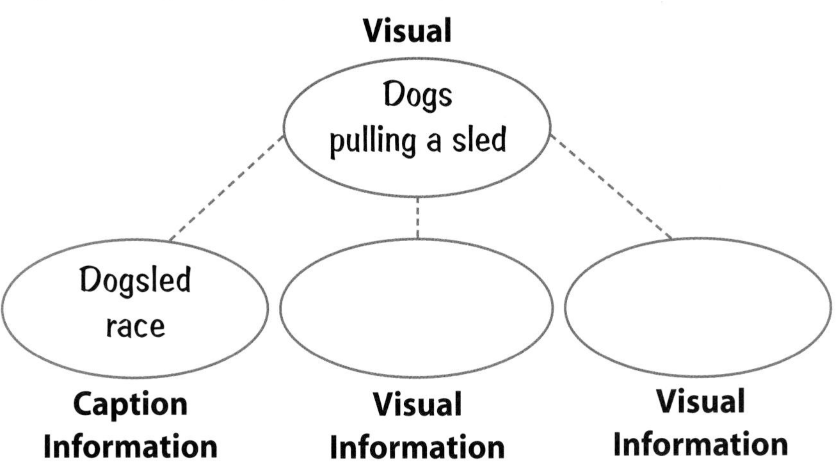

Practice Activities!

1. **Use Visuals** Study the photographs and read the caption on page 13. What can you learn from them?
2. **Create a Visual** Draw a picture of an important place in your community. Then write a caption. Exchange visuals with a classmate, and discuss them.

Keep in Mind

For more help in using visuals, keep these strategies in mind:

Study the pictures.
The pictures of people and events will help you understand what you are reading. The labels and captions give information about the pictures.

Study the maps.
The maps show you places where events have happened.

Study the chapter openers.
The first pages of a chapter give a preview of the chapter's information.

Welcome to Washington, D.C.

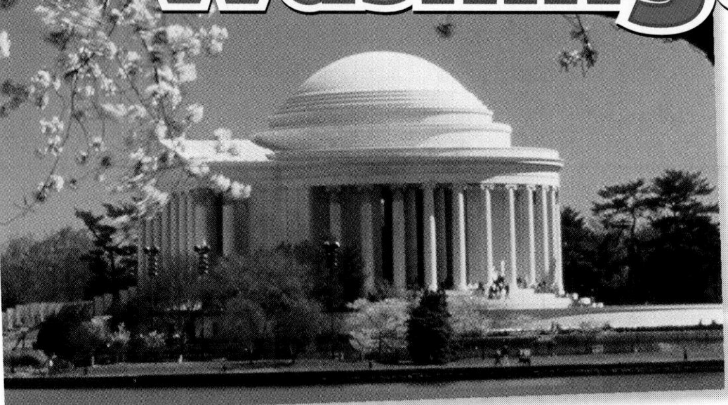

In the spring the cherry blossoms around the Jefferson Memorial are very colorful.

Lightning during a thunderstorm brightens the sky near the Washington Monument.

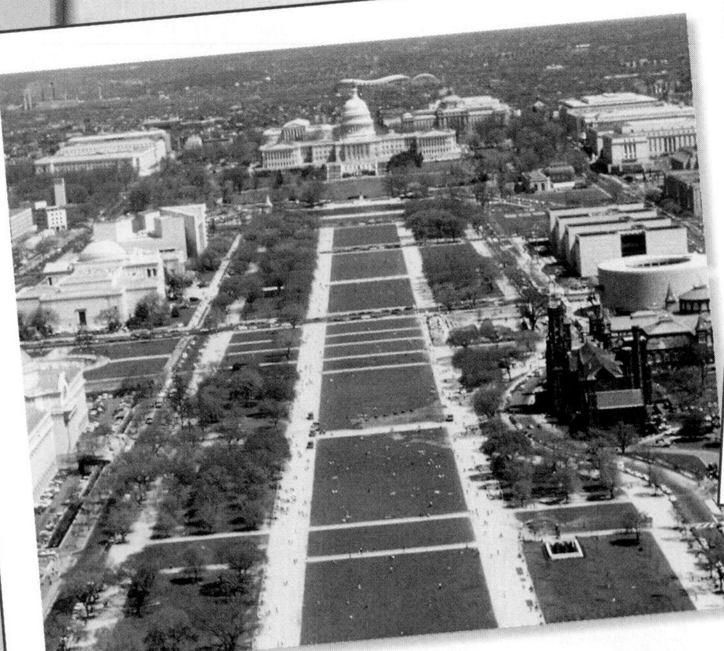

The museums of the Smithsonian are close to the Capitol.

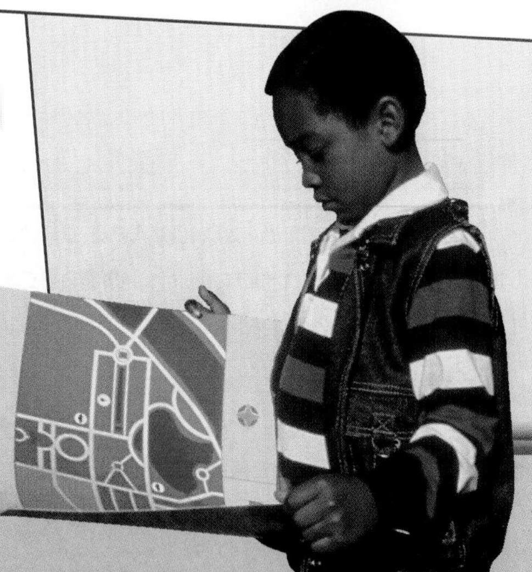

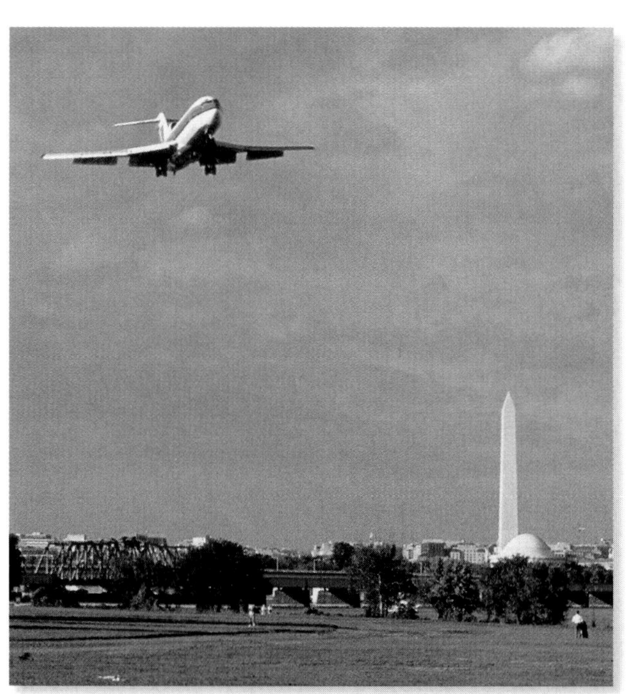

Airplanes move people and goods to and from the area.

People use maps to help them decide where to build roads, parks, and buildings.

People changed the land along the Potomac River. They built paths for walking, in-line skating, and bike riding.

Using Globes

VOCABULARY

North Pole
South Pole
equator

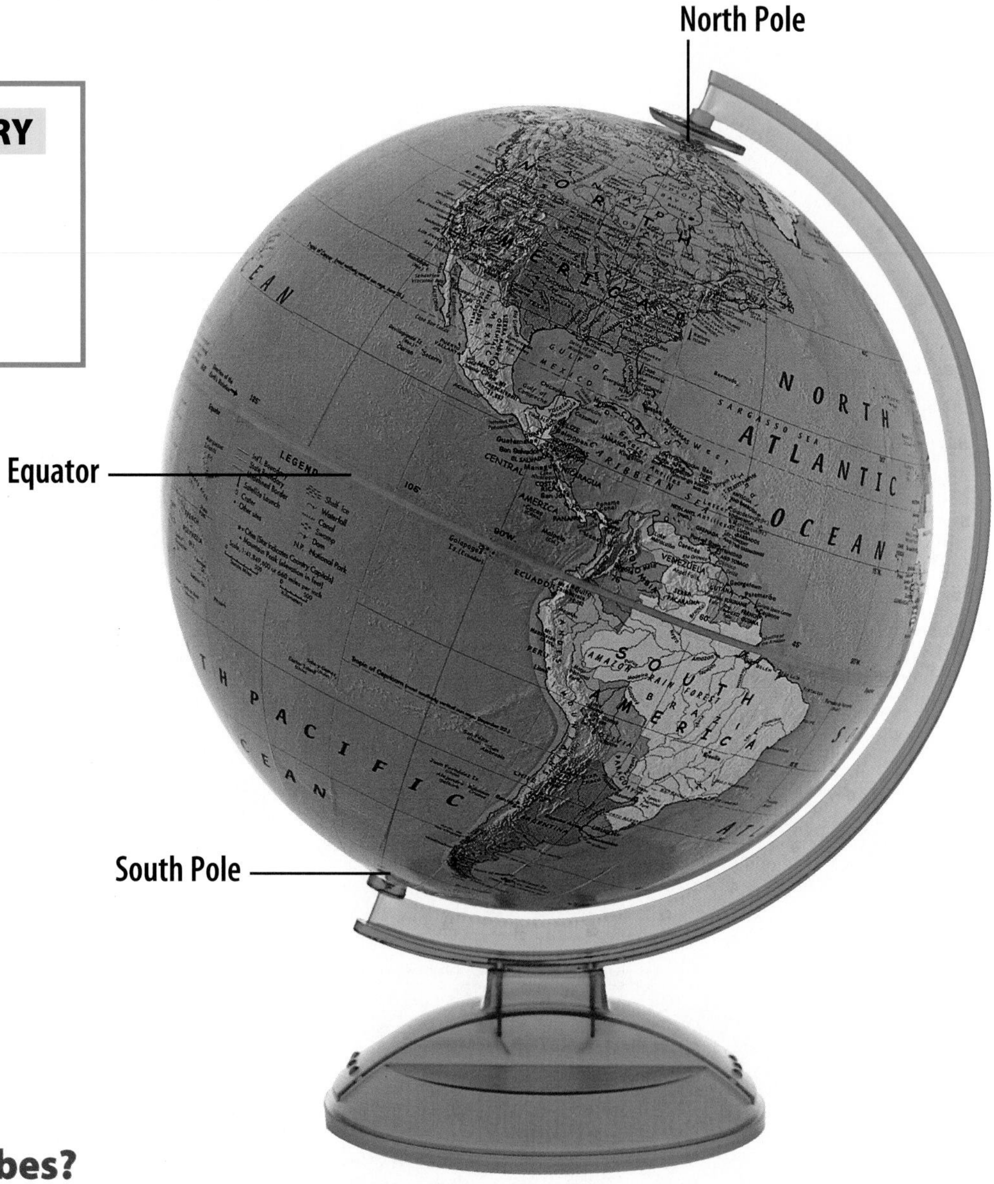

North Pole

Equator

South Pole

What are globes?

- A globe is a model, or copy, of Earth.
- Find the **North Pole** and the **South Pole** on the globe. The North Pole is the farthest place north on Earth. The South Pole is the farthest place south on Earth.
- Find the **equator** on the globe. The equator is an imaginary line circling Earth. It is halfway between the North Pole and the South Pole. Above the equator is the northern half of Earth. Below it is the southern half.

Using Maps

VOCABULARY

- continent
- ocean
- map symbol
- map key
- cardinal direction
- compass rose
- locator

What are maps?

- A map is a flat drawing of a place. This map shows the world.
- The world has seven **continents**. A continent is a very large body of land. Find and name the continents on the map.
- The world has four **oceans**. An ocean is a very large body of water. Find and name the oceans on the map.

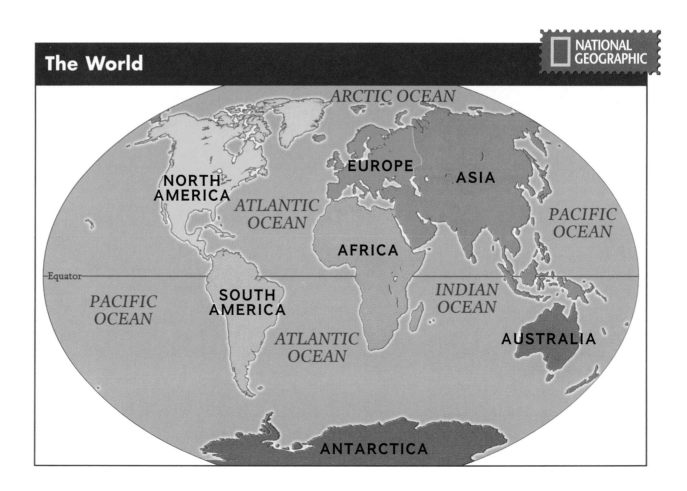

The World

NATIONAL GEOGRAPHIC

ARCTIC OCEAN
NORTH AMERICA
EUROPE
ASIA
ATLANTIC OCEAN
PACIFIC OCEAN
AFRICA
Equator
PACIFIC OCEAN
SOUTH AMERICA
INDIAN OCEAN
ATLANTIC OCEAN
AUSTRALIA
ANTARCTICA

Why do maps use symbols?

- The photo below shows a real place. The map on the next page shows the same place. How are the photo and the map alike? How are they different?
- Many maps have **map symbols**. Map symbols are drawings that stand for real things.
- Symbols can be lines, colors, or pictures. The same kind of symbol sometimes stands for different things on other maps. The color green, for example, could stand for parks on one map and farmland on another. What symbols do you see on the map?

What can the map title and map key tell you?

- The map title tells you what the map shows. Find the title on this map.
- A **map key** tells you what the symbols on a map stand for. What does the blue circle stand for on the map below? What symbol means tree?

NATIONAL GEOGRAPHIC

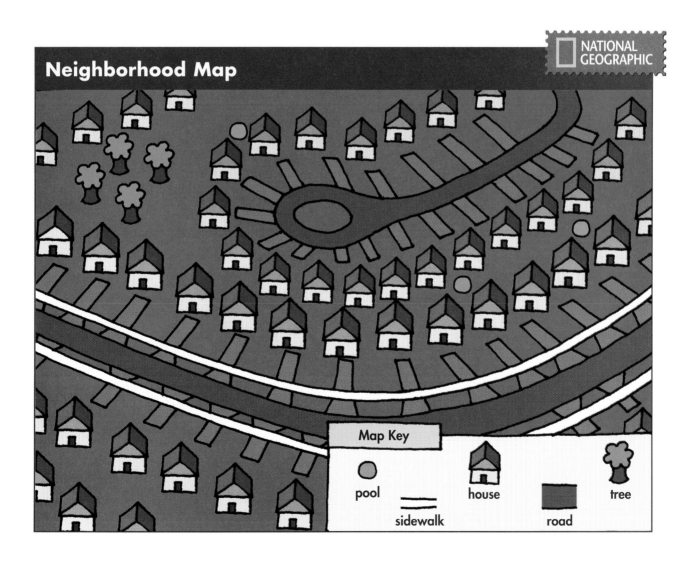

Neighborhood Map

Map Key

pool
sidewalk
house
road
tree

Reviewing Geography Skills

What are cardinal directions?

- There are four **cardinal directions**. They are north, south, east, and west.
- North is the direction toward the North Pole. When you face the North Pole, you are facing north. South is directly behind you.

What is a compass rose?

- A **compass rose** is a small drawing on a map that helps you find directions.
- Look at the compass rose on this page. North is shown by the letter **N**. What letters stand for east, south, and west?
- Look at the map of Texas on this page. Find its compass rose. What cities are north of Austin? What city is directly east of Austin?

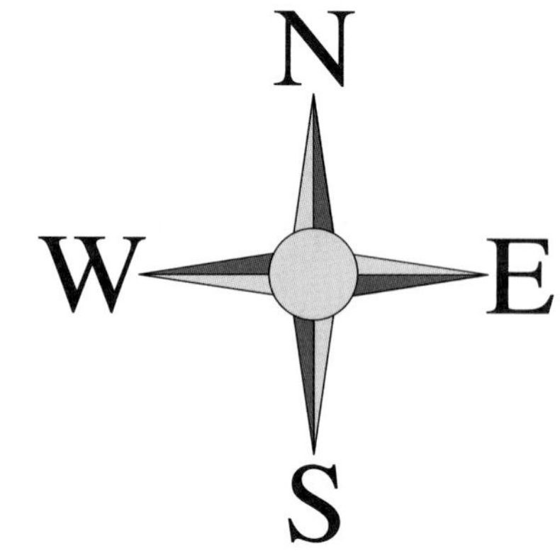

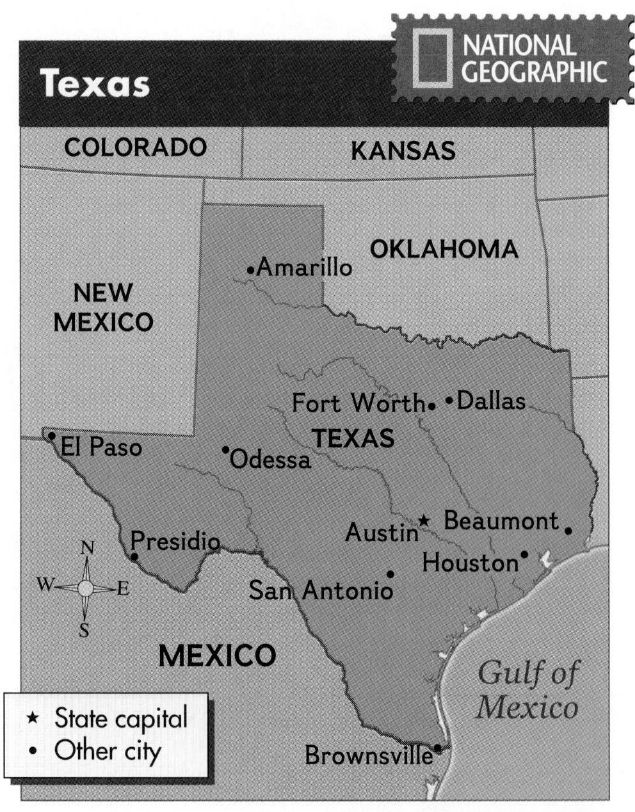

What is a locator?

- A **locator** is a small map on a bigger map. It shows where the area shown in the bigger map is located. The area of the main map is shown in red on the locator.
- Find the locator on the map. What area does it show?

The United States

NATIONAL GEOGRAPHIC

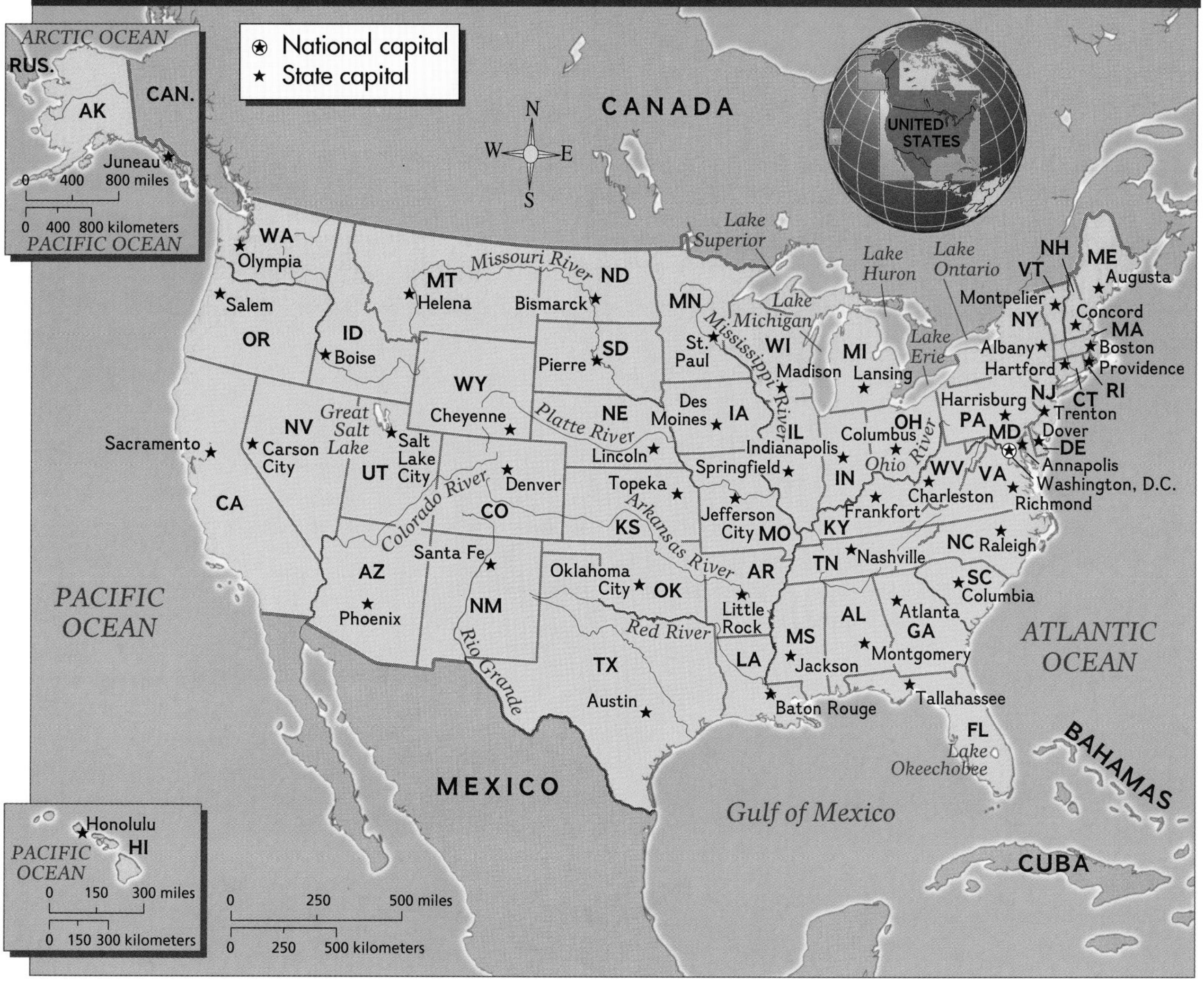

⊛ National capital
★ State capital

Using Different Kinds of Maps

VOCABULARY

landform map
grid map

What is a landform map?

- A **landform map** shows the different landforms on Earth. Many landform maps use different colors to show the different kinds of land.
- Look at the landform map of South Dakota on this page. Find the map key. What color shows mountains? What other landforms does the map show?

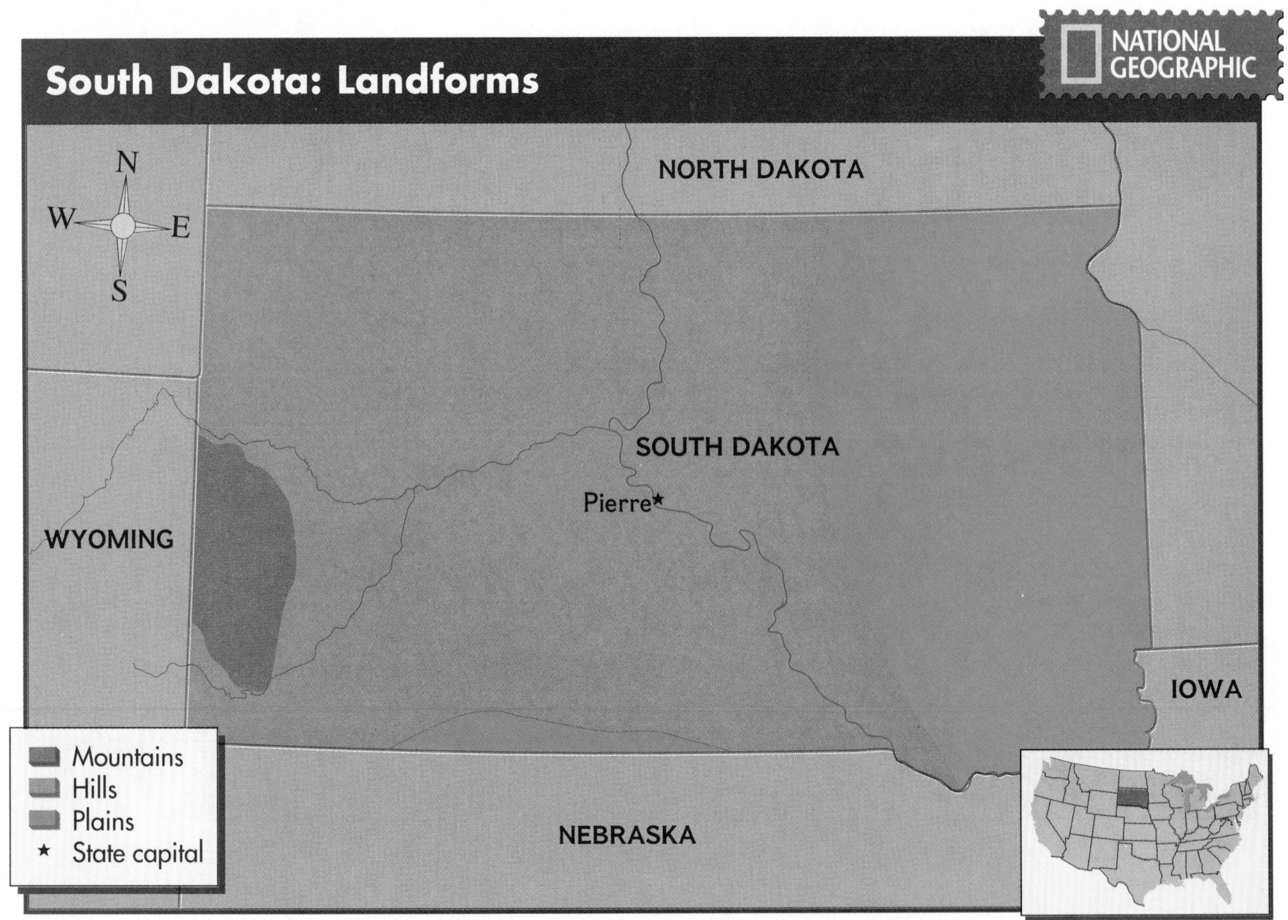

What is a grid map?

- A **grid map** can help you locate things. A grid map uses a set of boxes, or a grid, to locate places. Each box is named with both a letter and a number.
- Look at the grid map of Santa Fe, New Mexico. All the boxes on the first row across are named with the letter *A*. All the boxes on the first row down are named with the number 1. The first box to the left in the top row is named A1. What place is located in box C4?

Santa Fe, New Mexico

NATIONAL GEOGRAPHIC

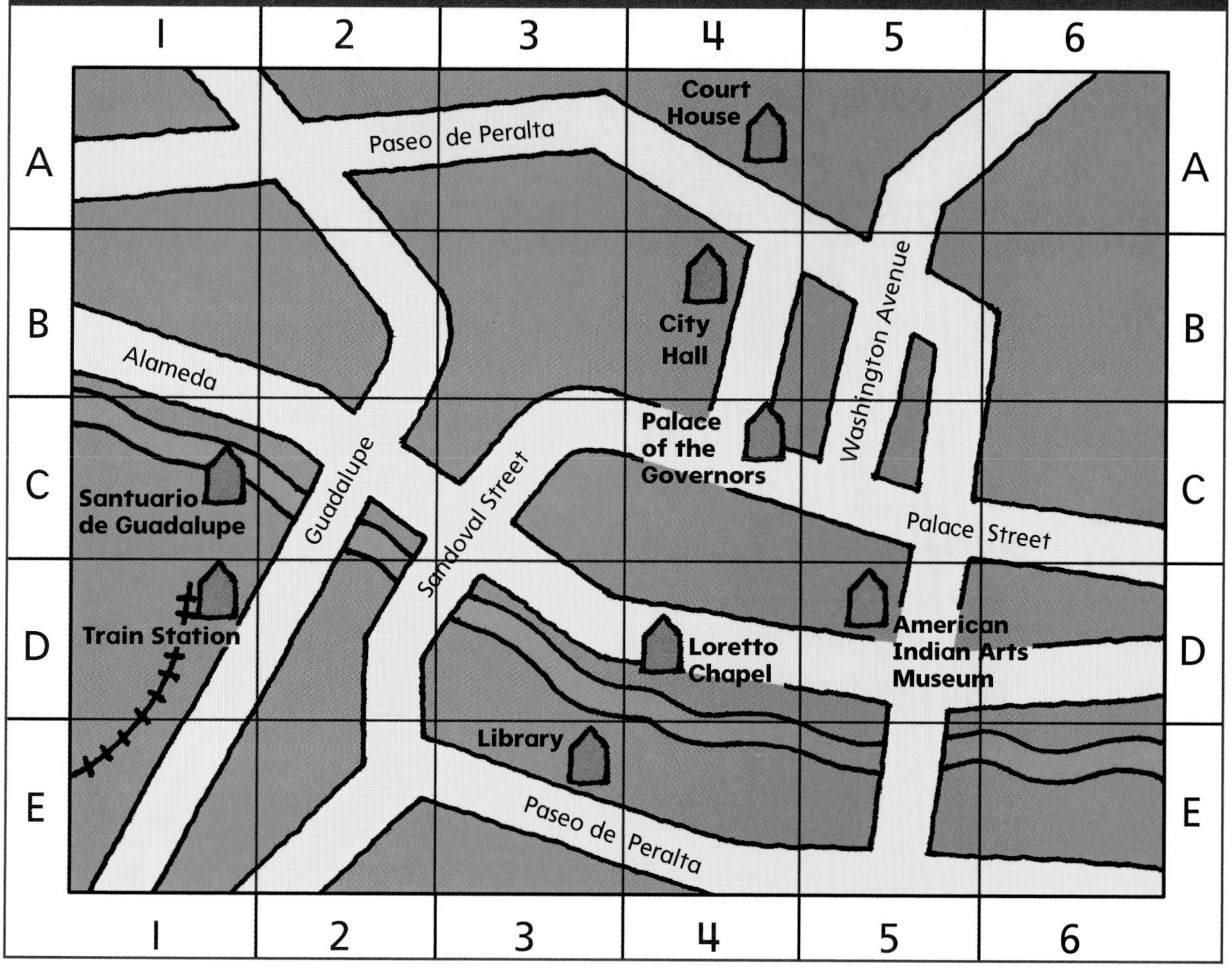

1 2 3 4 5 6

A B C D E

Court House
Paseo de Peralta
City Hall
Washington Avenue
Alameda
Palace of the Governors
Guadalupe
Sandoval Street
Santuario de Guadalupe
Palace Street
Train Station
American Indian Arts Museum
Loretto Chapel
Library
Paseo de Peralta

LITERATURE

The Town That Moved

Story by Mary Jane Finsand
Illustrations by Bob Dorsey

This is a true story about Hibbing, Minnesota. One day news came that would bring a big change to Hibbing. The whole town had to move! How do you do this? It would be hard to do this today, but it was even more difficult in the early 1900s.

Hibbing became famous for its rich **iron ore**. The town grew and grew. Everyone who lived there was very proud of Hibbing. They wanted to make it a beautiful city. They built fancy theaters and lovely parks and fine houses. They started excellent schools for their children, and they took wonderful care of their town. Then one day the mine owners made a discovery: THE VERY BEST IRON ORE WAS RIGHT BENEATH THE TOWN OF HIBBING!

---

iron ore (ī′ərn ôr) a mineral or rock that contains the metal iron

The people of Hibbing would have to move. If they didn't, the mines would have to be shut down. The miners would be out of work. Soon the other businesses would have to close down too. The people of Hibbing were very upset. They had worked so hard to build their beautiful town. How could they leave it? How could they watch it be torn down to make way for new mines?

"Where will we go?" they asked. "We will build you a new town," said the mine owners. "But what about our fine homes and our fancy theaters and our beautiful hotels?" the people asked. The mine owners thought and thought, and finally they came up with a **solution**.

---

solution (sə lü′shən) the answer to a problem

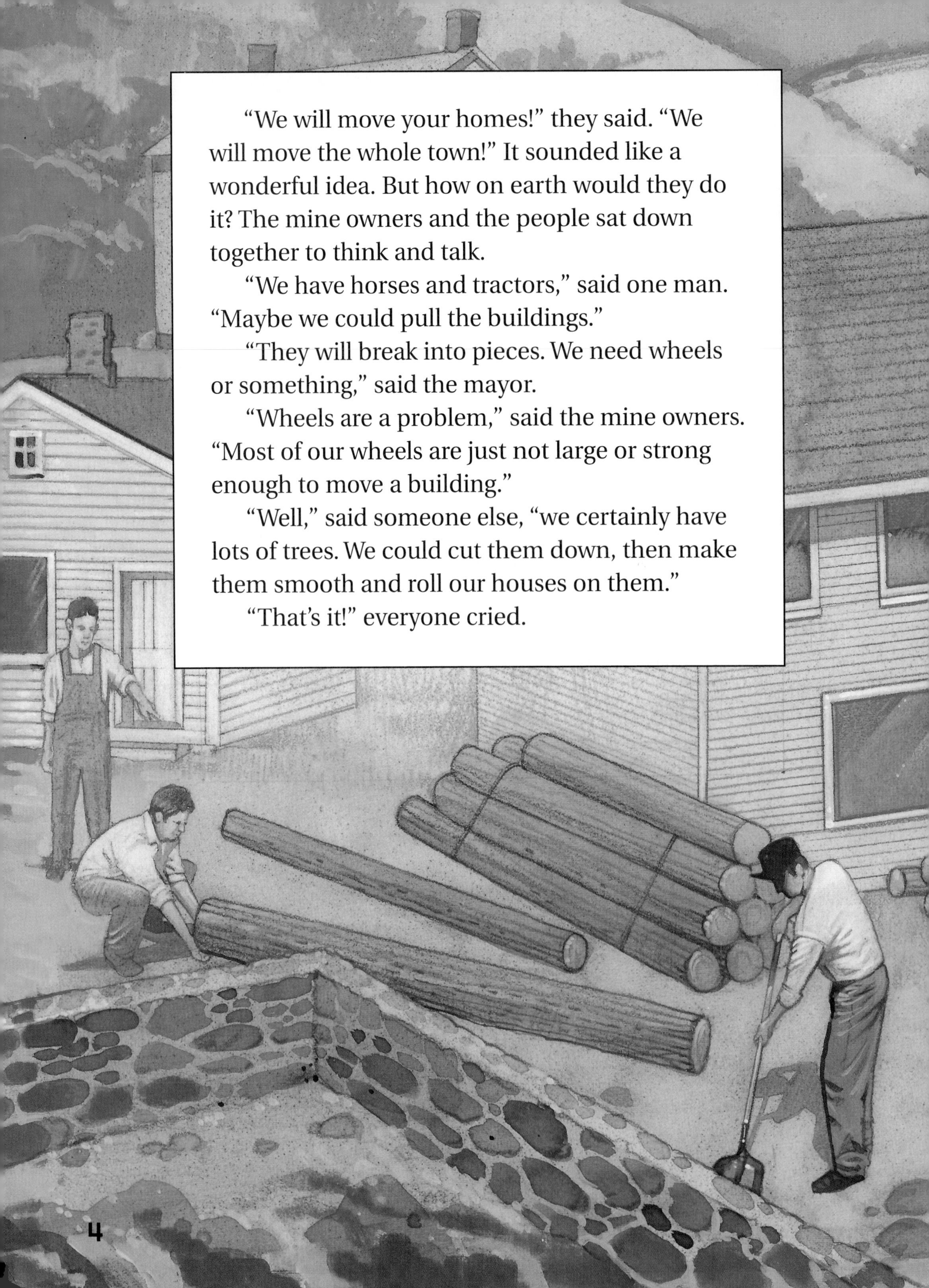

"We will move your homes!" they said. "We will move the whole town!" It sounded like a wonderful idea. But how on earth would they do it? The mine owners and the people sat down together to think and talk.

"We have horses and tractors," said one man. "Maybe we could pull the buildings."

"They will break into pieces. We need wheels or something," said the mayor.

"Wheels are a problem," said the mine owners. "Most of our wheels are just not large or strong enough to move a building."

"Well," said someone else, "we certainly have lots of trees. We could cut them down, then make them smooth and roll our houses on them."

"That's it!" everyone cried.

So the mine owners and the people began to get ready for moving day. They separated all the buildings from their basements. Then they dug new basements for all those buildings. They chopped down trees. Then they cut away branches. They made the logs smooth. People all over the world heard about Hibbing's plan to move. "Impossible!" they said. One big city newspaper wrote: "HIBBING GONE CRAZY!"

No one believed that the people of Hibbing could move their whole town. Finally moving day arrived. The Hibbing Hotel would be the first building moved. The miners attached large chains and ropes to **cranes** from the mine. The cranes would be powered by steam engines. Then the chains were wrapped over and under the Hibbing Hotel.

cranes (krānz) large machines with a long moveable arm for lifting heavy weights

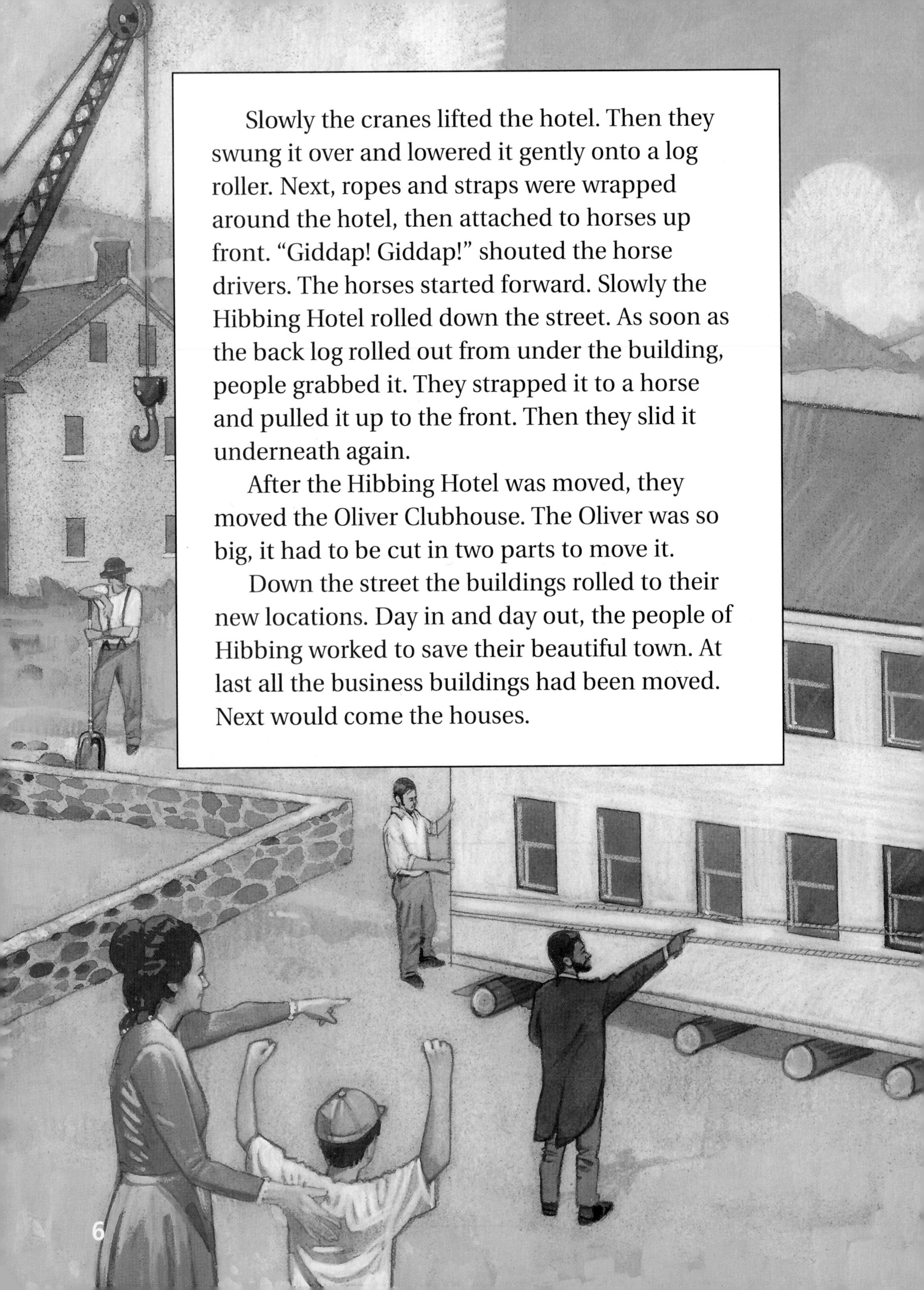

Slowly the cranes lifted the hotel. Then they swung it over and lowered it gently onto a log roller. Next, ropes and straps were wrapped around the hotel, then attached to horses up front. "Giddap! Giddap!" shouted the horse drivers. The horses started forward. Slowly the Hibbing Hotel rolled down the street. As soon as the back log rolled out from under the building, people grabbed it. They strapped it to a horse and pulled it up to the front. Then they slid it underneath again.

After the Hibbing Hotel was moved, they moved the Oliver Clubhouse. The Oliver was so big, it had to be cut in two parts to move it.

Down the street the buildings rolled to their new locations. Day in and day out, the people of Hibbing worked to save their beautiful town. At last all the business buildings had been moved. Next would come the houses.

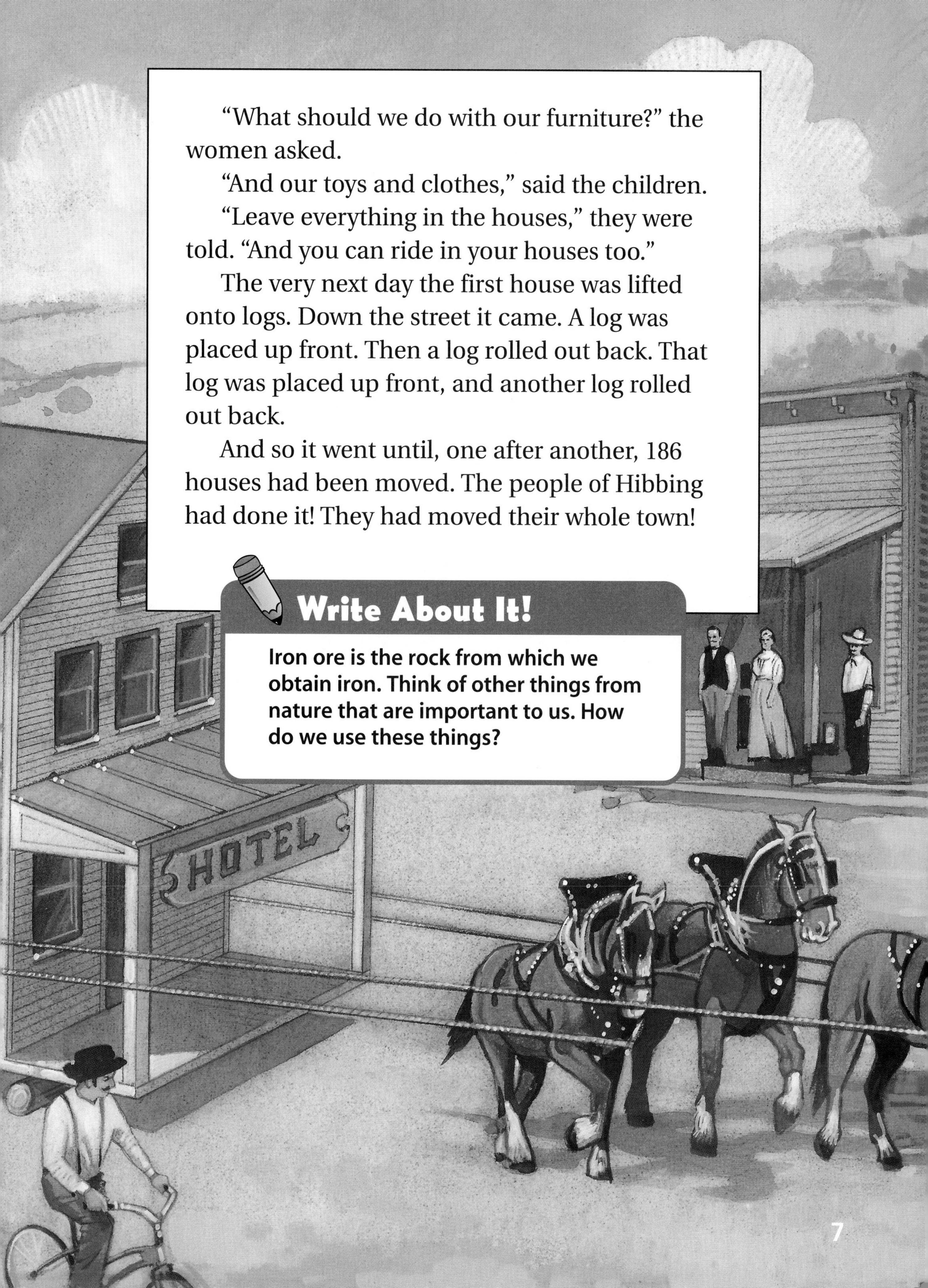

“What should we do with our furniture?” the women asked.

“And our toys and clothes,” said the children.

“Leave everything in the houses,” they were told. “And you can ride in your houses too.”

The very next day the first house was lifted onto logs. Down the street it came. A log was placed up front. Then a log rolled out back. That log was placed up front, and another log rolled out back.

And so it went until, one after another, 186 houses had been moved. The people of Hibbing had done it! They had moved their whole town!

Write About It!

Iron ore is the rock from which we obtain iron. Think of other things from nature that are important to us. How do we use these things?

Unit 1

People Build Communities

TAKE A LOOK

How does the land shape a community?

The things people do for work and for fun often depend on where a community is located.

Explore more about people and their communities at our Web site www.mhschool.com

Chapter 1

THE Big IDEAS ABOUT...

Life in Communities

A community is a place where people live together. Our country is made up of many communities. Some are large. Some are small. However, all communities have some things in common, and each one is special in its own way. In this chapter you will read about what makes a community.

LEARNING ABOUT A COMMUNITY

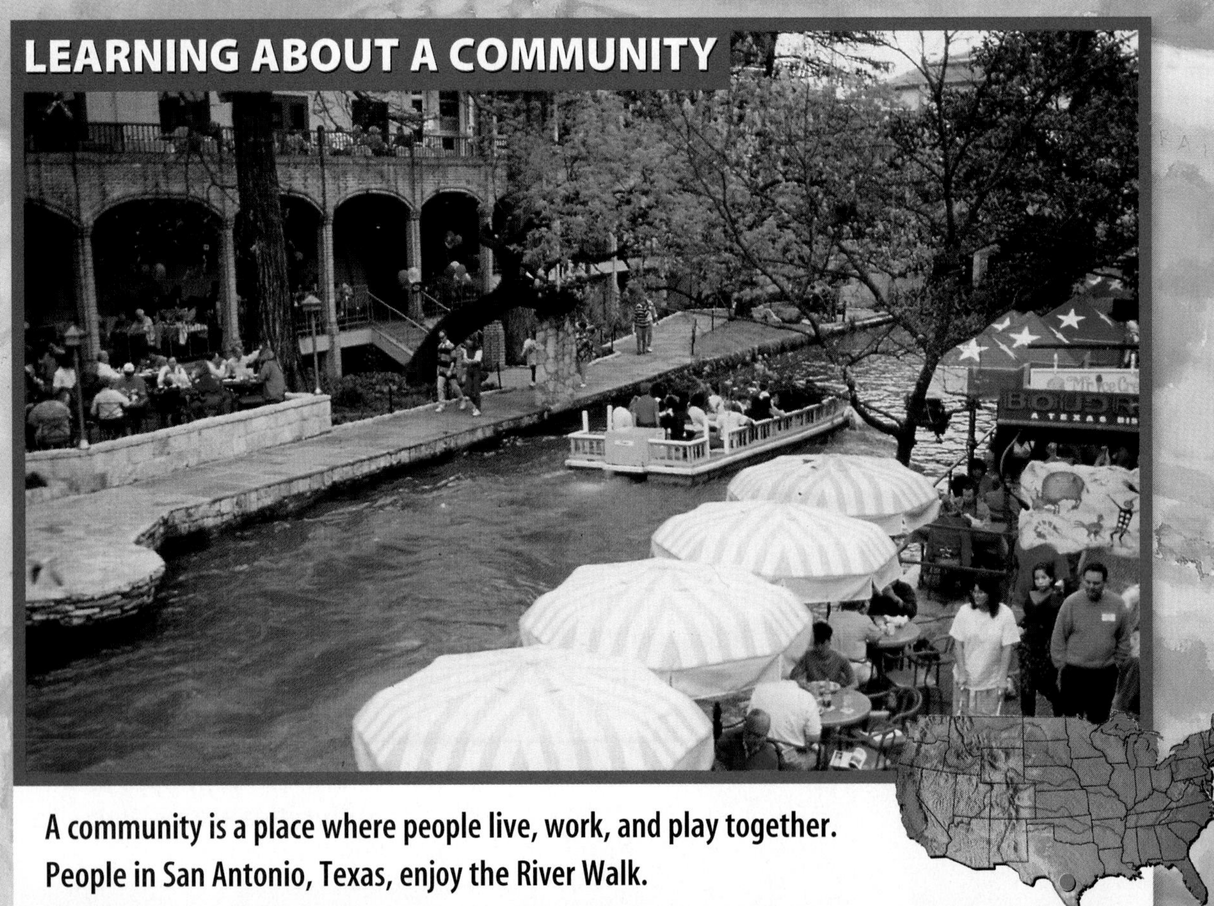

A community is a place where people live, work, and play together. People in San Antonio, Texas, enjoy the River Walk.

COMMUNITIES IN OUR COUNTRY

There are all kinds of communities in our country. Some are big cities. Others are small towns, like Telluride, Colorado. Read the lesson to find out more about communities in our country.

Foldables

Make this Foldable to help organize what you learn about "Life in Communities."

1. Fold a large sheet of construction paper like a hamburger.
2. Fold two sheets of white copy paper in half like hamburgers.
3. Glue the two hamburgers inside the sheet of construction paper.
4. Make two cuts equal distances apart forming three tabs on the front of each hamburger.

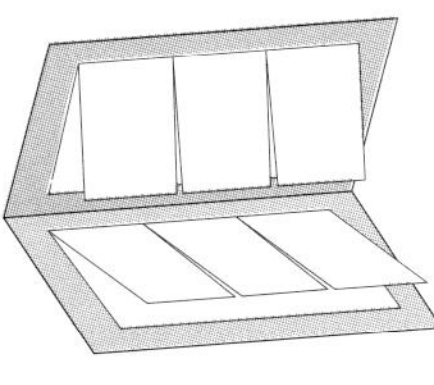

Lesson 1

Learning About a Community

VOCABULARY

community

construction

citizen

What makes up a community?

Lesson Outline

- People and Communities
- Communities at Work
- Community Fun

READING STRATEGY

In a diagram like this, write a **main idea** about communities. Then describe some features of a community.

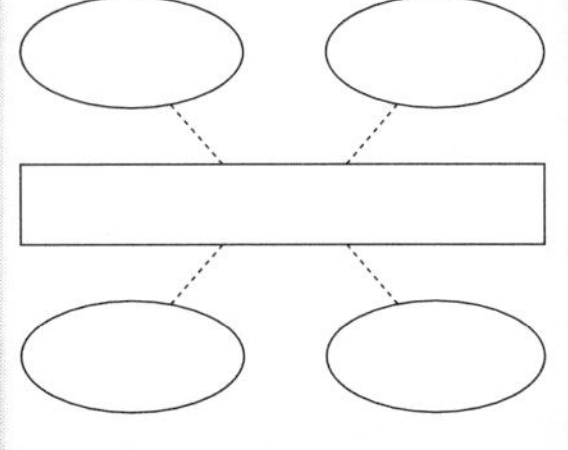

BUILD BACKGROUND

A **community** is a place where people live, work, and play. Communities are made up of neighborhoods where people live. Communities have stores and businesses where people work. They also have parks and other places where people can have fun. Read about one community and the people who call it home.

PEOPLE AND COMMUNITIES

San Antonio, Texas, is a large community. It is home to more than one million people, and it is still growing.

People in San Antonio care about their community and work to make it better. To make room for new roads and houses, many old trees must be cut down. People in different neighborhoods get together to fix this by planting new trees almost every week. That is one way they make their community a better place to live.

The people of San Antonio are proud of their community. Visitors from all over the world come to see it. One sight they never miss is The Alamo. That is where many heroes gave their lives to free Texas from Mexico, the country that once owned it.

Three million people visit The Alamo (above) in San Antonio (left) every year. People plant trees (below) to make their community a better place to live.

How can you tell that the people of San Antonio care about their community?

These **construction** workers are building new homes.

COMMUNITIES AT WORK

People in communities have many kinds of jobs. Some people in San Antonio have jobs in **construction**. Construction is the act of building something. Construction workers in San Antonio build not only houses, but libraries, offices, and stores as well.

Construction companies in San Antonio hire workers who live in the community. Mary Anna Gannon works at one construction company. She says, "The construction workers move from job to job together, and they all know each other. It's a real local, real together feel. It's a sense of community."

Helping Hands in a Community

People in communities depend on each other for help. In 2002 San Antonio had a terrible flood. Heavy rains caused the San Antonio River to rise so high that water spilled over onto the land.

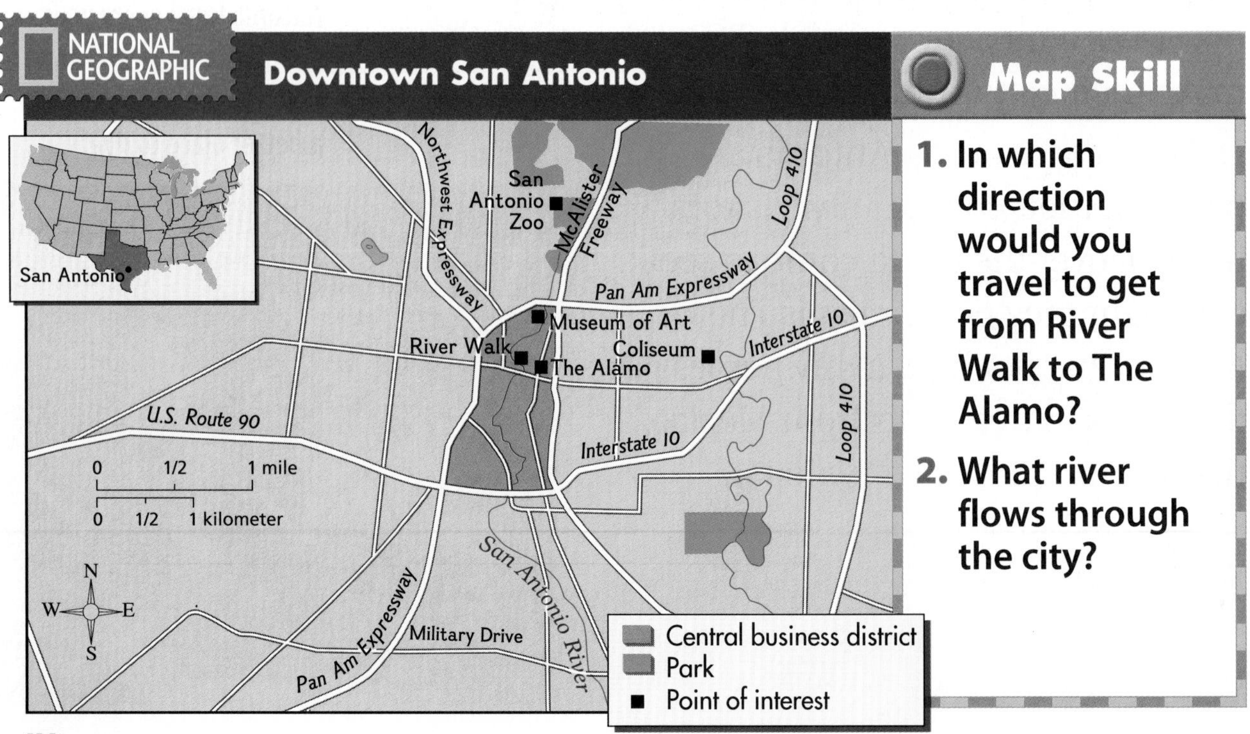

Map Skill

1. **In which direction would you travel to get from River Walk to The Alamo?**
2. **What river flows through the city?**

In 2002 a flood hit parts of San Antonio (above). **Citizens** helped clean up (below).

The roads were filled with water, so cars could not get through. Many homes were filled with water, too. People had to climb to their rooftops and wait for boats to rescue them. Take a look at the map on page 14. Why might a flood of the San Antonio River cause so much harm?

During the flood the **citizens** of San Antonio helped each other. A citizen is a person who lives in a community and has certain rights and duties. The citizens of San Antonio cleaned homes that were not even their own. Stores gave clothes and food to people in need.

With the help of its citizens, San Antonio got through the flood. Today the community is still working together. Now it is working on plans to prevent more floods.

How did the people of San Antonio help each other during the flood of 2002?

COMMUNITY FUN

There are many other ways to have fun in San Antonio. Nine-year-old Rachel Gomez goes to the Garza Community Center in her neighborhood. The center has a dance class that teaches Folklórico, the many beautiful folk dances of Mexico. It has an art class, where Rachel learned how to tie Chinese knots. It also has sports, such as basketball, which Rachel likes to play.

The end of April is Fiesta time in San Antonio. *Fiesta* (fee ES tuh) means "festival" in Spanish. For ten days the community celebrates Texas's independence. Fiesta time is fun for everyone. People ride in floats made of flowers. Parades with bands and dancers fill the streets. Everyone has a chance to try foods from different places around the world.

Fiesta Flambeau, San Antonio, Texas

— Pete Ortiz, Jr., parade director, 2001

I work on the Fiesta Flambeau (flam BOH). That is the illuminated [lit up] night parade. There are so many happy faces at Fiesta. A lot of people look forward to this parade all year. They want to see all the floats and what kind of costumes people will be wearing. People have great imaginations! We had 12,000 marchers, 200 horses, and 58 floats last year. People dress up in costumes. They also throw confetti at each other—that's for good luck!

How many people marched in Fiesta Flambeau in 2000?

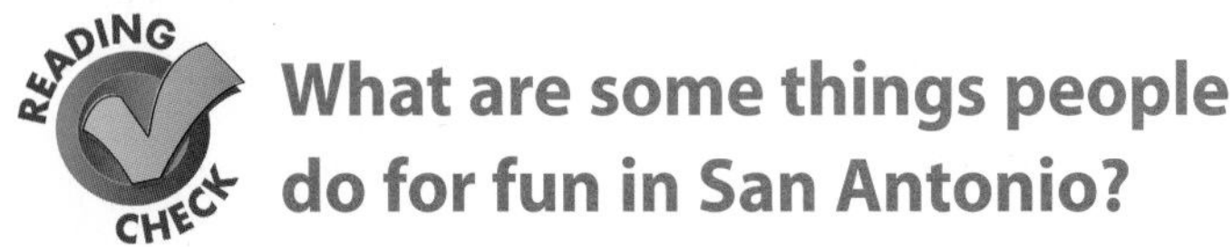

What are some things people do for fun in San Antonio?

PUTTING IT TOGETHER

In this lesson we have looked at the community of San Antonio, Texas. We have seen how the people work together to help each other and their community. A close look at one community can help us understand others, including our own. All communities have citizens who work and play together.

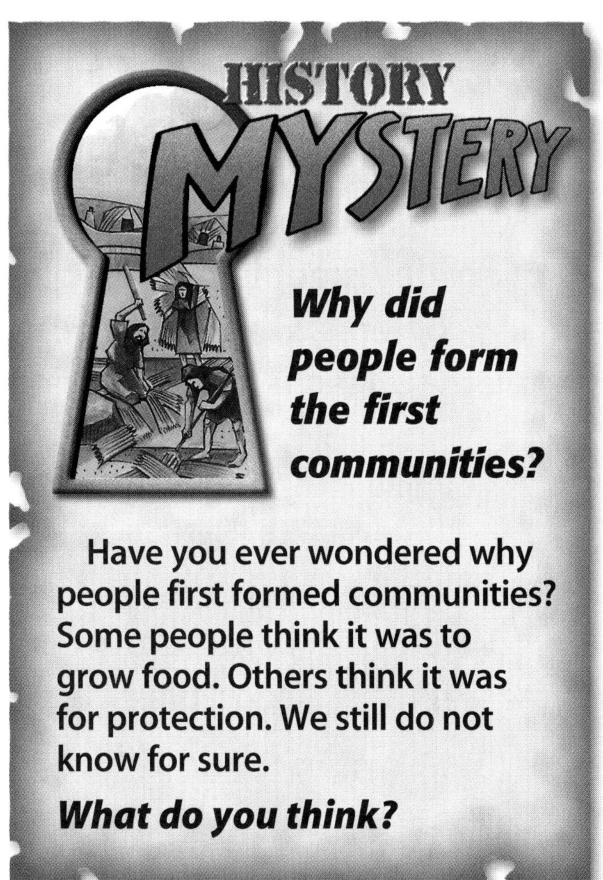

HISTORY MYSTERY
Why did people form the first communities?
Have you ever wondered why people first formed communities? Some people think it was to grow food. Others think it was for protection. We still do not know for sure.
What do you think?

Review and Assess

1. **Write** one sentence for each of the vocabulary words.

   citizen **community**
   construction

2. Why might the people of San Antonio be proud of their community?
3. Identify the things that make up a community. Find out!
4. Give an example of **citizens** in San Antonio working together.
5. In what ways are your community and San Antonio **alike and different?**

Look at the map of San Antonio on page 14. Draw your own map of a pretend city that you design. Show a business district, points of interest, and a river.

Suppose you have a friend in another town. **Write** a letter telling him or her how the people in your community live, work, and play.

Problem Solving

Every day, people face problems. Some are small problems, while others can be big ones. Problem solving is a way to find answers.

VOCABULARY

option

consequence

solution

LEARN THE SKILL

Follow these steps to solve a problem.

1. **Identify the problem.**
   Karen has arranged to spend two hours playing with her friend Sara. Karen wants to play tennis, but Sara would like to go swimming. They identify their problem: What will they do?

2. **Gather information.**
   Although each wants to do something different, they are both willing to work out their problem.

3. **Identify the options.**
   An **option** is a possible choice. Karen and Sara have four options. They can play tennis, go swimming, do neither, or do both.

4. **List the possible consequences.**
   A **consequence** is the result of an action. If the girls only play tennis, the consequence is that Sara will be upset. If they only swim, Karen will be upset. If they do neither, both will be upset. If they play tennis and swim, both girls will be happy.

5. **Choose a solution. Check your solution with your parents, your teacher, or another adult.**
   Karen and Sara choose a **solution** with the help of their parents. A solution is an answer to a problem. They agree to play tennis for one hour and to swim for one hour.

6. **Think about the solution.** Karen and Sara enjoyed playing together because each got to do something she wanted to do. They chose the best solution to their problem.

TRY THE SKILL

Mr. Eden's class has a problem. Use the steps on these pages to help the class solve its problem.

The students in Mr. Eden's third-grade class want to go to the museum. Mr. Eden tells them that to make the visit, five adults must go with the class. So far Mr. Eden is the only adult going.

Peter thinks the class should forget the trip. Carla thinks they should wait for four more adults. Kim has another idea. She thinks the students should tell their parents how important the trip is and urge them to go along.

1. What problem does Mr. Eden's class have?
2. What information will help solve the problem?
3. What are the options that the class has?
4. What are the possible consequences of each option?
5. What do you think is the best solution? Why?
6. What other problems might occur in a third-grade class, and how would problem-solving skills be useful?

EXTEND THE SKILL

Communities often have problems. They use problem-solving skills to find solutions. In the last lesson you read about the 2002 flood in San Antonio.

- What problems did the 2002 San Antonio flood create?
- What solutions to the problems did San Antonio find? Can you think of other solutions?

Communities in Our Country

VOCABULARY

rural
urban
suburb
transportation

READING STRATEGY

In a chart like this, write a **summary** of three different communities. Use a separate column for each summary.

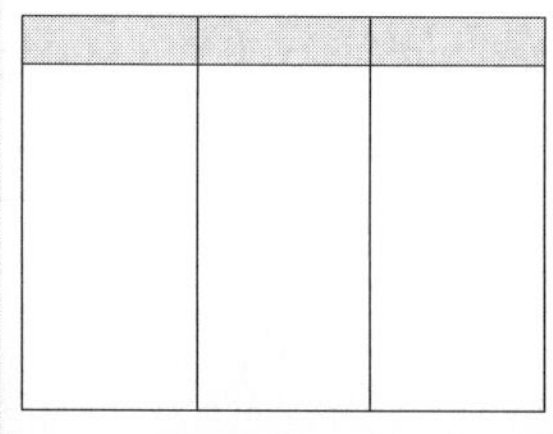

What are some different kinds of communities?

Lesson Outline
- On the Farm
- Exploring a City
- Life in a Suburb

BUILD BACKGROUND

There are all kinds of communities in our country. Some communities are big and crowded. Some are small with few people. In this lesson you will read about the three different kinds of communities in our country.

ON THE FARM

There are few buildings in **Beatrice** (bee A tris), **Nebraska**. However, there are rows and rows of corn plants. Corn grows well in Nebraska's soil. That is why Nebraska is called the Cornhusker State. Beatrice is a **rural** community. A rural community is a place of farms or open country. In Beatrice many people farm.

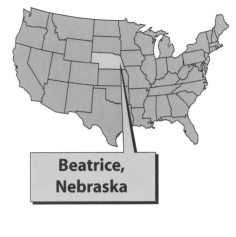

Beatrice, Nebraska

Farming is hard work. To take care of their crops, farmers get up as the sun rises. Growing a crop like corn requires lots of land and equipment. These are becoming more costly.

For fun, farmers in Beatrice attend the Gage County Fair. There they show off their best farm animals and crops.

What is a rural community?

Farming communities have few people (far left). Farmers work hard to grow crops like corn (above), but they still find time for fun at rural fairs (left).

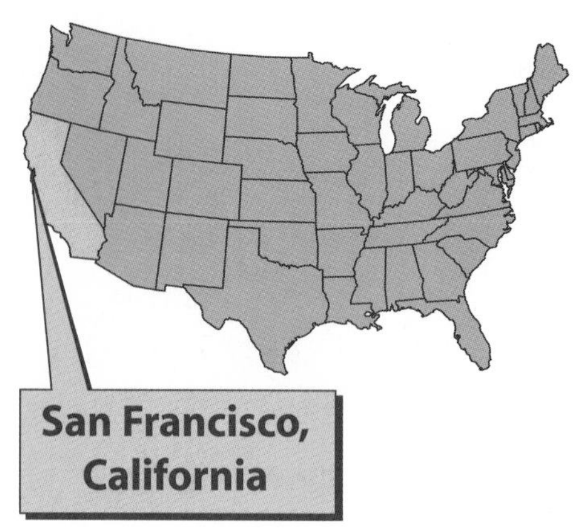

EXPLORING A CITY

Another kind of community often has lots of businesses and workers. There are many big buildings and many people. **San Francisco, California**, is a place like this. San Francisco is an **urban** community. An urban community is a city and its many neighborhoods.

Many people in San Francisco travel on cable cars. A cable car is a car that runs on a track and is pulled by a cable. People love the cable cars. They even passed a law to use them there forever!

Look at the photo below. It shows a Chinese American neighborhood in San Francisco called Chinatown. People from China first came here over one hundred years ago during the Gold Rush. Today San Francisco's Chinatown is one of the biggest Chinese communities outside of China.

What is an urban community?

Cable cars (below) and Chinatown (bottom) are only two features of San Francisco's busy **urban** community.

Each day people travel from Alexandria (left) to work in Washington, D.C. Many use trains (below) for **transportation**.

LIFE IN A SUBURB

Alexandria, Virginia, is another kind of community. It is a **suburb** of Washington, D.C. A suburb is a community that is near a city. A suburb is smaller than a city. Many people work in Washington, D.C., but live in Alexandria. Today suburbs like Alexandria are growing. That is because there are many jobs in and around these communities.

Alexandria is just across the Potomac River from Washington, D.C. People take different kinds of **transportation** to get from their homes to work. Transportation is a way of getting from one place to another. People may use cars, buses, or trains.

What is a suburb?

Different Types of Communities

People live in different kinds of communities. In which type of community do people live most closely together?

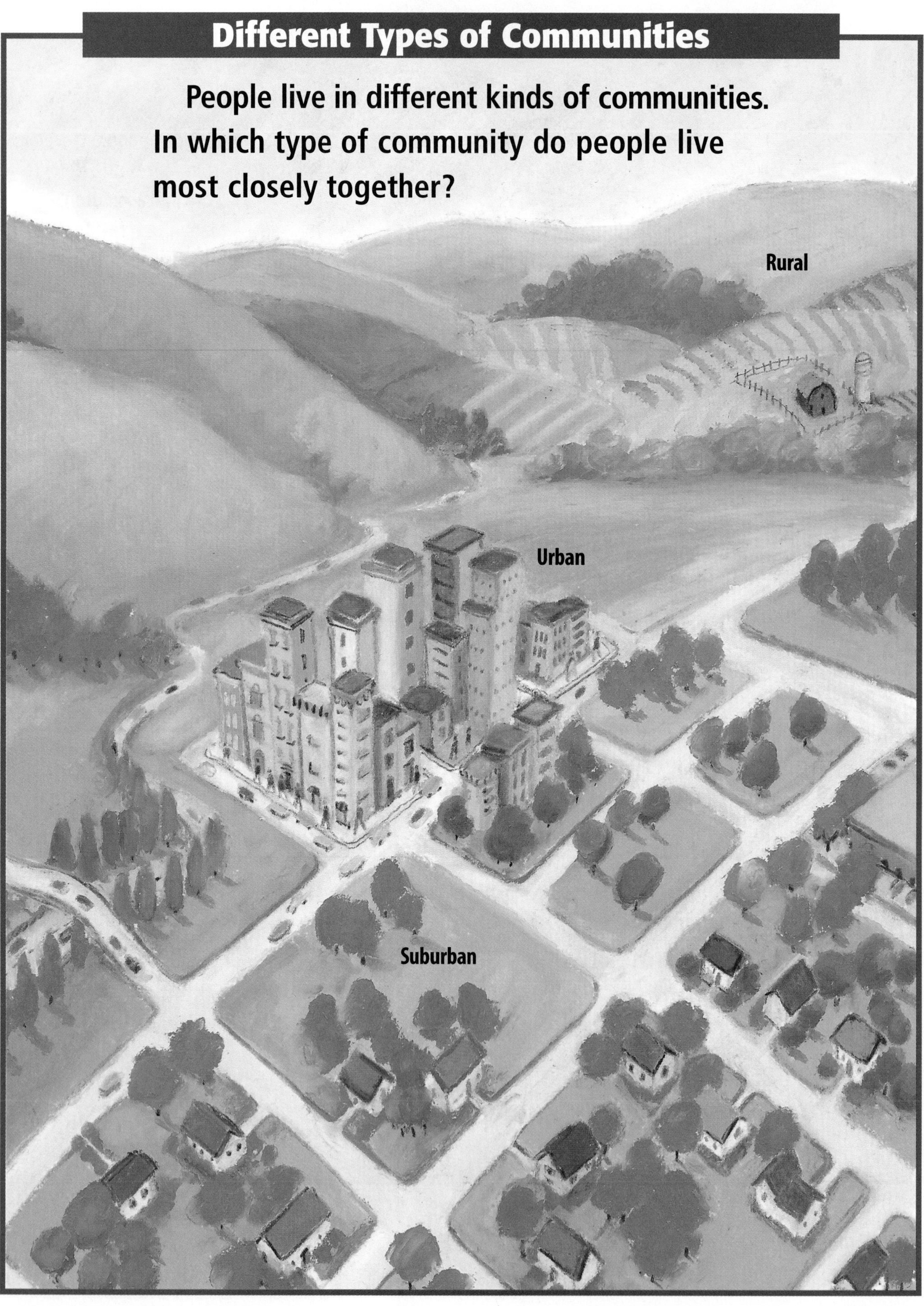

PUTTING IT TOGETHER

There are different kinds of communities in the United States. These include rural communities, urban communities, and suburban communities. The way we live depends on where we live. Some people live on farms and others in big buildings. Some have few neighbors, and others have many. Understanding what makes each kind of community special helps us respect people who live differently than we do.

Our families and friends are what make a community our home.

Review and Assess

1. Write one sentence for each of the vocabulary words.

   rural **suburb**
   transportation **urban**

2. What kind of work do many people do in Beatrice, Nebraska?
3. Analyze the three different kinds of communities.
4. Why do many people travel each day from suburban to urban communities?
5. What **sort** of community do you live in? Explain your answer.

Draw a picture showing the kinds of transportation that people in your community use.

Write a poem about any kind of community. You might write about what the community looks like, the people who live there, or both.

Chapter 1 REVIEW

VOCABULARY REVIEW

Number a sheet of paper from 1 to 3. Beside each number write the word from the list below that completes each sentence.

citizen **community**

rural

1. A person who lives in a town or city and has certain rights and duties is a ___.
2. A place where people live, work, and play is a ___.
3. A place with farms or open country is a ___ community.

CHAPTER COMPREHENSION

4. Describe three things that you might find in every community.
5. What are three kinds of communities in the United States? Describe one thing that makes each kind of community special.
6. Write about two kinds of transportation people in a suburb might use to get to work.

SKILL REVIEW

Read the paragraph below. Then answer the questions that follow.

Martha and Colin want to go to their friend Joe's house. It is too far to ride their bikes. Their mom is home, but she is busy. If they wait an hour, their older sister can drive them. They could ask their friend to come over now, or they could play with their friend tomorrow.

7. **Reading/Thinking Skill** Identify the problem in this paragraph.
8. **Reading/Thinking Skill** What are two possible options?
9. **Reading/Thinking Skill** Why is problem solving an important skill?

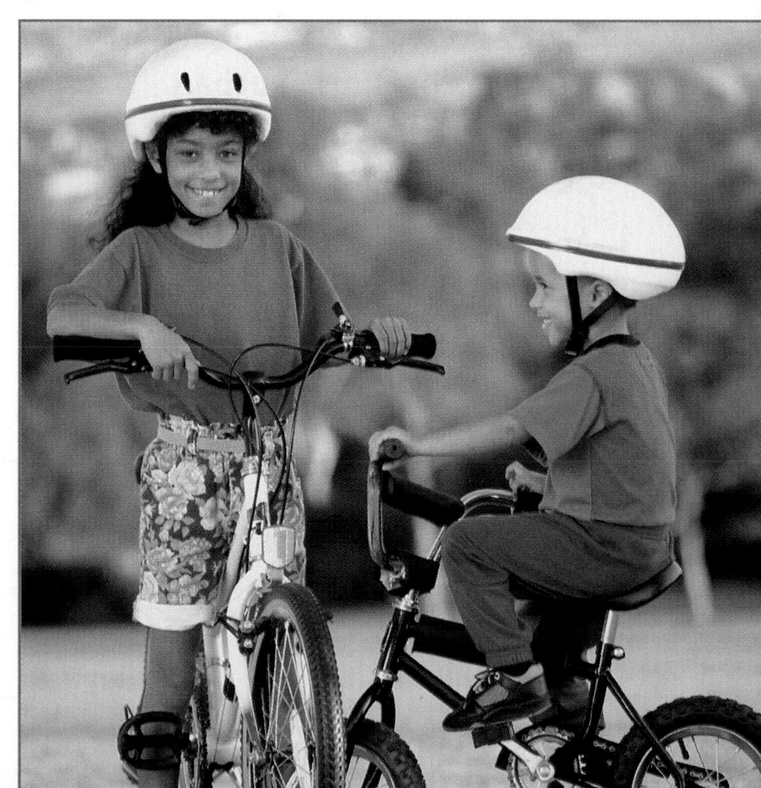

Chapter REVIEW

USING A CHART

10. Use the chart to answer the following question. Which type of community might be located between a city and farmland?

Type of Community	Description
Rural	**Farms or open country, few people**
Urban	**City or town, many buildings, many people**
Suburban	**Outside a city or town, houses, medium number of people**

Activity

Make a Model Community Is your community urban, suburban, or rural? What things make your community a certain type? Use paper, cardboard, and clay to construct a model community. Label your model "Urban," "Suburban," or "Rural."

Use your Foldable to review what you have learned about life in communities. As you look inside your Foldable, review what you learned about urban areas, rural areas, and suburbs. Think about ways in which people live, work, and play in communities. Review your notes under the tabs of your Foldable to check your memory. Record any questions that you might have.

Chapter

THE Big IDEAS ABOUT...

Communities and Geography

Communities are in different places. Each place has its own land, water, and weather. People use the land, water, and other resources to live.

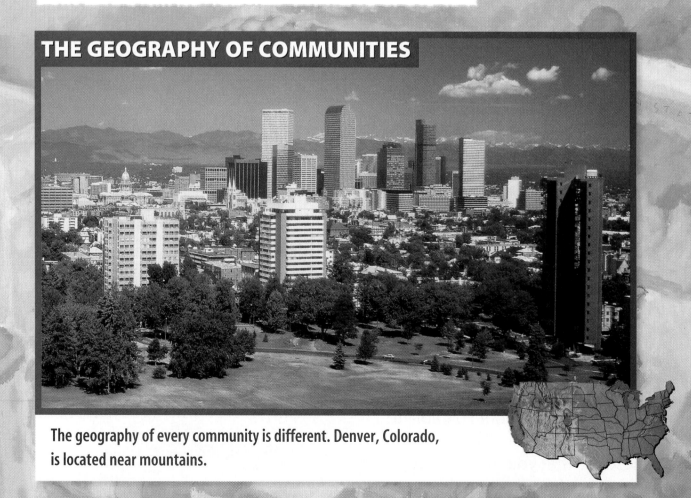

THE GEOGRAPHY OF COMMUNITIES

The geography of every community is different. Denver, Colorado, is located near mountains.

COMMUNITIES NEED RESOURCES

People in communities use resources. Many communities in Oregon use trees to make things.

PROTECTING OUR ENVIRONMENT

In Ine, Japan, the sea provides a way of life.

Foldables

Make this Foldable study guide and use it to record what you learn about "Communities and Geography."

1. Fold a large sheet of paper into fourths, forming four rows.
2. Open and fold the paper into fourths again, forming four columns and 16 rectangles.
3. Write the chapter title in the top left corner.
4. Label the rows and columns.

Lesson 1

The Geography of Communities

VOCABULARY

geography
landform
plain
plateau
climate
adapt

READING STRATEGY

Draw this chart. In column one **predict** what you will learn about geography. In column two write what you learned.

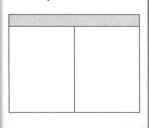

What kinds of land and water does our country have?

Lesson Outline

- People and Geography
- Land and Water
- Climate or Weather?

BUILD BACKGROUND

Suppose you were making a model of your community. Would it show that the land is mostly flat or that there are many hills? Would it include a river, a lake, or maybe a stream? The answers depend on where your community is. In this lesson you will see why one community might be quite different from another. You will also see how land and water affect people and communities.

PEOPLE AND GEOGRAPHY

When you answered the questions in Build Background, you were describing the **geography** of your community. Geography is the study of Earth's natural features. It describes the surface of the land and the bodies of water that cover it.

Building bridges is one way that people have learned to work with **geography** (above). In dry areas many houses are made from dried bricks called adobe (below).

Geography is an important part of how people live in communities. It affects transportation in and between communities. It affects the kinds of homes people live in and even the kinds of clothes they wear.

Just as geography affects people, so do people affect geography. When people change the land or water around them, they are changing geography.

READING CHECK **Why is it important to learn about geography?**

LAND AND WATER

If you took a trip across the United States, you would see different kinds of **landforms**. A landform is the shape of the surface of the land.

A large area of flat land is called a **plain**. The **Great Plains** stretch from North Dakota all the way south to Texas. Some places that look like plains are actually **plateaus**. A plateau is a large area of flat land that is raised high above the land around it. The **Colorado Plateau** can be found in New Mexico, Colorado, Arizona, and Utah. The **Rocky Mountains** stretch north from New Mexico and up past Montana.

Landforms affect people's daily lives. In mountain communities, for example, people often need cars with special tires to get around.

People also affect landforms. The longest tunnel in the United States was built through Maynard Mountain in Alaska. The tunnel changed parts of the land, making it easier for people to travel between two communities, Whittier and Portage.

People change the land in many ways, such as building tunnels (above). Much farming is done on plains (below).

Cedar shingles protect this house on Cape Cod from storms and salt air.

Water, Water Everywhere!

Did you know that much of Earth is covered by water? From oceans to rivers, and lakes to ponds, water flows through and around almost all land.

The largest bodies of water are oceans. The **Atlantic Ocean** borders the United States on the east. The **Pacific Ocean** borders it on the west. Lakes and rivers are smaller than oceans. Lakes are surrounded by land, while rivers run across land.

Oceans are made of salt water. Most lakes and rivers, however, are made of fresh water. Ponds and streams, which are the smallest bodies of water, are fresh water, too.

People, animals, and plants need water to live. People also use water for transportation and for fun. Many people enjoy vacations in places that are near the water. Cape Cod, Massachusetts, on the Atlantic Ocean, gets very crowded in the summertime. People go there to swim, sail, and fish.

How does geography affect people's lives?

CLIMATE OR WEATHER?

If you lived in **Little Rock, Arkansas**, you would get good use out of your umbrella. Lots of rain falls in Little Rock every year. In **Phoenix, Arizona**, however, it almost never rains. Phoenix has a dry **climate**, while Little Rock has a wet one. Climate describes what a place's weather is like over a long period of time. It tells how hot or cold, rainy or dry, windy or calm a place can be. Climate is part of a place's geography.

People need warm clothes in cold **climates** (below). In warm climates people wear lighter clothes (bottom).

Climate is different from daily weather. For example, it may be rainy in Phoenix for a day or two. However, over a long period of time, it is mostly dry. In the United States the climate is most often cooler in the north than it is in the south.

People learn to **adapt** to the climate of their communities. To adapt means to become used to something. People who live in cold climates are used to wearing warm clothes. People in warm climates are used to wearing light clothes.

Tornadoes often strike on flat plains areas.

Weather Watch

Some kinds of weather can be dangerous. A tornado, for example, is a strong spinning wind that looks like a cone. The winds of a tornado can reach up to 300 miles per hour. A tornado is called a natural hazard because it happens in nature and can be very dangerous to people and property.

Hurricanes and blizzards are also natural hazards. Hurricanes are rainstorms with high winds and usually thunder and lightning. Blizzards are snowstorms with strong winds and cold temperatures. Blizzards usually happen in the northern half of the United States, especially in the mountains.

Exploring TECHNOLOGY

Storm Warning!

People today have more warning about storms than ever before. Scientists take pictures of storms by using cameras that circle Earth. These pictures help them see where a storm is headed. Scientists can then warn a community if a hurricane, blizzard, or tornado is coming its way.

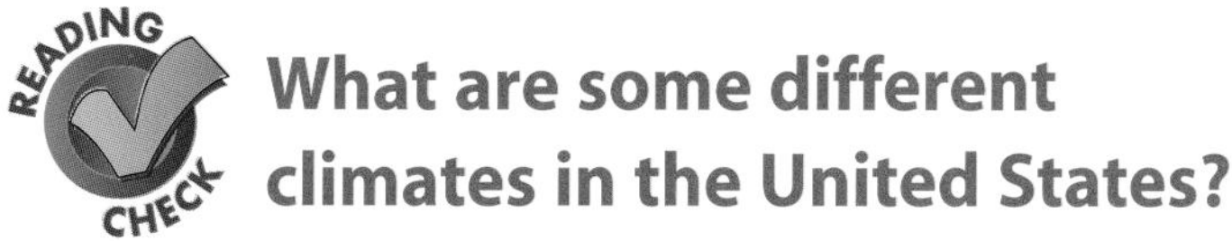

What are some different climates in the United States?

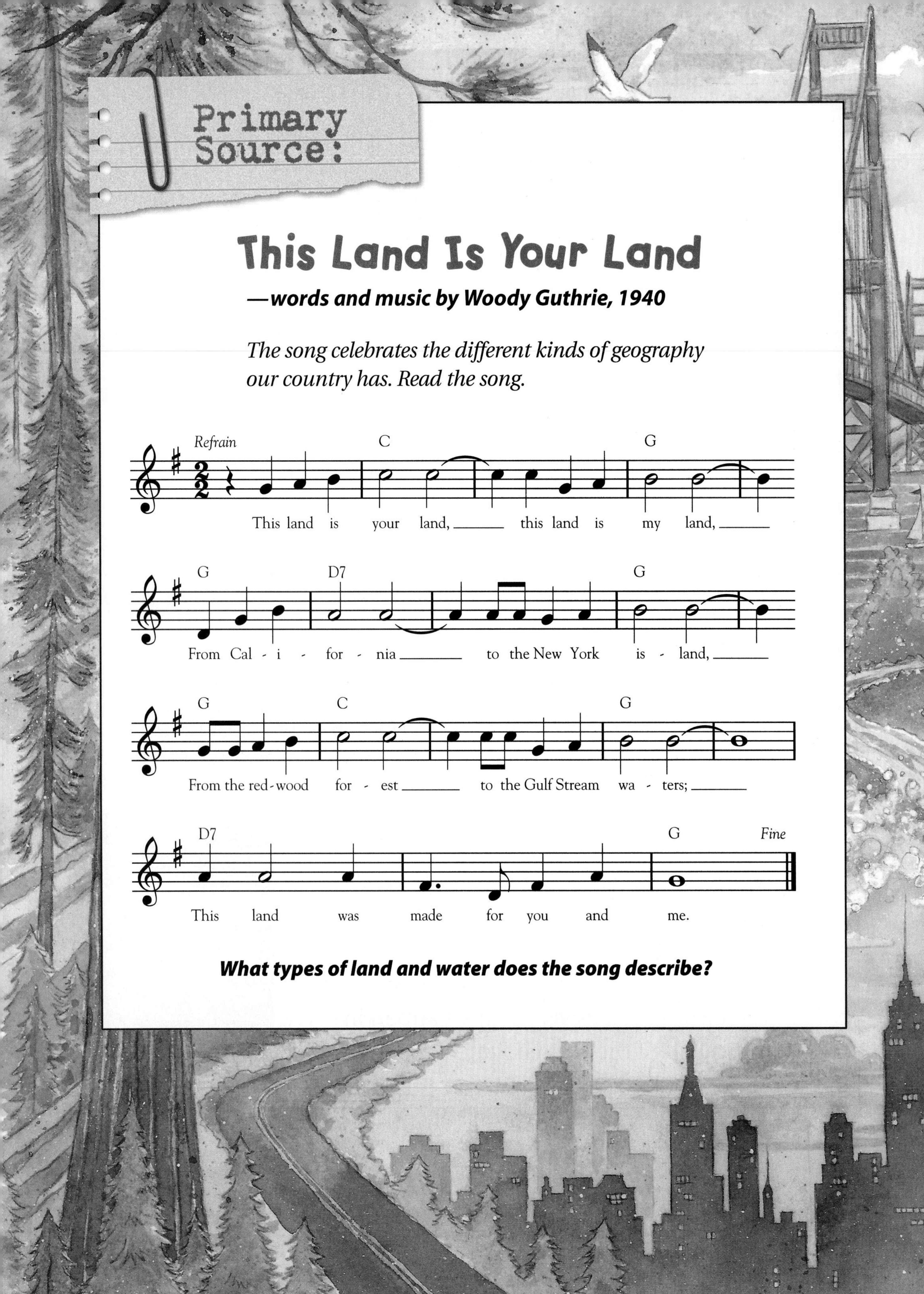

Primary Source:

This Land Is Your Land

—*words and music by Woody Guthrie, 1940*

The song celebrates the different kinds of geography our country has. Read the song.

What types of land and water does the song describe?

PUTTING IT TOGETHER

You have seen that different communities have different geography. They have different landforms, bodies of water, and climates. The people in these communities learn to live with the land, water, and climate around them. Knowing about the geography of different communities helps us understand the different ways people live.

Review and Assess

1. Write one sentence for each of the vocabulary words.

   adapt **climate**
   geography **landform**
   plain **plateau**

2. Describe three kinds of landforms found in the United States.
3. What are some of the landforms and bodies of water in our country?
4. How have people in your community adapted to its **geography**?
5. **Sort** the following into two groups—mountains, lakes, rivers, plateaus, plains, and oceans. Say whether they are landforms or bodies of water.

Activities

Make a landform model. Use clay to model mountains, plateaus, and plains.

Write a postcard to a friend at home telling of a pretend trip to a mountain or seaside community. Describe the geography of the community.

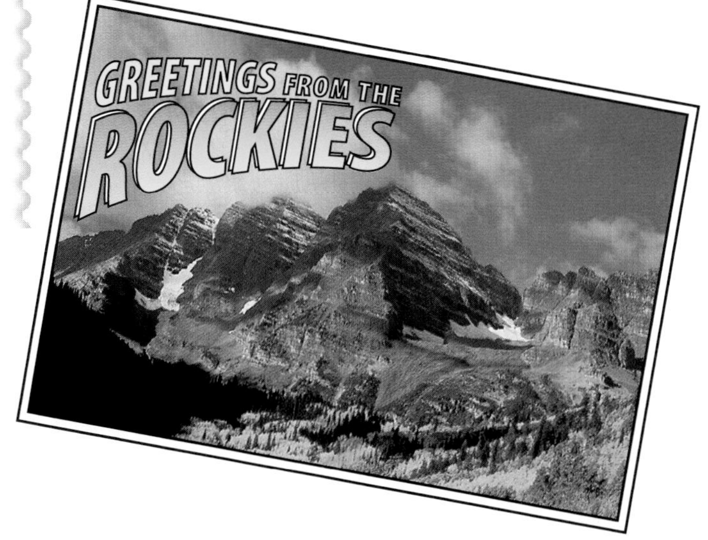

Using a Landform Map

A **landform map** uses different colors to show where different kinds of landforms are found. You might use a landform map when planning a trip.

VOCABULARY

landform map

compass rose

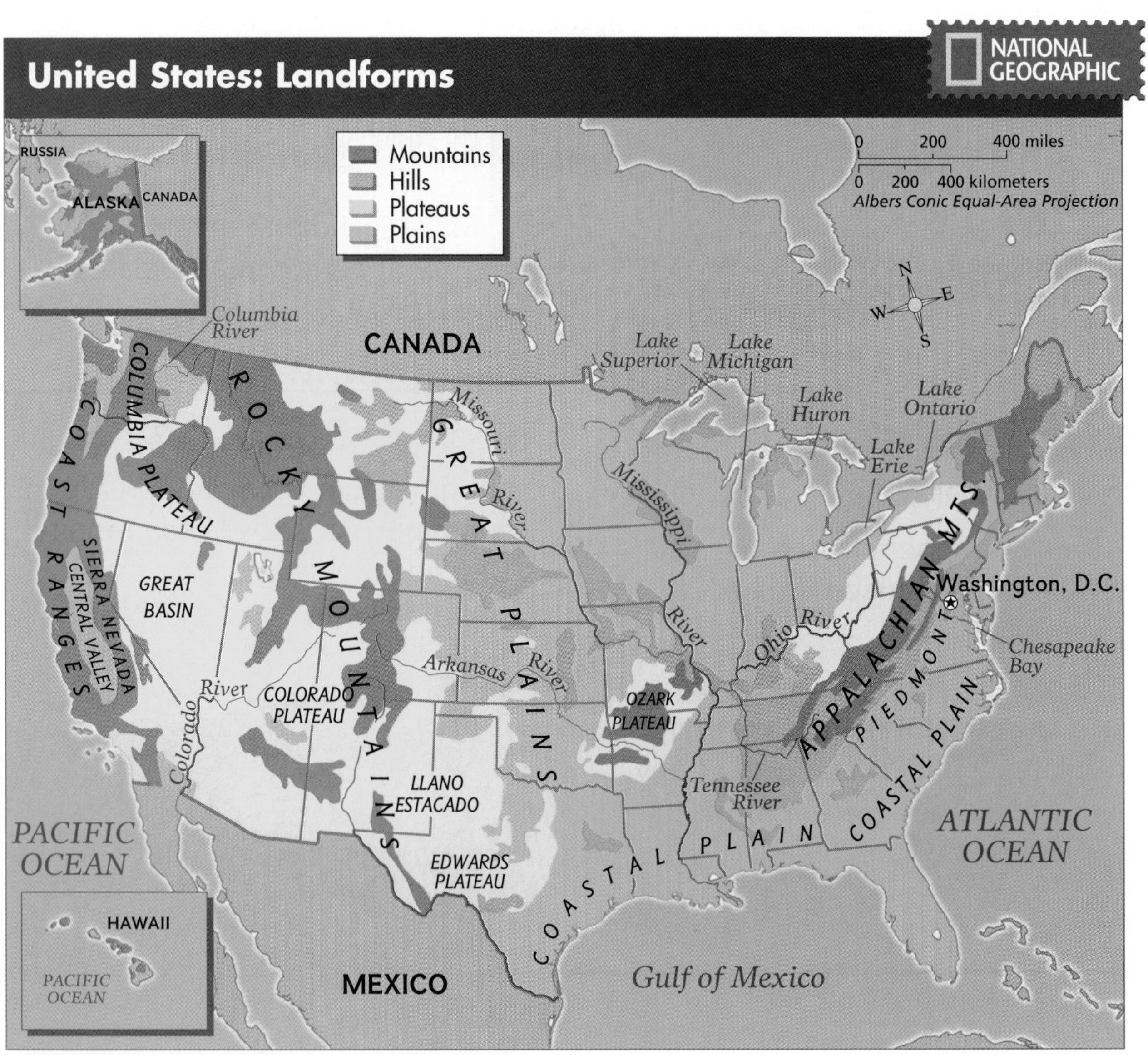

LEARN THE SKILL

Follow these steps for using a landform map. Look at the map on page 38 as you read.

1. **Read the map title.**
   The title tells you what area is shown on the map.
2. **Look at the map key.**
   The key shows what kind of landform each color stands for. On this map yellow shows plateaus.
3. **Check the compass rose.**
   The **compass rose** shows directions.
4. **Look for other information printed on the map.**
   Some landform maps show boundaries for countries and states. They can also give the names of specific mountains, rivers, and lakes.

TRY THE SKILL

Now study a landform map using the information you have read. Use the map on this page to answer the questions.

1. What state does the map show?
2. Name the different landforms found in this state.
3. In what part of the state are plateaus found?
4. In what direction would you travel if you drove from either of the mountain groups to the Missouri River?

EXTEND THE SKILL

Use the maps on pages 38 and 39 to answer the questions below.

- Look at the landform maps of the United States and Missouri. What plateau is in the southern part of Missouri?
- Find the Missouri River. In what part of our country does it begin? What landforms does it cross? Where does it end?

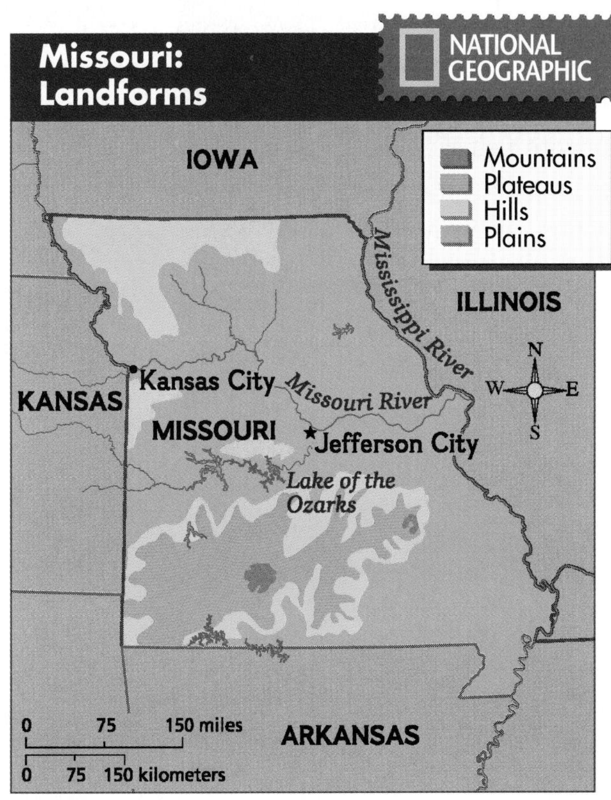

Lesson 2

Communities Need Natural Resources

VOCABULARY

natural resource
mineral
renewable resource
nonrenewable resource
environment
recycle

READING STRATEGY

Help solve problems in our environment. Write "recycle" in a word web like this. Then write items that can be recycled.

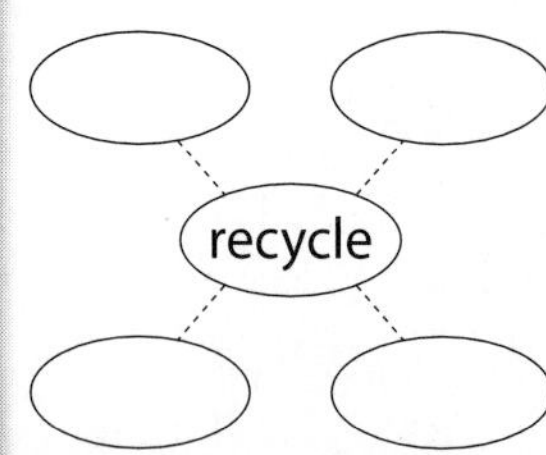

What is a natural resource?

Lesson Outline

- Resources Help Us Live
- Communities Use Natural Resources
- Protecting Our Natural Resources

BUILD BACKGROUND

Did you ever think about all the things you use that come from nature? The paper and pencil you write with both come from trees. Nature also provides us with the water we drink and the air we breathe. In this lesson you will read about other things in nature that are useful to people. You will also read about why it is important to take care of nature.

RESOURCES HELP US LIVE

People in communities depend on the **natural resources** around them. A natural resource is something found in nature that people use.

Water is one of our most important natural resources. People, plants, and animals need fresh water to live. People enjoy swimming, fishing, and boating at lakes, rivers, and oceans. We can also use rivers to travel or to move goods.

Minerals are another natural resource. Minerals are things found in the earth that are not plants or animals. Iron, salt, and coal are all minerals.

Forests are a natural resource, too. The trees in forests are used to build houses and furniture. Trees are also used to make paper for books like the one you are reading now!

Different communities have different natural resources. People in communities plan ways to use the resources that they have. They also plan ways to get other resources that they need. What natural resources are found in your community?

People depend on **natural resources** such as fresh water (above) and rich soil (below).

How do people use natural resources?

Wood (right) is a **renewable resource**. People drill for oil, a **nonrenewable resource**, on land and at sea (below).

COMMUNITIES USE NATURAL RESOURCES

There are two kinds of natural resources. One is called a **renewable resource**, which is something found in nature that can be replaced. Wind, sunlight, water, and trees are renewable resources. Communities need to plan how to replace their renewable resources. For example, the community of Cascade, Idaho, uses its forests. The trees there are used for wood to make houses and paper. Every time a tree is cut down, a new one is planted.

The other kind of natural resource is a **nonrenewable resource**. Nonrenewable resources are things found in nature that are limited and cannot be replaced. Minerals such as copper, iron, coal, and gold are nonrenewable resources. These minerals are mined, or removed from the earth, and made into products that people can use.

What is the difference between renewable and nonrenewable resources?

DATAGRAPHIC

Natural Resources in the United States

This map shows where some natural resources can be found in the United States. Use the chart to find out some products that are made from these natural resources.

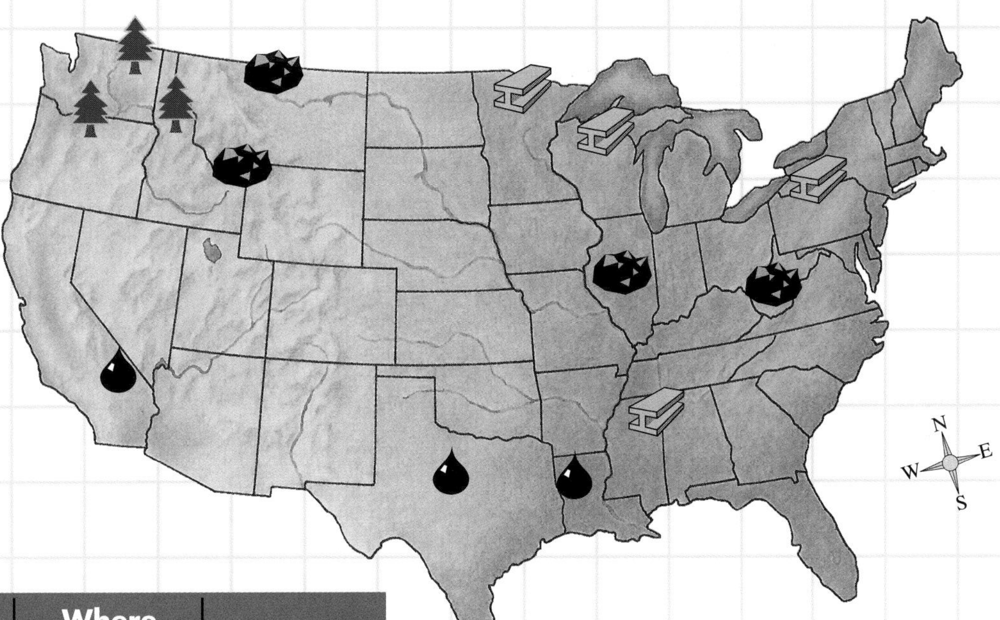

Natural Resources	Where Found	Products
Trees	Idaho Washington Oregon	Building lumber, paper, pencils, tissues, napkins
Oil	Texas Louisiana California	Gasoline, diesel fuel, plastics, fertilizers
Coal	Montana Wyoming Illinois West Virginia	Fuel, electricity
Iron	Minnesota Michigan Alabama Pennsylvania	Steel, cars, bridges, wires, paper clips, pots and pans

Questions

1. Which states have oil as a natural resource?
2. In which parts of the United States is oil found: north, south, east, or west?

Visit **www.mhschool.com** *for more information about natural resources.*

PROTECTING OUR NATURAL RESOURCES

What can people do to help care for their natural resources? Melissa Poe is a nine-year-old from Nashville, Tennessee. She got a group of kids together to help protect trees in the United States. She named the group Kids For a Clean Environment (Kids F.A.C.E.). Now the group has over 300,000 members! Kids F.A.C.E. has worked to plant new trees all over the world.

Kids F.A.C.E. and other groups of people are working to help the **environment** (en VIGH ruhn muhnt). The environment is the air, the water, the land, and all the living things around us. We need a clean environment to help us live. Animals and plants also need a clean environment to live.

There are many things you can do to help take care of our natural resources and protect our environment. One way is to **recycle** things instead of throwing them in the garbage. To recycle means to use something over again. You can recycle paper, tin, plastic, and glass.

How do people protect natural resources?

Exploring
ECONOMICS

Ghost Town: Bodie, California

Sometimes communities rely too much on their natural resources. In the 1800s gold was found in California. New towns sprang up as people came to look for gold. Soon, Bodie had ten thousand people. For a few years people had lots of money and enjoyed their life. However, the gold ran out. The people moved away. Bodie became a "ghost town."

Activity

What is the price of gold today? Use the Internet to find out!

These children are helping the **environment** by cleaning trash from a beach.

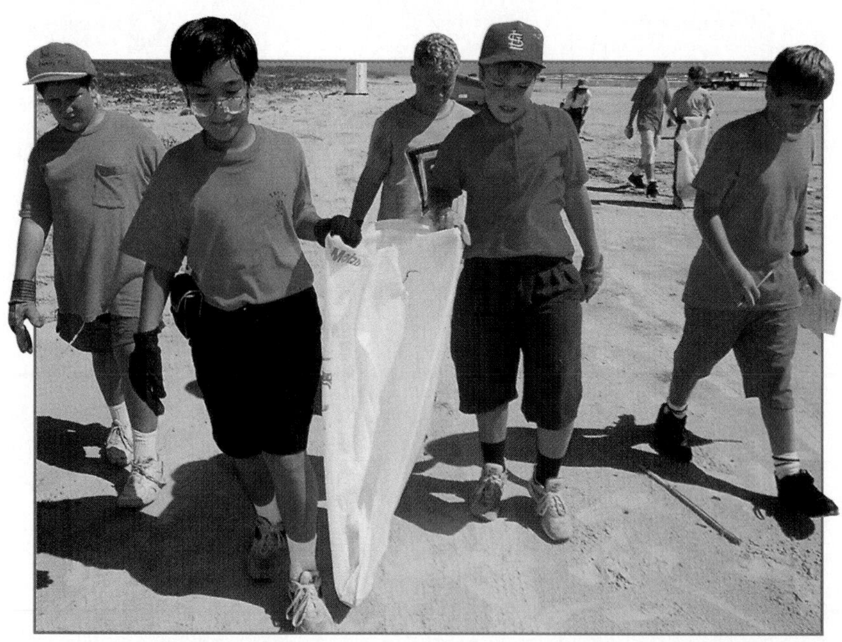

PUTTING IT TOGETHER

It is amazing to think about the natural resources we use every day. The water we drink, the air we breathe, even the wood used for the furniture are all natural resources. There are many other natural resources that we may not think about. These are things such as coal, oil, gas, and sunlight. People in every community depend on natural resources. Natural resources are so important because they help us live. That is why we need to learn ways to care for natural resources and our environment.

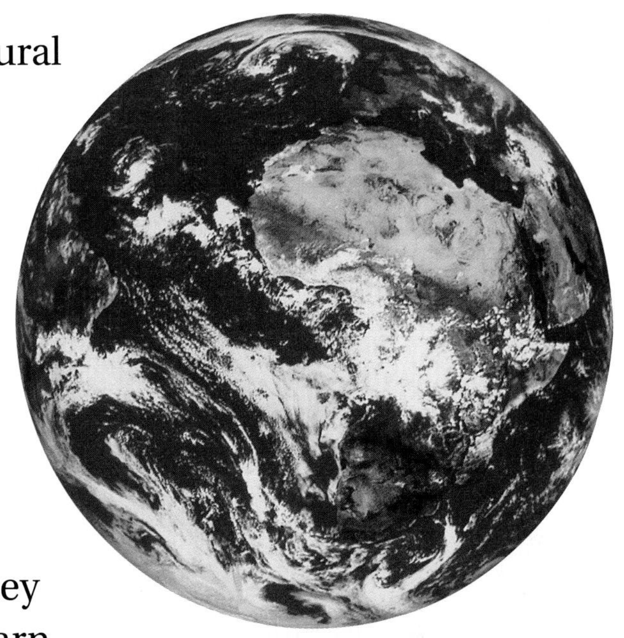

Earth's natural resources provide us with everything we need to live.

Review and Assess

1. Write one sentence for each of the vocabulary terms.

   environment **mineral** **natural resource** **nonrenewable resource** **recycle**

2. What is something you use that is made from trees?

3. What are natural resources?
4. What are two natural resources all people need, no matter where they live?
5. **Sort** the following into two groups—oil, coal, water, trees, gold, salt, sunlight, and copper. Say whether they are renewable resources or nonrenewable resources.

Make a poster showing ways that you and your family use natural resources.

Write about things you can do to help protect our environment. Choose one of them, and explain why it is important.

BIOGRAPHY Focus on Responsibility

Marjory Stoneman Douglas

"There are no other Everglades in the world. . . . Nothing anywhere else is like them."

Marjory Stoneman Douglas had a way of changing people's minds. For more than 50 years, she wrote and spoke about the need to preserve the Florida Everglades. Thanks to her, the Everglades are now a national park.

The Everglades are a one-of-a-kind natural environment. They are home to alligators, crocodiles, birds of all kinds, butterflies, and even panthers. Many of the plants and animals there are found nowhere else.

THE LIFE OF MARJORY STONEMAN DOUGLAS

1890 | 1910 | 1930 | 1950 | 1970 | 1990

1890 Douglas is born in Minnesota.

1947 Douglas writes *The Everglades: River of Grass.*

1947 Everglades National Park is created.

1969 Douglas forms the Friends of the Everglades.

1993 Douglas gets the Medal of Freedom.

1998 Douglas dies at the age of 108.

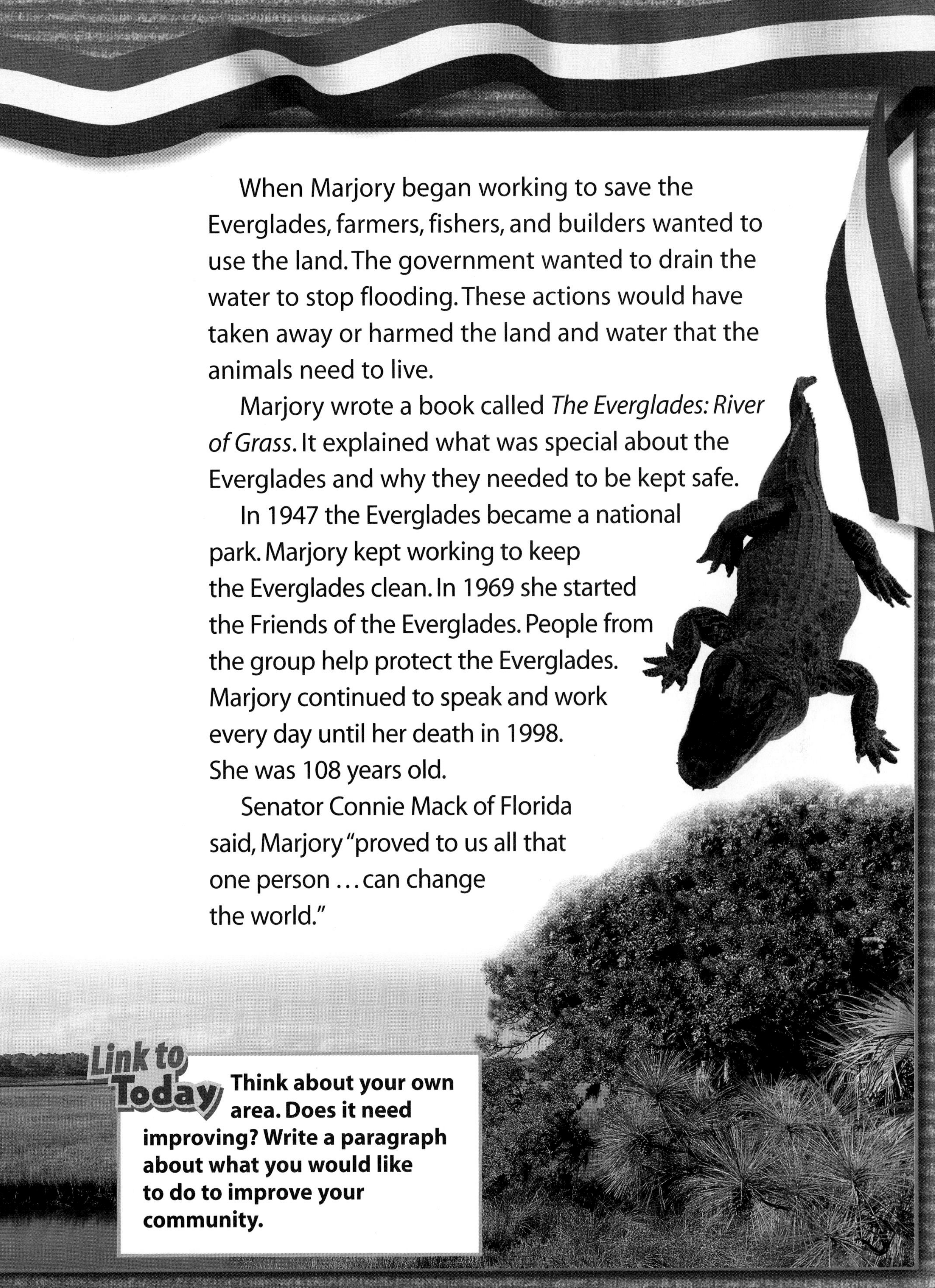

When Marjory began working to save the Everglades, farmers, fishers, and builders wanted to use the land. The government wanted to drain the water to stop flooding. These actions would have taken away or harmed the land and water that the animals need to live.

Marjory wrote a book called *The Everglades: River of Grass*. It explained what was special about the Everglades and why they needed to be kept safe.

In 1947 the Everglades became a national park. Marjory kept working to keep the Everglades clean. In 1969 she started the Friends of the Everglades. People from the group help protect the Everglades. Marjory continued to speak and work every day until her death in 1998. She was 108 years old.

Senator Connie Mack of Florida said, Marjory "proved to us all that one person . . . can change the world."

Link to Today **Think about your own area. Does it need improving? Write a paragraph about what you would like to do to improve your community.**

Being a Good Citizen

Frogwatch!

Every month Sean Carollo, age ten, and his family go searching for frogs at a pond near their home in Glenwood, Maryland. They are members of a group called Frogwatch USA. Frogwatch members help scientists count frogs in all our country's ponds, swamps, and marshes.

Frogs are dying in many parts of the country. Sometimes it is because of changing weather patterns or water that has become unhealthy.

"By keeping track of the frogs, we can know if they are starting to disappear," says Sam Droege. He is a scientist with Frogwatch. "Maybe then we can do something to protect them."

Sean and other volunteers help track the frogs by recording their calls. Volunteers learn to know the calls of different frogs.

"Counting frogs is a way of telling us how our environment is doing."

Sean Carollo

"Bullfrogs," Sean says, "have very deep voices. Cricket frogs make clicking sounds. Green frogs, American toads, and spring peepers each have their own calls."

At night, when frogs are most active, volunteers listen for their calls. They write down how many kinds of calls they hear and how often. They also record the temperature and wind speed. This is because heat and wind affect how many frogs come out.

Sean likes being a Frogwatch volunteer. "Counting frogs is a way of telling us how our environment is doing," he says.

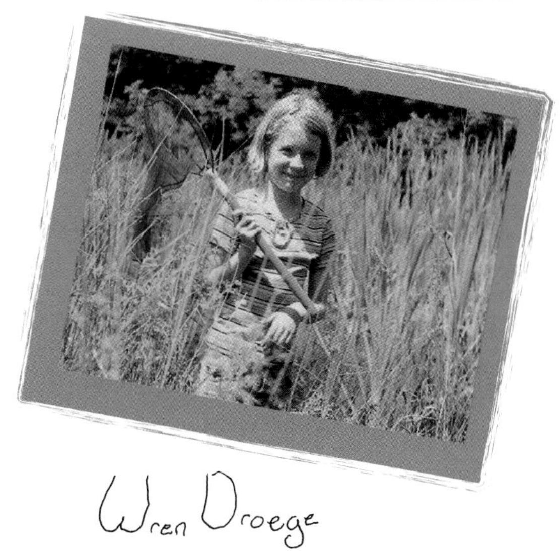

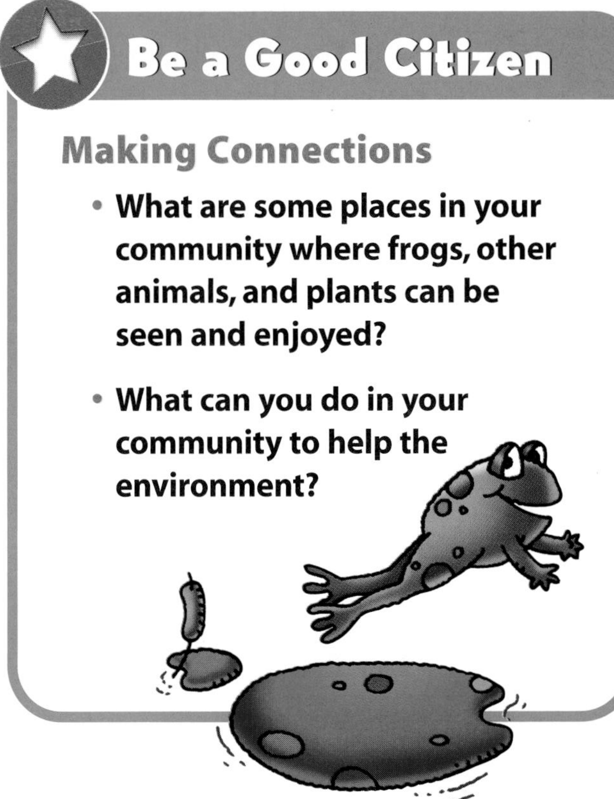

Be a Good Citizen

Making Connections

- **What are some places in your community where frogs, other animals, and plants can be seen and enjoyed?**
- **What can you do in your community to help the environment?**

Acting On It

In the Classroom

Observe the environment around your own school and community. How many different plants and animals live there? List as many as you can think of. Then choose one to study further.

Our Environment

Maple Trees
Oak Trees
Deer
Rabbits
Butterflies

Reading Bar Graphs and Line Graphs

You have read that different states have different natural resources. Suppose you want to look at natural resource production in different states. Maybe you want to know about production in different states at the same time. Maybe you want to know how production changed in one state over a period of years. A **graph** could help you. A graph is a special kind of picture that shows information in a way that is easy to understand. There are several different kinds of graphs.

VOCABULARY

graph
bar graph
line graph

LEARN THE SKILL

Look at the graphs on these pages as you follow the steps below.

1. **Identify the type of graph.** The graph on this page is a **bar graph**. A bar graph has bars to show amounts at one time. The graph on the next page is a **line graph**. A line graph shows how something changes over time. A line connects dots that give information for different dates.

2. **Look at the graph title to tell what the graph shows.** The graph on this page shows the leading oil-producing states in 2000.

3. **Look at the labels on the graph.** The labels along the bottom of the bar graph name states. The labels along the left side show oil production in millions of barrels.

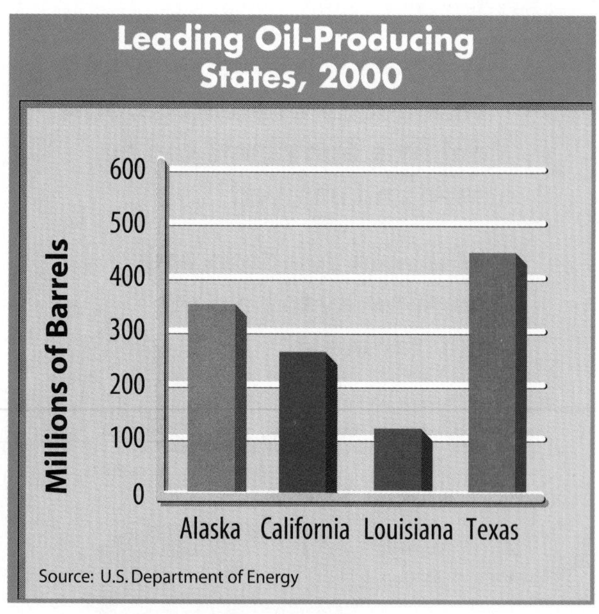

4. **Use the graphs to find information and to see similarities and differences.** By looking at the bar graph, you know that in 2000 California produced more oil than Louisiana. The line graph on this page shows how much oil Alaska produced in different years.

TRY THE SKILL

Look at the graph on this page to answer the questions.

1. What type of graph is this?
2. What does this graph show?
3. About how much oil did Alaska produce in 1980?
4. In what year did Alaska produce the most oil? The least oil?

EXTEND THE SKILL

Make a line graph to show information about a third-grade class recycling project. In the first month they collected 290 cans; in the second month, 360 cans; in the third month, 480 cans; in the fourth month, 390 cans; and in the fifth month, 450 cans.

- What is the title of your graph?
- What information will you put along the bottom of the graph? The side?
- In which month did they collect the most cans?
- How many cans did the class collect in five months?

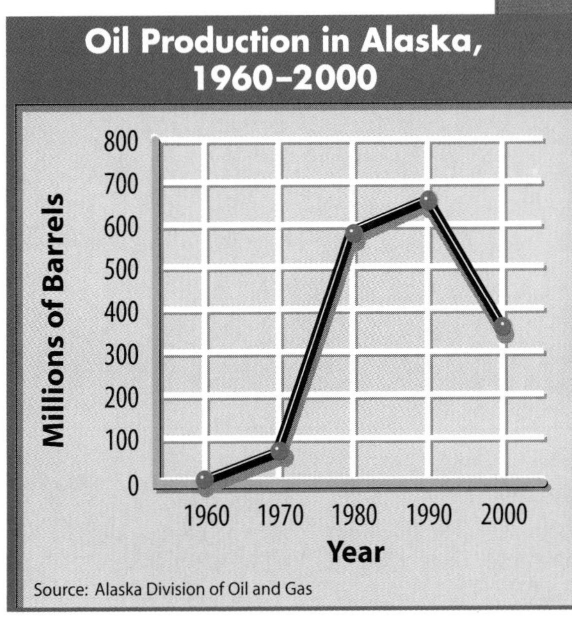

Protecting Our Environment

VOCABULARY

coast
peninsula
island
wildlife

How are natural resources important to people in Ine, Japan?

Lesson Outline

- Life in a Fishing Community
- Rich in Wildlife
- Caring for Our Resources

READING STRATEGY

Copy this chart. In the top write "Ine, Japan." Below write two **main ideas** about Ine. In the bottom write facts about each idea.

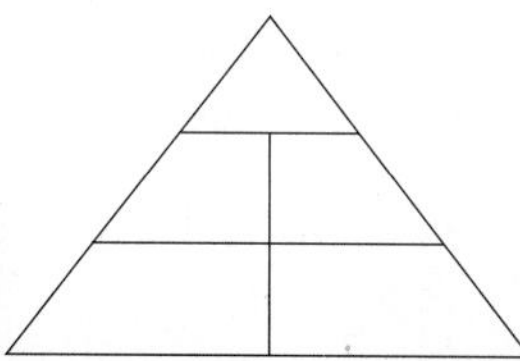

BUILD BACKGROUND

People around the world build their communities near natural resources. In this lesson we will travel to another country and visit a community by the sea. The plants and animals that live in the ocean are an important natural resource to the people who live here.

LIFE IN A FISHING COMMUNITY

Ine (EE nay) is on the **coast** of **Japan**, a country in Asia. A coast is land next to a large body of water. When you are in Ine, water is all around you. That is because Ine is on a **peninsula**, or land that has water on three sides. Japan itself is an **island**. An island is land that is completely surrounded by water.

The sea around Ine is home to many kinds of animals. There are birds, seals, turtles, whales, and, of course, lots of fish!

Prawns (above) are a type of shrimp found in the Sea of Japan.

How is a peninsula different from an island?

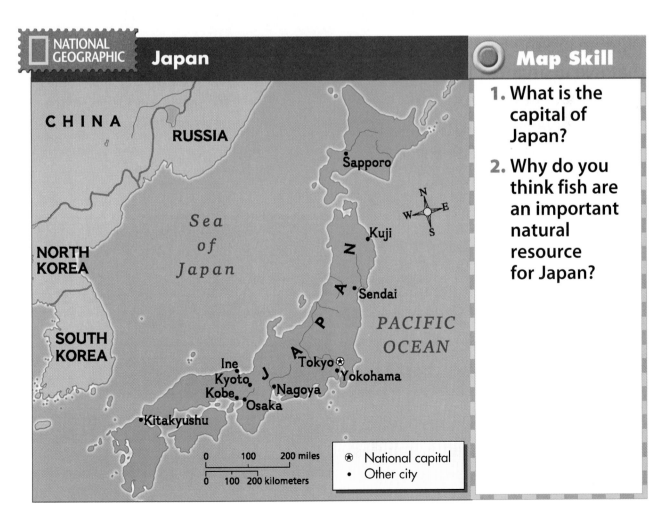

NATIONAL GEOGRAPHIC **Japan**

CHINA
RUSSIA
NORTH KOREA
SOUTH KOREA
JAPAN
Sea of Japan
PACIFIC OCEAN
Sapporo
Kuji
Sendai
Tokyo
Yokohama
Ine
Kyoto
Kobe
Osaka
Nagoya
Kitakyushu
N S E W
0 100 200 miles
0 100 200 kilometers
⊛ National capital
• Other city

Map Skill

1. What is the capital of Japan?
2. Why do you think fish are an important natural resource for Japan?

RICH IN WILDLIFE

The people of Ine use the resources around them. Many people in this community have jobs in fishing. The most important fish resource is a small fish called a sardine. A type of shrimp called prawns is another important fish resource in Ine. Millions of these fish are netted and shipped to markets in Japan and around the world.

Part of Ine is a reserve. That means it is a protected area for plants and **wildlife**. Wildlife are the wild animals that live in an area. The reserve in Ine covers both land and water. It gives many animals a safe place to live. The reserve is one important way that people in Ine work to protect their environment.

One reason there is so much wildlife in Ine is because of a special mix of warm and cold ocean water that meets here, in the Sea of Japan. Plants that fish eat grow well in this water. The large number of fish in turn allows for large numbers of birds, whales, and other animals that eat fish.

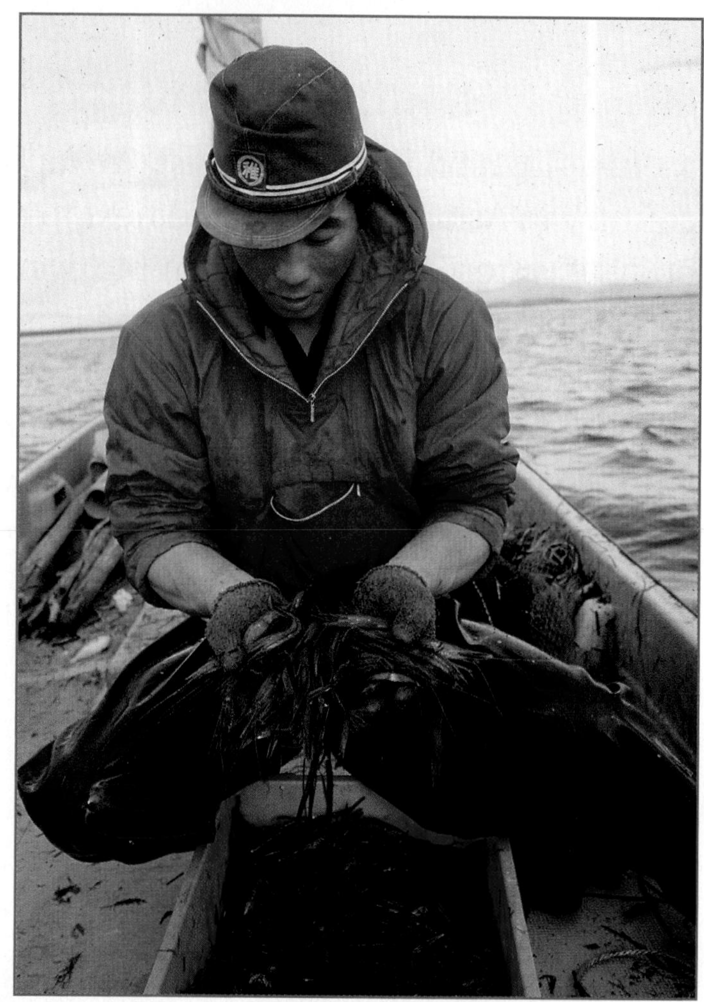

Fishers catch lots of shrimp (above) and snow crabs (below) in the waters off Ine.

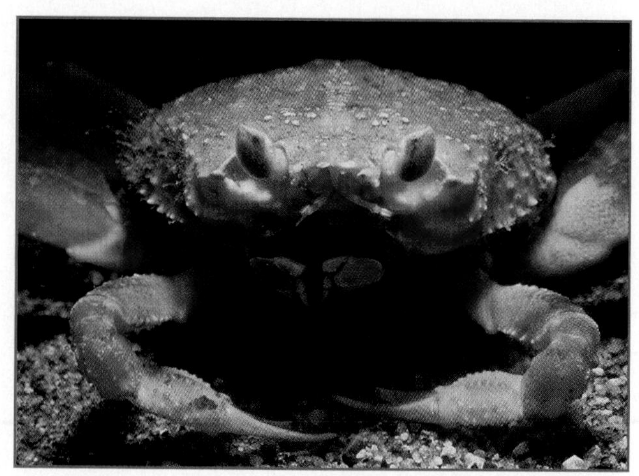

Visitors Come to Ine

People come from all over the world to see the wildlife here. Some people in Ine have jobs taking visitors on tours of the area around Ine. Visitors also go to nearby Aoshima (ay oh SHEE muh) Island. The rich wildlife of this area provides both food and jobs for the people who live here.

READING CHECK **In what ways is the wildlife of Ine important to the people who live here?**

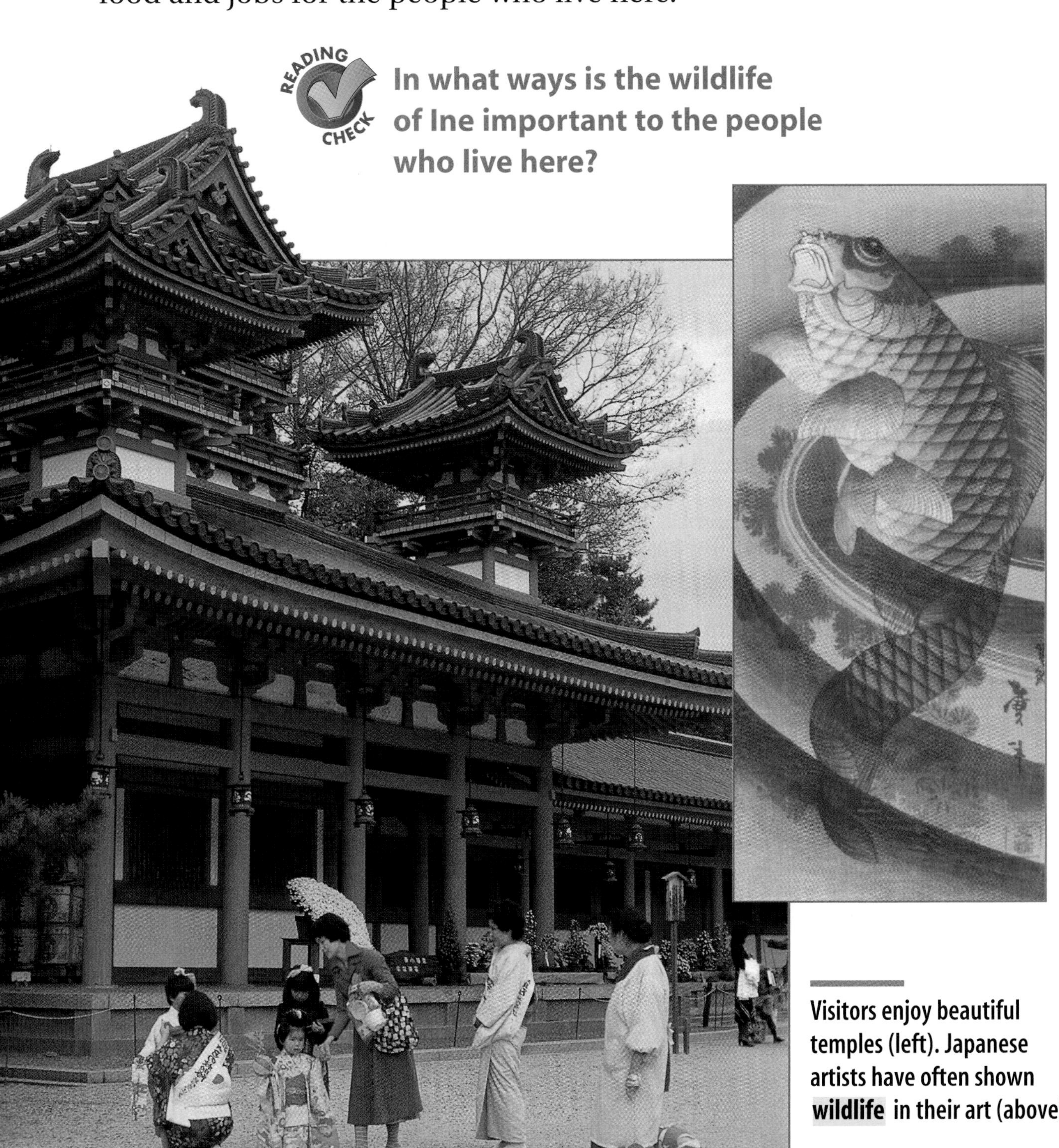

Visitors enjoy beautiful temples (left). Japanese artists have often shown **wildlife** in their art (above).

CARING FOR OUR RESOURCES

The people in Japan care about the natural resources in their environment. Like many other communities around the world, Ine has a problem with pollution. Pollution is something that makes air, water, or soil dirty. Garbage left in the ocean, such as plastic bottles, plastic bags, and old fishing nets, can kill fish and other ocean life.

Using very large modern fishing nets, people are also catching too many fish, especially sardines. With fewer sardines in the water, larger fish and dolphins do not have enough to eat. Fishing nets also endanger dolphins and other wildlife.

All of these actions are harmful to the wildlife in and around Ine. People are working hard to make the environment better, though. The Kyoto government is making laws to clean up the sea. Factories are changing their machines to create less pollution. Safer nets are also being designed.

What are the people of Ine doing to take care of their environment?

People in Ine use and care for natural resources like the Sea of Japan.

PUTTING IT TOGETHER

Natural resources are very important to the community of Ine, Japan. Many people make their living by fishing. Other people have jobs bringing travelers to places where they can watch and enjoy wildlife. You have also seen that people can destroy their natural resources, or use too many of them. It is important for communities to find ways to protect their resources. If they do, the resources will be there to use and enjoy for many years to come.

The Japanese art called origami often depicts creatures from the natural world.

Review and Assess

1. Write one sentence for each of the vocabulary words.

   coast **island**
   peninsula **wildlife**

2. What are three natural resources found in Ine, Japan?
3. Analyze how the people of Ine use their natural resources.
4. Describe a peninsula. What might life be like on a peninsula?
5. How are the wildlife in your community and the wildlife in Ine **alike** and **different**?

Make a wildlife poster. Go through old magazines to find pictures of different kinds of wildlife. Cut out the pictures, and paste them onto a piece of oaktag.

Suppose you know a student in Ine, Japan. **Write** him or her telling about wildlife in your community.

Chapter 2 REVIEW

VOCABULARY REVIEW

Number a sheet of paper from 1 to 3. Beside each number write the term from the list below that best completes each sentence.

environment **landform**

natural resource

1. A(n) ___ is something that helps people live.
2. A plateau is a kind of ___.
3. We help the ___ by recycling.

CHAPTER COMPREHENSION

4. How might the geography of a mountain community affect the way people there live?
5. Which natural resource is used to make paper? Is this a nonrenewable resource?
6. Write about the environment in Ine, Japan. Give one example of what people there are doing to take care of their environment.

SKILL REVIEW

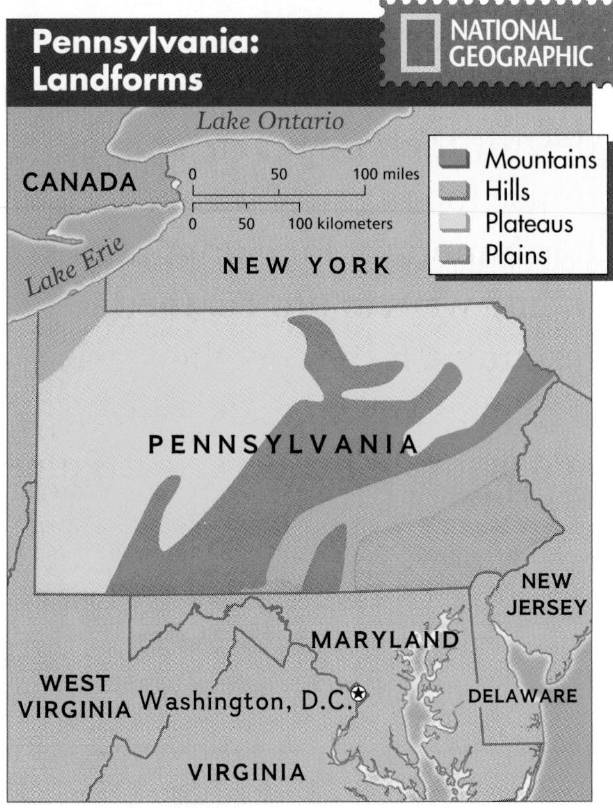

7. **Geography Skill** How many different landforms does the state of Pennsylvania have?
8. **Geography Skill** Which kind of landform covers the greatest area of Pennsylvania? Which covers the least?
9. **Study Skill** What is a bar graph? How is it used?

USING A CHART

10. Look at the chart. What are two things we get from oil?

Natural Resources	Uses
Water	Drinking, watering crops
Trees	Building, lumber
Oil	Fuel, plastic
Iron	Steel, building

Activity

Talking About Geography and Natural Resources Choose a community you know of that has a special feature. The feature can be a natural resource, a landform, a body of water, or the climate.

Write a short speech about how this special feature changes the way people in the community live. Include maps or pictures you have drawn. Make a presentation, and read your speech to the class.

Use your Foldable to review what you know, would like to know, and what you learned about communities and geography. As you look at the front of your Foldable, mentally recall how geography and natural resources affect how people supply their basic needs—food, shelter, clothing, and transportation. Review ways in which communities can protect their environment and natural resources.

Your Community's Geography

In this unit you have been reading about the geography of communities. What is your local geography like? What can geography tell you about your community?

Cindy had fun learning about her community. She lives in Seattle, Washington. She went to the library and went on-line to look at maps. To show what she learned, Cindy built a 3-D map out of clay.

- ***What would a similar map of your community look like?***

Activity

Build a 3-D Map with Clay

Materials

- cardboard
- map of your community
- clay of different colors
- paper
- tape
- markers

Step 1 After learning about your community, decide what to include on your map.

Step 2 Gather your materials.

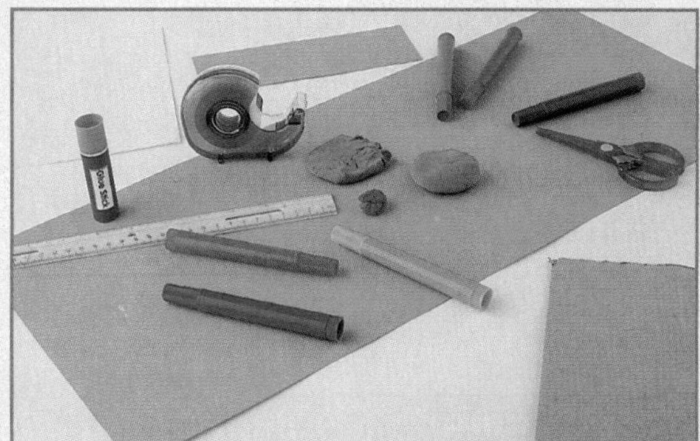

Step 3 Cover the cardboard with a thin layer of clay. Build up the features using different colors of clay.

Step 4 Identify the features with labels. Use toothpicks to place the labels into the clay. Give your map a title.

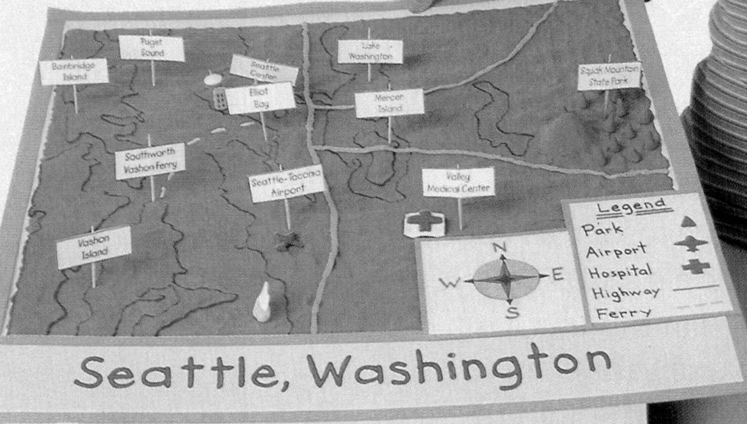

Unit 1 REVIEW

VOCABULARY REVIEW

Number a sheet of paper from 1 to 6. Beside each number write the word from the list below that matches the description.

citizen **climate**
community **environment**
geography **landform**

1. The study of Earth's natural features
2. A person who lives in a community
3. A place where people live, work, and play
4. What a place's weather is like over a long period of time
5. The air, water, land, and living things around us
6. The shape of the surface of the land

SKILL REVIEW

7. **Reading/Thinking Skill** People in Ine, Japan, depend on fishing for food and jobs. If they take too much fish from the sea, though, there will be a shortage. How might they solve this problem?
8. **Study Skill** What is a bar graph? What is a line graph?
9. **Geography Skill** What do the colors on the map on this page represent?
10. **Geography Skill** What landforms does West Virginia have?

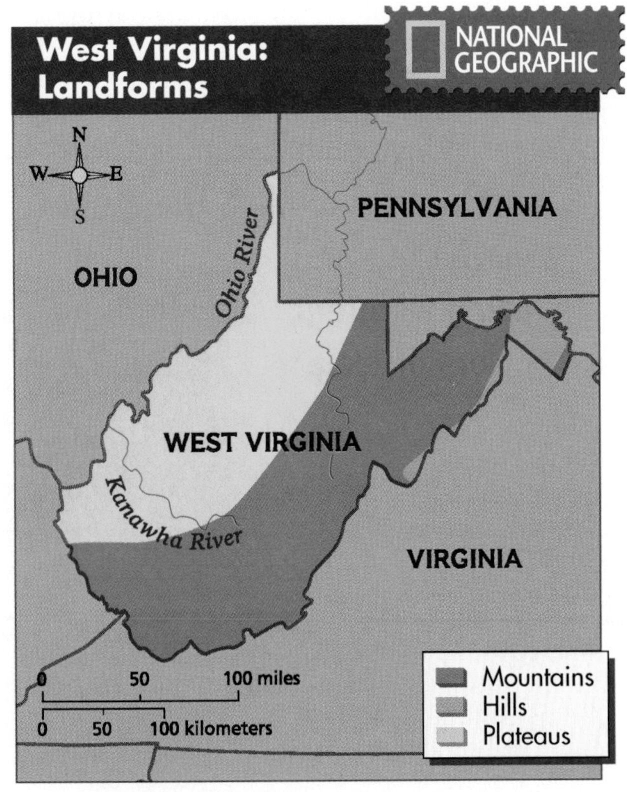

TECHNOLOGY

For more resources about the people and places you studied in this unit, visit **www.mhschool.com** and follow the links to Grade 3, Unit 1.

TEST PREP

Read the passage. Then read the questions that follow. Decide which is the best answer to each question, and write it on a piece of paper.

Climate is different from daily weather. For example, it may be rainy in Phoenix for a day or two. However, over a long period of time, it is mostly dry. In the United States the climate is most often cooler in the north than it is in the south.

People learn to adapt to the climate of their communities. To adapt means to become used to something. People who live in cold climates are used to wearing warm clothes. People in warm climates are used to wearing light clothes.

1 What problem might a family from a warm climate have when they move to a cold climate?

- They would not like wearing light clothing.
- They would not be used to the cold.
- They would have to move again.
- They would be too hot in the north.

2 One year El Paso had 50 days of rain and 315 days of sun. The climate there is mostly

- cool and cloudy
- wet and windy
- cold and snowy
- hot and dry

WRITING ACTIVITIES

Writing to Persuade One way to help keep your community clean and also preserve natural resources is to recycle. Write a speech. Tell other students why they should save and recycle bottles, cans, and paper.

Writing to Inform Suppose you are a tour guide in the community of Ine, Japan. Write a script in which you tell visitors about Ine, including the things they will see and places they will visit.

Writing to Express Write the words for a song or poem about our country's geography and the natural features that are found in different places.

LITERATURE

A Poem About History

I Have Heard of a Land

Selection by Joyce Carol Thomas
Illustrated by Floyd Cooper

In the late 1800s many people started new communities in the western part of our country. These settlers came with hopes and dreams to start new lives.

I have heard of a land
Where the crickets **skirl** in harmony
And babies wrapped to their mothers' backs in the field
Laugh more than they cry

I have heard of a land where worship
Takes place in an outdoor church
Under an **arbor** of bushes
And the hymns sound just as sweet

---

skirl (skûrl) to make a high-pitched sound

arbor (är′bər) a place that is covered by trees, shrubs, or vines growing on a frame

I have heard of a land
Where a woman sleeps in a **sod** hut
    dug deep in the heart of the earth
Her roof is decorated with brush
A hole in the ground is her stove
And a horse saddle is her pillow
She wakes thinking of a three-room log cabin

And soon that morning her neighbors
    and their sons and daughters
Help lift the logs and chock them into place
Together they **hoist** the beams high
After dinner, they finish the porch
    where they sit and tell stories

---

sod (sod) the top layer of soil that has grass growing on it
hoist (hoist) to lift or pull up

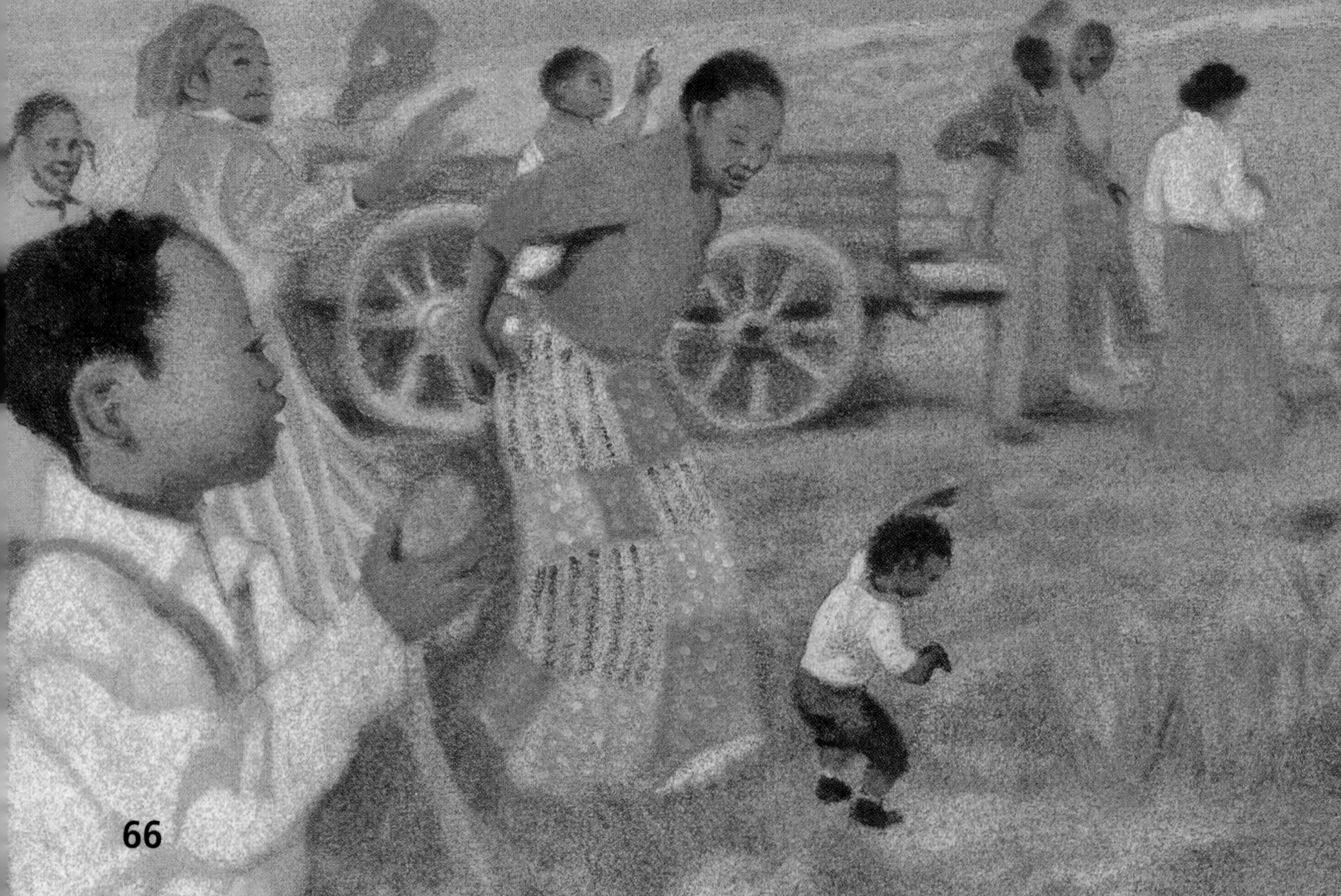

Finally when everyone else has gone home
She saws the planks for the steps
by herself

That night by the glow of an oil lamp
She writes in her journal:

I raise nearly everything I eat
The land is good here
I grind corn for meal
Raise me some cane and make ***sorghum*** *syrup*
And if I feel real smart
I make ***hominy*** *grits from scratch*

I have heard of a land
Where the **pioneer** woman still lives
Her possibilities reach as far
As her eyes can see
And as far as our imaginations
can carry us

---

sorghum (sôr′gəm) a plant from which syrup, similar to cane syrup, is made

hominy (hom′ə nē) kernels of white corn that are hulled and ground up

pioneer (pī′ə nîr′) a person who is among the first to explore an area not known to him or her

Write About It!

Life was very difficult for the new pioneers. What do you think life was like for children during this time? Explain your answer in one paragraph.

Unit 2

Communities Have History

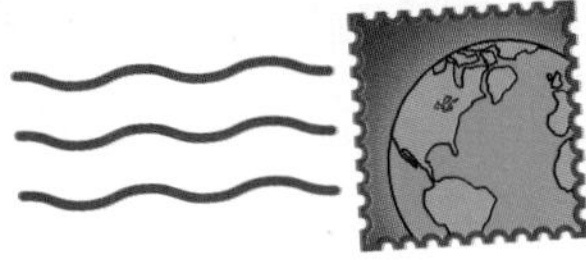

TAKE A LOOK

How have communities changed?

Your community did not always look the way it does today. Communities change over time.

Explore our country's
history at our Web site
www.mhschool.com

Chapter

Early Communities in America

Native Americans formed the first communities in America.

About 400 years ago new people came from other lands.

They too built communities in North America.

Native Americans used the natural resources in the environment to build communities.
This community that we now call Mesa Verde was home to the Anasazi people for hundreds of years.

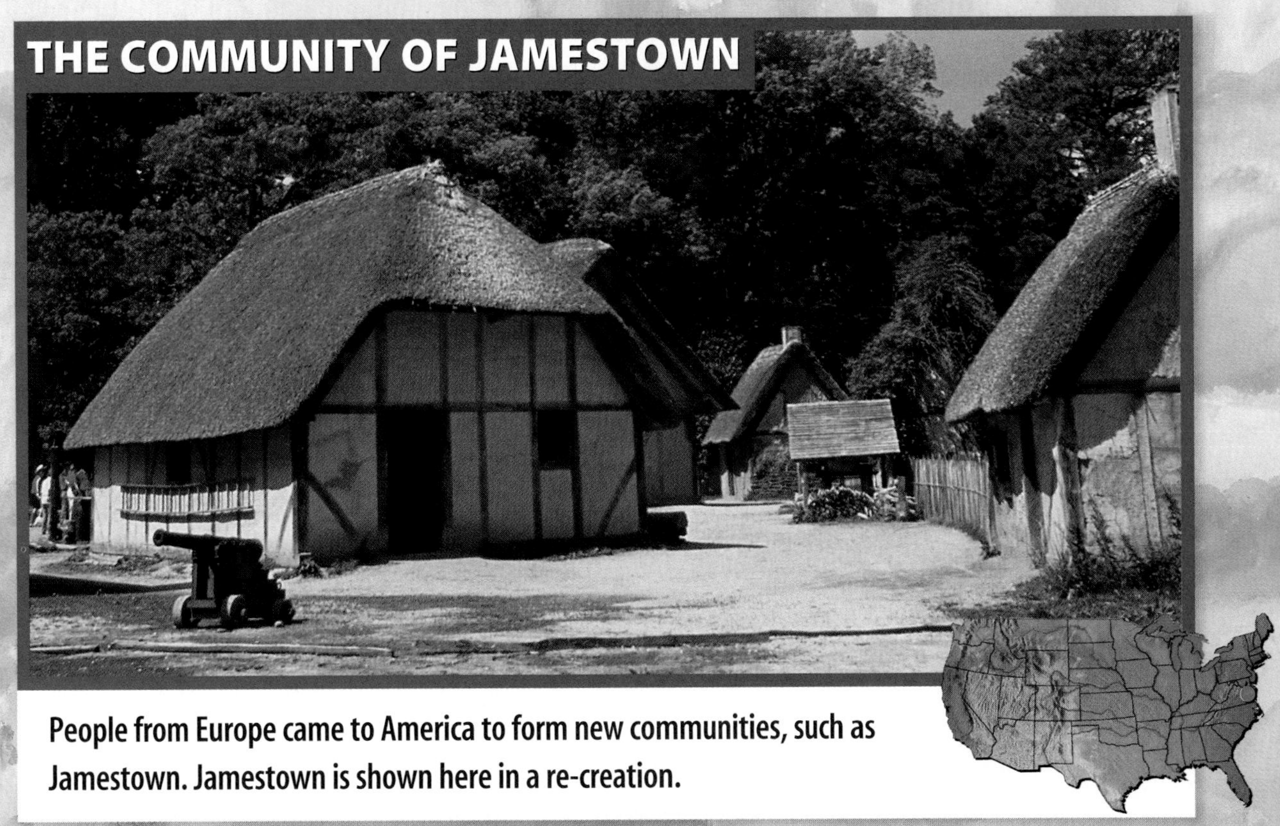

People from Europe came to America to form new communities, such as Jamestown. Jamestown is shown here in a re-creation.

Foldables

Make this Foldable study guide, and use it to record what you learn about "Early Communities in America."

1. Fold a sheet of paper like a hot dog, but make one side 1" longer than the other.
2. On the short side of the paper, make two cuts, equal distances apart to form three tabs.
3. Draw two ovals to form a Venn diagram.
4. Label the 1" tab with the chapter title. Label the two outside tabs with lesson titles. Label the middle tab "Both."

Lesson 1

Native American Communities

VOCABULARY

ancient
culture
desert
technology
canyon
mesa
cliff

READING STRATEGY

In a chart like this, **sort** the natural resources used by the Iroquois and the Anasazi. Tell how each resource was used.

What were the first communities in North America like?

Lesson Outline

- Storytelling and Culture
- Native American Groups
- A Native American Community of Long Ago
- Searching for the Anasazi

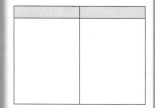

BUILD BACKGROUND

Native Americans have lived in North America since **ancient** times. *Ancient* means having to do with times long ago. Native Americans are also known as Indians. In this lesson you will read about how some Native Americans lived long ago. You will also read about life in one Native American community.

STORYTELLING AND CULTURE

Native Americans have lived in what is now the United States for thousands of years. In that time they developed many **cultures**. Culture is the way of life of a group of people.

Native Americans today preserve their **culture**. This boy (opposite page) is showing the grass dance.

Storytelling is an important part of many Native American cultures. Stories are told to explain the natural world, to teach proper behavior, or just to have fun. Stories are passed down from parents to children. The Cherokee story below tells how Earth got its shape.

from **"Between Earth and Sky"**
— by Joseph Bruchac

The ground was still as wet as a swamp, too soft for anyone to stand.

Great **Buzzard** said, "I will help dry the land." He began to fly close above the new Earth. Where his wings came down, valleys were formed, and where his wings lifted, hills rose up through the mist....

And so it is that the Cherokee people, aware of how this land was given, know that the Earth is a **sacred** gift we all must respect and share.

---

buzzard (buz′ərd) a very large bird
sacred (sā′krid) deserving respect

How is storytelling part of culture?

NATIVE AMERICAN GROUPS

Native Americans lived in different groups. Each group had its own culture, with different languages and beliefs. Often the way of life of an Indian group was shaped by the environment. Look at the map on page 77. It shows some Native American groups and where they lived. It also shows how some Native American groups shared similar cultures.

The Chinook lived in an area of tall trees and many rivers. From the trees they built boats called canoes. They used the canoes to fish for salmon. Each year the salmon returned from the ocean to the rivers. The Chinook marked this return as a special time of year.

The Iroquois lived in a wooded area. They used trees to build homes, tools, and canoes. They used the rich soil for growing corn, beans, and squash. They hunted deer for both meat and skins. Deerskins made warm clothing for the winter.

Salmon (above) were an important part of the Chinook culture. The Iroquois built large "longhouses" (below).

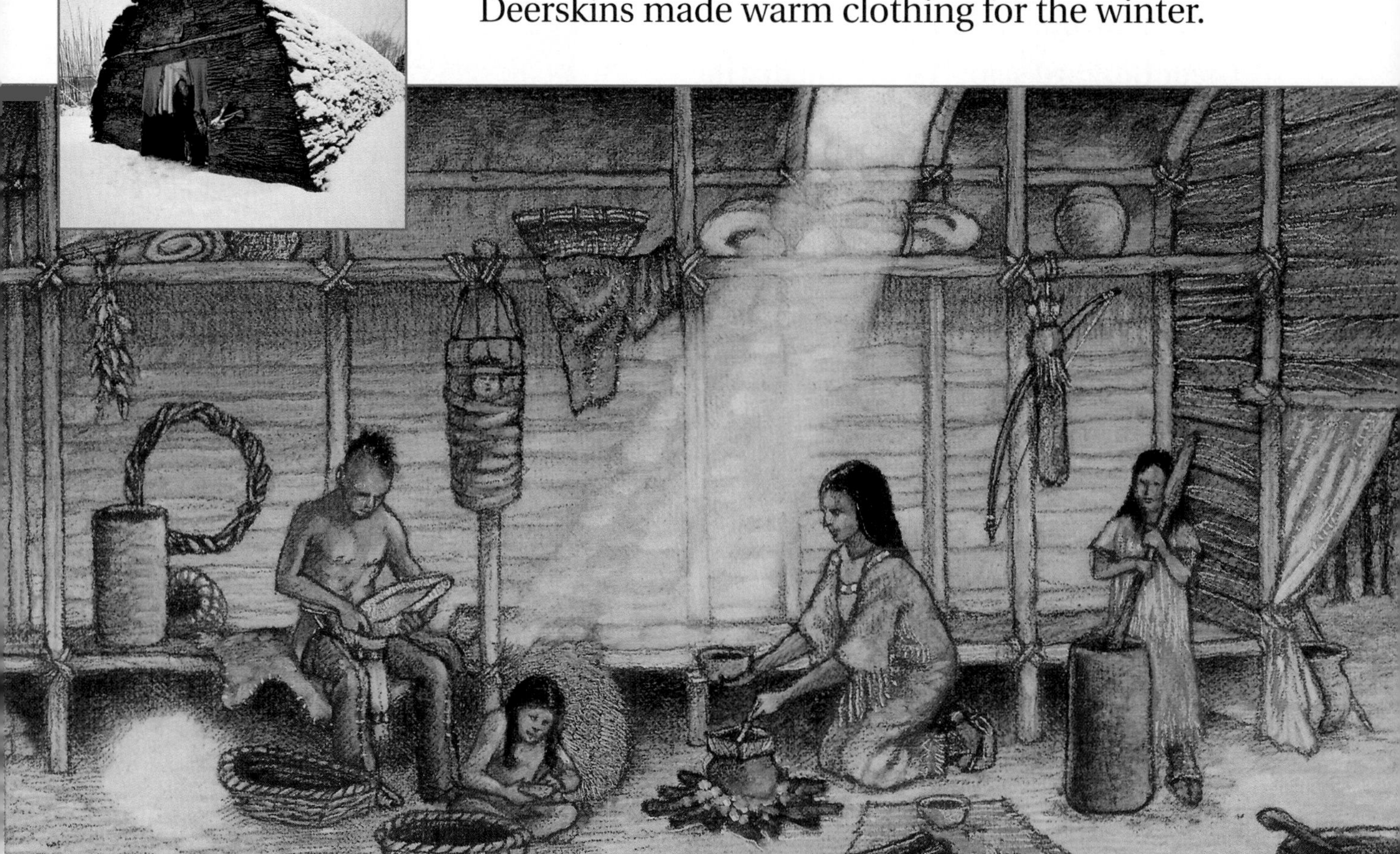

Native American Cultural Areas

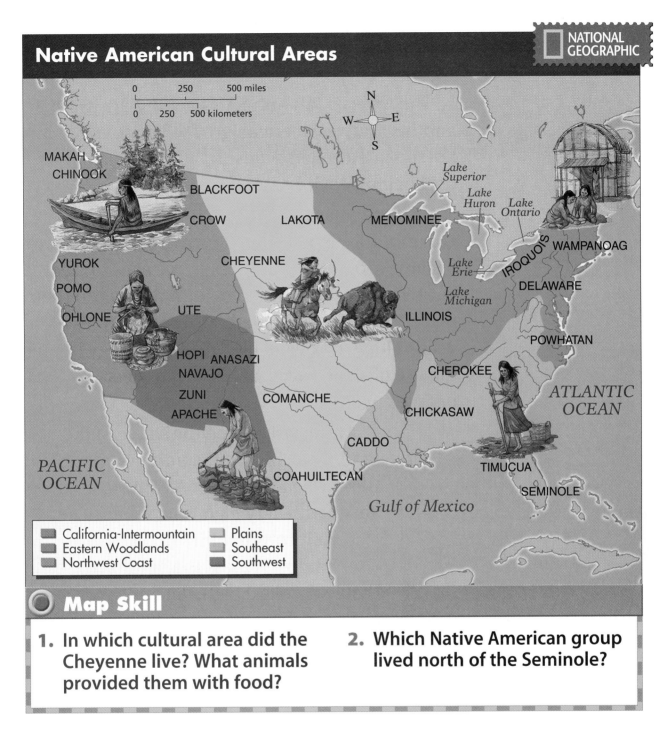

NATIONAL GEOGRAPHIC

Map Skill

1. **In which cultural area did the Cheyenne live? What animals provided them with food?**
2. **Which Native American group lived north of the Seminole?**

Wherever they lived, each Native American culture used materials from the environment. Natural resources were used for food, clothing, and shelter. Each Native American group used the resources in its environment in its own way.

How was the environment important to Native American peoples?

A NATIVE AMERICAN COMMUNITY OF LONG AGO

The Anasazi (ah nuh SAH zee) Indians were another Native American group. They lived in a hot, dry area called a **desert**. It was a harsh and challenging environment.

Still, the Anasazi were able to build communities in this difficult environment. They became farmers. They made stone axes to clear land. They dug ditches to carry rainwater to their fields. These farming methods are examples of **technology** (tek NOL uh jee). Technology is the use of skills, ideas, and tools to meet people's needs.

The Anasazi used the shape of the land, too. They built communities on the walls of **canyons**. A canyon is a deep valley with very high, steep sides. They also built communities on **mesas** (MAY suhz). A mesa is a landform that looks like a high, flat table.

Life at Mesa Verde

One of the largest Anasazi communities was at a place we call **Mesa Verde**. At Mesa Verde the Anasazi built their homes right on the **cliffs**. A cliff is the steep face of a rock. These buildings protected the Anasazi from enemies and bad weather.

Almost everyone at Mesa Verde worked to help the community. Women usually cared for children, ground corn, and cooked. They made clothing and baskets from the yucca plant. They also made pots from clay. Men worked in the fields. They hunted rabbits, deer, and small desert animals. Men also built and fixed the houses. Older children helped adults in many ways. This helped the children learn important skills.

The Anasazi used natural resources to make clothing (above) and pottery (below). They built their homes (bottom) right into the **mesa** (opposite).

READING CHECK **How did the Anasazi use resources in their environment?**

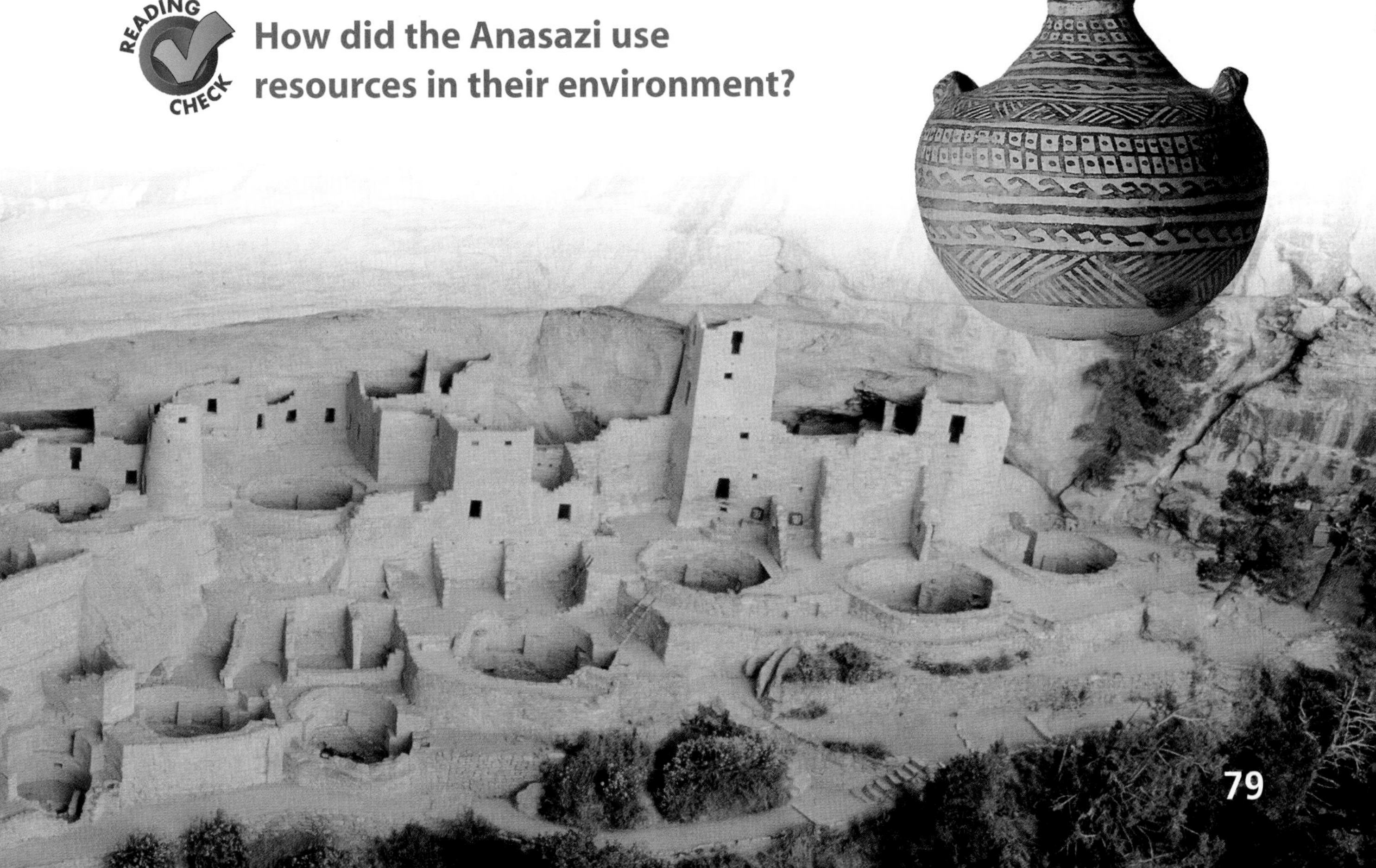

SEARCHING FOR THE ANASAZI

About 700 years ago the Anasazi left Mesa Verde and their other communities very suddenly. No one really knows why. For hundreds of years Mesa Verde lay empty. When scientists began to explore the cliff buildings, they found wall paintings, tools, clothing, pottery, and toys. The dry climate had helped to keep these things in good shape.

The Pueblo (PWEB loh) Indians of today share important parts of the Anasazi culture. The Pueblo make pottery similar to the Anasazi pottery of long ago.

READING CHECK **What happened to the Anasazi culture?**

This Pueblo potter (below) is making a vase. Pueblo pottery (below, left) looks a lot like ancient Anasazi pottery.

PUTTING IT TOGETHER

Native Americans were the first people to live in what is now the United States. Native American cultures were shaped by their environment. Native American people also shaped their environment to fit their needs. For thousands of years Native Americans were the only people living on this continent. Later other people came to live here.

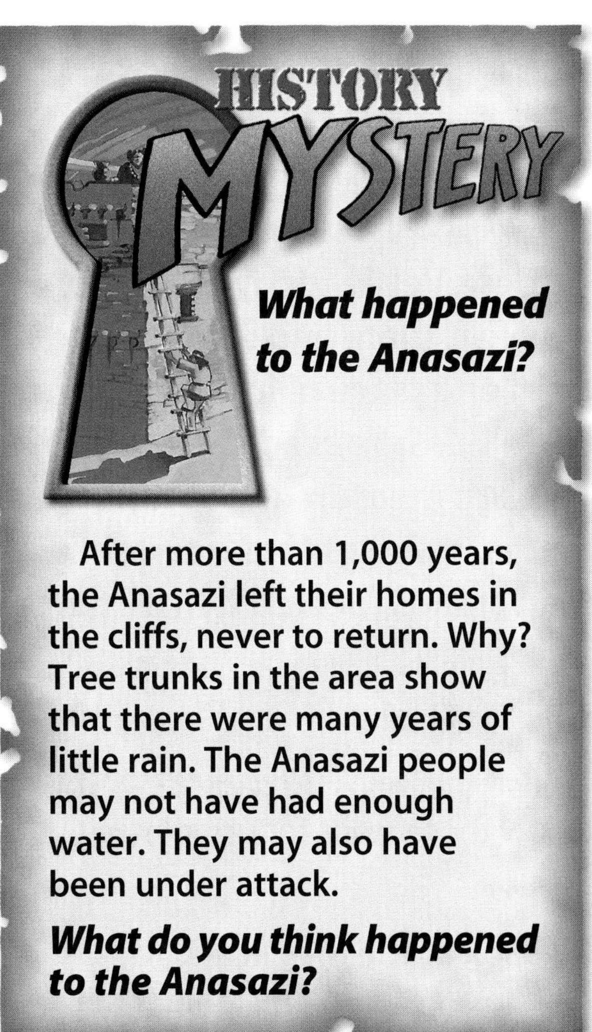

What happened to the Anasazi?

After more than 1,000 years, the Anasazi left their homes in the cliffs, never to return. Why? Tree trunks in the area show that there were many years of little rain. The Anasazi people may not have had enough water. They may also have been under attack.

What do you think happened to the Anasazi?

Review and Assess

1. Write a sentence for each word.

   ancient **canyon**
   desert **technology**

2. Why are stories important to Native American cultures?
3. What were the first North American communities like? Find out!
4. How did the Anasazi use landforms for their buildings?
5. How did the Anasazi use technology to **solve** the **problem** of their harsh environment?

Look at the map on page 77. Which Native American groups are shown along the Pacific Ocean?

Write a description of the picture of Mesa Verde on pages 78 and 79. What do you think it might have been like to live at Mesa Verde?

Using Map Scales

Mesa Verde today is a national park. Suppose you visit there and want to find out how far it is from one place of interest to another. One way to do this is to read the **scale** of a map. The scale helps to measure the real distance between places. It shows that a certain distance on the map stands for a certain distance on Earth.

VOCABULARY

scale

LEARN THE SKILL

Use the maps on page 83 as you follow these steps for using map scales.

1. **Look at the map scale.**
   Look at Map A. The scale is the line with marks that stand for miles. It shows that 1 inch on Map A stands for 8 miles.

2. **Make a map scale using a paper strip.**
   Look at the map scale on this page. Place your own strip along the top of the scale. Mark every inch to show 8 miles.

3. **Use your scale to measure distances on Map A.**
   How far is it from the Museum to the Far View Visitor Center? To find out, place the strip so that the 0 is at the dot for the Museum. Now read the number closest to the Far View Visitor Center. The distance between them is about 4 miles.

4. **Remember that not all maps have the same scale.**
   Maps have different scales because they show larger or smaller parts of Earth. Even though the scales are

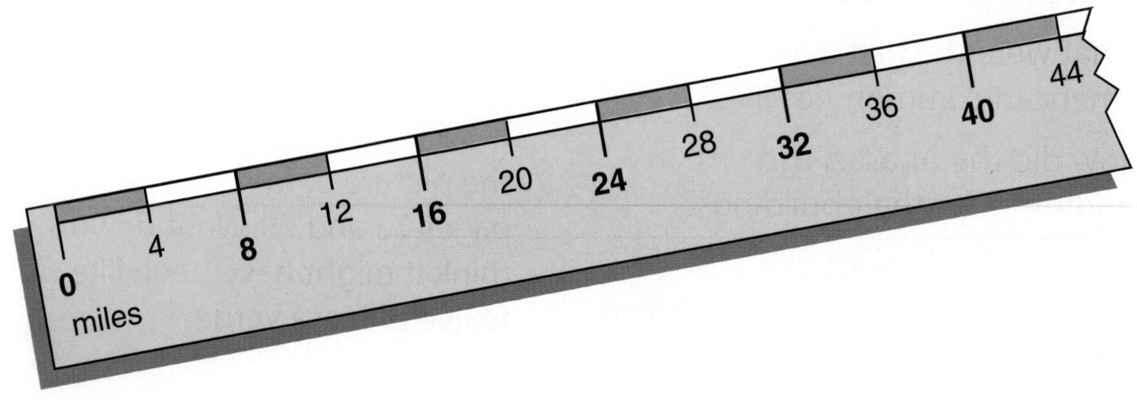

different, the real distances remain the same. The scale on Map B is different from the scale on Map A. Make a scale strip for this map. Use a ruler to help you mark the strip. Every inch will equal 4 miles.

TRY THE SKILL

Use the maps and your map-scale strips to answer the following questions.

1. What is the distance between Cortez and Mancos?
2. What is the distance between the Cliff Palace and the Balcony House?
3. How far is it from the Park Entrance to Morefield Village and campground?
4. At its widest point, how many miles is it across the park from west to east?

EXTEND THE SKILL

Turn to the map of North America on page R16 in the Atlas at the back of this book. Use the map scale to create a scale strip. Then find the distance from Washington, D.C., to Houston, Texas. What other distances can you find using your scale strip?

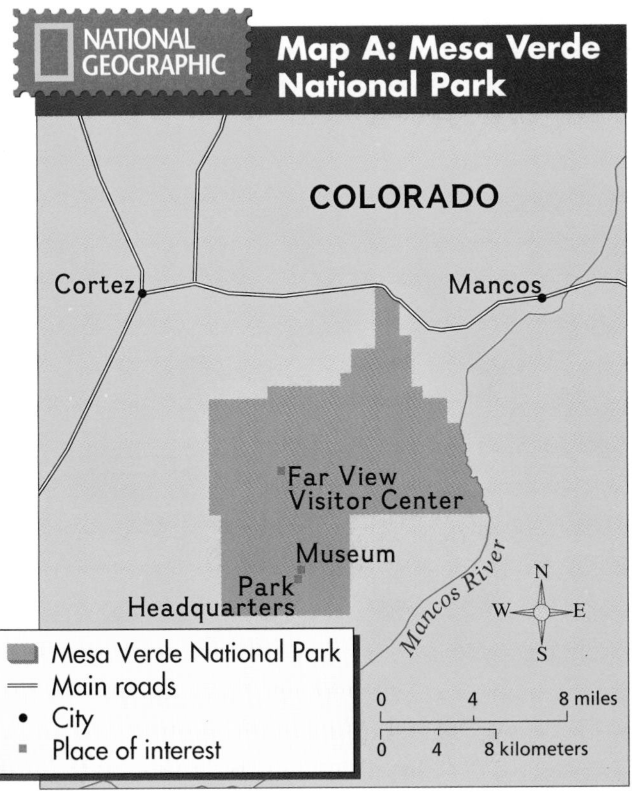

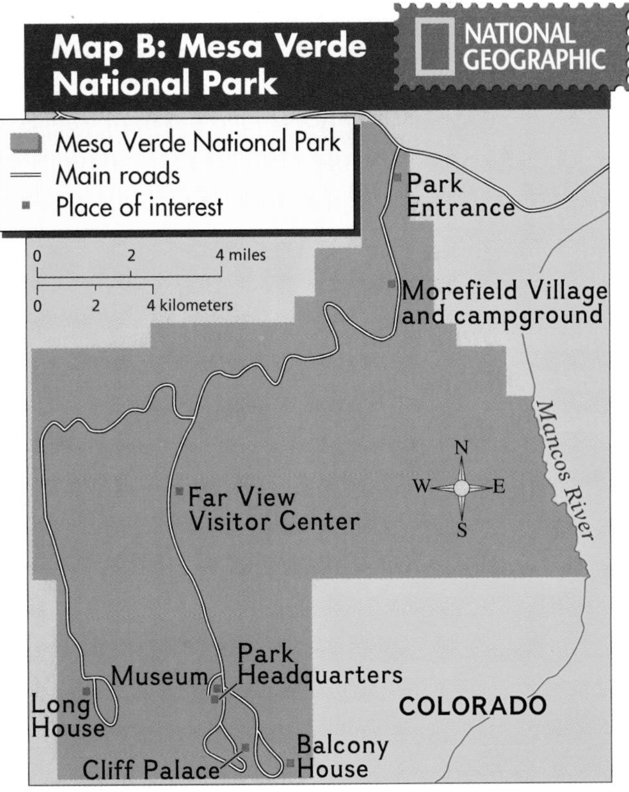

The Community of Jamestown

VOCABULARY

colony

bay

colonist

slavery

PEOPLE

Christopher Columbus

John Smith

Powhatan

John Rolfe

Pocahontas

READING STRATEGY

Copy the diagram. In the bar write this main idea: "Problems in Jamestown." In the circles identify the problems.

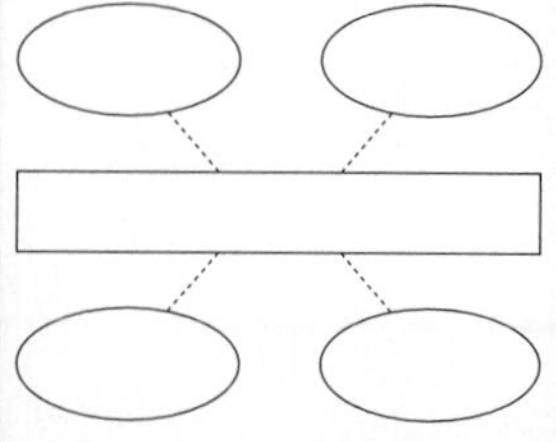

What was life like at Jamestown?

Lesson Outline

- The Powhatan Indians
- The English at Jamestown
- The Colony Struggles
- Slavery Comes to the Colonies

BUILD BACKGROUND

More than 500 years ago, Christopher Columbus sailed from Europe to the Americas. Other Europeans would follow and build communities in North America. This forever changed the lives of the Native Americans. They had lived here for thousands of years.

THE POWHATAN INDIANS

In 1607 English settlers sailed to the area that is now the state of Virginia. They set up a **colony** there. A colony is a place that is ruled by another country. They named it **Jamestown**, after the king of England, James I.

When the English arrived, the Powhatan Indians were already living in this area. The Powhatan fished in the rivers and **bay**. A bay is a part of the ocean that is partly enclosed by the coast. The Powhatan people also farmed and hunted for food. They used pine trees to build houses and make bows and arrows. They made canoes by carving out trees.

What natural resources did the Powhatan Indians use?

Christopher Columbus (above) reached the Americas in 1492. English settlers arrived more than 100 years later. The English met the Powhatan Indians, who lived in villages like this re-creation (top).

THE ENGLISH AT JAMESTOWN

Captain John Smith (above) had help from Chief Powhatan (below).

The English had high hopes for their new colony. The land was rich in natural resources. One settler wrote that it had "fair meadows and goodly tall trees." Meadows could become farmland. Trees and furs could be sent back to England. Some settlers even dreamed they would find gold and silver in their new home.

The Jamestown **colonists** soon found life hard in the new environment. A colonist is someone who lives in a colony. Many colonists refused to do the work needed to survive. They went off to look for gold and silver. Many became sick from drinking unhealthy water. By winter more than half of the colonists had died of diseases and hunger.

Help for the Colony

Things improved a little the following year. **John Smith**, a leader of the group, took control. He made a new rule, saying, "He that will not work, shall not eat." He told the settlers to build houses and plant crops. Some of the settlers did not like Smith, but he helped to keep them alive.

Smith got help from the powerful Indian chief also called **Powhatan**. Take a look at the map on page 87. It shows the Jamestown colony and the lands of the Powhatan people.

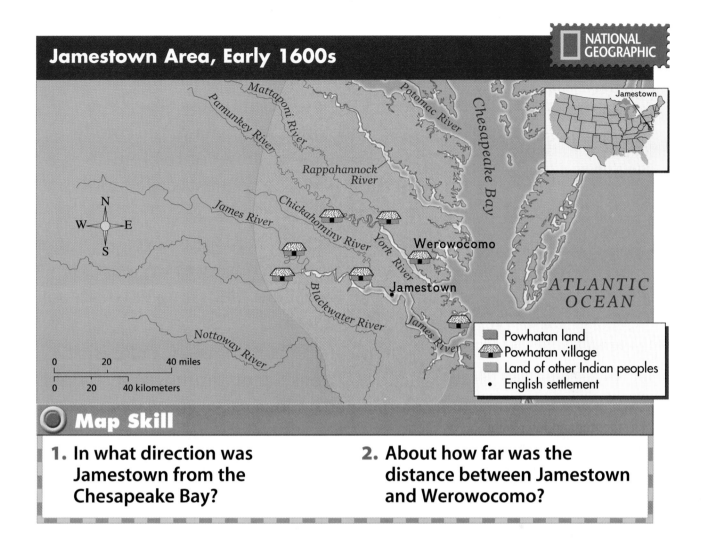

Jamestown Area, Early 1600s

Map Skill

1. In what direction was Jamestown from the Chesapeake Bay?
2. About how far was the distance between Jamestown and Werowocomo?

The Powhatan had lived in this area for more than a thousand years. They knew the land well. They knew how to use its natural resources.

Powhatan and his people showed the colonists how to hunt and fish in the area. They also taught the colonists how to grown corn, beans, and squash. The Powhatan had been growing these crops for many years. The crops were new to the colonists, though.

Why did the colonists have a hard time in Jamestown?

THE COLONY STRUGGLES

NOVA BRITANNIA.

OFFERING MOST

Excellent fruites by Planting in

VIRGINIA.

Exciting all ſuch as be well affected to further the ſame.

LONDON

Printed for SAMVEL MACHAM, and are to be ſold at his Shop in Pauls Church-yard, at the Signe of the Bul-head.

1609.

Even with the help of the Powhatan, the colonists found it difficult to stay alive. When John Smith went back to England, the colony fell on hard times. The winter of 1609–1610 was especially bad. The colonists called it "the starving time."

One settler wrote, "There were never Englishmen left in such misery as we were. The settlers began to feel the sharp hunger which no man can truly describe."

Despite the many hardships, the colonists struggled on. Things did not improve much until one colonist had an idea.

Pocahontas and John Rolfe were married in 1614.

This statue of Pocahontas is in Jamestown.

Conditions Improve

In 1612 **John Rolfe** started growing a new kind of tobacco that was very popular in Europe. The tobacco crop was shipped to England. There it was sold for a great deal of money. Although the colonists never found gold or silver, some of them became rich by growing and selling tobacco. Tobacco helped save Jamestown.

In 1614 Rolfe married **Pocahontas**, the daughter of the powerful Chief Powhatan. Their marriage led to a long period of peace between the colonists and the Native Americans. Now Jamestown began to grow.

How did tobacco help the Jamestown colony?

Exploring ECONOMICS

The Crop That Saved Jamestown

Tobacco was like gold to the people in Jamestown. The colonists even used it as money. Why was it so valuable? The answer is that it gave the colonists something to sell.

Dried tobacco could make the long sea trip to London. Unlike food, tobacco did not spoil. Also, tobacco grew well in Virginia but poorly in England. That made it rare in England.

With the money they got from selling tobacco, the colonists could buy the English goods they needed. They could also buy more land to grow more tobacco.

Activity

Think of another crop to research. Where is your crop grown? Where is it sold? How are crops brought from the farms to the local markets?

SLAVERY COMES TO THE COLONIES

The colonists wanted to make more money by growing more tobacco. To do this, they needed more workers. At first they hired workers. Later they bought enslaved people to do the work. The practice of one person owning another person is known as **slavery**.

Many African people were brought to the Americas and sold into **slavery**.

Most people who were enslaved came from West Africa. There, they were often captured by African and European slave traders. Then they were brought to the Americas. Many of them died on the long ocean trip. Once in the Americas, the survivors were sold.

The first shipload of enslaved people to Jamestown came from Africa in 1619. Enslaved Africans worked in the fields. They also cooked, sewed, took care of children, and built houses. They were not free to go to school, to work at their own jobs, or to live where they wished. Slavery did not end until the 1860s.

What happened to the people who were captured in West Africa?

PUTTING IT TOGETHER

About 500 years ago Europeans began to come to the Americas and start colonies. Virginia was the first colony started by the English. At first life was very difficult for the colonists at Jamestown. Later tobacco helped Virginia become a successful colony for the English. By the late 1700s the English had 13 colonies in North America.

However, Native Americans who lived here before the colonists lost their land. Many lost their lives. Many Africans were enslaved and brought to the Americas by force.

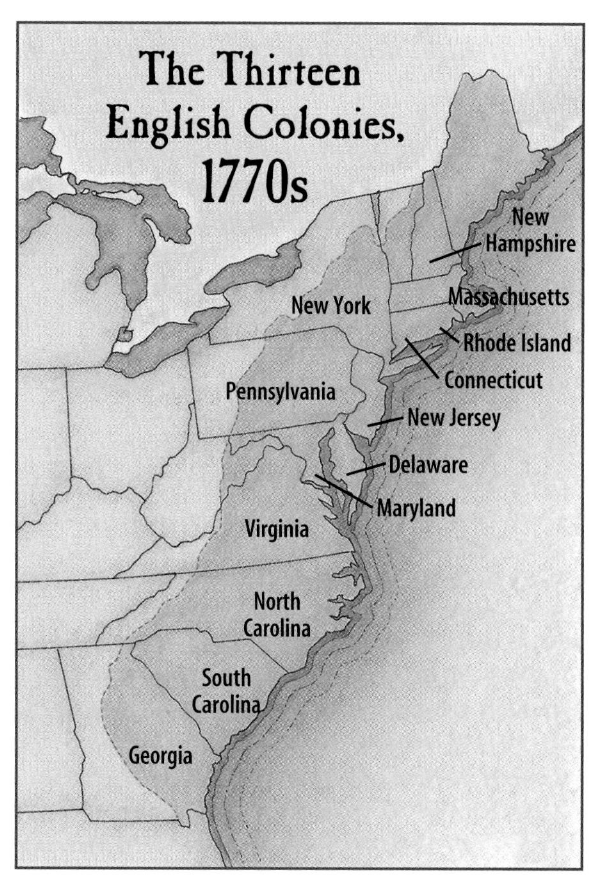

Review and Assess

1. Write one sentence for each of the vocabulary words.

   bay **colonist**
   colony **slavery**

2. Who was John Rolfe?
3. What was life like at Jamestown?
4. Name four natural resources of the area around Jamestown.
5. How did the people of Jamestown **solve** the **problem** of not having enough money?

Use an atlas to add these modern communities to a copy of the map on page 87: Richmond, Norfolk, Petersburg, and Newport News. Show the location of each by a dot, and label each dot.

Write a diary entry for one day as if you were living in Jamestown in 1610.

Chapter 3 REVIEW

VOCABULARY REVIEW

Write the word from the list below that matches the description.

canyon **slavery**

technology

1. A deep valley with high, steep sides
2. The use of skills, ideas, and tools to meet people's needs
3. The practice of one person owning another

CHAPTER COMPREHENSION

4. Name at least three different things that make up a people's culture.
5. Describe three ways Native Americans used the natural resources around them.
6. Write about some of the struggles the people of Jamestown faced. What helped the conditions there improve?

SKILL REVIEW

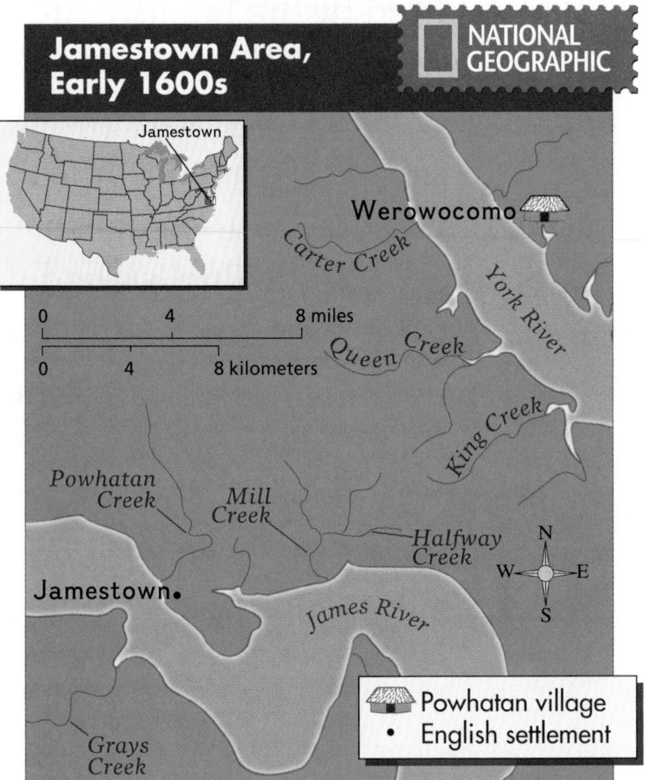

7. **Geography Skill** Why is it useful to be able to read a map scale?
8. **Geography Skill** What is the scale of the map above?
9. **Geography Skill** How far was Jamestown from the York River?

USING A CHART

10. Use the chart below to answer the following question. What natural resources did the Powhatan use?

The Powhatan's Needs	Natural Resources Used
Homes	Trees
Canoes	Trees
Food	Plants, animals, fish

Activity

Use Natural Resources Suppose you had to live without modern comforts. What things would you need? How would you get these things? Make a chart listing things you would need in one column. In another column explain how you would get each thing.

Use your Foldable table to review what you read in the chapter. Look at the Venn diagram, and think about what you learned about Native American communities and the English community at Jamestown. Lift the tabs to review your notes. Think of ways in which all communities are similar.

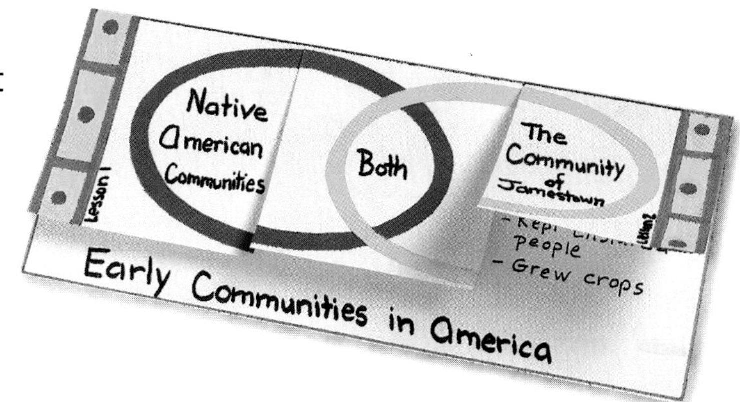

Chapter

THE Big IDEAS ABOUT...

People on the Move

People often move to new places to search for a better life. Some start new communities. Others join old communities, bringing growth and change.

BUILDING NEW COMMUNITIES

In the 1800s people like Lewis and Clark and Sacagawea led the way for new communities in the West.

MOVING TO A NEW HOME

In the late 1800s and early 1900s, people from around the world came to the United States.

CITIES GROW AND CHANGE

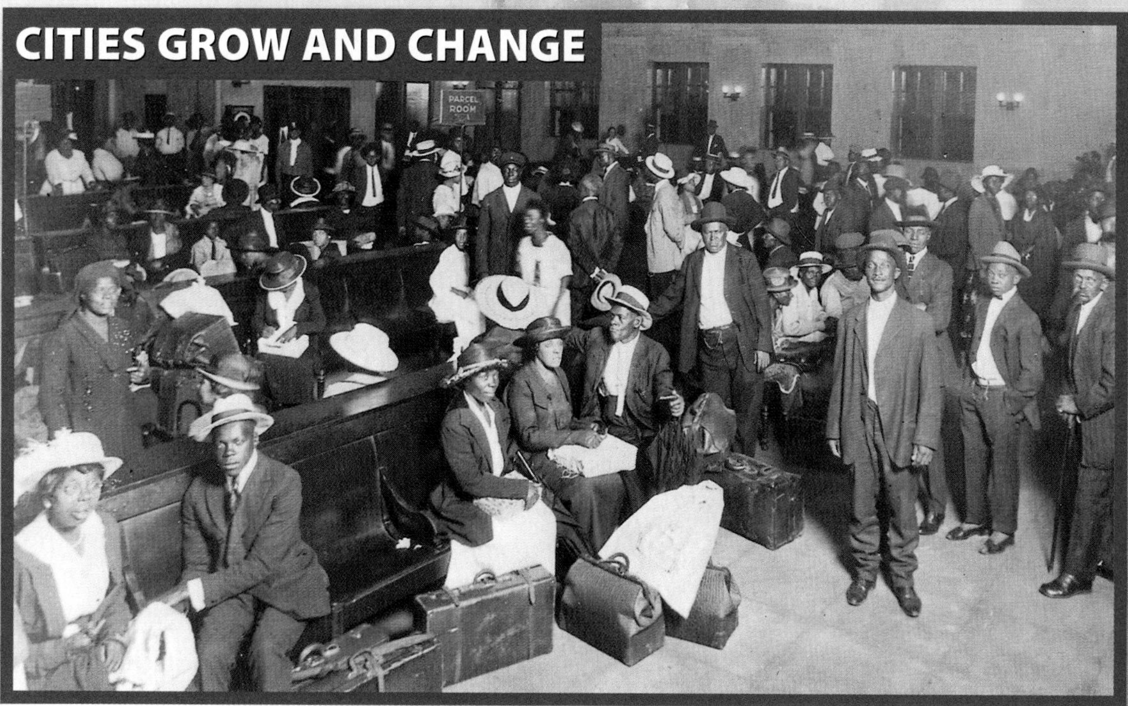

In the early 1900s many African Americans left the South and moved to cities in the North in search of a better life.

Foldables

Make this Foldable study guide, and use it to record what you learn about "People on the Move."

1. Fold a sheet of paper like a hot dog, but make one side 1" longer than the other.
2. On the short side of the paper, make two cuts, equal distances apart to form three tabs.
3. Label the 1" tab with the chapter title. Label the small tabs with the name of each lesson.

Lesson 1

Building New Communities

VOCABULARY

century

frontier

pioneer

transcontinental

PEOPLE

George Washington

Daniel Boone

Meriwether Lewis

William Clark

Sacagawea

How did communities spread in the United States?

Lesson Outline

- The Pathfinder
- An Incredible Journey
- Heading West
- Train Travel

BUILD BACKGROUND

In 1775 war broke out between England and the 13 colonies. For six years Americans, led by **George Washington**, fought to become free, or independent. In 1781 a new nation was born—the United States of America. During the next **century**, or one hundred years, new communities spread all the way to the Pacific Ocean.

READING STRATEGY

Use a word web to **summarize** Lewis and Clark's journey. Write their names in the center. Then add information about the trip.

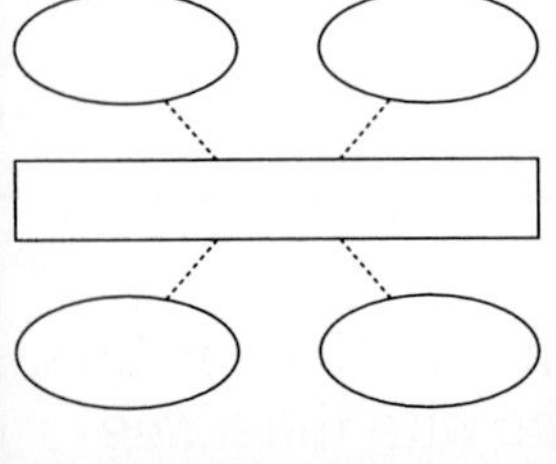

1700	1750	1800	1850	1900	1950	2000

You Are Here
1760 – 1870

THE PATHFINDER

Daniel Boone is shown here leading a group of settlers west.

Daniel Boone was known as the "Pathfinder." He found new trails, or paths, that led west. He explored the **frontier**. A frontier is the far edge of a country where a group of people is just beginning to settle. In 1769 Boone found Native American trails that went west through the mountains. From these trails he created the Wilderness Road. It led into what is now Kentucky.

Thousands of **pioneers** followed Boone into Kentucky and settled there. A pioneer is one of the first of a group of people to settle in an area new to them. As Kentucky grew, it became too crowded for Boone. "Too many people! Too crowded," he said. In 1779 he moved west again. He led a group of settlers into what is now Missouri. Daniel Boone is still admired today for his courage, leadership, and independent spirit.

READING CHECK **How did Daniel Boone contribute to the spread of communities in our country?**

AN INCREDIBLE JOURNEY

In 1803 the United States bought land from France. The land, called the Louisiana Territory, was west of the Mississippi River. The new land almost doubled the size of our country. President Thomas Jefferson hired **Meriwether Lewis** and **William Clark** to explore, or find out about, the newly bought land.

Lewis and Clark began their trip near St. Louis, Missouri, in May 1804. They returned to St. Louis more than two years later. In that time they explored and mapped more than 2,000 miles of land. Their maps later helped settlers to move west.

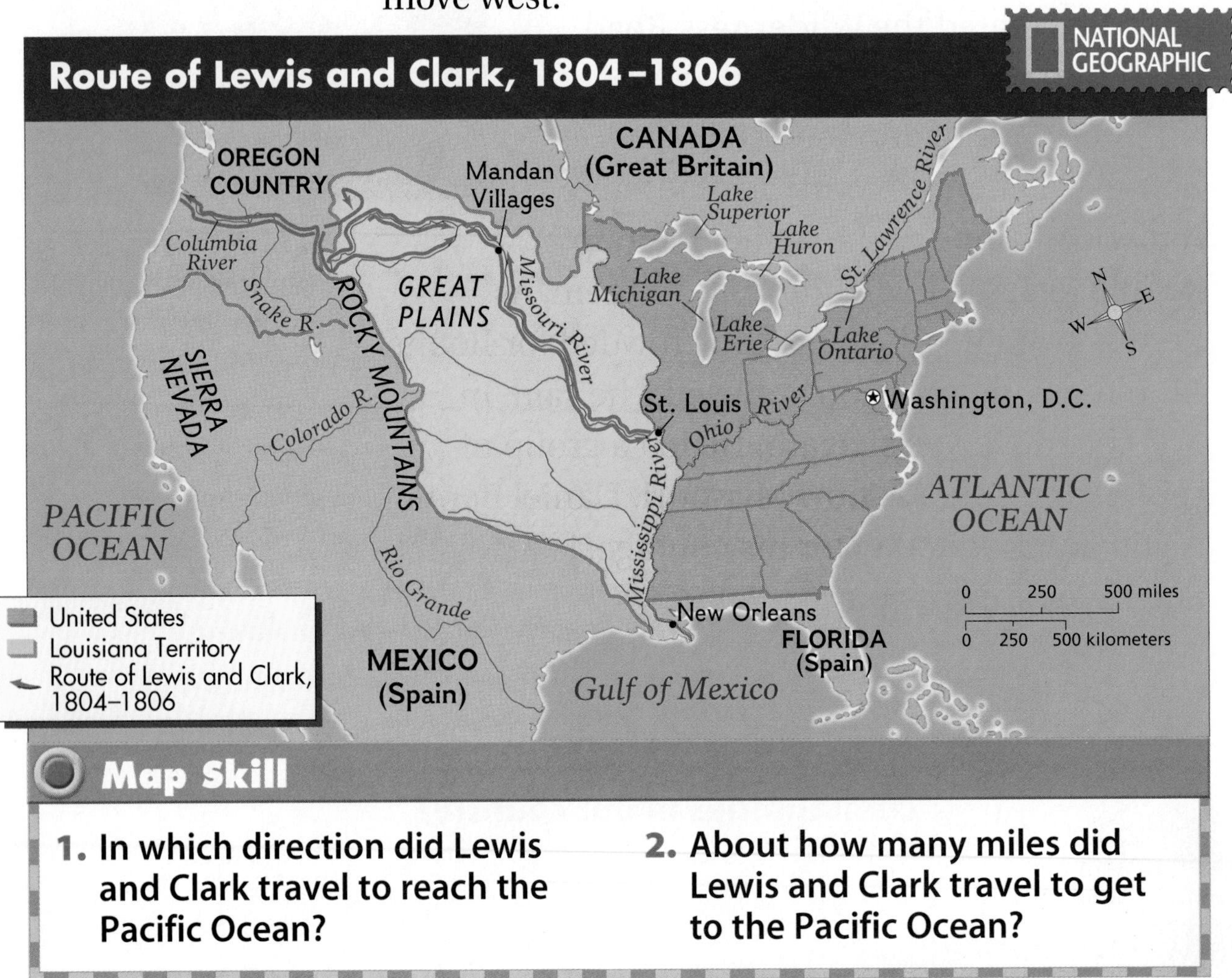

Map Skill

1. **In which direction did Lewis and Clark travel to reach the Pacific Ocean?**
2. **About how many miles did Lewis and Clark travel to get to the Pacific Ocean?**

Along the Way

A Shoshone Indian woman, **Sacagawea** (sak uh juh WEE uh), helped Lewis and Clark during their journey. She translated the languages of Native Americans they met. With help from Native Americans like Sacagawea, Lewis and Clark explored the Missouri River and found their way west. In November 1805 they reached the Pacific Ocean.

Sacagawea points the way for Lewis and Clark.

Lewis and Clark kept a journal during their trip. Read the entry below to see how they felt when they reached the Pacific Ocean.

excerpt from the journals of Lewis and Clark

— written by William Clark, November 7, 1805

We set out early . . . the fog so thick we could not see across the river. . . . We proceeded [went] down the channel with an Indian . . . as our pilot. . . . [We] had not gone far when the fog cleared off. . . . Ocean in view! O! the joy!

What route did Lewis and Clark take—land or water—on the day they reached the Pacific Ocean?

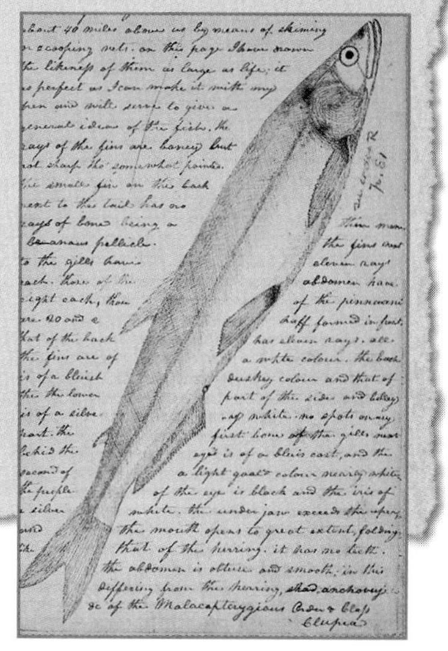

What did Lewis and Clark do on their journey?

HEADING WEST

Explorers such as Daniel Boone, Meriwether Lewis, and William Clark helped open trails that led west. In the 1840s and 1850s, thousands of United States citizens followed these trails to start new lives. The map below shows some of the routes they used. One of the most used routes was the Oregon Trail.

Pioneers on the Oregon Trail often started their trip in Independence, Missouri. They traveled in groups of wagons, called wagon trains. The trip was very difficult and dangerous. It took about five months and covered 2,000 miles. Sometimes settlers and Native Americans fought over who owned the land.

The journey west was difficult. Still, families brought along things from home.

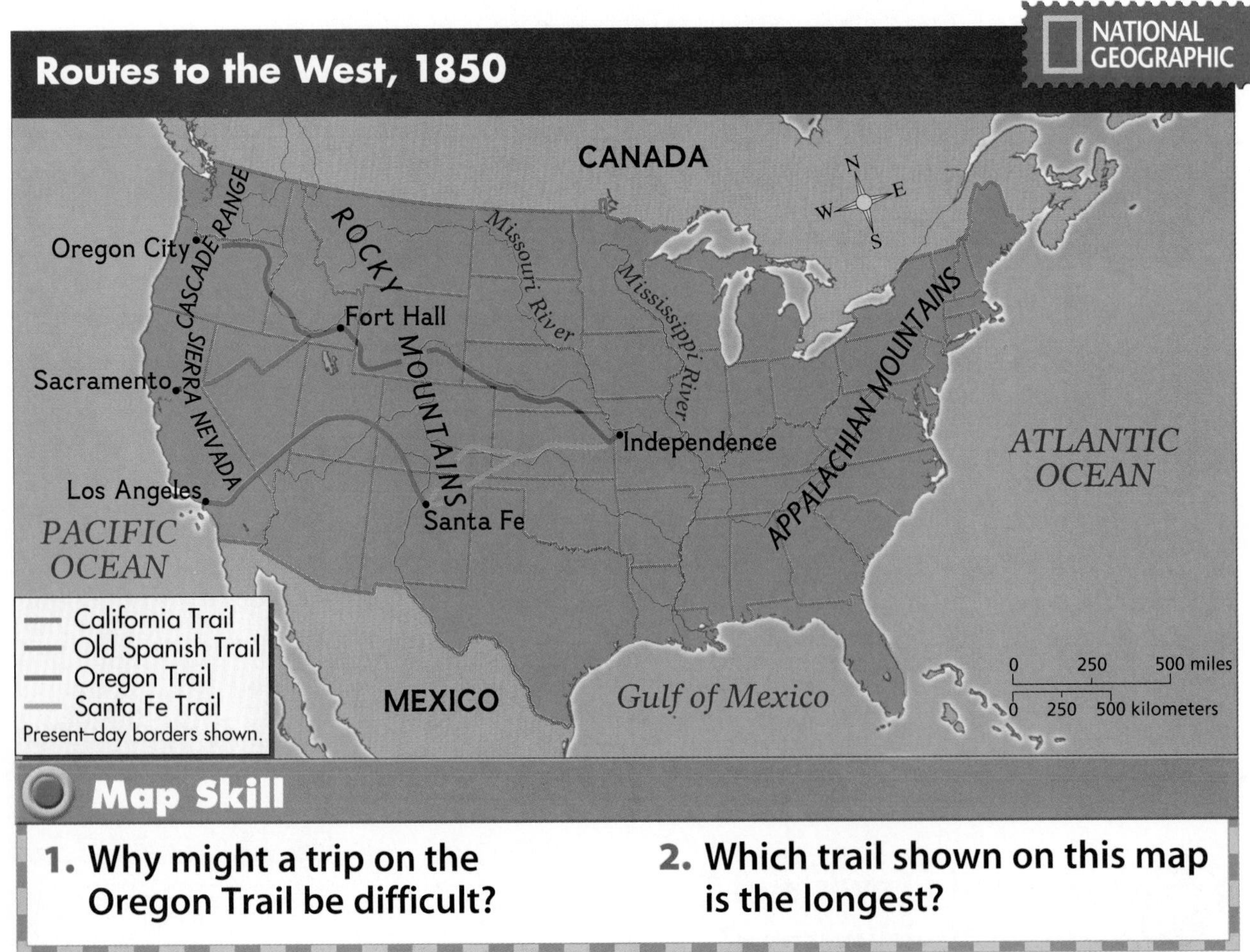

Map Skill

1. **Why might a trip on the Oregon Trail be difficult?**
2. **Which trail shown on this map is the longest?**

Communities in the West

Often pioneers reached Oregon with few belongings and no money. Many also lost family members and friends along the way. One traveler wrote of his trip, "Our journey across the Plains was a long and hard one. We lost everything but our lives."

Pioneers had to stop each night and make camp (above). Oregon Trail wagon ruts (below) can still be seen today.

Most pioneers planned to settle in new communities and farm the land or start businesses. By 1869 about 12,000 pioneers had traveled in wagon trains along the Oregon Trail. They set up new communities and began to use the natural resources of the area to build new lives.

Why was the journey west so hard?

TRAIN TRAVEL

In 1869 the last spike was hammered down to connect a railroad in the west with one in the east. The **transcontinental** railroad, a railroad that stretched across the continent, was finished. People could now travel across our country by train. They could get from place to place much faster than before. Travel that used to take months now took days. In time other railroads were connected to the transcontinental railroad.

The railroads helped cities and towns in the western part of our country to grow. Railroads made it easier for people to move there to live. They also made it easier to ship goods between east and west.

READING CHECK **How did the transcontinental railroad change the way people lived?**

The railroad (bottom) was a big improvement over harsh wagon trails (below).

PUTTING IT TOGETHER

From 1760 to 1870, citizens of the United States pushed the frontier west. They started communities on land they had not seen before. Along the way pioneers met many different Native Americans. Native Americans had lived on the land for centuries. Sometimes pioneers and Native Americans fought over the land. Later the transcontinental railroad connected the eastern and western parts of our country. In about a century the United States had spread from coast to coast.

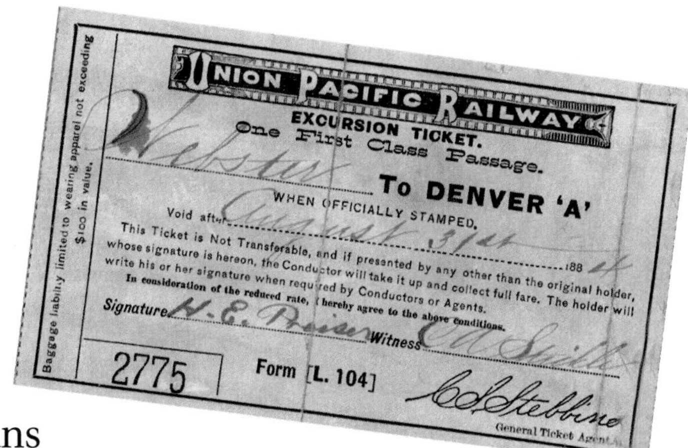

In the 1880s a trip from New York to San Francisco on the **transcontinental** railroad cost $150.

Review and Assess

1. Write one sentence for each of the vocabulary words.
   century **frontier** **pioneer**
2. What was the Oregon Trail?
3. Find out! Explain how communities spread after the United States became a country.
4. Identify the reasons that people moved west.
5. **Summarize** how Lewis and Clark's trip helped to change the United States.

Draw a picture of pioneers on a wagon train traveling west. Include items you would take if you were a pioneer, and draw what pioneers hoped to find when they arrived.

Write a poem as though you are Meriwether Lewis and have just reached the Pacific Ocean.

Using and Making Time Lines

You have read about many important events that took place in the past. It is not always easy to remember the order in which events happened. What happened first and what happened next might be unclear. A **time line**, tells the time order in which events occurred. Learning to use time lines will help you to better understand history.

VOCABULARY

time line

decade

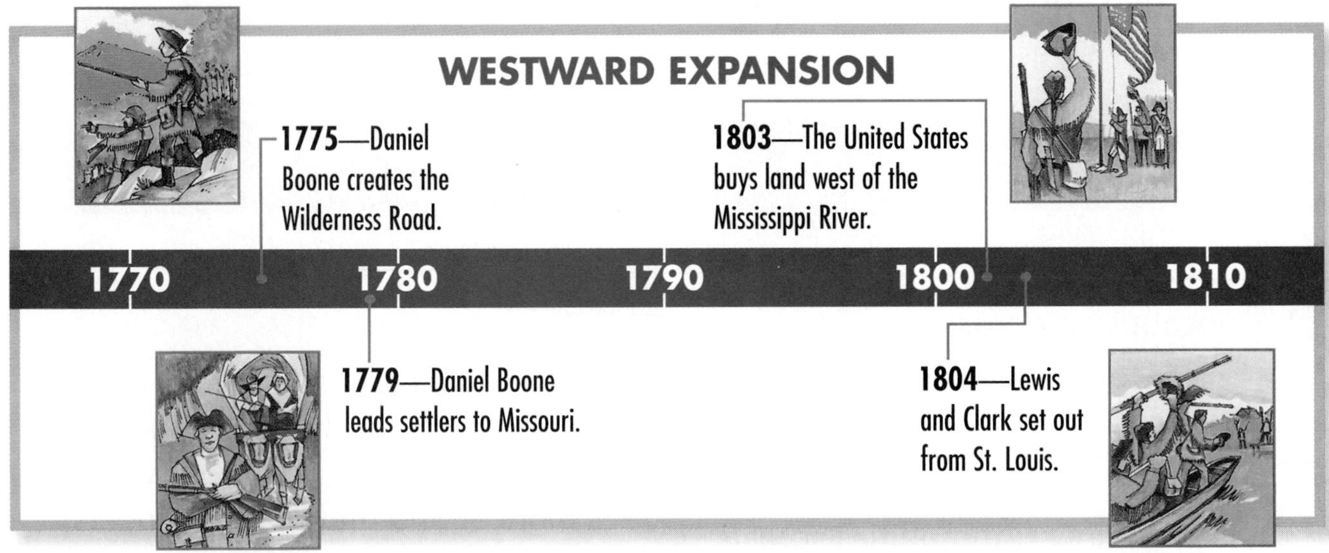
WESTWARD EXPANSION
1775—Daniel Boone creates the Wilderness Road.
1803—The United States buys land west of the Mississippi River.
1770
1780
1790
1800
1810
1779—Daniel Boone leads settlers to Missouri.
1804—Lewis and Clark set out from St. Louis.

LEARN THE SKILL

Follow these steps, and look at the time line above as you read.

1. **Look at the dates to see what time span is covered.**
   Time lines are usually divided by years, **decades**, or centuries. A decade equals ten years. This time line covers the decades between 1770 and 1810.

2. **Look at the order of events.**
   Events are given in time order from left to right. An event to the *left* of another event took place earlier. An event to the *right* of another event took place later. This time line shows that Daniel Boone created the Wilderness Road before he led settlers to Missouri.

3. **Use the dates given for events to tell the number of years between them.**
   To tell the number of years between two events, subtract the date of the earlier event from the date of the later event. For example, Daniel Boone led the settlers to Missouri in 1779. Lewis and Clark began their expedition in Missouri in 1804. 1804 – 1779 = 25. Daniel Boone's journey was 25 years before Lewis and Clark's.

TRY THE SKILL

Use the time line below to answer the questions.

1. What period of time does this time line cover?
2. How many centuries does this time line cover? How many decades is this?
3. Was the Declaration of Independence written before or after the transcontinental railroad was completed?
4. How many years passed between the time Christopher Columbus reached North America and the beginning of Lewis and Clark's journey?

EXTEND THE SKILL

In Chapter 3 you read about the Jamestown colony in Virginia. Create a time line that shows the events that occurred at Jamestown. Will your time line be divided into years, decades, or centuries?

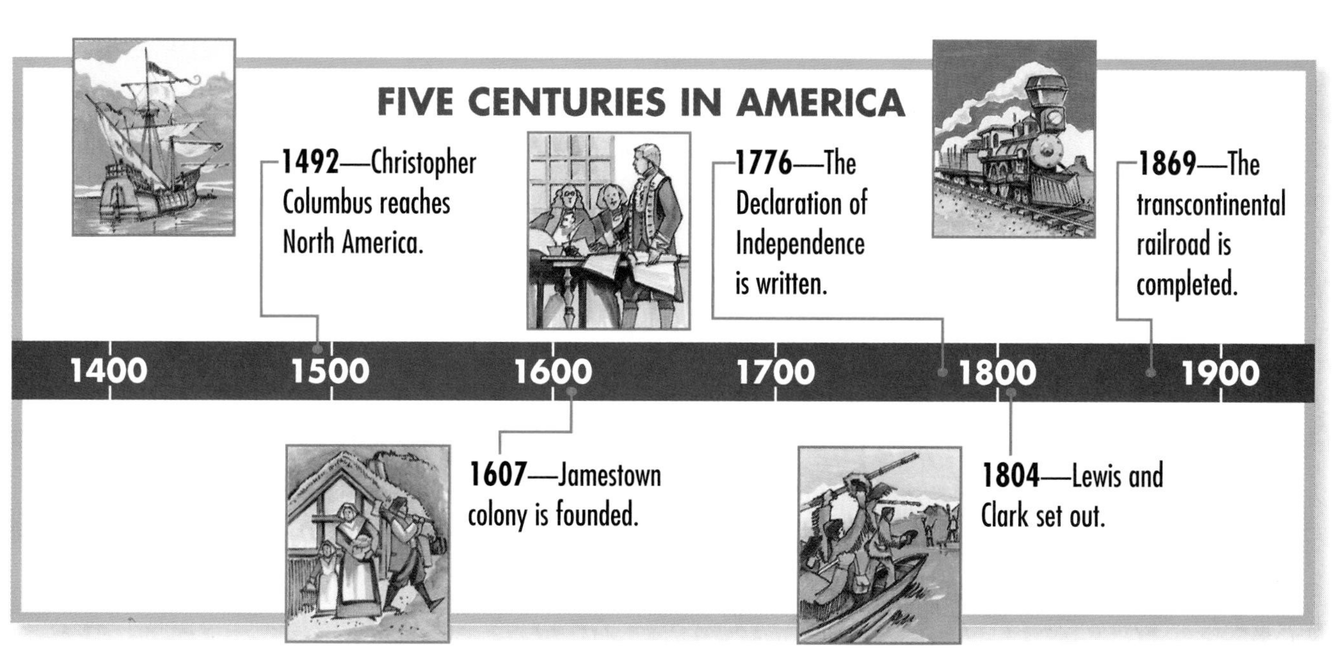
FIVE CENTURIES IN AMERICA
1492—Christopher Columbus reaches North America.
1607—Jamestown colony is founded.
1776—The Declaration of Independence is written.
1804—Lewis and Clark set out.
1869—The transcontinental railroad is completed.
1400
1500
1600
1700
1800
1900

Moving to a New Home

VOCABULARY

immigrant

database

READING STRATEGY

Use a **main idea** pyramid to write about immigrants. Tell why they came to this country and what they brought to it.

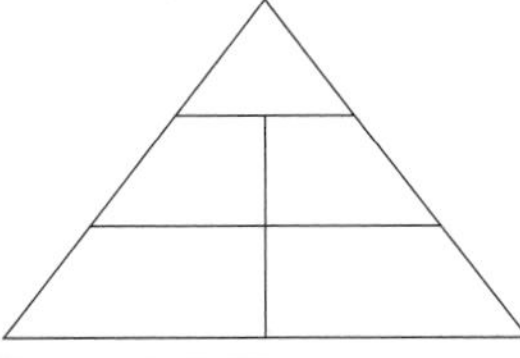

Why did people from other places come to the United States?

Lesson Outline

- Starting New Lives
- Immigrant Communities
- Immigrants Help Build a Nation

BUILD BACKGROUND

The Statue of Liberty is a symbol of the United States and of freedom. It welcomes people from other countries who come to live in the United States. It has been greeting people for more than a century.

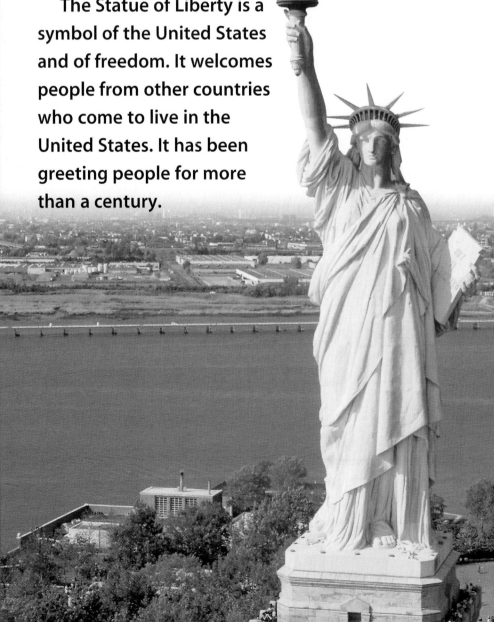

1700 1750 1800 1850 1900 1950 2000

You Are Here
1880 – 2000

STARTING NEW LIVES

The Statue of Liberty is in the harbor of **New York City**. For many years it was the first thing that many **immigrants** saw when they arrived in the United States. An immigrant is a person who comes from one country to live in another. Throughout our history many immigrants have come to the United States. Some came in search of freedom. Others came in search of jobs. Like the pioneers who moved west, the immigrants were seeking new and better lives.

Many immigrants sailed across the Atlantic Ocean and landed at **Ellis Island** in New York City. Ellis Island was an immigration center. Officers there decided who could stay in the United States. Immigrants who were sick or who did not know anyone in this country might be sent back to their native lands.

Immigrants were often packed onto crowded ships (above). Many entered the United States through Ellis Island (below).

How were immigrants in the early 1900s like the pioneers?

IMMIGRANT COMMUNITIES

Immigrants to the United States came from many different places around the world. Some entered the United States through Ellis Island. Other immigrants came through cities such as **Boston** or San Francisco.

Once they were here, immigrants settled in communities throughout our country. They worked hard to make a life in their new homes. Many immigrants had to work from dawn to dusk, six days a week, just to earn enough money to live. Children often worked, too. Some worked in factories. Others shined shoes or sold newspapers or pencils.

Busy immigrant communities were crowded, but they were also full of life.

Many Italian immigrants settled in New York's Little Italy (above). Dancers perform at Korean Day in Queens, New York (below).

Neighborhoods in a Community

When they arrived in the United States, people from one part of the world often settled together in a neighborhood or community. This made sense, since not everyone speaks English. German immigrants, for example, often lived in communities with other German-speaking people.

One of the oldest immigrant neighborhoods in New York City is called Little Italy. Many Italian immigrants settled there when they came to New York City in the early 1900s. A few blocks south of Little Italy is Chinatown. Many Chinese immigrants settled there. Immigrants continue to come to New York and many other cities in our country today.

READING CHECK **In what ways was life difficult for immigrants in the United States?**

Many immigrants had to start new lives with nothing more than they could carry.

IMMIGRANTS HELP BUILD A NATION

Immigrants to the United States came from many countries. Each group brought different languages, religions, customs, and traditions to communities across our country. The immigrants helped our country grow. Many immigrants came to the United States between 1880 and 1920. Look at the graph below to see the pattern of immigration in those years.

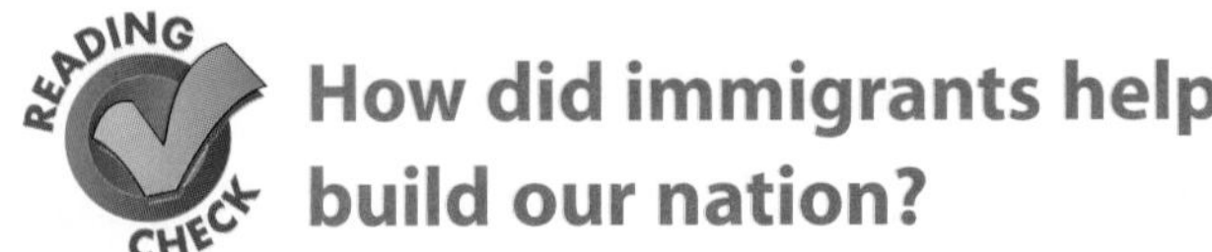

How did immigrants help build our nation?

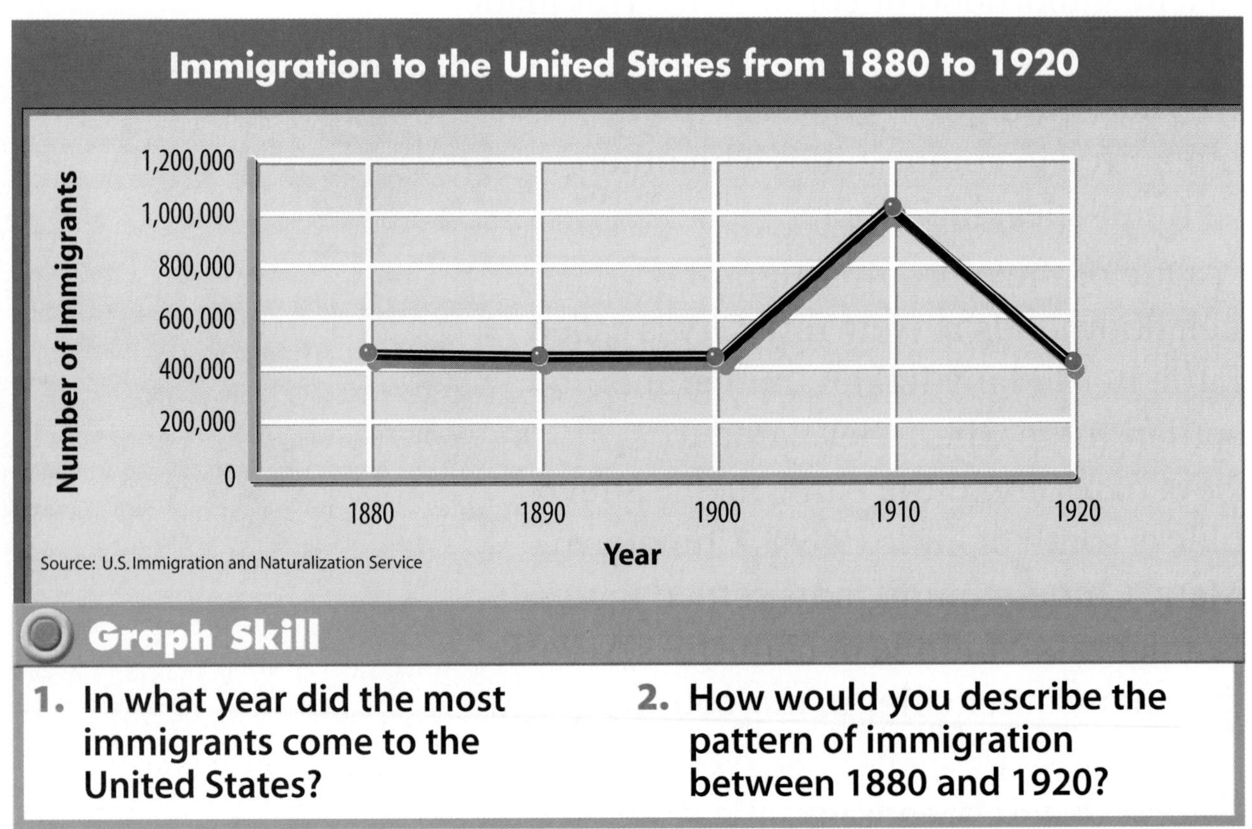

Graph Skill

1. In what year did the most immigrants come to the United States?
2. How would you describe the pattern of immigration between 1880 and 1920?

PUTTING IT TOGETHER

Immigrants have been coming to our country for hundreds of years. Immigrants are still coming today. They help our country grow. They share their cultures. Immigrants are an important part of what makes our country special.

Exploring TECHNOLOGY

From Present to Past

Today the Ellis Island museum keeps a **database** of information about immigrants. A database is a computer program that holds lots of similar information.

You can visit the Ellis Island website to search through the database and learn more about the immigrant experience. Go to **www.mhschool.com** and follow the links.

Review and Assess

1. **Write** one sentence for each of the vocabulary words.

   database **immigrant**

2. In what New York City community did many Italian immigrants live?
3. Identify reasons why immigrants came to the United States. Find out!
4. Give an example of how immigrants contributed to the **culture** of the United States.
5. **Summarize** what life was like for many immigrants when they first came to the United States.

Look at the line graph on page 110. Use the information to make a bar graph. Show in bar graph form how many immigrants came to the United States for the years 1880, 1890, 1900, 1910, and 1920.

Write a journal entry as though you are an immigrant coming to the United States. Tell how you feel when you first see the Statue of Liberty.

Using Intermediate Directions

Immigrants who come to the United States do not always stay in the cities where they arrive, such as New York or San Francisco. They may move in other directions to other communities. They might move in one of the cardinal directions: north, east, south, or west. They might also move in an **intermediate direction**. An intermediate direction is halfway between two cardinal directions.

VOCABULARY

intermediate direction

LEARN THE SKILL

A compass rose shows directions on a map. Follow these steps for using a compass rose to find both cardinal and intermediate directions.

1. **Find the cardinal directions.** The long points of the compass rose show the cardinal directions. North is shown by the letter **N**, east by the letter **E**, south by the letter **S**, and west by the letter **W**.
2. **Find the intermediate directions.** The short points of the compass rose show the intermediate directions. They are named by combining the names of the cardinal directions they fall between: northeast, southeast, southwest, and northwest. They use the abbreviations **NE**, **SE**, **SW**, and **NW**. Intermediate directions are not always labeled on a compass rose.

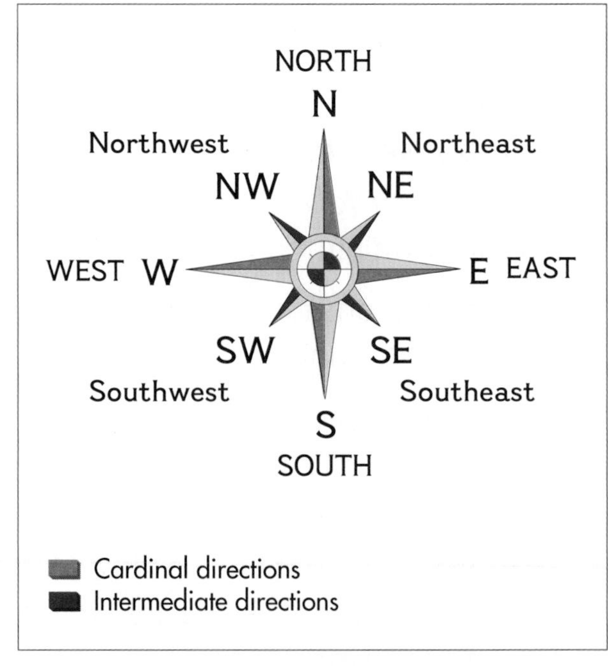

TRY THE SKILL

Use the map below to answer the questions.

1. In what direction would you travel to go from Los Angeles, California, to Carson City, Nevada?
2. In what direction would you travel to go from Denver, Colorado, to Las Vegas, Nevada?
3. In what direction would you travel to go from the capital of California to the capital of Arizona?
4. What city is about 200 miles northeast of Los Angeles, California?

EXTEND THE SKILL

Many immigrants from Asia arrived at Angel Island. Angel Island is in the San Francisco Bay, near the city of San Francisco. Some families then traveled to other cities in the southwestern United States.

If the families traveled northwest from San Francisco, in what city may they have settled? What if they traveled northeast? Directly east? Southeast?

Make a chart showing this information. In one column list cardinal and intermediate directions. In another column list cities.

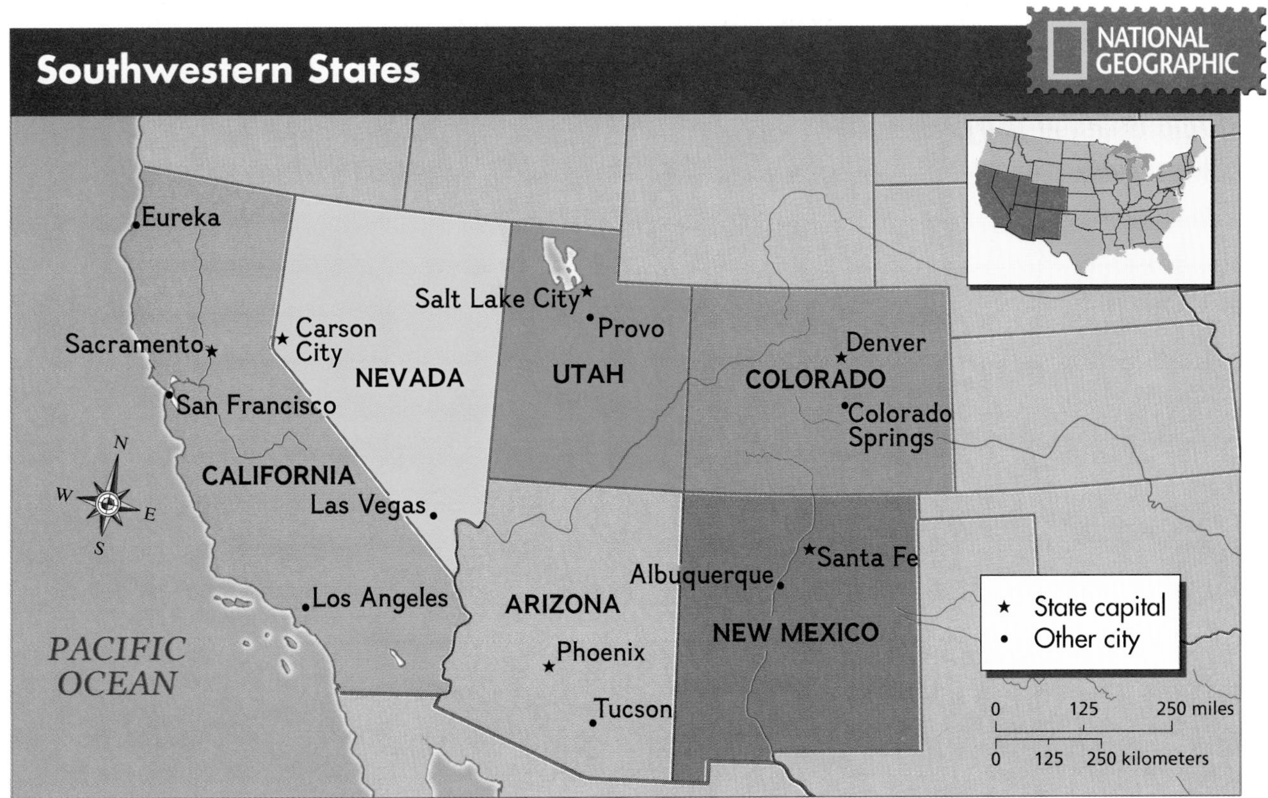

Cities Grow and Change

VOCABULARY

migration

Great Migration

Civil War

PEOPLE

Abraham Lincoln

Jacob Lawrence

Martin Luther King, Jr.

READING STRATEGY

Copy this chart. In column one **predict** what you will learn about the Great Migration. In column two write what you learned.

Why did many African Americans move to the North?

Lesson Outline

- War Between the States
- A Difficult Choice
- Changes over Time

BUILD BACKGROUND

In the early 1900s a great journey took place in the United States. It was a journey made by thousands of African Americans who moved from the South to the North. Moving from one part of the country to another is called migration. So many African Americans made this journey that it became known as the Great Migration.

1700 | 1750 | 1800 | 1850 | 1900 | 1950 | 2000

You Are Here
1860 – 1970

WAR BETWEEN THE STATES

Since colonial times most African Americans had lived as slaves. They were bought and sold. They were forced to work for the people who owned them.

Many people believed that slavery was wrong. **Abraham Lincoln** was one of those people. After Lincoln became President in 1861, a war broke out between the Northern states and the Southern states. This war is called the **Civil War**.

The Southern states believed in slavery. They thought that Lincoln would free the slaves, so they wanted to form their own country. The Northern states wanted to keep the country united. The Civil War ended in 1865. The Northern states won. African Americans were no longer enslaved.

President Lincoln led the United States during the Civil War.

READING CHECK **Why was the Civil War important?**

A DIFFICULT CHOICE

After the Civil War many African Americans still worked in Southern cotton fields (top). Often schools for African Americans in the South were poor (above).

The Civil War brought an end to slavery. African Americans were still treated unfairly, especially in the South. They were prevented from voting. They could not eat in the same places or live in the same neighborhoods as white people. In the South many African Americans became tenant farmers. They rented land from white landowners and paid for their rent with crops. Sometimes they paid so much that they had little food left for their families.

New Lives

By the early 1900s many African Americans in the South were making a difficult choice. They left their homes and moved to cities in the North. There they hoped to find jobs and a chance for a better life. The Great Migration began.

Life in the North was better for many African Americans. They found jobs. Some started their own businesses. One woman wrote to her family back home, “I am well and thankful to be in a city. . . . The houses are so pretty, we [have] a nice place. Hurry up and come to Chicago. It is wonderful.”

Many African American families, like this one, moved from the South to the North in search of better lives.

Jacob Lawrence was an artist whose parents moved north during the Great Migration. In 1941 Lawrence made a series of paintings about the Great Migration. What does his painting below tell you about it?

How was life in the North different from life in the South for many black people?

Harlem in the 1920s was home to many famous artists and writers (above). Martin Luther King, Jr. (facing page), was an important leader for change in the 1950s and 1960s.

CHANGES OVER TIME

When they moved to the North, many African Americans settled together in communities. One such community was **Harlem**, a neighborhood in New York City. Like Chicago, New York offered the promise of jobs and a better life. Many artists, including Jacob Lawrence, settled in Harlem.

A Great Man

Life was better for African Americans in the North. They still faced unfair treatment there and in the South, however. In the 1950s and 1960s, people joined together to work for change.

Martin Luther King, Jr., was an African American leader. He believed that all people should be treated fairly. Look at the picture on page 119. What does it tell you about the work that he did?

Why was moving north a disappointment for some African Americans?

PUTTING IT TOGETHER

Enslaved African Americans gained their freedom after the Civil War. However, they were still treated unfairly in some Southern states. During the early 1900s many African Americans moved from the South to the North. They were like the pioneers who moved west and the immigrants who moved to this country. The people who made the Great Migration to the North were seeking new and better lives.

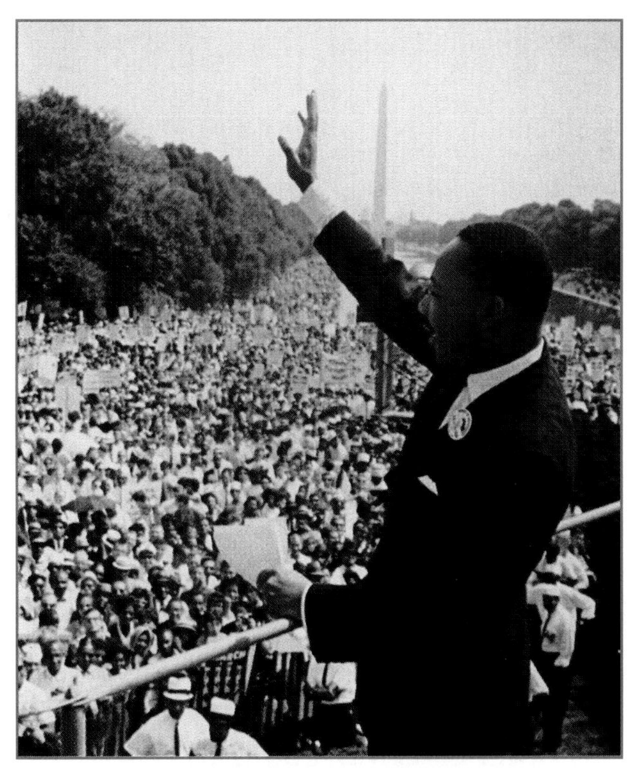

Review and Assess

1. Write one sentence for each of the vocabulary terms.

   Civil War **Great Migration** **migration**

2. What happened as a result of the Civil War?
3. Explain why many African Americans migrated to the North in the early 1900s.
4. What are some ways both the North and South changed because of the Great Migration?
5. How were slavery and tenant farming **alike** and **different** for African Americans?

Look at the map of the United States on pages R18–R19 of the Atlas of this book. Then suppose you were migrating from Georgia to Illinois. Write down the states you would pass through and the directions in which you would travel.

Write a letter to a friend as though you were one of the people who took part in the Great Migration. Explain why you made the trip and what you left behind.

Chapter 4 REVIEW

VOCABULARY REVIEW

Number a sheet of paper from 1 to 3. Write the word or term that best completes each sentence.

Great Migration **immigrant**

pioneer

1. A(n) ___ comes to live in a new country.
2. The ___ was when many African Americans moved north.
3. One of the first people to settle in an area that is new to them is a(n) ___.

CHAPTER COMPREHENSION

4. How did Daniel Boone and Lewis and Clark help to change the United States?
5. How are immigration and migration alike and different?
6. Write two reasons for the Great Migration.

SKILL REVIEW

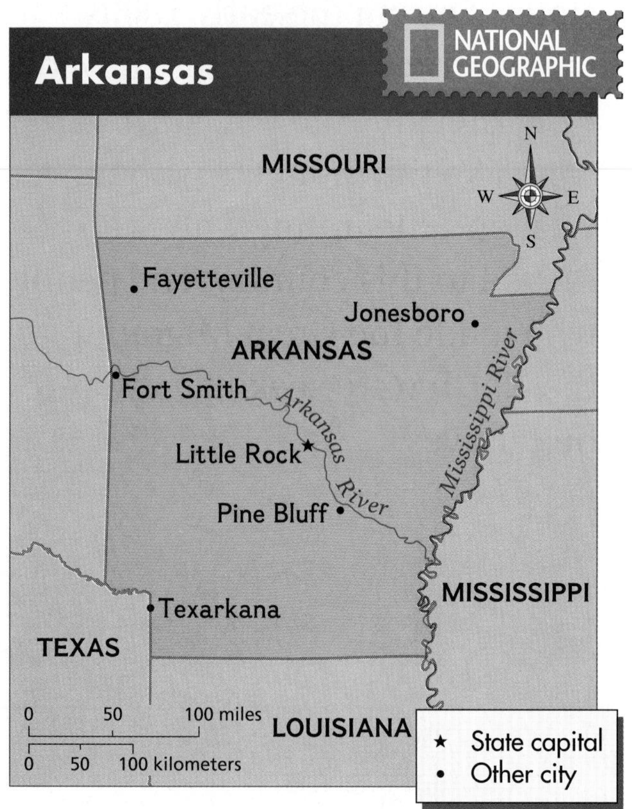

7. **Geography Skill** What are the four intermediate directions?
8. **Geography Skill** In which direction is Fayetteville from Little Rock?
9. **Study Skill** What is a time line? When are time lines useful?

USING A TIME LINE

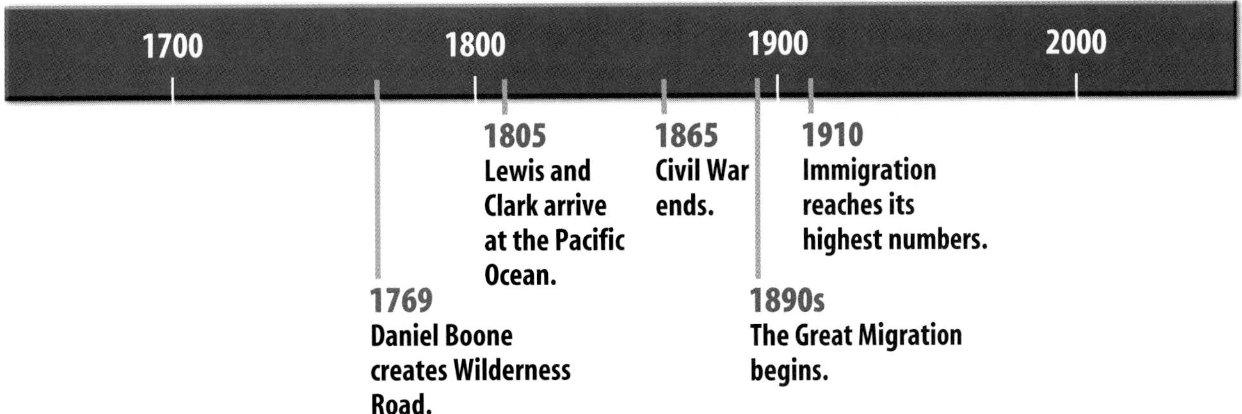
1700
1800
1900
2000
1805
Lewis and Clark arrive at the Pacific Ocean.
1865
Civil War ends.
1910
Immigration reaches its highest numbers.
1769
Daniel Boone creates Wilderness Road.
1890s
The Great Migration begins.

10. Look at the time line above. Did the Great Migration begin before or after the Civil War ended? When did immigration reach its highest numbers?

Activity

Planning a New Community

Suppose you and everyone in your community moved to a new place with few people and houses. Make a list of things you would need to live there. Are there things you might need to leave behind?

Foldables

Use your Foldable to review what you have read about people moving from one place to another. As you look at the front of your Foldable, think about reasons people move to new areas. Review your notes on the inside of your Foldable to check your responses. Record any questions that you have, and review the chapter to find answers.

People Build New Communities
Lesson 1
Moving to a New Home
Lesson 2
Immigrants help our country grow.
Cities Grow and Change
Lesson 3
People on the Move

New Ideas Change Communities

Communities are always changing. In the past 200 years, people with new ideas have changed how we build our communities. Other people have worked to make communities better places to live.

New ideas in building have changed the face of cities like Chicago, Illinois.

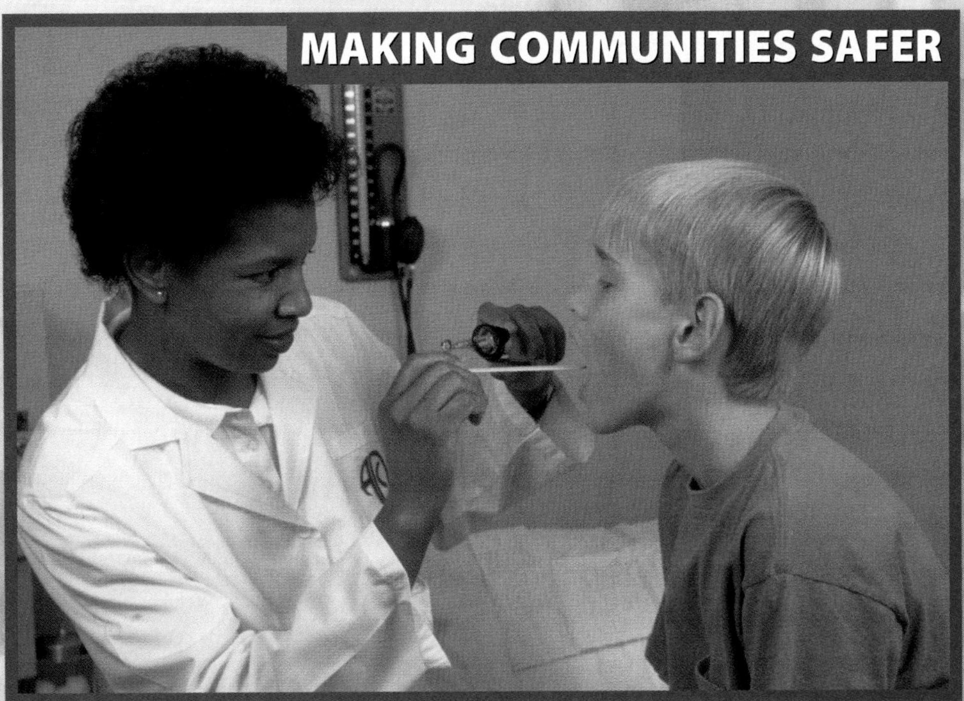

New ideas in health and science have made communities better places to live.

Foldables

Make this Foldable study guide, and use it to record what you learn about "New Ideas Change Communities."

1. Fold a sheet of 8½" x 11" paper in half like a hamburger, but leave one side of the paper 1" longer than the other.
2. On the short side make one cut in the middle, dividing it in half, forming two tabs.
3. Label the two tabs with the lesson titles. Label the 1" tab with the chapter title.

Lesson 1

Inventions Shape Communities

VOCABULARY

skyscraper

invention

elevator

PEOPLE

Elisha Otis

Henry Bessemer

Andrew Carnegie

Thomas Edison

William Le Baron Jenney

READING STRATEGY

Use the chart to put the following in the correct sequence: first skyscraper, Chicago Fire, safe elevators, first light bulb, first telephone.

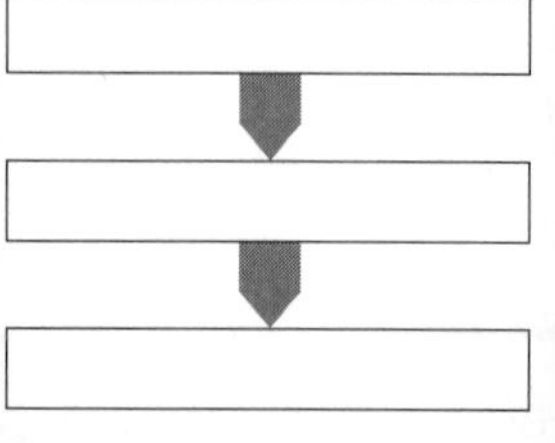

How have some inventions helped to shape communities?

Lesson Outline

- The Great Chicago Fire
- A New City Takes Shape
- The Changing Face of Cities

BUILD BACKGROUND

When you think of a big city, you probably think of very tall buildings, or **skyscrapers**. However, big cities have not always had skyscrapers. Skyscrapers only became possible about 140 years ago, because of new technologies. In this lesson you will read how new technologies have changed the way we build and live in cities.

1825 | 1850 | 1875 | 1900 | 1925 | 1950 | 1975 | 2000 | 2025

You Are Here
1852 – 1974

THE GREAT CHICAGO FIRE

Chicago today is known as the "home of the skyscraper." Back in 1871, though, it was a town of mostly small buildings. On October 8, 1871, a fire started in a barn in southwest Chicago. The fire quickly spread. Read the Primary Source to learn what happened.

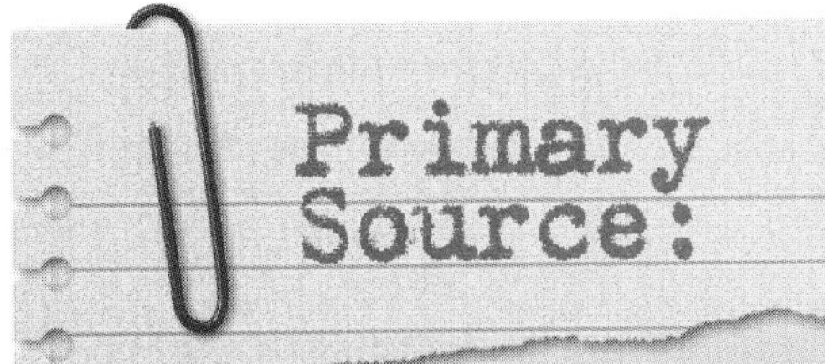

Chicago Historical Society

— letter of William A. Wieboldt, 13 years old, to his parents, October 30, 1871

[Most] of the lovely, beautiful, yes magnificent city of Chicago burned down in less than 24 hours. . . . Oh, it looks terrible . . . you can hardly imagine.

How long did it take for much of Chicago to burn down?

What happened during the Great Chicago Fire?

Chicago began rebuilding shortly after the fire in 1871 (above). Otis's **invention** made **elevators** safer (below).

A NEW CITY TAKES SHAPE

The Great Chicago Fire, as it became known, cleared the ground for a new city. Within 15 years of the fire, the first skyscrapers sprang up. At first these buildings were only about 10 stories tall. That is about 100 feet. By 1974, about a century after the fire, the Sears Tower in Chicago rose over 110 stories. That is about 1,400 feet! How did it happen?

Skyscrapers brought together three **inventions**. An invention is something that has been made for the first time. The first invention was a safe **elevator**. An elevator moves people up and down in a building. Early elevators had a problem. Too often the rope holding them broke. In 1852 **Elisha Otis** made elevators safe for people to use. He invented brakes that would stop the elevator from falling even if a rope broke.

Making the First Skyscraper

Skyscrapers also need a very strong building material—and lots of it. Steel is very strong. It can hold a lot of weight. In 1856 an English inventor named **Henry Bessemer** invented a way to turn iron into steel. His invention made steel cheap to make. **Andrew Carnegie** in the United States used the invention to begin producing great amounts of steel. Now there was plenty of steel.

Skyscrapers also need a way to bring light into the middle of a building. In 1879 **Thomas Edison** invented the light bulb. By 1881 Edison found a way to bring electric power and light to an entire building. Edison's light bulb solved the problem of bringing light inside a building.

In 1885 a Chicago builder brought these inventions together to build the first skyscraper. **William Le Baron Jenney**'s Home Insurance Company Building was built on a steel frame. It moved people with a safe elevator. Edison's light bulb made the building bright enough to work in. The skyscraper was born!

What inventions led to the skyscraper?

The Home Insurance Company Building in Chicago was the world's first skyscraper.

DATAGRAPHIC

Inventing the Skyscrapers

During the late 1800s many inventions were created that changed the way people in communities lived and worked. Most of these inventions are still used today in places like the Sears Tower.

Elisha Otis invents a safety device for elevators.

1852

Andrew Carnegie uses Bessemer's invention to produce great amounts of steel.

1875

1850 1860 1870 1880

1856

Henry Bessemer invents a way to produce large amounts of steel quickly.

1879

Thomas Edison invents the light bulb.

Questions

1. Which invention was made in the decade of the 1870s? Who invented it?
2. If you stacked one Home Insurance Building on another, how many would it take to reach as high as the Sears Tower?

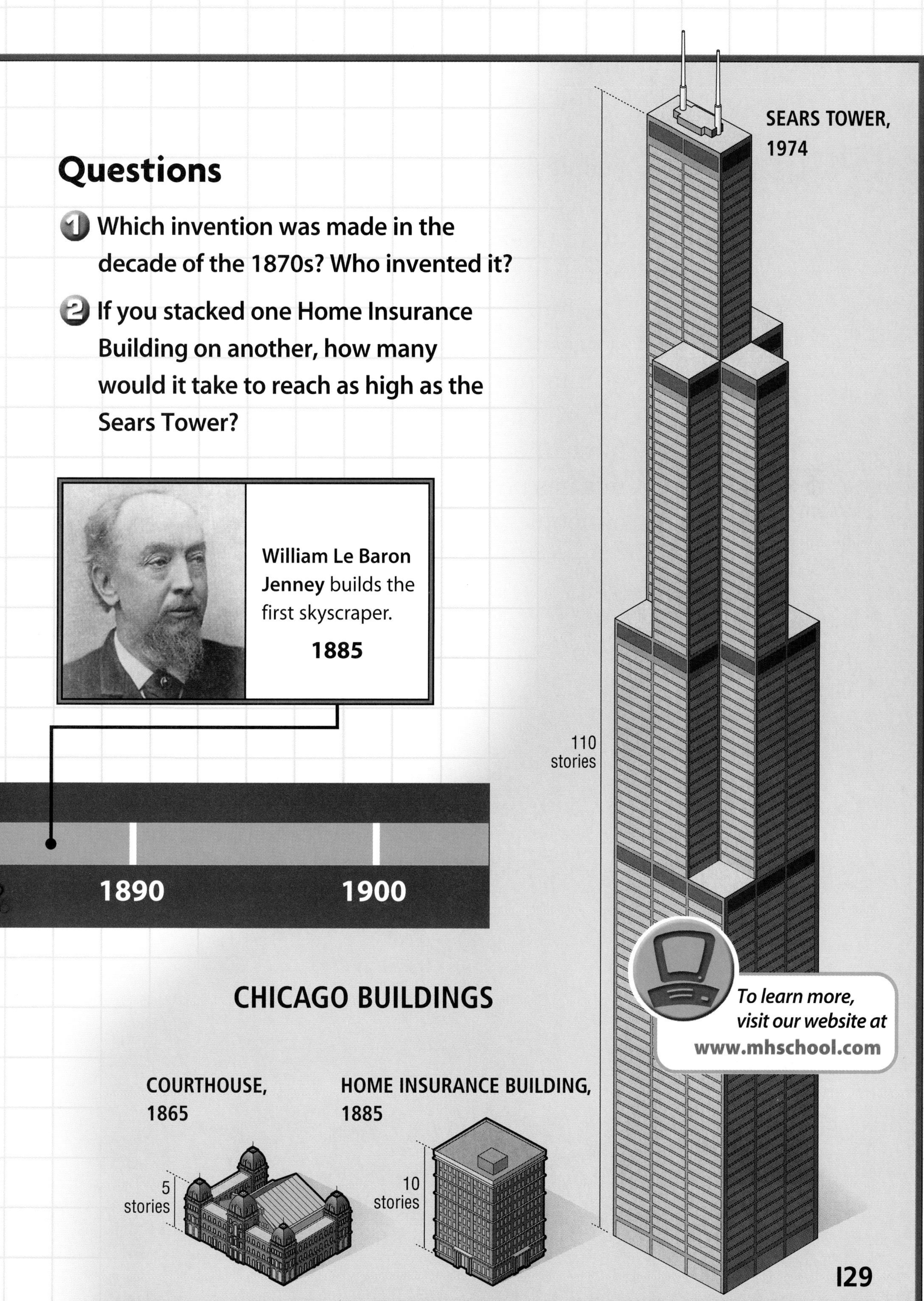

THE CHANGING FACE OF CITIES

Today Chicago, like many cities, is a city of skyscrapers. Skyscrapers have changed the way people live and work. A building like the John Hancock Center in Chicago is like a little city in itself. Over 20,000 people work in the building. Another 3,000 call its upper 45 stories home. The building has 50 elevators and parking spaces for 1,400 cars. It also has a pool, a gymnasium, its own supermarket, and a post office. A person can live, work, shop, and have fun without ever leaving one building. All of this has been made possible by the inventions of people like Elisha Otis and others.

Modern cities like Chicago are home to millions of people.

How have skyscrapers changed the way people in communities live and work?

PUTTING IT TOGETHER

We have read about how inventions have changed communities. We saw how a fire burned down the city of Chicago in the late 1800s. Then we saw how the city was rebuilt with new buildings taller than before. In the next lesson we will see how discoveries in science also changed the lives of people living in communities.

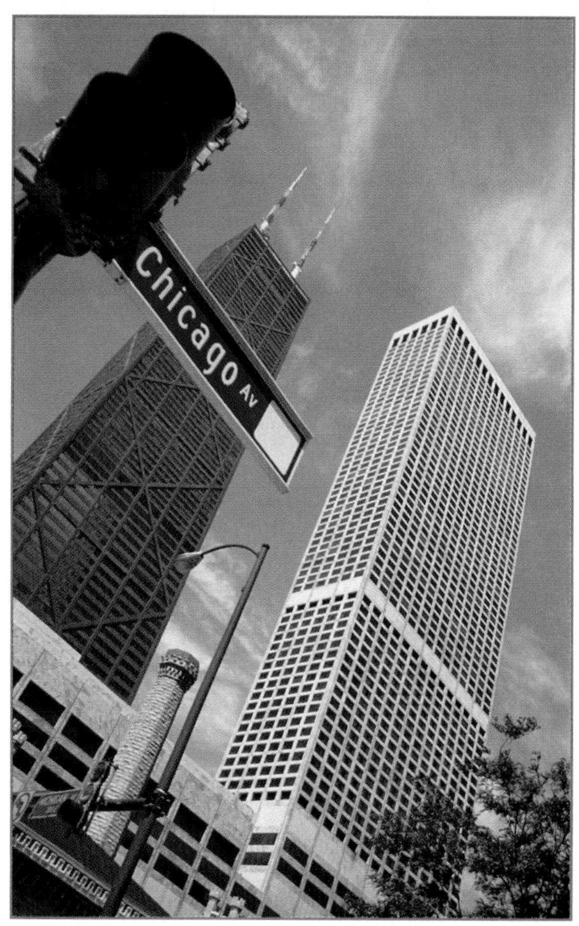

Review and Assess

1. Write one sentence for each of the vocabulary words.

   elevator **invention** **skyscraper**

2. What was the first skyscraper built in Chicago?
3. How have some inventions helped to shape communities?
4. Events such as the Great Chicago Fire changed the **history** of communities. How did Chicago change after the fire?
5. What **problems** did Chicago have after the Great Fire? How did people there solve the problems?

The Sears Tower is a special landmark in the community of Chicago. Make a model of a landmark in your community. Add a sign with the name of the landmark and the date it was built.

You read a letter from a young boy describing the Great Chicago Fire. **Write** your own letter to someone describing an event that happened in your community.

BIOGRAPHY **Focus on Leadership**

Alexander Graham Bell

"Leave the beaten track occasionally and dive into the woods. Every time you do so you will be certain to find something that you have never seen before."

Alexander Graham Bell's invention of the telephone changed the way people communicate. As a young boy Bell had a special way of having a conversation with his mother, who was almost completely deaf. Most people spoke to her through a tube connected to her ear. Aleck, the name his family used for him, spoke in a low voice very close to his mother's forehead. He thought she could best feel the vibrations of his words this way.

Young Aleck was also good at inventing things. He and his brother made a speaking machine that copied how a person talks.

THE LIFE OF ALEXANDER GRAHAM BELL

1850 1860 1870 1880 1890 1900 1910 1920

1847
Alexander Graham Bell is born in Edinburgh, Scotland.

1876
Bell invents the telephone.

1883
Bell starts a school for deaf children.

1888
Bell helps to found the National Geographic Society.

1922
Bell dies in Nova Scotia, Canada.

Aleck used his childhood ideas to continue experimenting with sound. In the 1870s he worked on the idea of sending sound over a wire. Along with electrician Thomas Watson, Bell made the first telephone call ever on March 10, 1876.

The telephone was not Alexander Graham Bell's only invention. He also designed early airplanes and air conditioners. Bell's inventions, however, were not his only important work. He is also known for the work he did to help deaf people. He taught people who could not hear how to speak. He helped to set up schools around the United States. Bell's lifetime of hard work and good ideas helped people everywhere.

Bell tests an early telephone (above) and works with Helen Keller (right).

Link to Today **Think about a person today who has done something good because of an event in his or her family life. Write a paragraph that describes that person.**

Compare and Contrast

Two things that are alike in some ways may be different in other ways. When we **compare**, we tell how things are alike. When we **contrast**, we tell how things are different. For example, let us compare a banana and an orange. They are both types of fruit. They both have an outer skin that you peel off before eating. Now let us contrast a banana and an orange. They have different shapes. They also have different colors and tastes.

VOCABULARY

compare

contrast

LEARN THE SKILL

Read the story. Then follow the steps to compare and contrast.

Kevin's family is trying to decide which park to visit, Allen Park or Baker Park. Allen Park has a lake for boating, fishing, and swimming. There are also tennis and basketball courts. Baker Park has horseback riding and hiking trails. There is a swimming pool and a tennis court. Both parks have a picnic area and a playground.

1. **Think about the things you are comparing and contrasting.**
   There are two parks, Allen Park and Baker Park.

2. **Ask yourself, "How are these things alike?"**
   Both parks have a picnic area and a playground. You can swim and play tennis at both parks.

3. **Ask yourself, "How are these things different?"**
   Only Allen Park has a lake for boating and fishing. Only Baker Park has horseback riding and hiking trails. You can play basketball at Allen Park but not at Baker Park. At Allen Park you swim in a lake, but at Baker Park you swim in a pool.

TRY THE SKILL

Now read another passage.

Myra and Tina are third-grade classmates. They ride the same bus every morning and talk about their favorite things. Myra's favorite color is red, and Tina's favorite color is purple. Tina loves to play soccer, but Myra prefers basketball. Myra wants to be a doctor when she grows up, and Tina hopes to be a teacher. Both of them love to read and write stories.

1. Compare Myra and Tina. What are three things that are similar about them?

2. Contrast Myra and Tina. What are three things that are different about them?

EXTEND THE SKILL

Comparing and contrasting can help you better understand what you read. In Lesson 1 you read about changes in the city of Chicago. Make a two-column chart. In the first column compare the city of Chicago before and after the Great Fire of 1871. In the second column contrast the city of Chicago before and after the fire. Use the pictures below to help you.

Chicago Water Tower, 1870

Chicago Water Tower, Today

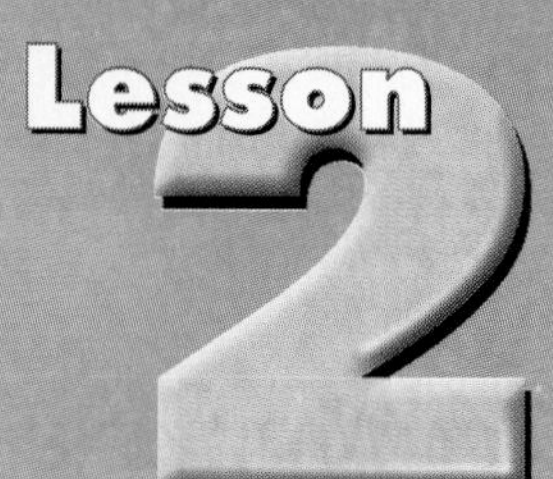

Making Communities Safer

VOCABULARY

pasteurization

preserve

vaccine

PEOPLE

Jane Addams

Louis Pasteur

Charles Drew

Jonas Salk

How have communities become better places to live?

Lesson Outline

- Improving City Life
- Discoveries in Health
- Community Safety

BUILD BACKGROUND

We have read about how inventions have helped to change communities. Over the years communities have also become safer places to live. In this lesson you will read about some people who have helped make communities better places to live.

READING STRATEGY

Copy the diagram. In the bar write this **main idea**: "Health and Safety." In the circles name people who worked for safe, healthy communities.

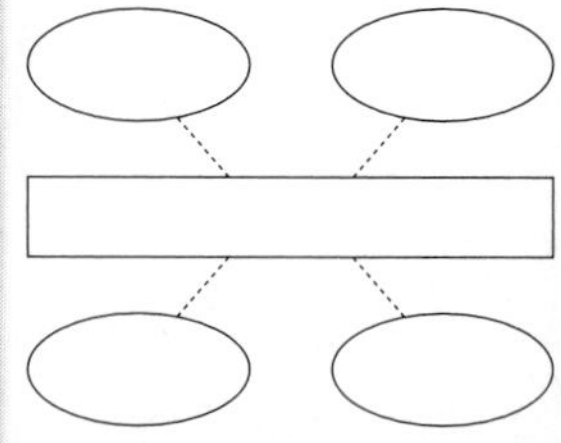

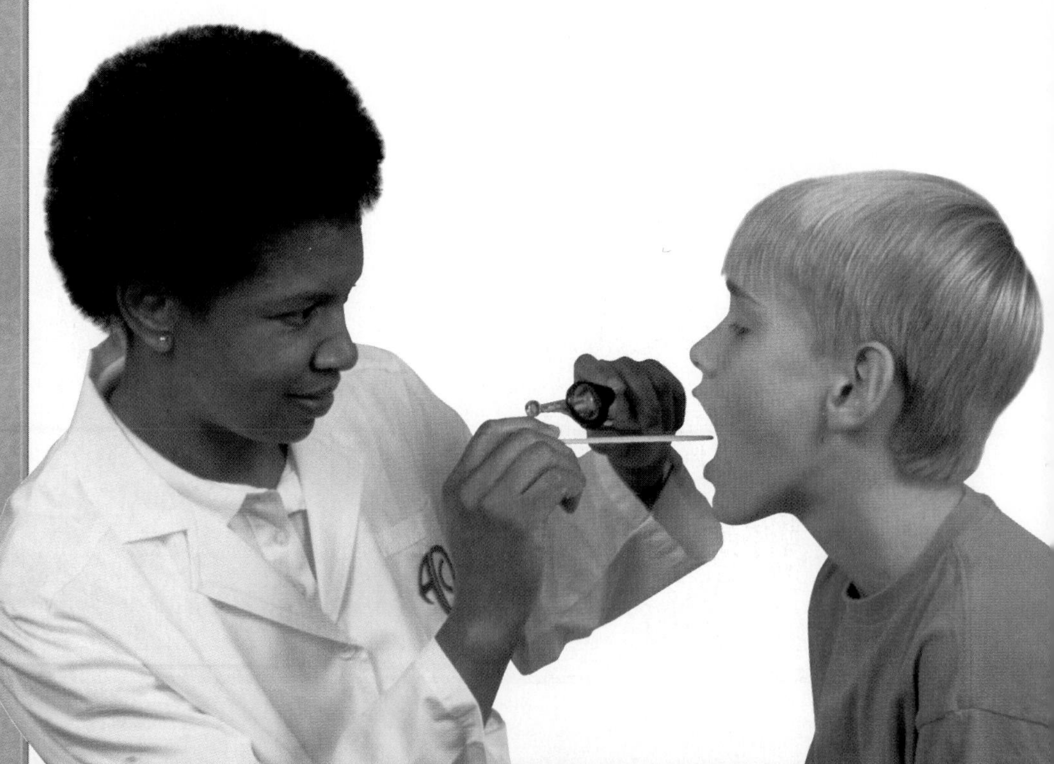

1825 | 1850 | 1875 | 1900 | 1925 | 1950 | 1975 | 2000 | 2025

You Are Here
1889–Present

IMPROVING CITY LIFE

Suppose you lived in the 1880s. There were not as many laws to keep people safe and healthy then. Cities such as Chicago were crowded. People worked long hours at dangerous jobs. When they came home, the water they drank was often dirty and unsafe. The food they bought was often rotten. Illnesses spread easily.

In 1889 a woman named **Jane Addams** decided that she wanted to do something about these problems. She opened a place in Chicago. It was called Hull House. At Hull House people could learn important skills, see a doctor, or get help finding a job. Addams worked with citizen groups to pass new laws making life better for people at work and at home.

Hull House, shown here in the 1940s, has helped people in Chicago for over 100 years.

Why was Hull House important to its community?

DISCOVERIES IN HEALTH

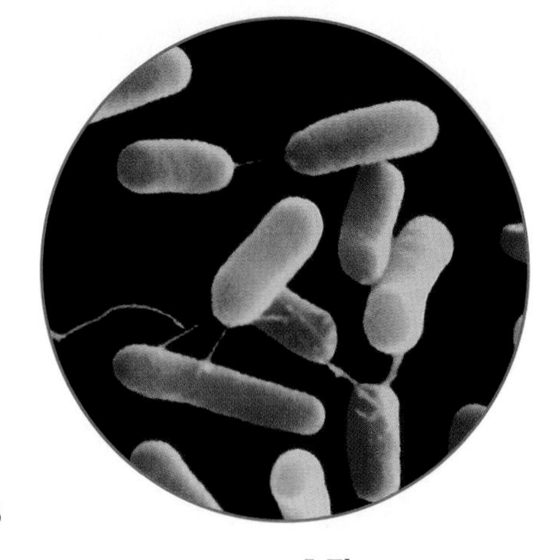

These germs are shown many times their real size.

In the 1860s a French scientist named **Louis Pasteur** (pas TUR) found that there are tiny living things called germs. Germs can grow in the food we eat and can make people sick. Pasteur found a way to stop germs from growing in food. He used heat to kill the germs. Today this discovery, called **pasteurization**, makes milk and other foods safer.

A scientist named **Charles Drew** made an important discovery in the 1940s. He found a way to **preserve** blood. To preserve means to store something so it can be used later. Drew created the American Red Cross Blood Program.

Jonas Salk also made an important discovery. In the 1950s he found a way to stop a serious disease called polio (POH lee oh). Polio could cause people to be unable to walk or move. Salk made a **vaccine** (vak SEEN) for polio. A vaccine is a liquid made from the dead or weakened germs of a disease. A vaccine can make a person sick but not very sick. The vaccine helps the body to protect itself against a disease. Salk's vaccine helped save many people from becoming sick with polio.

What discoveries improved community health?

Some People Who Have Made Communities Safer

Louis Pasteur **1822–1895**		• Discovered that germs cause infections • Discovered that heating liquids to a high temperature destroys harmful germs • Developed a process to make foods safer
Jane Addams **1860–1935**		• Founded Hull House in Chicago • Provided education and a safe place for children • Helped immigrants and women to find jobs and places to live
Charles Drew **1904–1950**		• Researched how to preserve blood • Started the American Red Cross Blood Program
Jonas Salk **1914–1995**		• Developed a vaccine for polio • Started a school for medical science

Chart Skill

1. Look at the chart. Who developed a vaccine for polio? In what year was this person born?
2. What do all of the people listed in the chart have in common?

COMMUNITY SAFETY

Think about everyone who works to make your community a safe place. There are doctors, nurses, and hospitals to take care of you when you are sick. There are people who make laws that protect you. There may be people who come to your school to talk about how to stay healthy.

There are people like Jane Addams, who help make life better at work and at home. There are scientists like Jonas Salk, who find ways to fight serious diseases. Maybe someday you will be a person who makes the world a healthier and safer place.

Who is someone who helps to make your community safe?

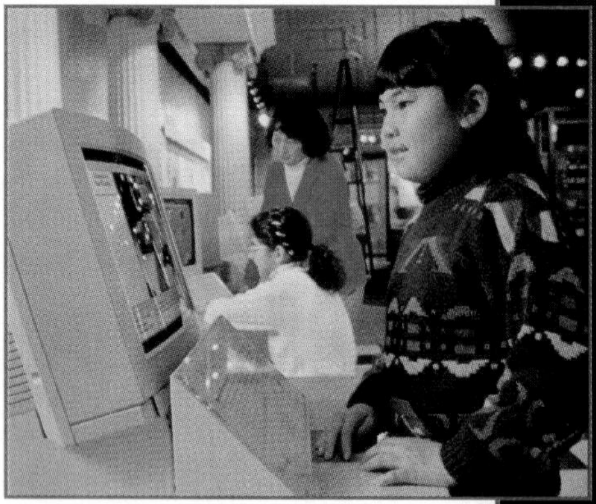

At a science museum children can learn about computers (above) or tornadoes (right).

PUTTING IT TOGETHER

We have seen how growing cities long ago were unhealthy places. We have seen how people such as Jane Addams worked for safety and health in cities. We have also read about how discoveries in health have changed the world. Certain diseases, such as polio, are almost completely gone in the United States today. This is because scientists such as Louis Pasteur, Jonas Salk, and Charles Drew have worked to find out more about illnesses and cures. In our communities today many people work to keep us healthy and safe.

Review and Assess

1. Write one sentence for each of the vocabulary words.

   pasteurization **preserve** **vaccine**

2. How did Jonas Salk improve community health?
3. What are some ways communities have become better places to live?
4. How did Jane Addams help the people in her community?
5. **Contrast** what Jane Addams did and what Louis Pasteur did.

Think about the people who work to make your community safe. Make a chart to show the information. In one column write what each person does. In another tell how each makes your community safer.

Write a short biography about Louis Pasteur, Jane Addams, Charles Drew, or Jonas Salk. Use information you find at the library or on the Internet.

Points of View

What is the most important invention of the last century?

There are many inventions that have greatly changed the way Americans live today. Which has changed our lives the most? Read three different points of view on this issue. Think about each, and then answer the questions.

OMAR KHALID
East Elmhurst, New York
Excerpt from an interview, 2001

"The telephone is so important because it gave us a new way to communicate. It is used for business calls as well as for talking to friends and other personal calls. We use the telephone to call our friends and family in New Jersey, Pennsylvania, and Pakistan."

KATHERINE PAUL
La Conner, Washington
Excerpt from an interview, 2001

"The electric automobile is the most important invention because it does not pollute Earth. Cars that run on gasoline use too much oil and pollute the air. Polluted air is not healthy for people or animals. In the future the electric car will lead to cleaner air."

ROSS DARY
Waupun, Wisconsin
Excerpt from an interview, 2001

"The polio vaccine is the most important discovery because it saved millions of lives. [Other inventions] are just for people's convenience, but the polio vaccine kept millions of people from dying. Maybe many people who got sick from polio might have been great leaders."

Thinking About the Points of View

1. Why does Omar believe that the telephone is the most important invention of the century?
2. Katherine and her family love the outdoors. They like to hike and camp in the woods. How might this have influenced her point of view on this issue?
3. What reasons does Ross give for his opinion?
4. What other points of view might people have on this issue?

Building Citizenship

Leadership

Discuss the inventors and scientists you have read about. How did each person take responsibility for the common good? How did the inventions and discoveries help people?

Write About It!

Make a list of five inventions that you think are important. List these inventions in order, starting with the most important one first. Write a paragraph explaining your choices and your ranking.

Chapter 5 REVIEW

VOCABULARY REVIEW

Number a sheet of paper from 1 to 3. Beside each number write the word from the list below that matches the description.

pasteurization

skyscraper

vaccine

1. A very tall building
2. A way to kill germs by using heat
3. A liquid made from the dead or weakened germs of a disease

CHAPTER COMPREHENSION

4. Name and describe two inventions that made it possible to build skyscrapers.
5. What was Jane Addams's goal? What did she do to reach that goal?
6. Write two examples of scientific discoveries that help to keep people healthier.

SKILL REVIEW

7. **Reading/Thinking Skill** What does it mean to compare and contrast two things?
8. **Reading/Thinking Skill** Compare and contrast life in Chicago before and after Jane Addams created Hull House.
9. **Reading/Thinking Skill** How were Louis Pasteur and Jonas Salk alike? In what ways were they different?

USING A TIME LINE

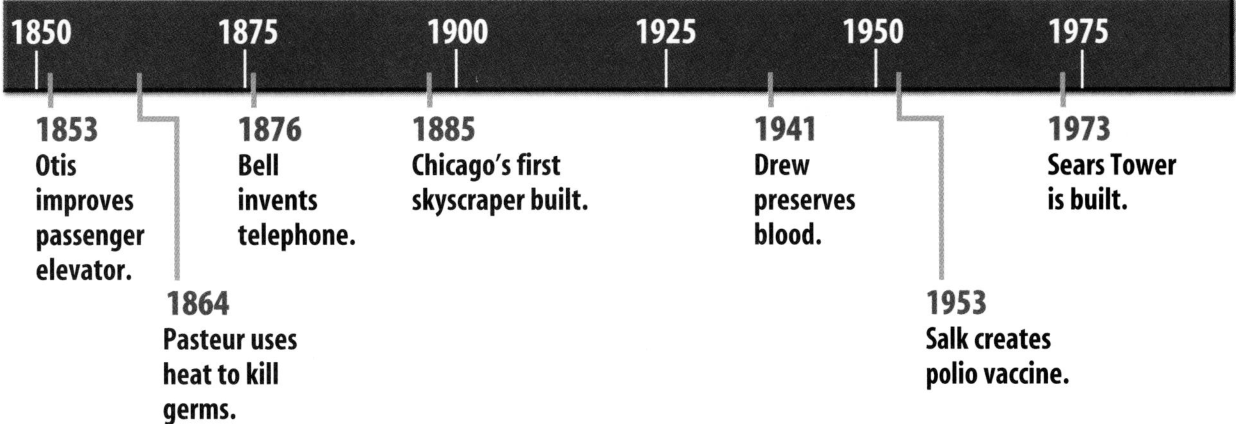
1850
1875
1900
1925
1950
1975
1853 Otis improves passenger elevator.
1864 Pasteur uses heat to kill germs.
1876 Bell invents telephone.
1885 Chicago's first skyscraper built.
1941 Drew preserves blood.
1953 Salk creates polio vaccine.
1973 Sears Tower is built.

10. Look at the time line to answer the question. How many years passed between the construction of the first Chicago skyscraper and the Sears Tower?

Activity

Make an Invention According to an old saying, "Necessity is the mother of invention." This means that inventions are created because people need things. Make a list of things people need today. Choose one need, and think of an invention that would fill the need. Draw your invention, and write a brief description.

Foldables

Use your Foldable concept map to review what you have learned about new ideas changing communities. Look at the lesson titles, and review what you learned about how inventions shape communities and how communities can be made safer through scientific discoveries. Lift the tabs to review your notes.

New Ideas Change Communities
People like Jane Addams and
Inventions Shape Communities
Lesson 1
Making Communities Safer
Lesson 2

Your Community's History

In this unit you have read that communities have history. Now you get to investigate. How has your community changed over the years? What can history tell you about your community today?

Rhonda lives in Philadelphia, Pennsylvania. She had fun digging into the rich history of her community. She interviewed an older neighbor. She also read books on local history and went to a museum. To show what she learned, Rhonda made a time line.

- ***What would a time line of your community's history look like?***

Activity

Making an Illustrated Time Line

Materials

- construction paper
- markers
- tape
- scissors
- your notes and sketches

Step 1 Learn about your community's past. Make notes of what you learn.

Step 2 Gather your materials.

Step 3 Make a time line. On the left write the year your time line begins. On the right write this year. In between mark the dates when something interesting happened. Draw pictures to illustrate the events you choose.

VOCABULARY REVIEW

Number a sheet of paper from 1 to 6. Read the definition of each underlined word. Write **T** if the definition is true and F if it is false. If it is false, write a sentence correctly defining the word.

1. A pioneer is one of the first of a group of people to settle in an area.
2. An immigrant is something that has been made for the first time.
3. Culture is the use of skills, ideas, and tools to meet people's needs.
4. A colony is a place that is ruled by another country.
5. Migration is the practice of moving from one country to another.
6. To preserve something means to store it so it can be used later.

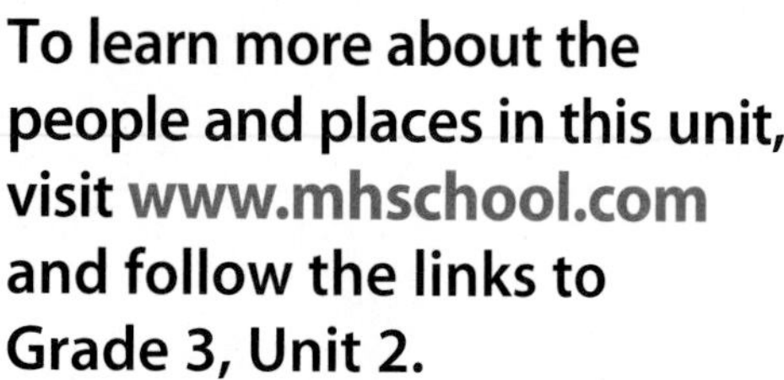

TECHNOLOGY
To learn more about the people and places in this unit, visit www.mhschool.com and follow the links to Grade 3, Unit 2.

SKILL REVIEW

7. **Study Skill** Explain how to find the number of years between two events on a time line.
8. **Reading/Thinking Skill** What is the difference between comparing and contrasting?
9. **Geography Skill** Use the map scale to find the distance between Albuquerque, New Mexico, and the state capital.
10. **Geography Skill** In what direction would you travel to go from Las Cruces to Roswell, New Mexico? In what direction would you travel to get from Roswell to Las Cruces?

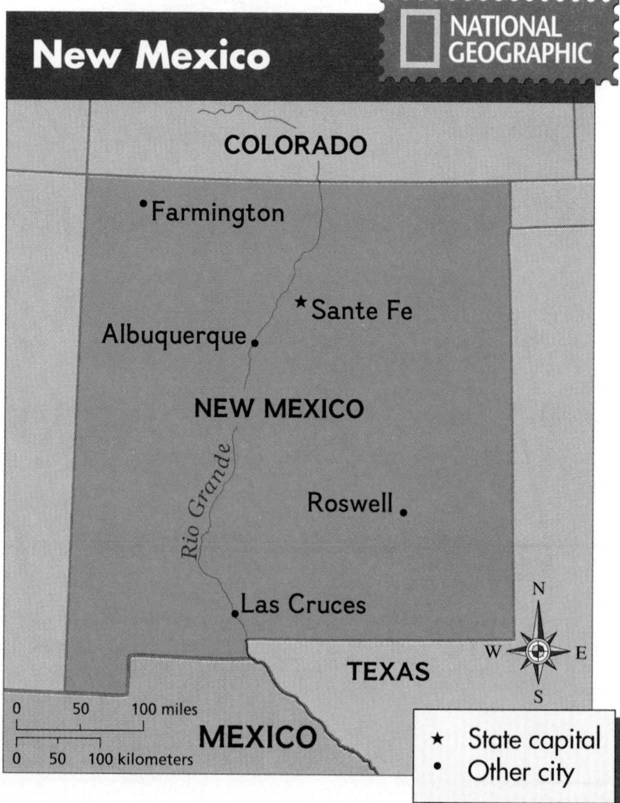

TEST PREP

Read the passage. Then read the questions that follow. Decide which is the best answer to each question, and write it on a piece of paper.

Explorers such as Daniel Boone, Meriwether Lewis, and William Clark helped open trails that led west. In the 1840s and 1850s, thousands of United States citizens followed these trails to start new lives.

1 Daniel Boone and Meriwether Lewis and William Clark all

- went to Missouri
- lived in Kentucky
- found the trail to Oregon
- helped open up trails that led west

2 In this passage the word trails means

- lands
- paths
- travelers
- states

WRITING ACTIVITIES

Writing to Express Write a pretend conversation between John Smith and Chief Powhatan. What questions and concerns might they have about each other?

Writing to Inform Suppose you were a pioneer who made the journey to Oregon. Write a newspaper article for people who are planning to make the same trip. Give advice about what to bring and what to expect.

Writing to Persuade Suppose you lived in the time of Thomas Edison. Write an advertisement for his new invention, the light bulb. Tell what the light bulb is and how it will make people's lives easier.

The Babe and I

by David A. Adler
illustrated by Terry Widener

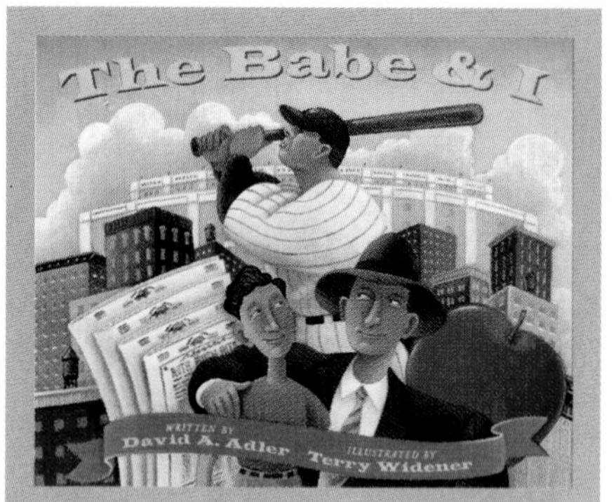

In the 1930s many people lost their jobs. Families worked together to get through hard times. In this story a father who has lost his job sells apples on the street. His son helps the family by selling newspapers. The boy and his friend Jacob learn that the name Babe Ruth sells a lot of newspapers.

"We're here," Jacob said. "That's Yankee Stadium."

He picked up a newspaper and looked through it. "Here it is," he said. "This is what they want."

"Babe Ruth hits home run!" he called out. "Read all about it!"

"Here, I'll take one," a man said, and gave Jacob two cents.

Jacob and I quickly sold our papers. When we left the stadium the coins in my pocket made a nice jingling sound.

When I got home I didn't tell Mom that I had seen Dad selling apples on Webster Avenue. Instead I told her about my job. She put the coins I earned in our money jar and said, "Don't say anything to your father about the newspapers. It might embarrass him to know you're helping out."

Later Dad came home and put some coins in the jar and said, "I was really busy at the office today. I'm tired." I wanted to tell him he didn't have to pretend he still had his job, but I couldn't. I just looked at Dad's briefcase and wondered what he had in there.

The next day Jacob and I called out about Babe Ruth again. He had hit his twenty-sixth home run! I quickly sold my newspapers. I knew I could have sold more, if only I had some way to get them to the stadium.

When I got home I searched the basement of our building for a wagon, or anything with wheels. All I found were boxes and a torn suitcase. Just before I went back upstairs I saw Mrs. Johnson pushing her baby in a carriage.

"Could I borrow that?" I asked.

"Why?" she asked. "You don't have a baby."

I told her about the newspapers.

"I suppose so," Mrs. Johnson said, thinking. "But this would have to be a business arrangement. With my carriage you'll make extra money, so I should make some, too." She offered to rent the carriage to me for ten cents an afternoon, and I agreed.

Thanks to Mrs. Johnson's carriage, I sold lots of papers. I had eighty cents to give Mom for the money jar.

When Dad came home he gave Mom a bottle of milk and a bag of apples, and said, "I bought the apples from an unemployed man I passed on my way home."

"Dad," I said, "that man is not unemployed. Selling apples is a job."

"No it's not," he said sharply. "It's just what you do while you wait and hope for something better."

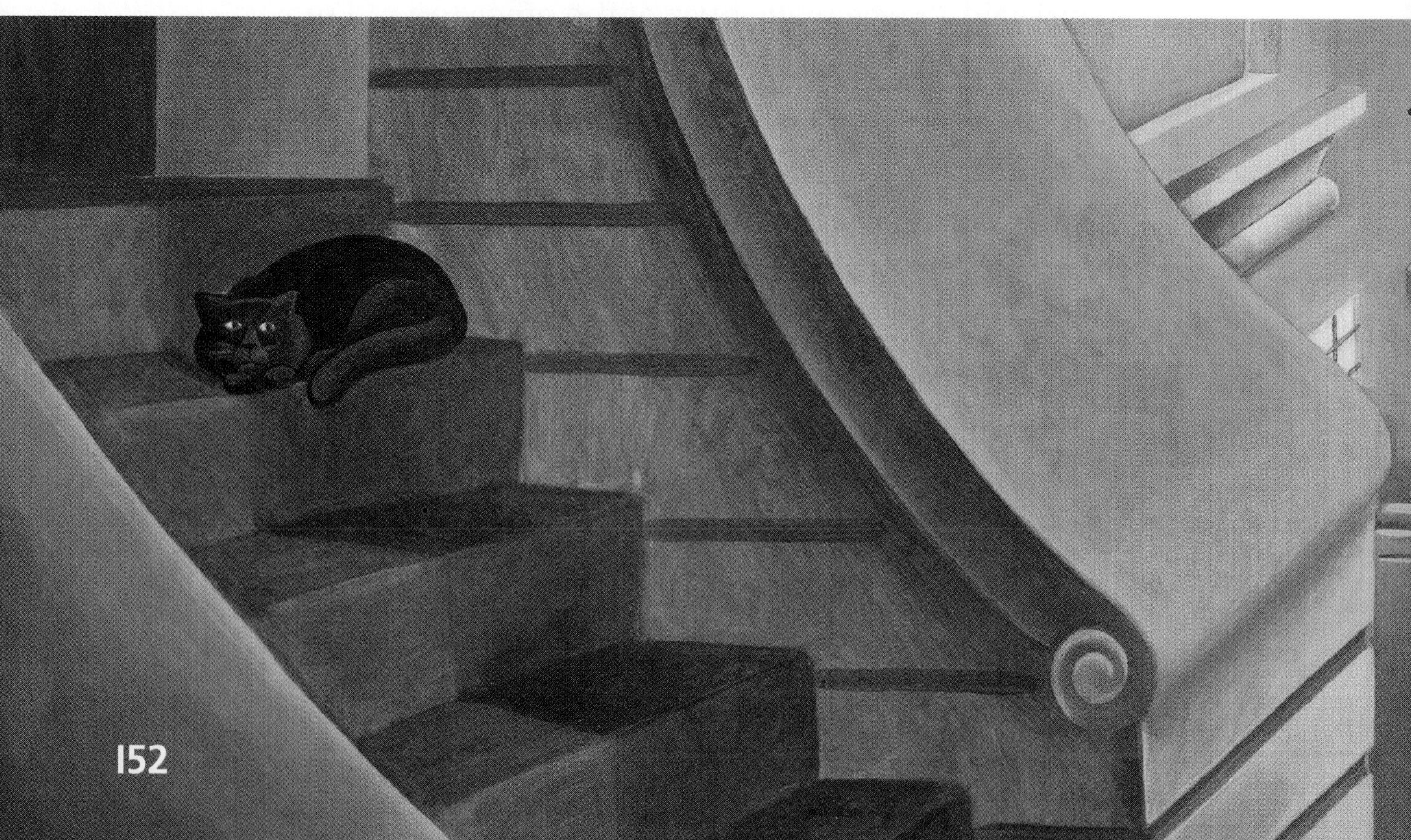

He looked upset, and I realized how important it was for him to keep his secret.

That night Dad asked me to walk with him. When we were a few blocks from home he said, "Today I saw you pushing Mrs. Johnson's baby carriage. I spoke with her, and she told me about the newspapers."

"I'm just trying to help, Dad."

He said, "I know."

Dad held my hand firmly. We walked quietly for a while. Then Dad asked, "Were you ever on Webster Avenue?"

"Once."

He squeezed my hand. Tears were rolling down his cheeks.

"I didn't tell Mom," I said.

Dad didn't say anything after that. I didn't either. We just walked.

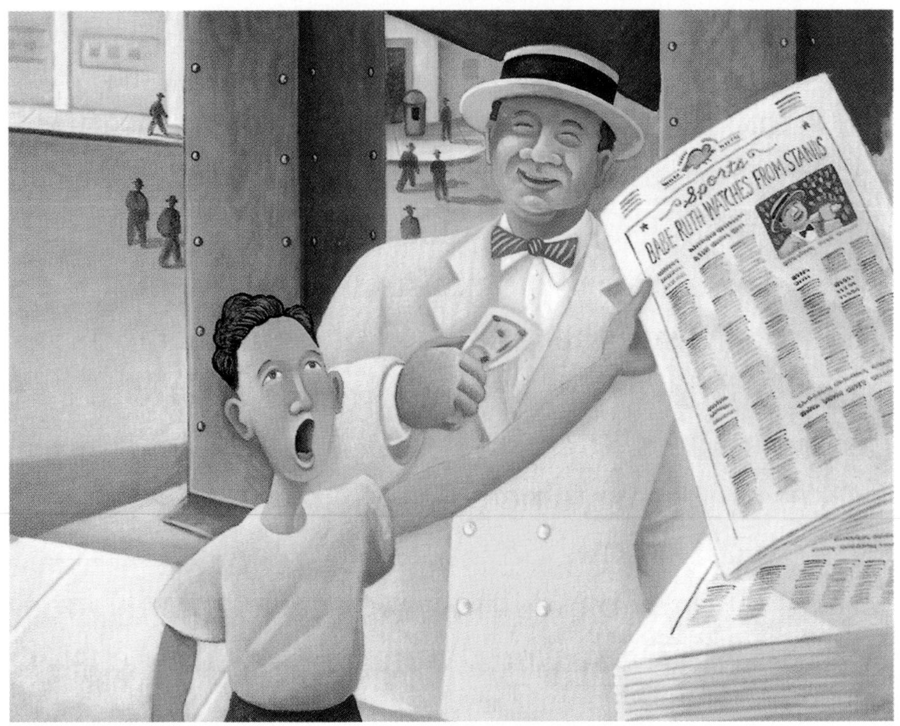

The next day Jacob and I called out, “Babe Ruth sits with fans! Read all about it!”

“Here, kid. I’ll take one.” A tall man gave me a five-dollar bill.

“I’m sorry,” I told him. “I can’t change that.”

“That’s okay, kid. Keep the change.”

I just looked at the money. I couldn’t believe anyone would pay that much for a newspaper.

Jacob ran to me. “Do you know who that was?” he asked. “You sold a paper to Babe Ruth.”

“Wow!” I said. “I just sold a newspaper to Babe Ruth!”

When all our papers were sold, I pointed to Yankee Stadium and told Jacob, “I’m going over there.” I needed to see Babe Ruth again.

I checked the prices and realized I could buy two tickets and still have plenty left for the money jar. So that’s what I did.

I think the Red Sox pitcher was afraid Babe Ruth would hit a home run. He purposely threw wide of the plate four times and walked the Babe.

We cheered again as Babe Ruth slowly walked to first base. We knew he couldn't hit a home run every time, but at least the Babe was there.

Babe Ruth was part of the 1932 Yankees. That year they were the best team in baseball. He and I were a team, too. His home runs helped me sell newspapers. As I left Yankee Stadium, with the coins I had earned making that nice jingling sound in my pocket, I knew Dad and I were also a team. We were both working to get our family through hard times.

Write About It!

The young boy in this story quickly learns how to work as part of a team. Think about his relationships with Jacob, Mrs. Johnson, Babe Ruth, and his dad. Write a paragraph telling why each was important to his success selling newspapers.

Unit 3

Communities at Work

TAKE A LOOK

What jobs do people do?

Whether they grow crops, make products, or build things, people around the world are busy working.

Explore our Web site www.mhschool.com to learn about some ways people earn money.

Chapter 6

THE Big IDEAS ABOUT...

Living and Working

People in communities work to earn money. They use the money to buy the things they need and want. Making good money choices is important for everyone.

PEOPLE EARN MONEY

Most people earn money by working at businesses. This business sells food.

MAKING MONEY CHOICES

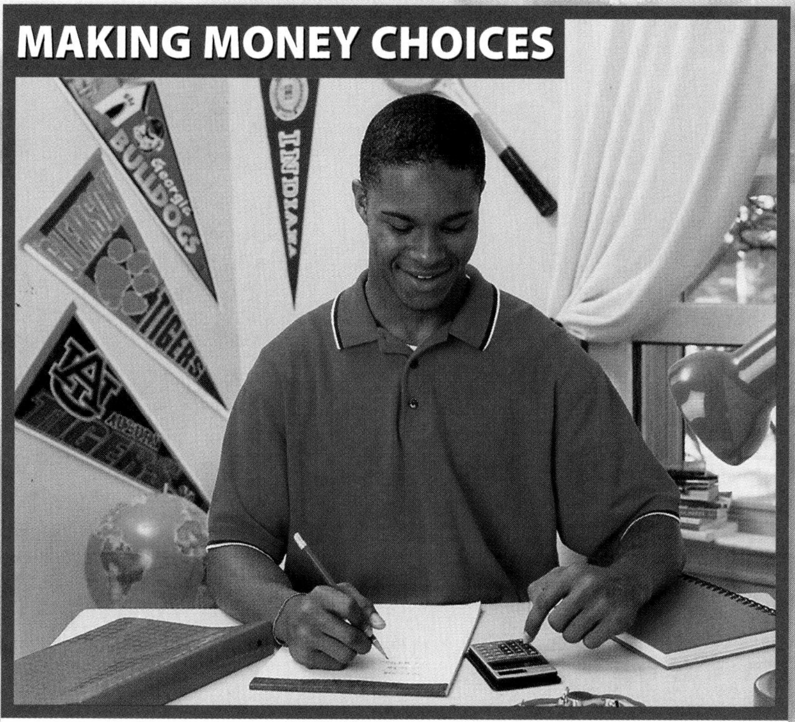

Making a plan for spending and saving can help us to make good choices about how to use our money.

Foldables

Make this Foldable study guide, and use it to record what you learn about "Living and Working."

1. Fold a sheet of paper like a hot dog, leaving one side 1" longer than the other.
2. Make one cut in the middle of the short side to form two tabs.

3. Label the 1" tab with the lesson titles.

Lesson 1

People Earn Money

VOCABULARY

goods
services
expenses
profit
employee
producer
consumer
economy

READING STRATEGY

Use the diagram to **compare and contrast** consumers and producers. Explain how they are different and how they are alike.

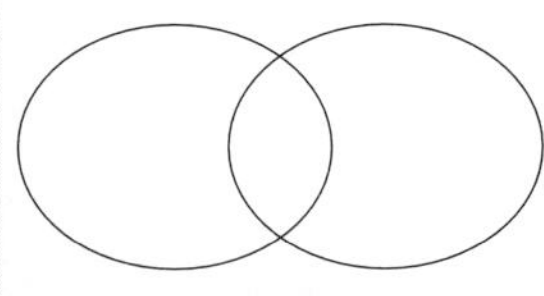

Find out!

How does a business operate?

Lesson Outline

- Businesses Provide Goods and Services
- Running a Business
- Businesses and the Economy

BUILD BACKGROUND

Most people work to earn money to buy what they need or want. They use the money for food, clothes, and a place to live. For some people this money comes from running a business. Let us look at how one business is run.

BUSINESSES PROVIDE GOODS AND SERVICES

The community of Seaside, Oregon, has many businesses. One of these businesses is Scoops Ice Cream Parlor. The shop has changed and grown over the years. John Haff opened the business over 40 years ago. At first it was a drugstore. Then John added a soda fountain and ice cream counter.

In 1992 John's daughter, Jean Rollins, took over the business. After a few years Jean decided to just sell ice cream. She also made a website. It tells Jean's customers about ice cream facts, special offers, and new flavors.

Jean's shop provides both **goods** and **services**. Goods—like ice cream—are things that people make or grow. Services—like providing information on a website—are things that businesses do for people.

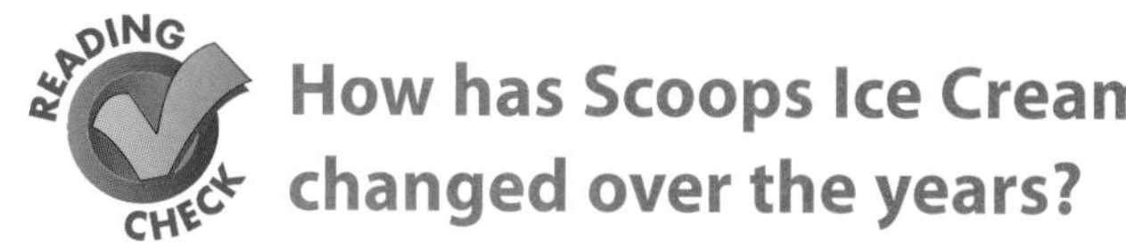

How has Scoops Ice Cream Parlor changed over the years?

This shop has been in business for so long, it has grown with the community.

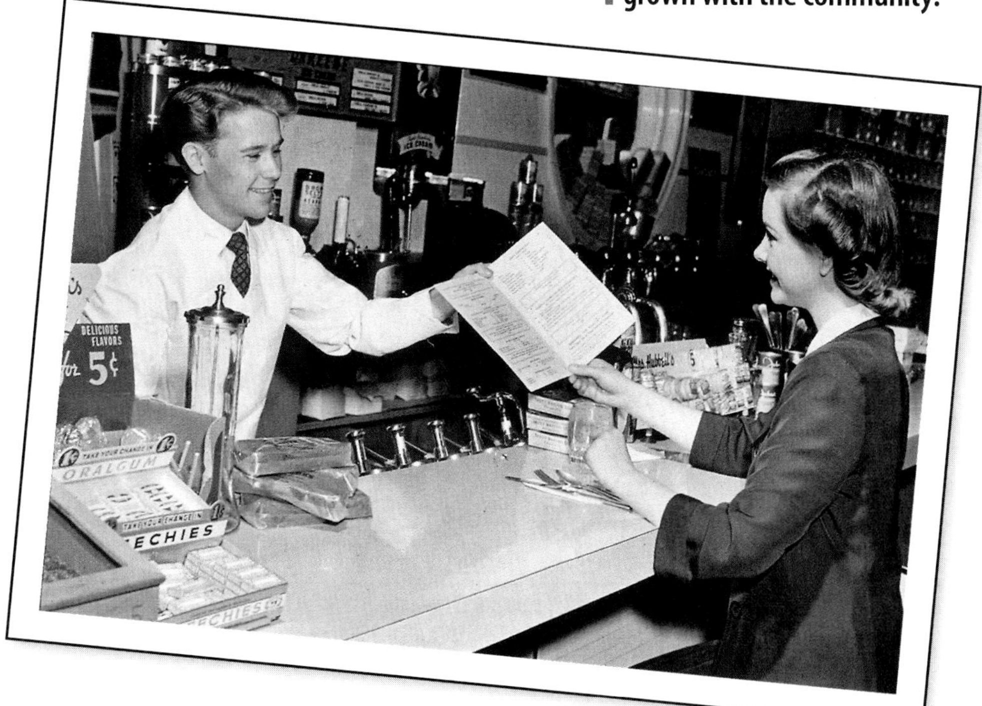

RUNNING A BUSINESS

Jean is in business to earn money. She needs to sell enough ice cream to pay her **expenses**. Expenses are all the things a business spends money on to stay in business. Jean's expenses include the shop's rent and electricity. The amount of money left after all the costs of running the business are paid is Jean's **profit**.

One of Jean's expenses is the money she pays her **employees**. An employee is a person who works for a person or business. Jean has two employees to help her run the shop.

Jean does not make all of the products she sells. She buys some from a **producer**. A producer is a person, company, or thing that makes or creates something. One of the things Jean buys from a producer is hot fudge sauce. This is one of Jean's expenses.

Running a Business—Expenses and Profit

1. **Producers** grow or make something to sell to other businesses.

2. Businesses like Jean's buy things from producers. These are business **expenses**.

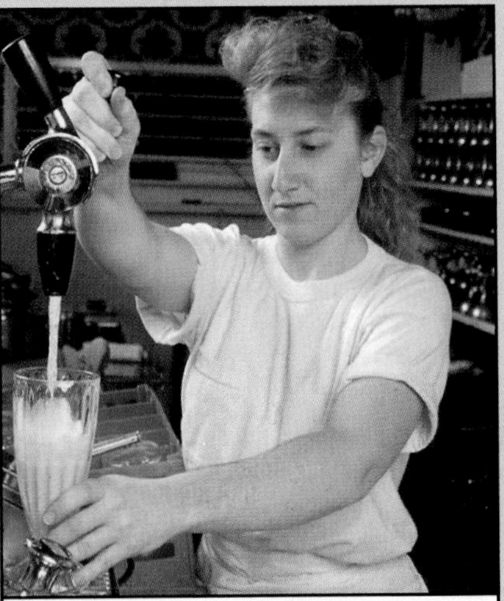

3. Jean sells to **consumers**. This is how her business makes a **profit**.

Knowing Your Customers

Business owners must know what consumers want.

The people who buy ice cream from Scoops Ice Cream Parlor are **consumers**. A consumer is a person who buys goods and services. You are a consumer when you buy something at a store. The chart on page 162 shows how goods move from producers to consumers.

Jean has to know her customers. She has to know what they want and how much they will pay. It is not easy. "It takes years of experience and years of making mistakes to know everything there is to do," Jean says. "You have to think, for example: Which flavors sell the best? How much should I charge so enough customers will buy our products? I also need to decide how much milk I need to buy to make enough ice cream. I don't want to buy more than I can sell, or the ice cream will not be fresh. Also, we sell more ice cream during summer months than in the winter. I need to know that, too."

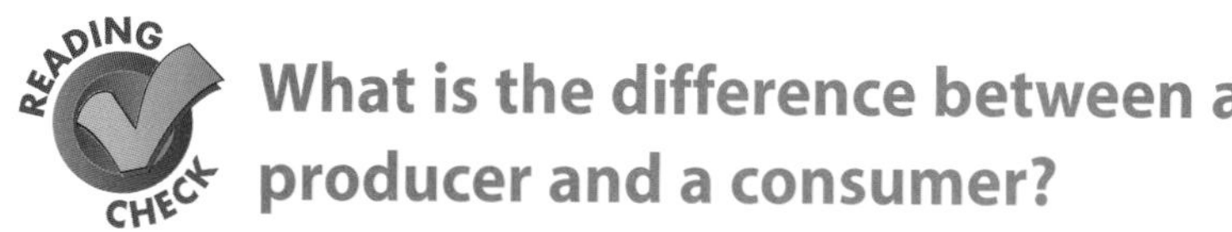

What is the difference between a producer and a consumer?

BUSINESSES AND THE ECONOMY

Scoops Ice Cream Parlor is just one small part of our country's **economy**. The economy is the way a country produces and uses its money, goods, natural resources, and services. In the United States' economy, people are free to choose what they will produce and consume.

Since consumers are free to choose where they will buy goods and services, businesses try hard to get customers to come to their store. Running a business is hard work. Jean says, "You need to be willing to work six or seven days a week. You need to work during lunch and dinner hours. You need to work hard to be successful."

How does the economy work in our country?

Exploring ECONOMICS

Must-Have Toys

Have you ever noticed that sometimes there is a toy that everyone seems to want? During this time stores charge full price and still sell all the toys they have. Then, after a time, not as many people want the toy. What happens then? Stores lower the price to sell the toy. When consumers want a product, prices stay high. When they do not want a product, prices come down.

Activity

Work in a group to think of a must-have toy and give it a price. Then see how much the other groups would pay for your toy. Is it higher or lower than the price you set?

PUTTING IT TOGETHER

Businesses are an important part of communities. Businesses provide jobs to people. They also provide goods and services.

Business owners work hard to earn a profit. They need to think about what consumers want and are willing to pay. In our economy people are free to choose what to make and what to buy.

Review and Assess

1. Write one sentence for each of the vocabulary words.

   consumer **employee** **profit**

2. From where does Jean Rollins get the hot fudge she sells?
3. Describe how a business operates.
4. What happens to prices when many people want certain goods or services?
5. **Compare and contrast** Scoops Ice Cream Parlor from the time the business first started to the business it is today.

Be a smart consumer. Find out the price of an item that is sold at three different stores. Make sure the item is the same each time. Make a chart that shows the names of the stores and the prices of the item. Where would you buy the item? Why?

Write an advertisement for a business. Choose any business that you wish. Decorate your advertisement with drawings or photos.

BIOGRAPHY Focus on Leadership

Maggie Lena Walker

"Let us have a bank that will take the nickels and turn them into dollars."

Maggie Lena Walker grew up at a time when many African Americans had just won their freedom from slavery. When she was a little girl, Maggie saw that blacks and whites were still being treated differently. She worked all her life to make things fair for all people.

When she was 14, Maggie joined a group called the Independent Order of St. Luke. The group helped African Americans improve their lives.

Maggie Lena Walker

THE LIFE OF MAGGIE LENA WALKER

1865 | 1875 | 1885 | 1895 | 1905 | 1915 | 1925 | 1935

- **1867** Maggie Lena Walker is born in Richmond, Virginia.
- **1881** Walker joins the Independent Order of St. Luke.
- **1902** Walker starts the St. Luke Penny Savings Bank.
- **1920** Walker's bank has helped people to buy 600 homes.
- **1934** Maggie Lena Walker dies.

Maggie believed that African Americans in Richmond, Virginia, would be better off if they had a bank. The bank would help people save and earn money. It would also help people buy homes and start businesses. In 1903 she started the St. Luke Penny Savings Bank. Maggie was the first woman in the United States to be president of a bank. Today that bank is still in business. It is the oldest bank run by African Americans.

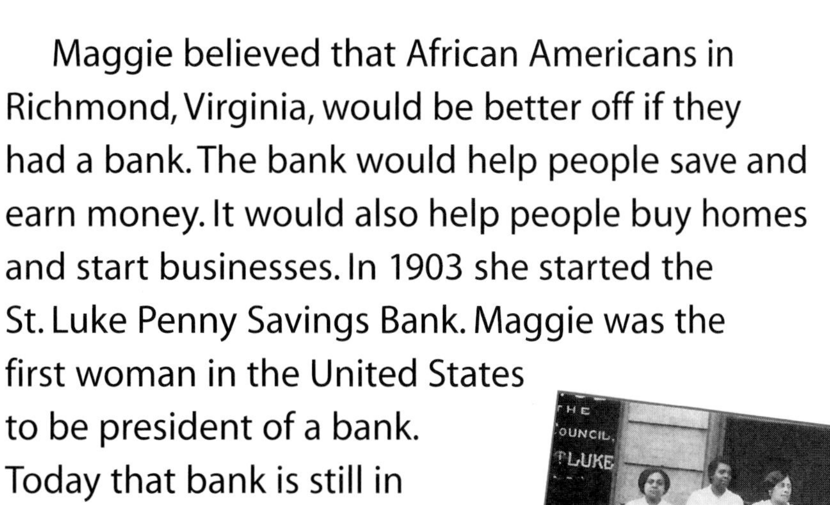

Maggie Lena Walker worked with her employees (top, right). Her house (right) is now a museum.

Link to Today **Find out about someone today who helps people to help themselves. Write a paragraph that compares and contrasts the person with Maggie Lena Walker.**

Classifying

Have you or someone you know ever moved to a new house? Think about all the things in the old house that had to be packed up and delivered to the new place. To make the move easier, everything was probably organized into boxes of similar things. There were probably boxes for kitchen items, toys, and clothing. This way of arranging things in groups is called **classifying**. Classifying can help a person better understand how items are related to each other.

VOCABULARY

classifying

LEARN THE SKILL

Follow these steps when you are classifying things.

1. **Look at the things you want to classify.**
   David's family is moving. David is helping to pack the things in the basement. He looks at all the things in the room to see what he will have to put in boxes. He wants to see if the items can be grouped together.

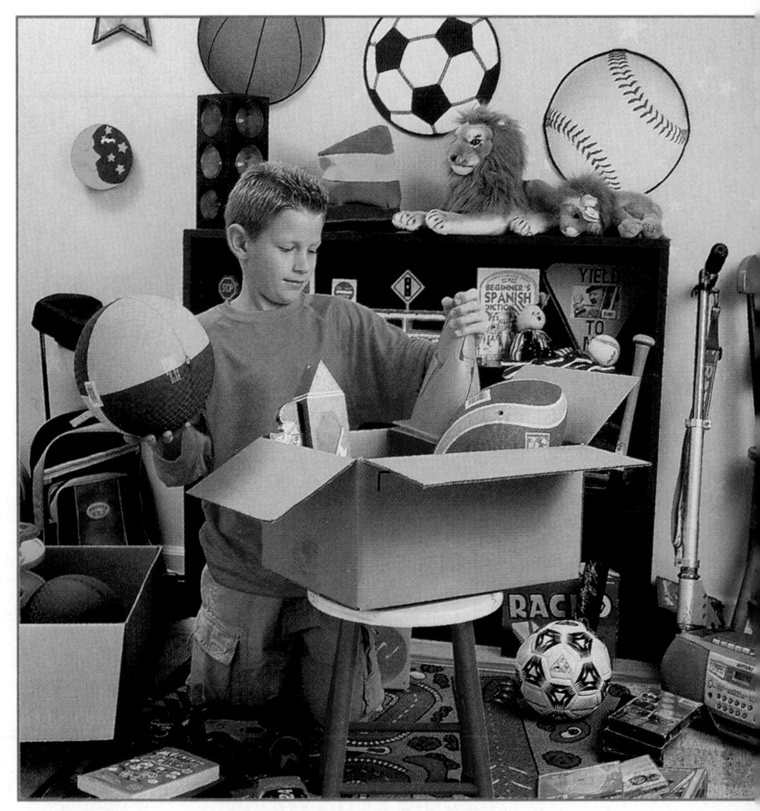

2. **Decide how you will group similar items.**
   David decides to classify the items into four groups. The groups are games, toys, books, and sports equipment.

3. **Put similar items together.** David puts the board games and handheld games into one box. He puts the cars, action figures, and other toys into a second box. He puts the comic books, coloring books, and paperback books into a third box. The balls, baseball glove, and tennis rackets go into a fourth box.

TRY THE SKILL

Mario has started a coin collection. So far he has collected the coins shown in the picture.

1. If Mario classifies the coins by their color, how many groups will he have? Which coins will go in each group?
2. If Mario classifies the coins by their shape, how many groups will he have? Which coins will go in each group?
3. What is a third way Mario can classify his coins? Which coins will go in each group?

EXTEND THE SKILL

Make a list of items you would expect to find at Scoops Ice Cream Parlor. Then classify those items into different groups, such as "Toppings for Sundaes," "Kind of Ice Cream," or "Equipment Used at Scoops Ice Cream Parlor."

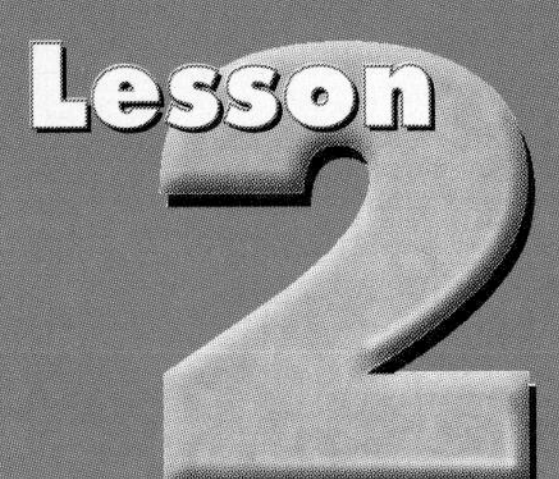

Making Money Choices

How can a plan help you spend and save money?

Lesson Outline

- Minding Your Money
- Making a Budget
- Different People Use Budgets

VOCABULARY

budget

income

interest

PEOPLE

Benjamin Franklin

READING STRATEGY

Use a word web to **summarize.** Write "Budget" in the center circle. Write ideas about budgets in the other circles.

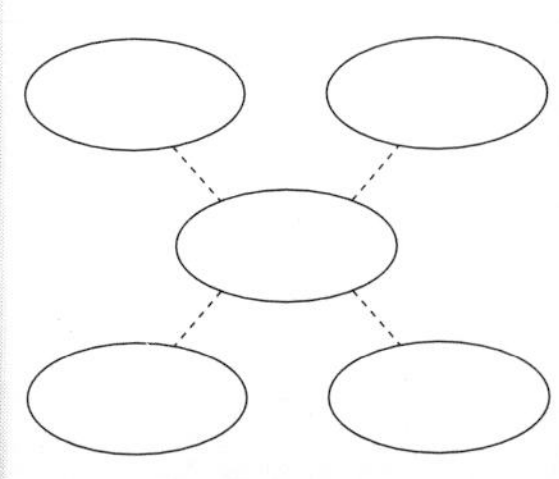

BUILD BACKGROUND

The money people earn goes toward paying for important things. People need to pay for a place to live. People need to buy food. People also spend money on things they want. There are a lot of choices to make. A plan can help. In this lesson we will find out about making money plans.

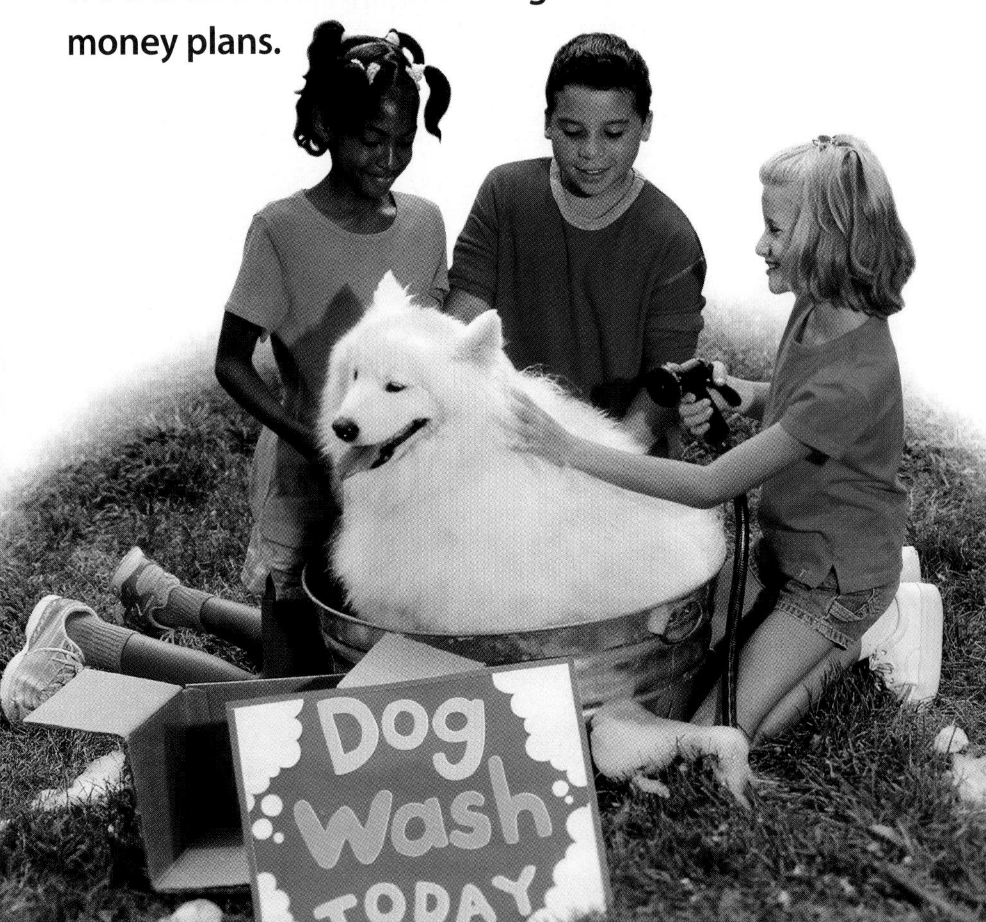

MINDING YOUR MONEY

"A penny saved is a penny earned." That was the advice **Benjamin Franklin** gave to people in the 1700s. That advice can also be used today. Saving money and spending money can be part of a plan. A plan for using money is called a **budget**. A budget can help you make money choices. It is a way to keep track of what you spend your money on. It can also keep you from spending too much.

A good budget balances your **income** and your expenses. Income is money you receive for work you do. Expenses are the things you spend money on. You look at the amount of your income for a week, a month, or a year. Then you decide how to spend and save it. There are things you need, such as food and clothes. Then there are things you might want, such as music CDs or going to the movies. People also save money for things they know they will need in the future.

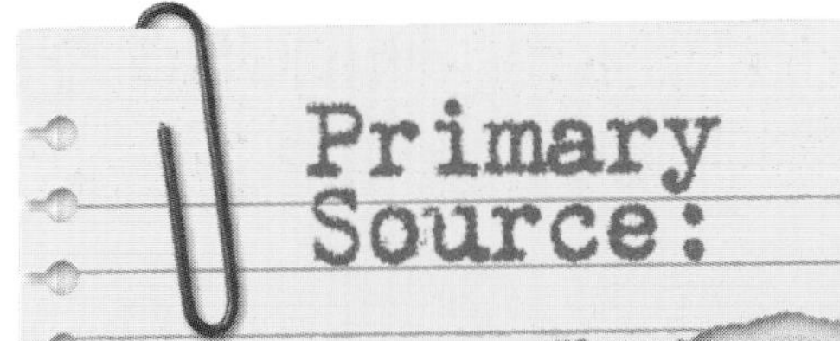

excerpt from **Poor Richard's Almanack (1732–1757)**
— sayings by Benjamin Franklin, politician, author, and inventor

- **Beware** of little expenses. A small leak will sink a great ship.
- Our **necessities** never equal our wants.
- A penny saved is a penny earned.
- He that goes a borrowing goes a sorrowing.

What did Benjamin Franklin think people should do with their money?

beware: be careful
necessities: needs

How do you use a budget?

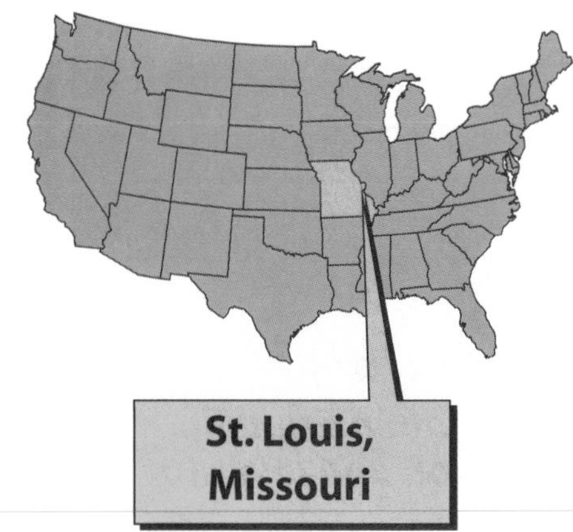

MAKING A BUDGET

Jason is 16 years old. He is working as a counselor at a day camp in **St. Louis, Missouri**. He earns $100 each week. Jason has some goals for his money. He wants to save money to buy a bicycle. He likes to go to the movies on weekends with his friends. Jason also wants to save money to go to college.

There are other things that Jason needs to spend money on so that he can have a job. He needs to pay for his bus fare to and from work. He needs to pay for lunch. These are his expenses.

Jason made a budget to help him make good money choices. His father's birthday is in July. Jason wants to get him a present. He decided to go to the movies less often. This way he will have money for the present. Jason also wants to buy a few music CDs.

Jason's job as a camp counselor helps him earn money.

A Savings Account

Putting money into a savings account is one way to save money. It is also a way to earn extra money. With a savings account a bank gives you **interest**. Interest is money that a bank pays you for borrowing your money. A penny saved is really a penny earned!

Here is Jason's budget for the month of July. His income for the month is $400. He listed the things he needs and the things he wants. Study the chart. How much will Jason save in July?

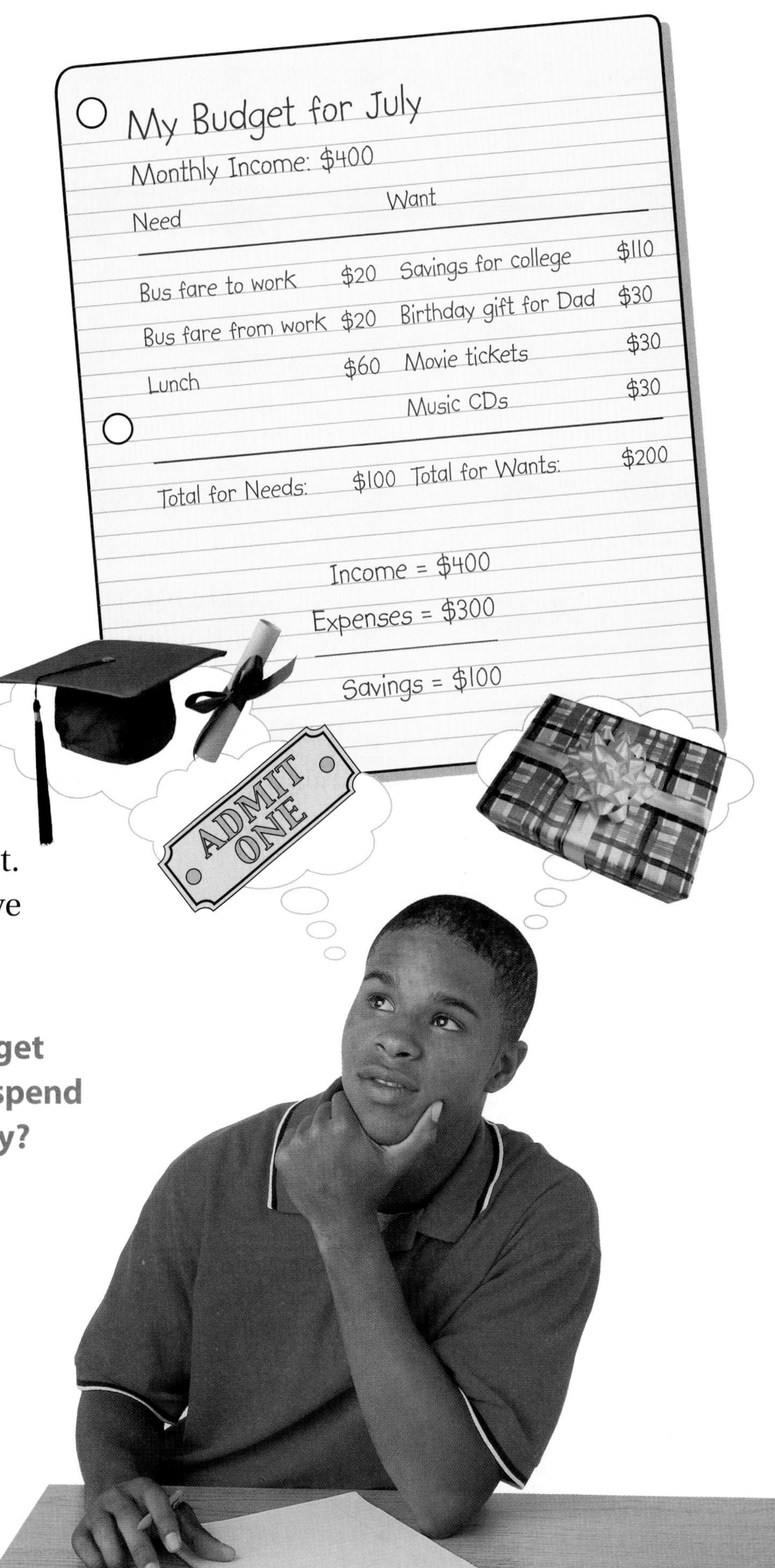

My Budget for July
Monthly Income: $400
Need
Want
Bus fare to work $20
Bus fare from work $20
Lunch $60
Savings for college $110
Birthday gift for Dad $30
Movie tickets $30
Music CDs $30
Total for Needs: $100
Total for Wants: $200
Income = $400
Expenses = $300
Savings = $100
ADMIT ONE

READING CHECK **How can a budget help people to spend and save money?**

DIFFERENT PEOPLE USE BUDGETS

Did you know that when you make a budget, you have something in common with the President of the United States? Our country's government gets money from its citizens. The President makes a budget for spending the money. Your state has a budget, also. A state government decides how to spend money for the things that people in the state need.

Families also make budgets. They figure out how much money they earn each month. Then they decide how to spend the money. Families need to pay for food, clothing, and a place to live. Families might also try to save money for important goals. Buying a house, going on a family trip, and helping children learn are some things a family might save money for.

This family is working on a **budget** (below). President Bush (next page) shows our country's budget.

What are some expenses in a family's budget?

PUTTING IT TOGETHER

It is important to make good choices with your money. A budget can help. People use budgets to plan how they will spend and save the money they earn. They may spend their money on the things they need and want. They may also save some of their money. Different people use budgets. People in government use budgets. Schools use budgets. Families use budgets. Knowing about budgets can help us to make wise choices about money.

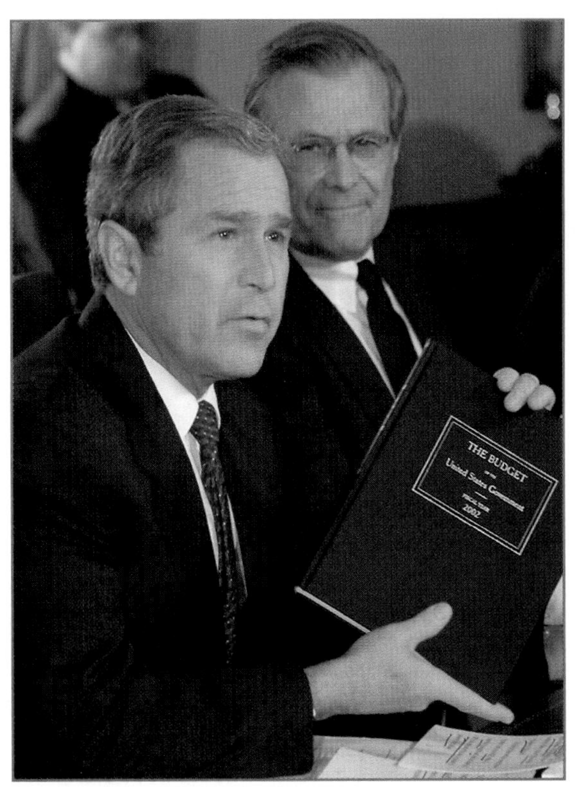

Review and Assess

1. Write one sentence for each of the vocabulary words.

   budget **income**
   interest

2. How do people usually get the money that they spend and save?
3. Explain how a plan can help people spend and save money.
4. Explain the **economic** term "bank interest."
5. **Compare and contrast** Jason's budget and a family's budget.

Suppose you have a job. You make $200 each month. Make a budget. List some things you need and want. Include what you might save. Make sure your budget is balanced.

Write a paragraph about why budgets are important. Give at least two examples.

Being a Good Citizen

Enterprise Village: Learning by Doing

Enterprise Village is in Largo, Florida. It is a special kind of shopping mall. Its stores and offices look just like real stores. However, students are the workers and the shoppers. The students get paid for their work. On their breaks or their lunch hour, they can shop.

Months before their visit students choose the stores they want to work in. They can work at a bank, a clothing store, or a newspaper. They might work at a video store, a fast-food restaurant, a radio station, or even a TV shopping channel.

Mrs. Schramek, a teacher at Orange Grove Elementary School, explains: "My students choose the business they want to work at. Then everyone works together to plan how to get customers and make their store a success."

"I learned to spend my money wisely."

Deadra Brown

Robert Powell worked as the bookkeeper for a video store at Enterprise Village. "I kept track of how much we were making. I learned a lot about how to run a business and be on time."

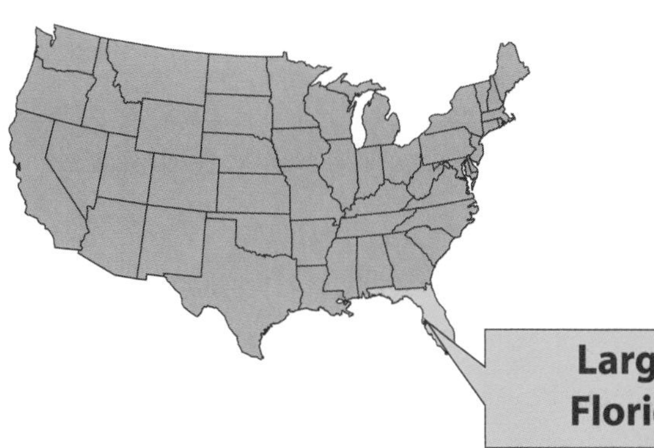

Deadra Brown tried to be a smart shopper. "You could go into one store and spend all your money in there and then go into the next store and see something you wanted more. I learned to spend my money wisely."

"I learned a lot about how to run a business."

Robert Powell

Be a Good Citizen

Making Connections

- **What are some different jobs people have in your community?**
- **How could you learn more about one of these jobs?**

Talk About It!

- **Why is being on time important in running a successful business?**

Acting on It

In the Classroom

Work in groups to create pretend businesses in your classroom.

Chapter 6 REVIEW

VOCABULARY REVIEW

Number a sheet of paper from 1 to 3. Beside each number write the word from the list below that matches the description.

budget **consumer**

profit

1. The amount of money left after all the costs of running a business are paid
2. A person who buys goods and services
3. A plan for using money

CHAPTER COMPREHENSION

4. Describe how people earn money from savings.
5. Identify one way each of earning, spending, and saving money.
6. Write a brochure advertising some services you might offer to your neighbors. Make sure your brochure tells why people should hire you and what you will charge.

SKILL REVIEW

7. **Reading/Thinking Skill** How do you classify things?
8. **Reading/Thinking Skill** What things do you classify in a normal day?
9. **Reading/Thinking Skill** How might you classify the things in your school?

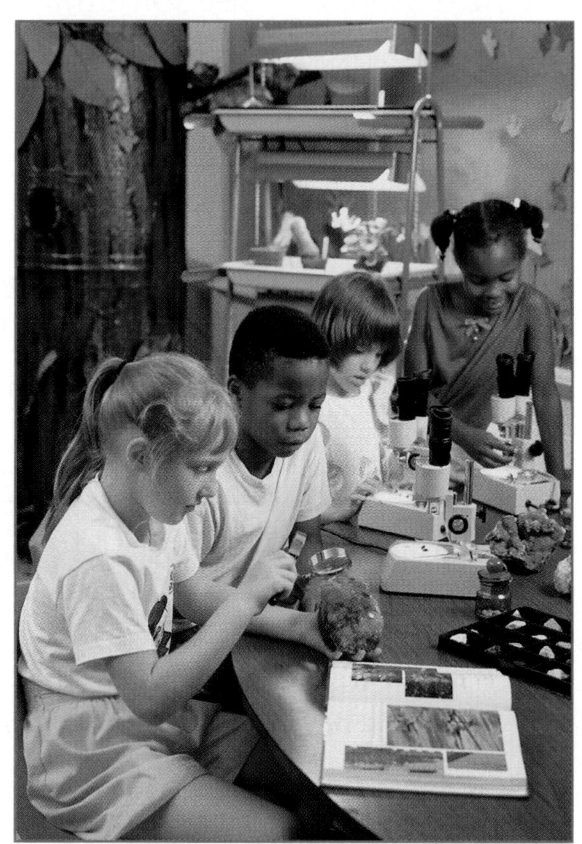

USING A CHART

10. Use the chart to answer the question. What service does the business provide?

Type of Business: Clothing Store

Goods/Services	Expenses
Shirts	Clothes
Pants	Employees
Dresses	Electricity
Sewing / Repairs	Clothing Racks

Writing About a Community Business Think about a business in your community, such as a grocery store, bookstore, repair shop, or restaurant. Write about the goods or services it sells. Who buys them? Who works there? How does this business help your community?

Use your Foldable to review what you have learned about living and working in communities. As you look at the front of your Foldable, think about ways in which you might earn money, save money, and spend money. Explain the importance of budgeting—to a person, community, and nation. Review your notes under the tabs to check your responses.

THE Big IDEAS ABOUT...

Working in Communities

In communities around the world, people are at work. They work on farms or in businesses. They make goods and provide services. In this chapter we will read about how people work.

LIFE IN A FARMING COMMUNITY

People work on farms, providing us with the food we eat. They grow crops and raise animals.

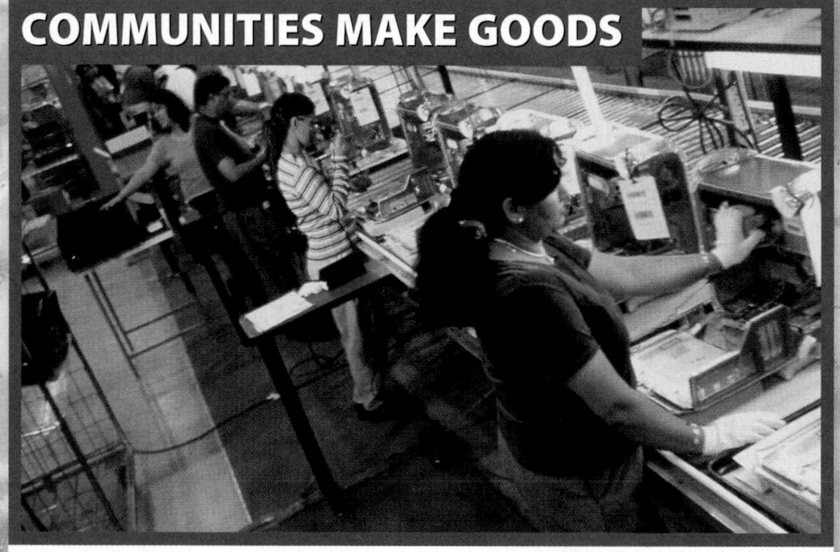

COMMUNITIES MAKE GOODS

People work to make the goods we need. These workers shown here are making computers.

TRADE LINKS COMMUNITIES

The goods we make in the United States are shipped to people around the world. In turn we buy the goods made by people in other countries.

Foldables

Make this Foldable study guide, and use it to record what you learn about "Working in Communities."

1. Fold an $8\frac{1}{2}$" x $8\frac{1}{2}$" paper square in half to form a taco.
2. Fold the taco in half again, and open to see the square divided into fourths.
3. Cut up one fold line, and stop at the middle.
4. Write lesson topics on three of the triangles.
5. Glue the blank triangle behind the tab next to it, forming a pyramid.

Lesson 1

Life in a Farming Community

VOCABULARY

harvest
agriculture
fertilizer
combine
Internet
supply
demand
scarcity

READING STRATEGY

Copy the **main idea pyramid**. Use it to show how supply and demand works.

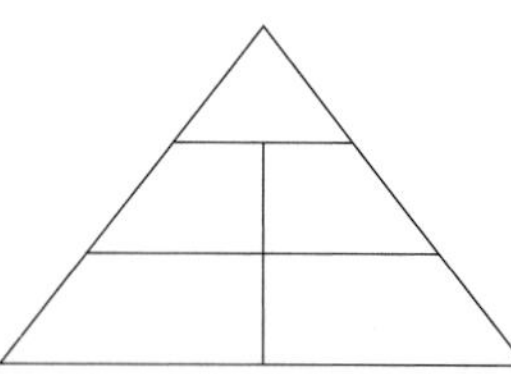

What is life like in a farming community?

Lesson Outline

- Welcome to a Farming Community
- A Farmer at Work
- From the Farm to Your Home
- Working Together

BUILD BACKGROUND

Do you know where the food you eat comes from? Most of it is produced on farms. Farmers work long hours to grow plants and raise animals. Most farmers live in farming communities. In this lesson you will read about a farming community in Pennsylvania.

WELCOME TO A FARMING COMMUNITY

Hundreds of people can live on one city block. In the country, though, the distance between neighbors can grow into miles.

In this lesson you will meet John and Susan Mason. They live in a rural community. During planting season John can sit on his tractor and look out and see rolling hills of rich, brown soil. At **harvest** time golden corn will cover those fields. The harvest is the ripe crops that are ready to be gathered. The Masons' closest neighbor lives nearly a mile away.

The nearest town is **Erie, Pennsylvania**. Pennsylvania has good soil and a good climate. There is plenty of rain for growing crops. Many of the people who work in town work at businesses that help the farmers. There are banks, farm supply stores, and places to sell crops.

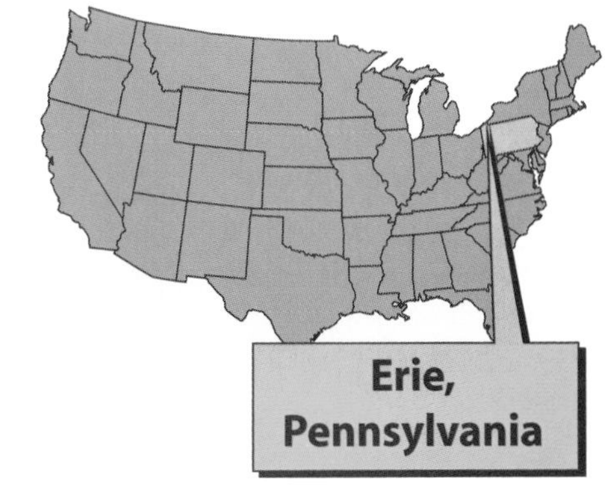

READING CHECK How is a farming community different from a city?

Susan and John Mason (below) are farmers. In farming communities (below) more land is used for crops than for housing.

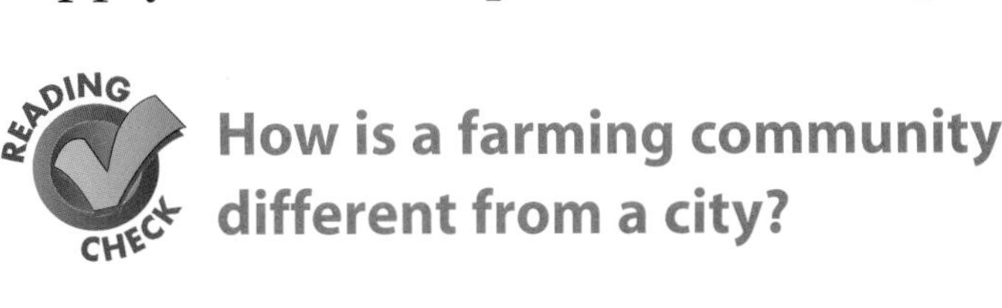

A FARMER AT WORK

In 1901 Addison Mason began a small farm, growing tomatoes, corn, and grapes. Over time his sons and then grandsons took over. Now the Mason farm grows strawberries and a wider variety of vegetables. Today the Mason family is still working in **agriculture**. Agriculture is the business of growing crops and raising animals.

Farm Technology

Like many farmers the Masons use technology to make farming easier. "We use machines to plant the corn and to spread **fertilizer**," John says. Fertilizers are chemicals that are used to help plants grow. Sometimes John is out in the fields, riding a **combine** or giving directions to other workers. A combine is a machine that makes harvesting faster. It cuts the corn and shakes the corn ears from the stalks. From there trucks haul the corn to storage tanks.

The Mason family has been farming in Pennsylvania for over 100 years. Addison Mason (top) started the farm. Today John Mason (left and above) and Susan Mason (above) run it—with the help of their grandchildren.

The Masons also use a newer tool. "I use the **Internet** to find out in a second the price of corn," Susan says. The Internet is a system of computers around the world that are connected to each other. When a computer is connected to the Internet, it can share information with other computers in the system.

"The Internet helps me make decisions about when and where to sell my crop," Susan says. "I also use it to check out what the weather will be."

Susan Mason uses a computer to keep track of things on the farm.

READING CHECK How does the combine make harvesting easier?

Exploring
TECHNOLOGY

The Mechanical Reaper

For thousands of years crops were harvested by hand. In 1831, however, Cyrus McCormick invented a mechanical reaper. It was pulled by horses and used a knife that cut wheat plants just like a saw cuts wood.

This new technology made harvesting faster, easier, and cheaper. It helped to change the way people farmed. McCormick's reaper led to today's modern combine.

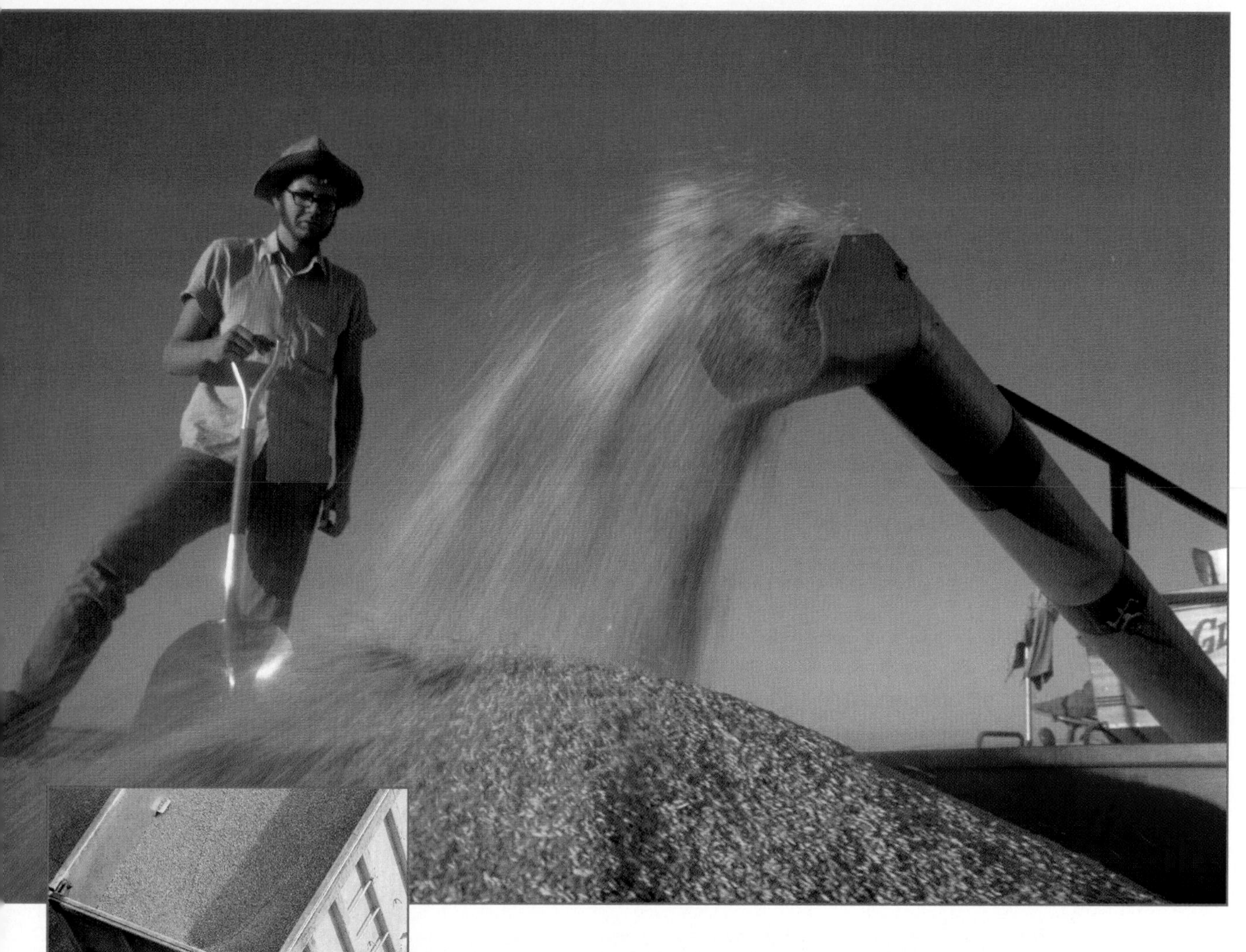

Corn is loaded into storage bins (top) before processing and shipping (above).

FROM THE FARM TO YOUR HOME

When John Mason brings his crop to town, the harvest work is finished. The Masons then need to make a profit on what they have grown. The amount of profit depends on **supply** and **demand**. Supply is the amount of goods that are available at any time. Demand is how many people want the goods that are in supply.

All around the world people need to eat, so there is always a demand for what the farmers grow. However, if there is low rainfall during the growing season, a crop such as corn will not grow as well. Then the farmer cannot produce all of the corn that is needed. There will be a **scarcity**, or shortage, of corn that year.

If there is a scarcity of corn, do you think the price will go up or down? The price will go up. This is because there will not be enough corn for everyone who wants it. If there is a scarcity of something, then there is not enough supply to meet the demand. When this happens, prices usually rise.

Workers in a large bakery make bread and rolls. These will be shipped to stores and bought by consumers.

The Food on Your Table

Some of your favorite foods begin with a handful of corn kernels. Some are cereal, tortilla chips, and anything cooked in corn oil. The corn is brought to a mill to be ground into flour. The corn is also processed to take out the oil. The flour and oil will be shipped to bakeries that make the goods you buy at the store. People at the bakeries put the food into packages. Truckers drive the packages to supermarkets and grocery stores. The stores sell the food to consumers—like you!

What happens when there is a scarcity of something?

WORKING TOGETHER

Farmers rely on each other. "The corn I grow helps feed people and also animals raised on someone else's farm," says John Mason. "The food on my own table comes from other farms—from all around the world."

Like everyone else, farmers buy their groceries at the local supermarket. They might buy oranges that grew in Florida or ice cream made in Wisconsin. People who make the ice cream might buy cereal made from the corn the Masons grew in Pennsylvania. People depend on each other for the goods and services they use every day.

Farmers, of course, rely on the weather every day. Read what this farmer said about how the weather shaped his business.

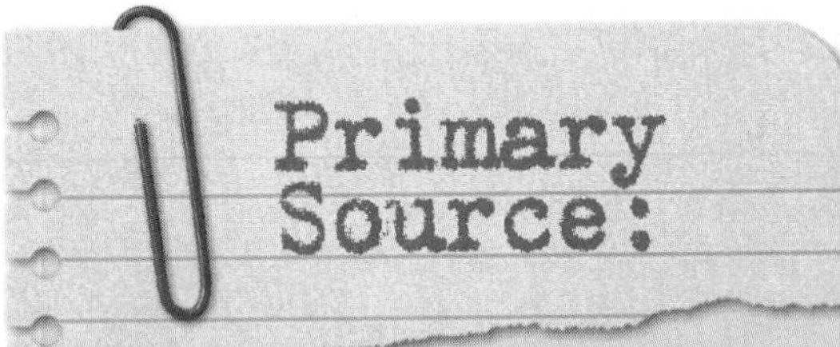

Pierce Walker

—interview with Studs Terkel, in* Working, *1972

Farming, it's such a **gamble**. The weather and the prices, and everything that goes with it. . . . Weather will make ya or break ya. The crops have to have enough **moisture**. If they don't have enough, they hurt. If you have too much, it hurts. . . . There's nothing you can do about it. You just don't think too much about it. . . . If you weren't proud of your work, you wouldn't have a place on the farm.

Why is the weather so important for farmers?

gamble: a risky act

moisture: rainfall

How do people depend on each other for goods and services?

PUTTING IT TOGETHER

Agriculture is important to people all around the world. No matter where they live, people need to eat! Farmers who make the foods we buy are consumers, too. They buy food, clothes, and anything else they might need. Today in Erie, Pennsylvania, John Mason and his wife, Susan, are farmers—just like John's grandparents were 100 years ago.

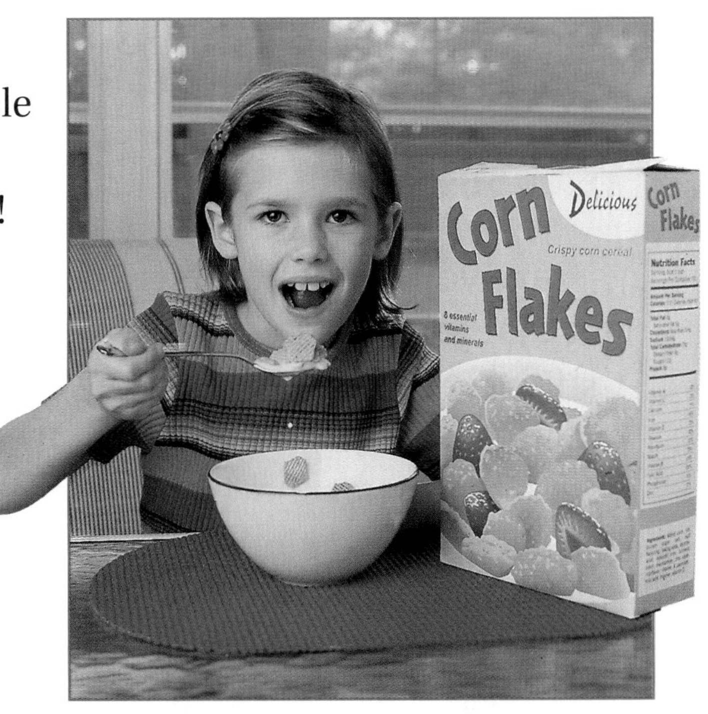

You might not realize it, but you probably eat something made with corn almost every day!

Review and Assess

1. Write one sentence for each of the vocabulary words.

   agriculture **harvest**
   Internet **scarcity**

2. What is the business of agriculture?
3. What is life like in a farming community? Find out!
4. How have changes in **technology** changed the way people farm?
5. Identify how scarcity **affects** the price of goods and services.

Activities

Refer to the Atlas at the back of the book. Locate the state of Pennsylvania. Is Pennsylvania north, south, east, or west of your state?

Write a story about what it might be like to live and work on a farm.

Reading a Flow Chart

Have you ever baked a cake? If so, you found out that several steps are involved. You learned that the steps have to be followed in a certain order. You could have used a flow chart to help you. A flow chart shows the different steps necessary to complete an activity or to produce something. Flow charts also show the order in which steps are performed.

VOCABULARY

flow chart

LEARN THE SKILL

Follow the steps in reading a flow chart. Refer to the chart below as you read.

1. **Look at the title of the chart.**
   This flow chart shows the steps a farmer must follow to grow corn and sell it for a profit.

2. **Look at the pictures and read the labels to see what steps are involved in the activity.**
   The labels tell you what the farmer has to do to grow and sell the corn. The pictures help you see what equipment is used to help the farmer.

3. **Look at the arrows to see the order in which the steps are taken.**
   The order in which the steps are taken is shown by the direction of the arrows. You can tell that the crops have to be harvested before the corn is stored in the tank.

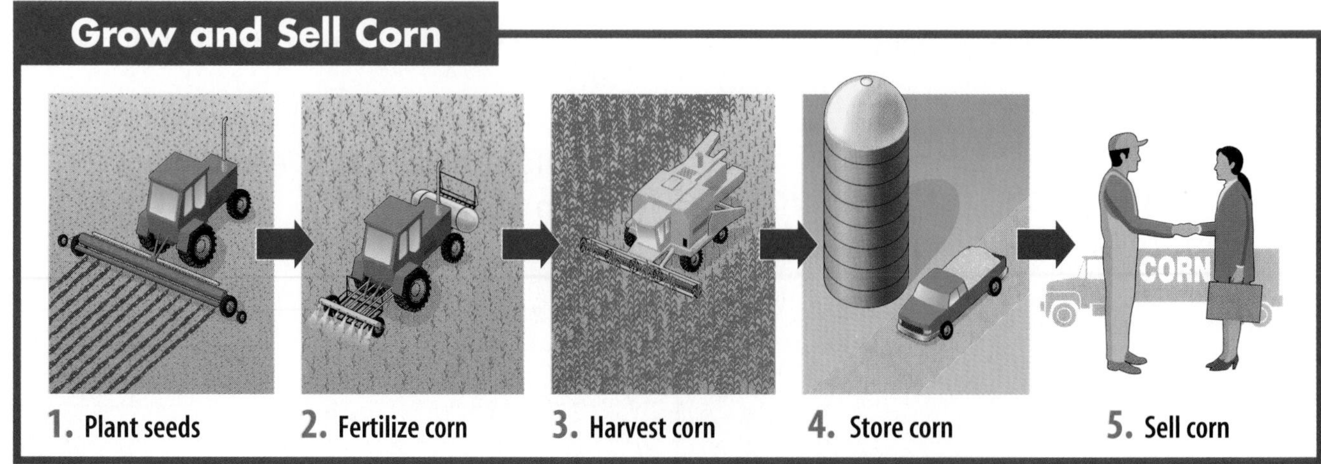

TRY THE SKILL

Answer the questions by reading the flow chart on this page.

1. What does the chart show?
2. How many steps are there in the activity? What is the first step? What is the last step?
3. What happens before the pretzel is twisted into its common shape?
4. What happens after the pretzels are moistened, salted, and baked?

EXTEND THE SKILL

Make a flow chart to show the steps in an activity or process that is familiar to you. Illustrate and label each step. Indicate the order of the steps by using arrows. Your flow chart might describe how to play a game, plant a garden, or make a craft.

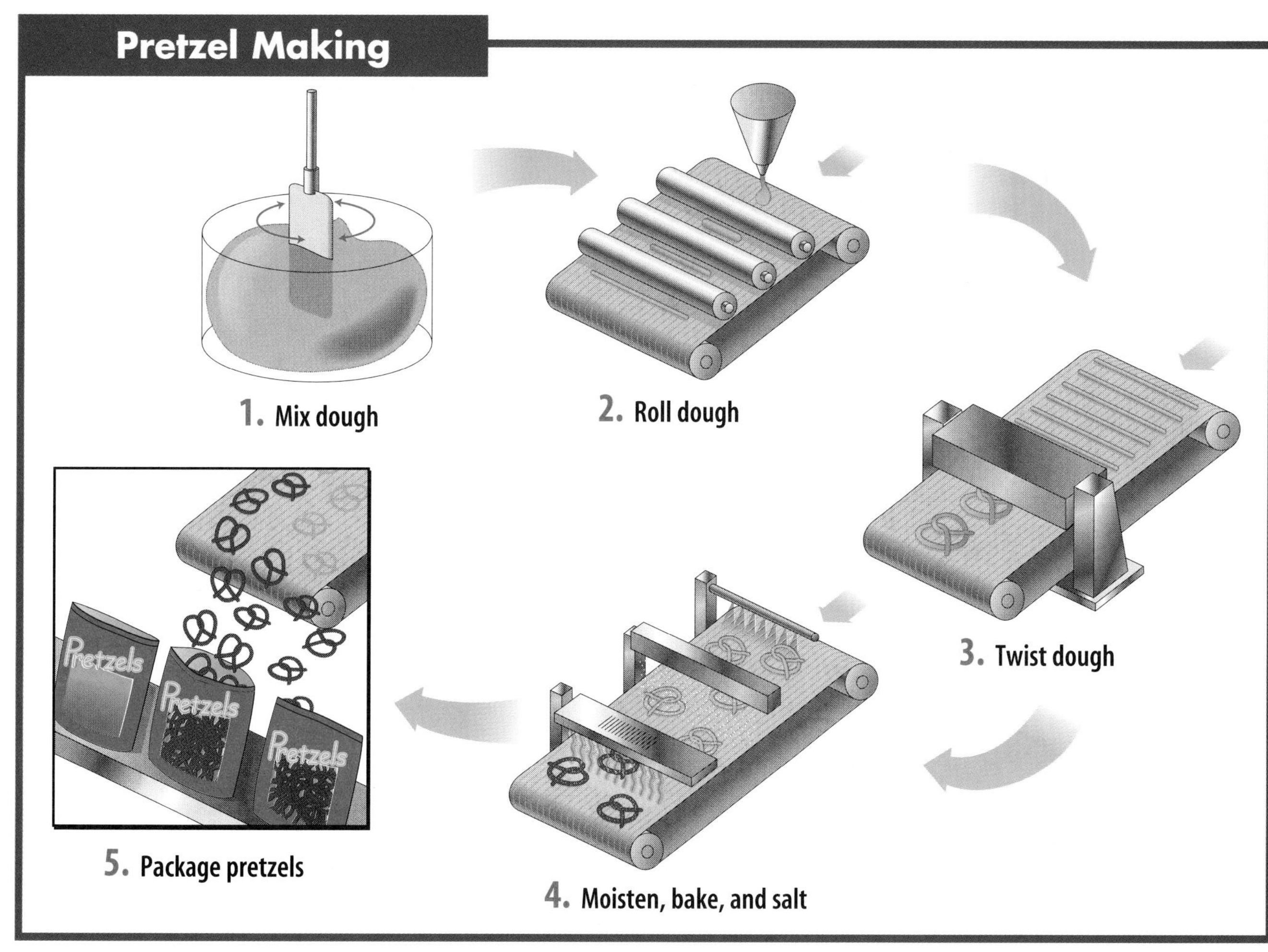

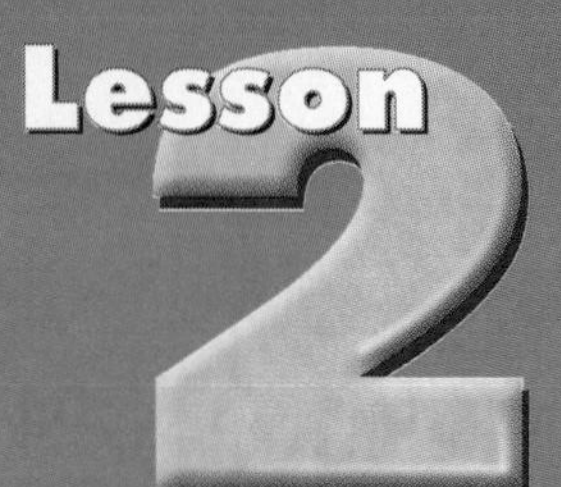

Communities Make Goods

VOCABULARY

manufacturing

factory

assembly line

PEOPLE

Henry Ford

READING STRATEGY

Use the diagram to **compare and contrast** Detroit factories in the past and present. Show what is different and what is the same.

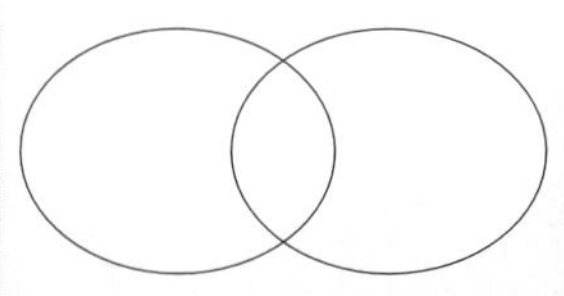

Find out! *What is manufacturing?*

Lesson Outline

- Detroit, the Motor City
- Making Cars
- Manufacturing Today
- Pride in Their Work

BUILD BACKGROUND

Manufacturing is an important part of our country's economy. Manufacturing is the business of making things. Cars, trucks, even the book you are now reading were all manufactured. People in communities across the country work to make these things and other products.

DETROIT, THE MOTOR CITY

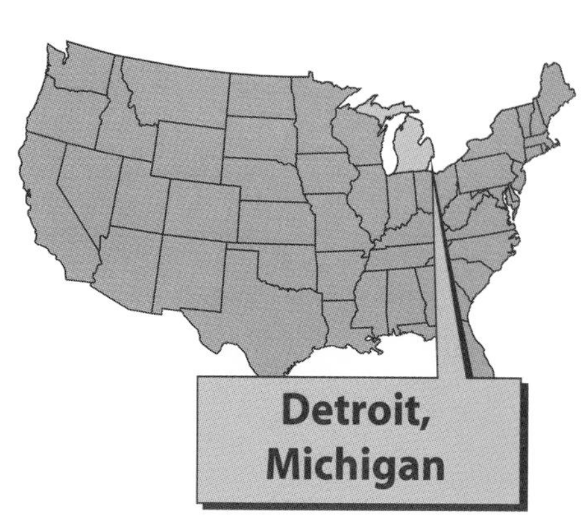

Detroit, Michigan, is one of the world's great manufacturing cities. It is known as a center of automobile production. More cars are made there than anywhere else in the world. That is why Detroit is called the "Motor City."

Many people who live in Detroit manufacture cars. Most manufacturing takes place in a **factory**. A factory is a place where things are manufactured. In the past manufacturing was done mostly by hand. Today high-tech machines, or robots, work alongside people in factories.

Detroit was a center for factories even before it became known for making cars. In the 1800s it was known for making carriages, wagons, and railroad cars. When the car was invented, skilled Detroit workers were hired to make cars.

Why is Detroit known as the "Motor City"?

Auto **manufacturing** (opposite page) helped Detroit (below) become a big city.

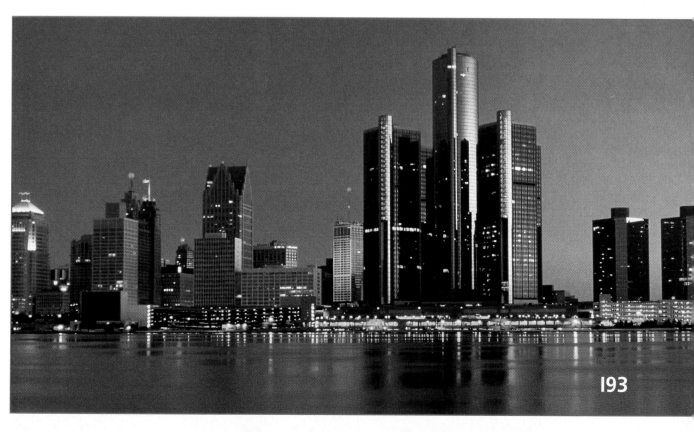

MAKING CARS

One person who helped turn Detroit into "Motor City" was **Henry Ford**. In 1903 Ford started a company in Detroit to manufacture automobiles. Cars were very expensive to make and buy in those days. Henry Ford dreamed of making a car that nearly everyone could afford.

The Assembly Line

Ford changed the way cars were made. In the past, two or three people built an entire car. Ford used a moving **assembly line** instead. An assembly line is a line of workers and machines all working together to make a final product. With a moving assembly line, workers stayed in one place, while the car moved past them. Each worker added a part until the car was done.

Building a Car on the Auto Assembly Line

1. The frame begins in pieces.

2. The frame is welded together.

3. The body panels and other parts are attached to frame.

The assembly line made cars more quickly and cheaply. This brought down the price of cars. People rushed to buy them. The more cars Ford sold, the greater his profit.

Ford sold his first "Model T" car in 1908. By 1923 almost half of the cars sold in the United States were Model Ts. While many manufacturing methods have changed, cars are still made on assembly lines today.

Henry Ford drives a Model T past a wagon wheel.

What did Henry Ford do to change automobile manufacturing?

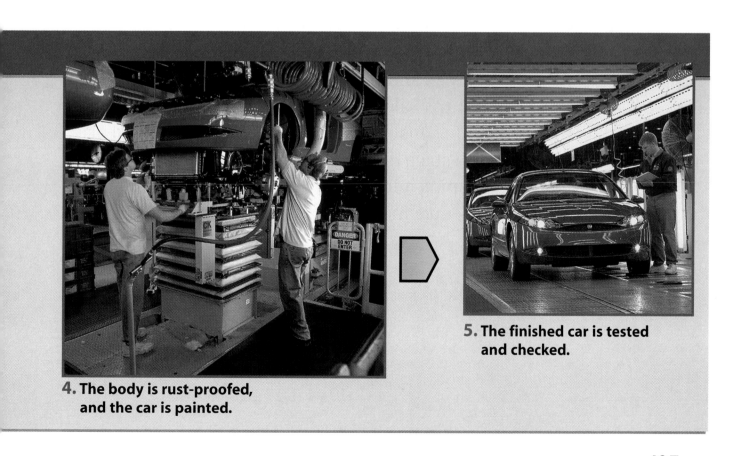

4. The body is rust-proofed, and the car is painted.

5. The finished car is tested and checked.

MANUFACTURING TODAY

Many people work together to make a car. Some people design, or plan, the car. Other people build the parts. Still other people put the parts together to make the car.

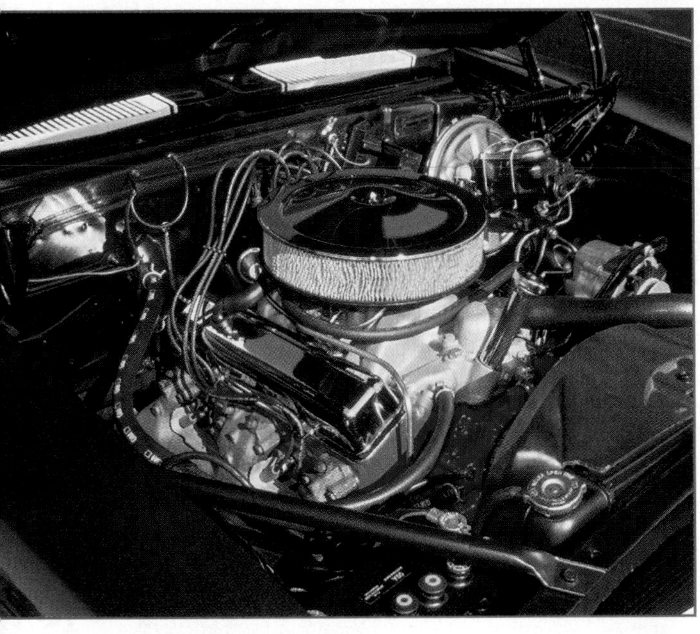

Modern car engines are made using parts from many countries.

In Henry Ford's time all of these jobs took place in one factory. Today people around the world work together to make the cars we buy. The auto glass may come from Canada. Motor parts may be made in India and put together in Taiwan. Seats may be manufactured in Mexico. Doors may come from the United States. All of the pieces are put together, or assembled, at the factory in Michigan.

From Manufacturer to Consumer

Once the cars are completed, they are shipped by truck and train to car dealers around the country. Salespeople at the car dealers sell them to the consumers. All of the people involved at each stage depend on each other. Building and shipping and selling cars ties together thousands of people in different parts of the world.

How has manufacturing changed since Henry Ford's time?

A World of Cars

Auto manufacturing is a global business. Cars assembled in Detroit use parts made in countries around the world.

Look at the map and the car diagram. They show some of the countries where car parts come from.

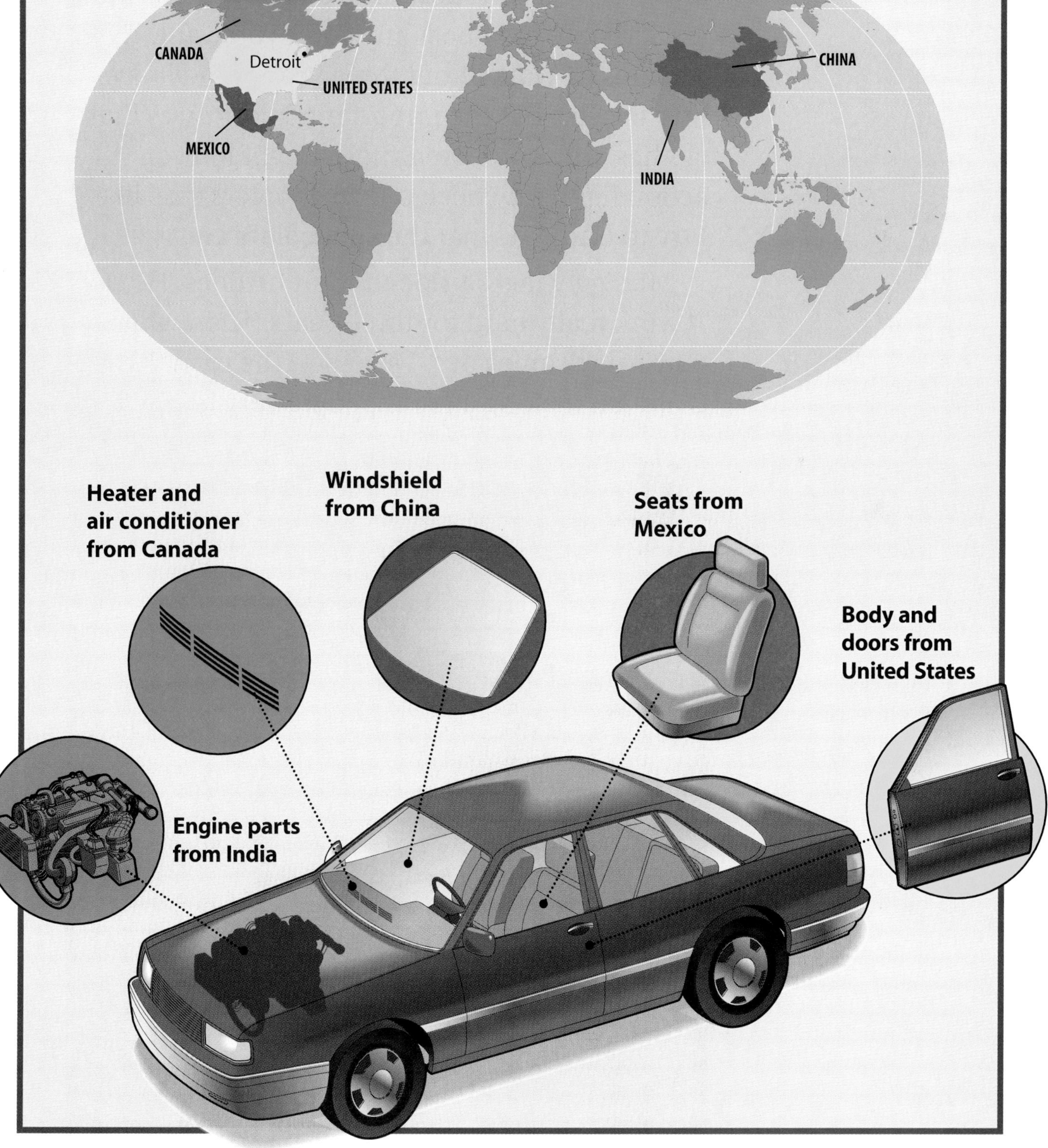

PRIDE IN THEIR WORK

As you have read, many people are needed to make a car. One of them is Allan Eggly. He picks the colors for the new cars and trucks.

Henry Ford once said, "The customer can have any color he wants so long as it's black." Mr. Eggly says, "That is certainly not true today. Cars and trucks come in almost any color you want." He explains, "I work about three years in advance. I try to see what the important colors are. What clothes are people wearing? I might look at action figures. I check out what colors kids like. I try to find out what the cool colors are."

Mr. Eggly takes pride in what he does. He says, "I work really hard for three years. Then when a new truck comes out, I see it on the road. I know that I am making a lot of people very happy."

How does Mr. Eggly help to make a car?

It takes thousands of people like Mr. Eggly to make a car.

PUTTING IT TOGETHER

Henry Ford used the moving assembly line nearly 100 years ago. It changed the way cars and other goods are manufactured. Most of the jobs in your community and around our country are connected to people who live in communities far away. In the next lesson we will see how products made in one community travel around the world.

Big trucks bring cars from the factory.

Review and Assess

1. Write one sentence for each of the vocabulary terms.

   assembly line **factory** **manufacturing**

2. What makes Detroit special?

3. **Define** and **describe** manufacturing.
4. How did Henry Ford's assembly line affect the way cars were made?
5. **Summarize** how an assembly line works.

Activities

Make a classroom assembly line. With three other students divide the job of folding sheets of paper into a "football" or other shape. Pass the paper down the line until the shape is complete.

Write a paragraph that compares how cars were made in the time of Henry Ford with how they are made today.

Using Transportation Maps

Cars like the ones made in Detroit are just one form of transportation. Planes, trains, and boats are ways to travel. People who travel or send goods need to know how to get from place to place. The information they need can be found on **transportation maps**. A transportation map shows routes from one place to another. A transportation map may show roads, railroads, waterways, and airports.

VOCABULARY

transportation map

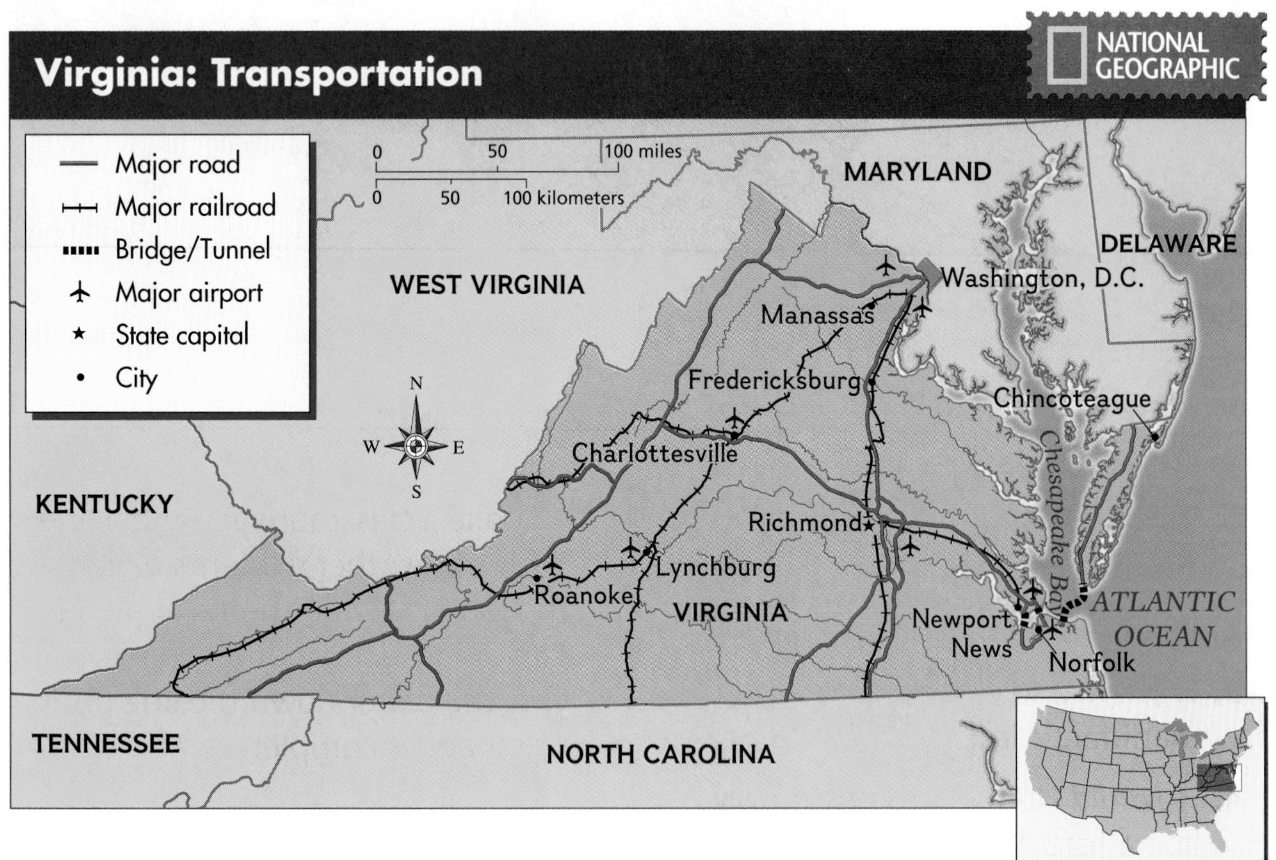

LEARN THE SKILL

Look at the map on page 200 as you follow the steps for reading a transportation map.

1. **Read the map title.**
   This map shows transportation in the state of Virginia.

2. **Look at the map key.**
   On this map a black line with cross marks stands for a major railroad.

3. **Use the map to find routes between places.**
   The map shows that you could travel by train from Charlottesville to Lynchburg.

TRY THE SKILL

Study the transportation map on page 200, and answer the questions.

1. What kinds of transportation routes does the map show?

2. In what ways could you travel or send goods between Richmond and Newport News?

3. If you traveled by highway from Norfolk to Washington, D.C., what cities shown on the map would you pass through?

EXTEND THE SKILL

Do you get from home to school by car, by bus, or by walking? Make a map of the area between your home and your school. Trace several routes you could take. Give your map a title. Provide a compass rose, a key, and a scale.

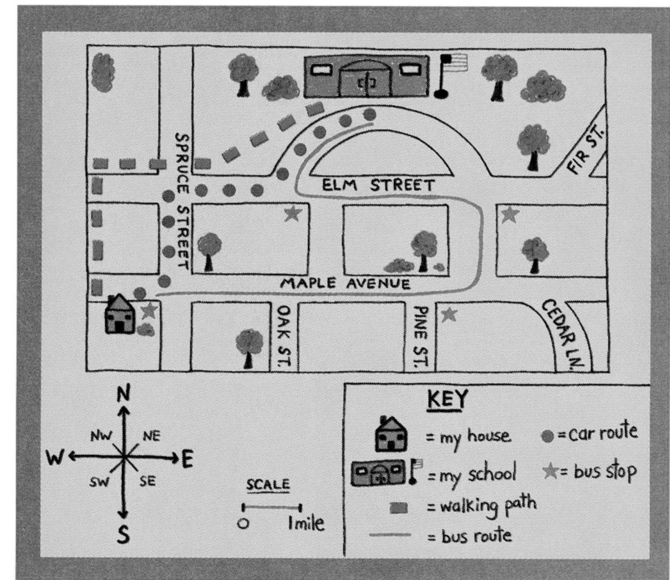

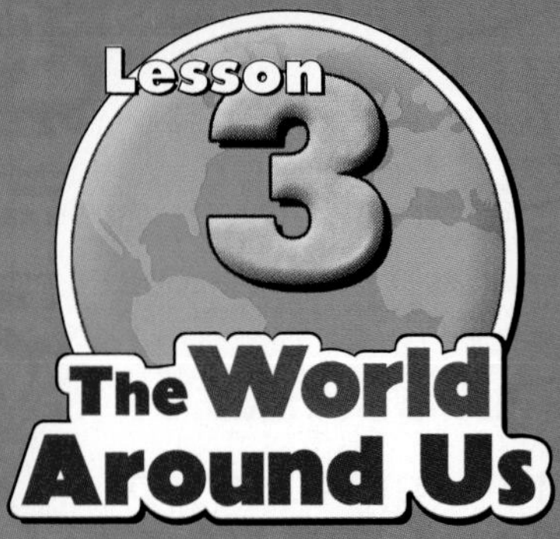

Trade Links Communities

VOCABULARY

trade
domestic trade
international trade
import
export
marketplace
global marketplace

READING STRATEGY

Copy the chart. Use separate columns to classify the trading partners, imports, and exports of the United States.

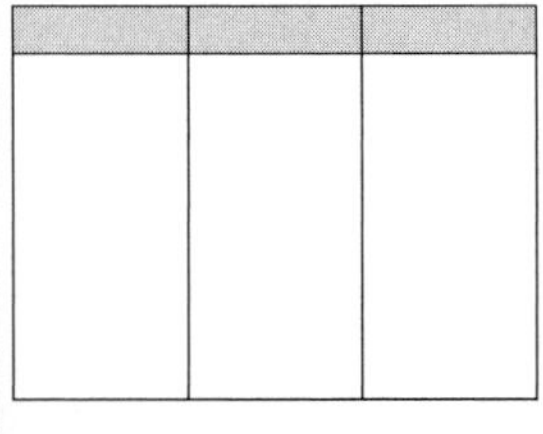

How do people around the world get things they need?

Lesson Outline

- Goods Move Around the World
- Why We Trade

BUILD BACKGROUND

What do you think of when you hear the word *trade*? Perhaps you think about trading cards or stickers. For businesses and governments, trade means buying and selling goods and services. People use trade because each side has something the other side needs or wants.

GOODS MOVE AROUND THE WORLD

Earlier in this chapter you read that Pennsylvania has good land for growing corn and other vegetables. Detroit, Michigan, has many automobile factories, but no farms. The people in Pennsylvania might buy cars and trucks made in Detroit. The people in Detroit eat food grown in Pennsylvania. Trade such as this, in one country, is called **domestic trade**.

International trade is trade between people in different countries. Most countries cannot produce everything they need. Instead they **import**, or buy goods made or grown in another country. Countries also **export**, or sell goods to other countries. Our country's two biggest international trading partners are Canada and Mexico.

Like cars, airplanes (above) are assembled using parts that come from around the world. Workers load goods for **international trade** (below).

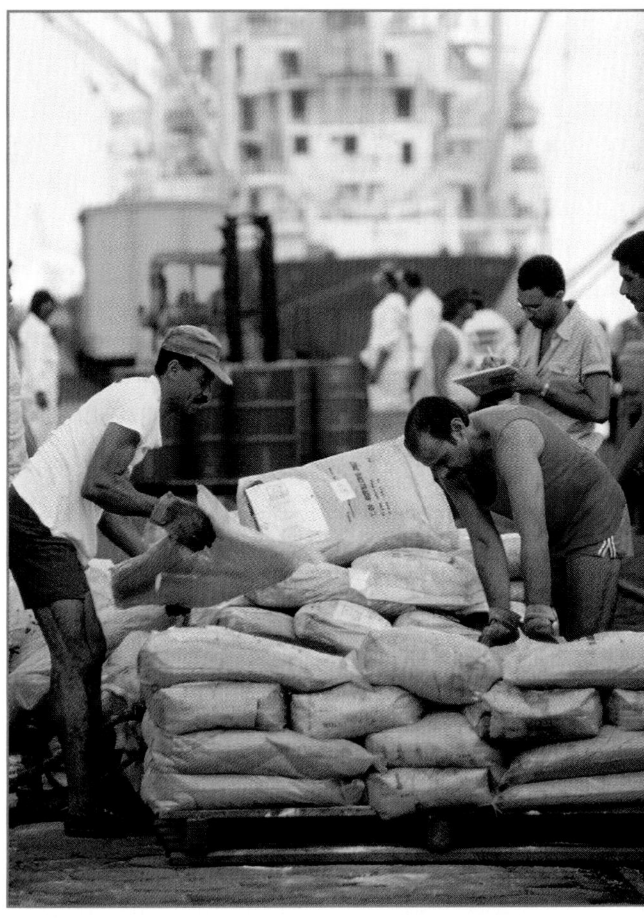

READING CHECK **How is international trade different from domestic trade?**

DATAGRAPHIC

International Trade

The United States has both domestic and international trade. Besides trade inside the United States, we have trade with many other countries. We import things from other countries. We export things to other countries.

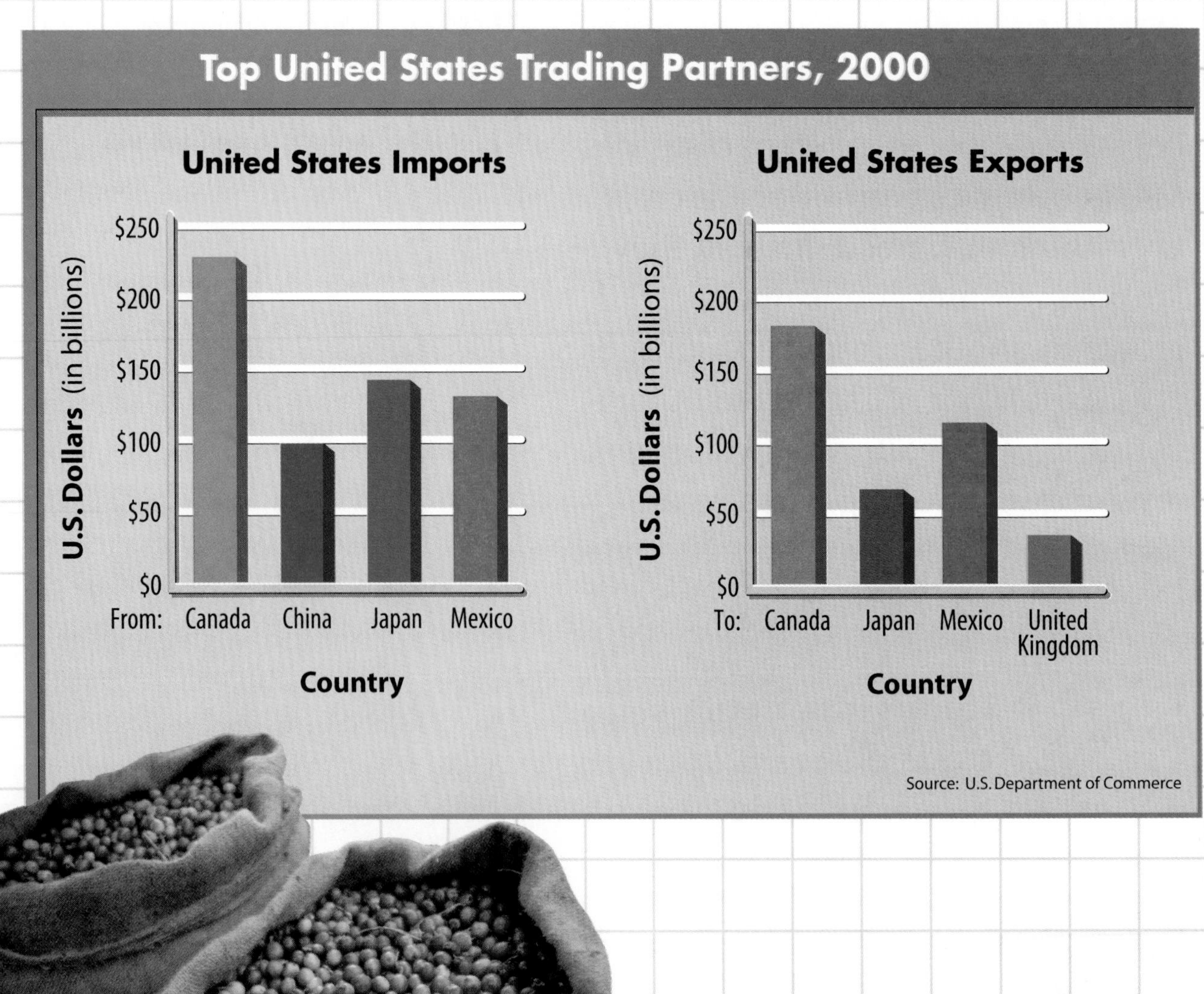

Coffee beans are grown in Africa and Central America. They are shipped around the world.

World Trade Products

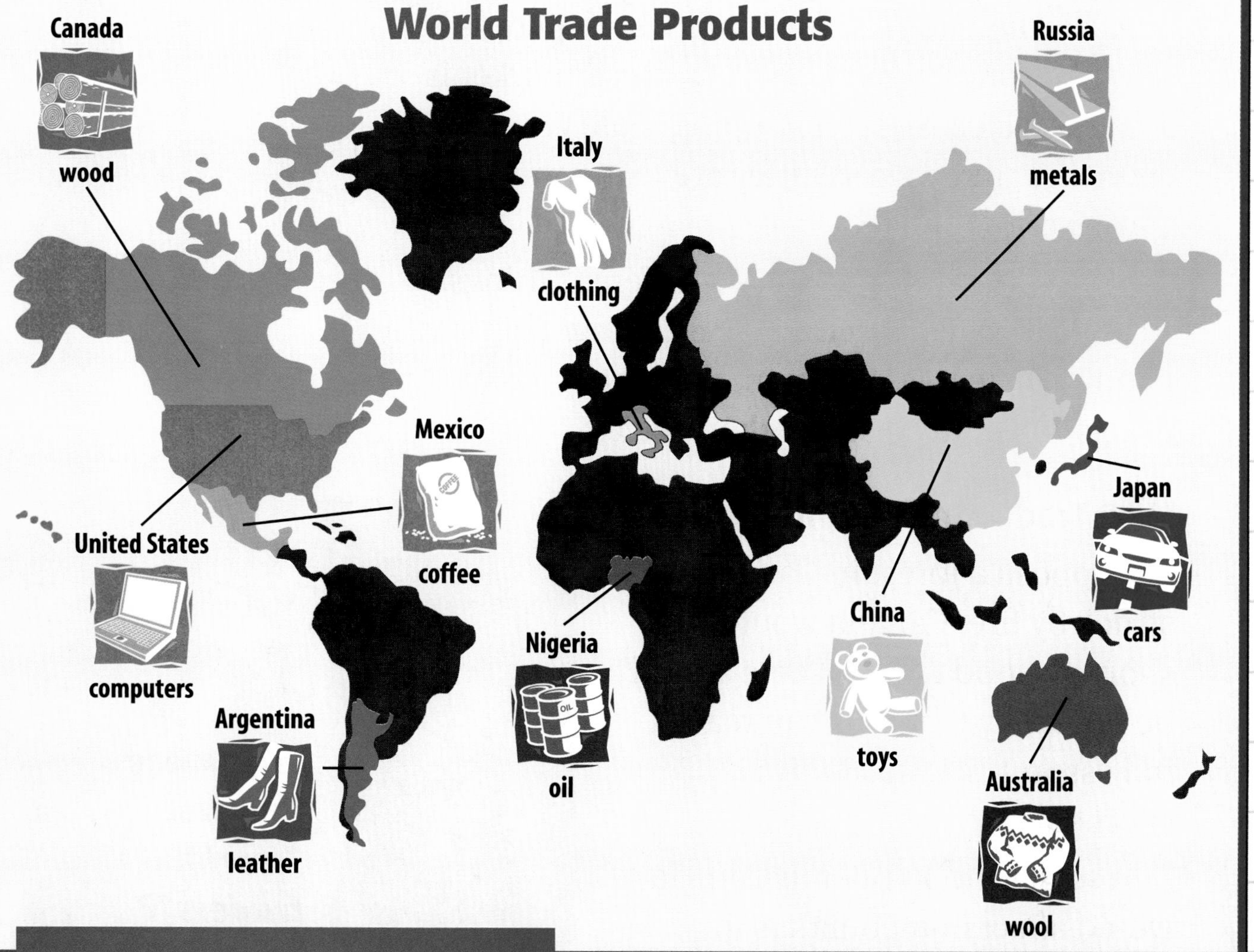

Canada
wood

Italy
clothing

Russia
metals

Mexico
coffee

United States
computers

Japan
cars

China
toys

Nigeria
oil

Argentina
leather

Australia
wool

World Trade, 1963–1999

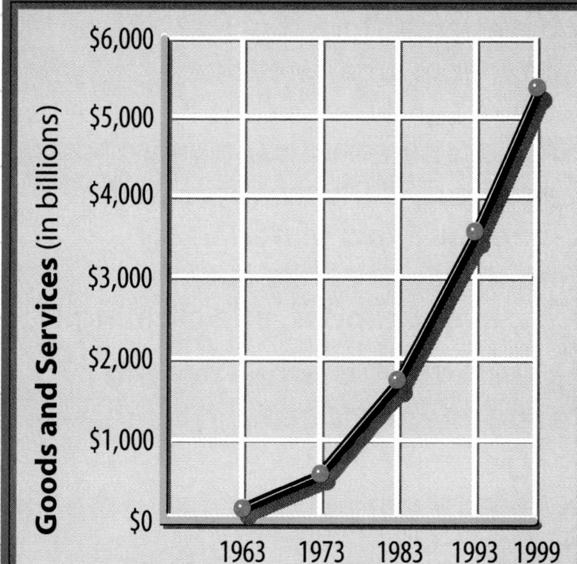

Source: World Trade Organization

Questions

1. From which country does the United States import the most?
2. What is one important export from Nigeria?
3. Has world trade increased or decreased in the past 40 years?

Visit **www.mhschool.com** *to learn more about domestic and international trade.*

WHY WE TRADE

A **marketplace** is any place where people sell things and buy things. A farmers' market is a marketplace. So is a shopping mall. When countries trade, we say they are using the **global marketplace**.

Everyone wants and needs different things. Nobody can actually make *everything*. This is why people come together in marketplaces—to get things they cannot make themselves.

How Trade Links Communities

Suppose a forest in Canada was struck by fire. Canada would run short of wood to sell. There would be a scarcity of wood. You read in Lesson 1 that scarcity is a short supply.

A scarcity of lumber in Canada would affect homebuilders in California. They would not have as much work to do. Then they would have less money to buy things.

Suppose some of those things are made in China. If people in California do not buy as much, a Chinese factory might have to lower prices. A scarcity of wood in Canada could affect workers in Canada, the United States, and China!

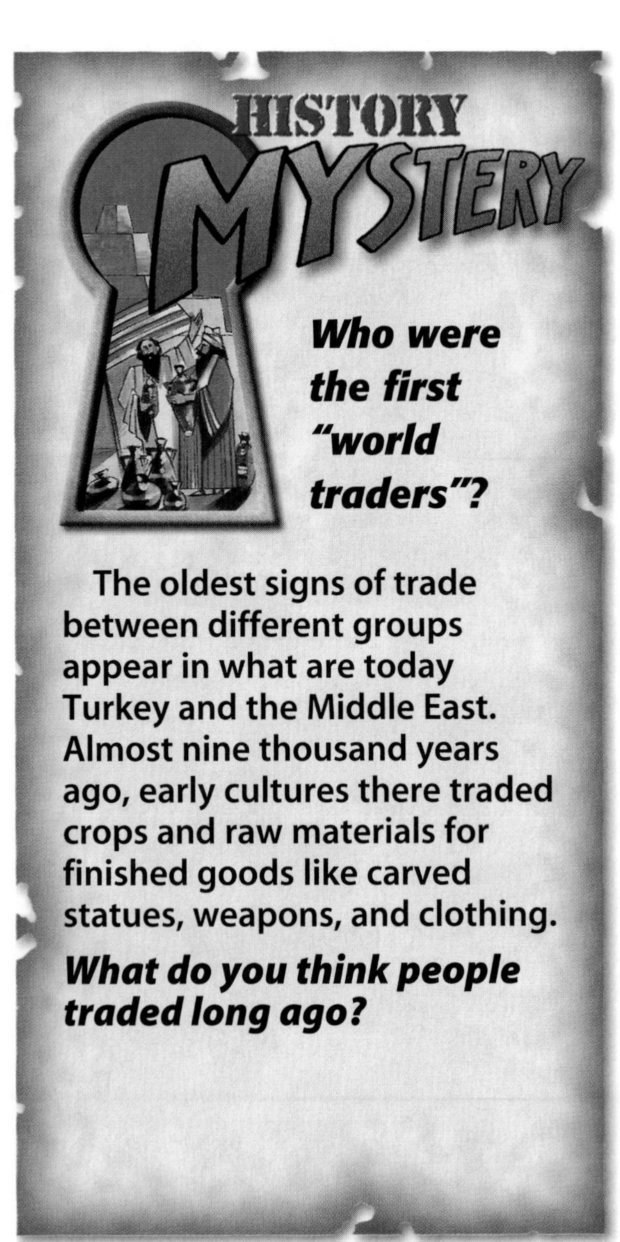

Who were the first "world traders"?

The oldest signs of trade between different groups appear in what are today Turkey and the Middle East. Almost nine thousand years ago, early cultures there traded crops and raw materials for finished goods like carved statues, weapons, and clothing.

What do you think people traded long ago?

What is a marketplace?

PUTTING IT TOGETHER

People in communities in the United States and around the world depend on each other in many ways. One of these ways is trade. Trade is a way for people to get more things than they could possibly make for themselves. If you read labels, you will notice that the things you use or wear every day come from all around the world. We all depend on each other. We are all part of the global marketplace.

In the **global marketplace**, people around the world work together and depend on each other.

Review and Assess

1. Write one sentence for each of the vocabulary words.

   export **import**
   marketplace **trade**

2. What is the difference between imports and exports?
3. Analyze how people in different parts of the world get things they want and need.
4. What is the global marketplace?
5. How do people solve the **problem** of getting things they cannot make themselves?

Make a list of five things you own. You might include clothes, sneakers, toys, or other items. Look at each to see where it was made. How many of the items were made outside the United States?

Suppose you had a pen pal in Japan, Mexico, or Canada. **Write** him or her about a product that the pen pal's country exports to the United States. Tell how it makes your life better.

Chapter 7 REVIEW

VOCABULARY REVIEW

Number a sheet of paper from 1 to 3. Beside each number write the word from the list below that matches the description.

agriculture **manufacturing**

scarcity

1. The business of making things
2. A shortage of goods or services
3. The business of farming

CHAPTER COMPREHENSION

4. Name two things about Detroit that helped it become a manufacturing center.
5. How did the moving assembly line change automobile manufacturing?
6. Write about how trade between countries helps people get the goods and services they need.

SKILL REVIEW

7. **Study Skill** What does a flow chart show? How can flow charts be helpful?
8. **Geography Skill** What clues tell you that this map is about transportation?
9. **Geography Skill** What different types of transportation are shown on this map?

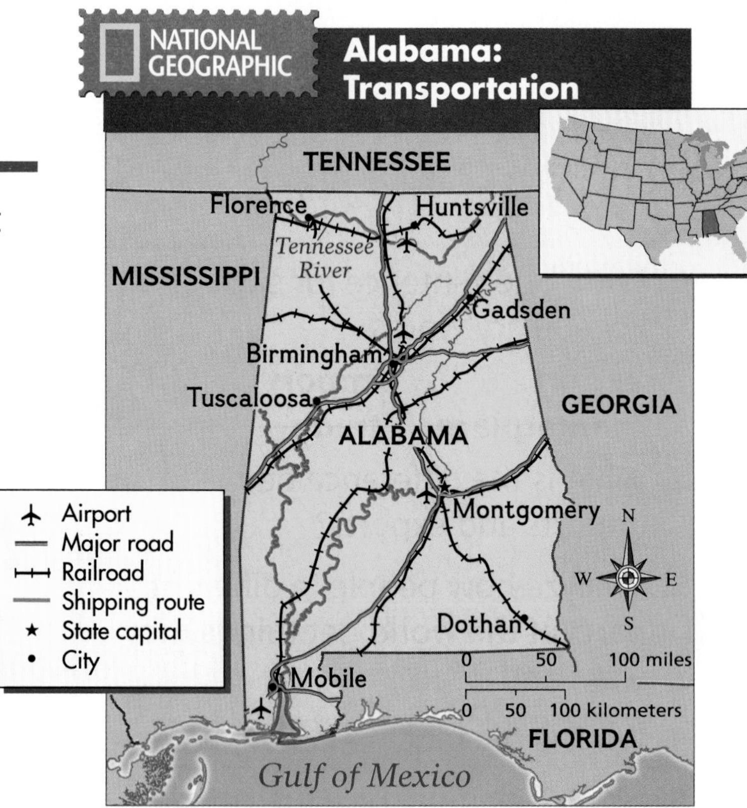

USING A CHART

10. Look at the flow chart shown here. What is the first step? At what point are handlebars added to the bicycle?

Activity

Writing About Food Manufacturing Suppose that you are in charge of setting up a school farm to raise money. You will grow things to eat. What will you grow? Tell why you think there is a need for your crops. Describe where you will sell them. Who will be your customers? What jobs will people need to perform in order to get the work done from start to finish? How will you and others work together?

Foldables

Use your Foldable to review what you have learned about making and trading goods. As you look at your pyramid of information, think about farming, manufacturing, and trade. Describe how they affect life and work in a community. Review your notes under the lesson titles on your Foldable to check your responses.

Your Community's Economy

In this unit you have learned about the many ways people work and the different kinds of jobs people have. What kinds of jobs do people in your community have?

Enrique lives in Raleigh, North Carolina. He found out the jobs his neighbors do. He talked to them about their jobs. He even visited some of them at work. He took pictures of people doing different jobs. To share what he learned, Enrique made an accordion book.

- ***What would an accordion book of jobs in your community look like?***

Activity

Making an Accordion Book

Materials
- oaktag
- stiff paper
- markers
- scissors
- glue
- ribbon

Step 1 Learn about your community's economy. Interview your neighbors about the jobs they have.

Step 2 Visit different businesses to see what people do at work. Take pictures of people working.

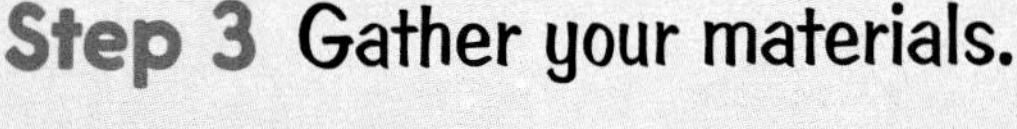

Step 3 Gather your materials.

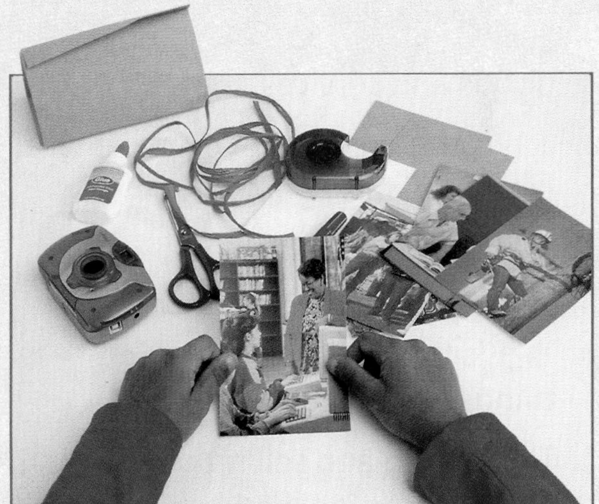

Step 4 Fold a large piece of stiff paper into even parts. Glue a photo to each page, and label the photos. Attach oaktag covers with string. Give your book a title, decorate the cover, and share it!

VOCABULARY REVIEW

Number a sheet of paper from 1 to 6. Beside each number write the word from the list below that best completes each sentence.

agriculture	**budget**
consumer	**manufacturing**
marketplace	**trade**

1. A(n) ___ is someone who buys goods and services.
2. ___ is the business of growing crops and raising animals.
3. A plan for using money is a(n) ___.
4. ___ is the business of making things.
5. The buying and selling of goods and services is called ___.
6. A(n) ___ is any place where people sell things and buy things.

TECHNOLOGY

To learn more about the people and places in this unit, visit www.mhschool.com and follow the links to Grade 3, Unit 3.

SKILL REVIEW

7. **Reading/Thinking Skill** What are the steps to take in classifying?
8. **Reading/Thinking Skill** Classify the following items you might see on a farm: barn, chickens, combine, cows, farmhouse, tractor.
9. **Study Skill** What does a flow chart show?
10. **Geography Skill** What are two ways you could travel between Boise and Idaho Falls, Idaho?

TEST PREP

Read the passage and the questions that follow. Write the best answers on a piece of paper.

"A penny saved is a penny earned." That was the advice Benjamin Franklin gave to people in the 1700s. That is still true today. Saving money and spending money are parts of a budget. A budget is a plan for keeping track of how you spend your money. It can also keep you from spending too much.

A good budget balances your income and your expenses. Income is money you receive for work you do. Expenses are the things you spend money on. You look at the amount of your income. Then you decide how to spend and save it. There are things you need, such as food and clothes. Then there are things you want, such as music CDs or going to the movies. People also save money for things they know they will need in the future.

1 Brooke is saving to buy a music CD and a new toy. These things are Brooke's

- wants
- needs
- budget
- income

2 Benjamin Franklin probably

- spent a lot of money on his wants
- wanted people to save less money
- thought budgets were important
- made a lot of money

WRITING ACTIVITIES

Writing to Inform Write a report explaining how a scarcity of milk would affect consumers and producers in your community.

Writing to Express Choose one of the jobs you read about in this unit. Write a paragraph telling what you would and would not like about doing that job.

Writing to Persuade Look at page 171, and reread Benjamin Franklin's sayings about saving money. Then write two sayings of your own about the same subject.

LITERATURE

This Is My Country

We Americans are proud of our country. One way we celebrate it is through song. Read and sing this song. It tells of feeling proud of the United States.

Words by Don Raye
Music by Al Jacobs
C F G7 C G7
This is my coun-try! Land of my birth.
C F G7 C Am G7
This is my coun-try! Grand - est on earth.
F C F G7
I pledge thee my al - le - giance, A - mer - i - ca the bold, for
C Am F G7 F G7 C
This is my coun - try, to have, and to hold!

allegiance (ə lē′jəns) loyalty

Write About It!

Think about what the words of this song are trying to say. Write a paragraph telling why you are proud to be an American.

Unit 4

Communities Have Governments

TAKE A LOOK

How does government work in our country?

In our country we have community, state, and national governments. Our national government is in Washington, D.C.

Explore governments in communities around the world at our Web site www.mhschool.com

Chapter

8 THE Big IDEAS ABOUT...

How Government Works

Citizens work together to solve problems. One way they do this is through government. In our country we have community governments, state governments, and a national government. Each does different things. They all work to meet people's needs.

LOCAL GOVERNMENT

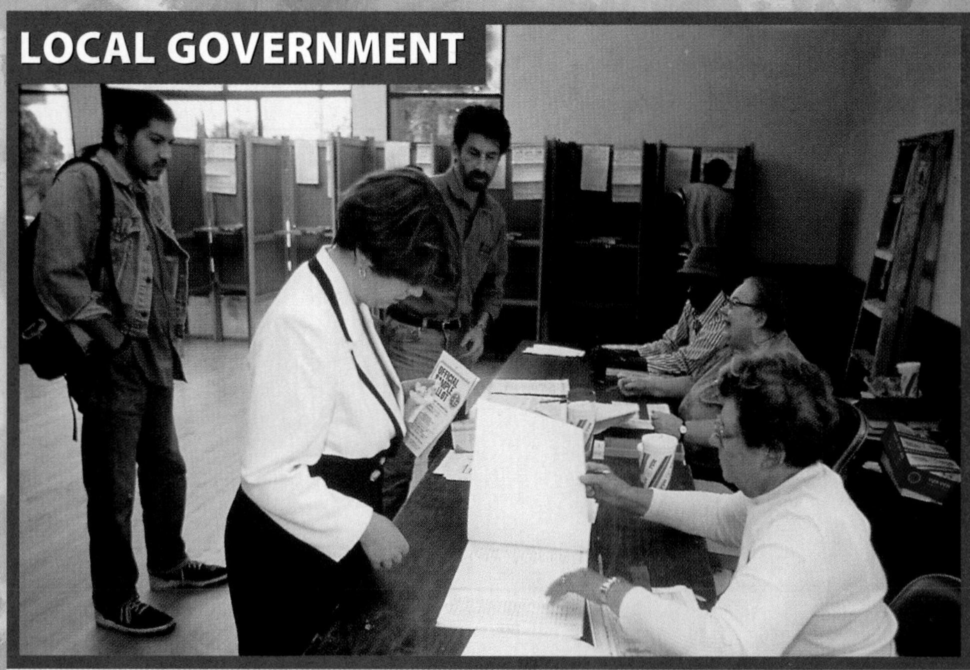

In communities around our country, citizens vote to elect people to make decisions about how to best meet their community's needs.

OUR COUNTRY'S GOVERNMENT

Our country's government is centered in Washington, D.C. Decisions made there affect our whole country.

MEXICO'S CAPITAL CITY

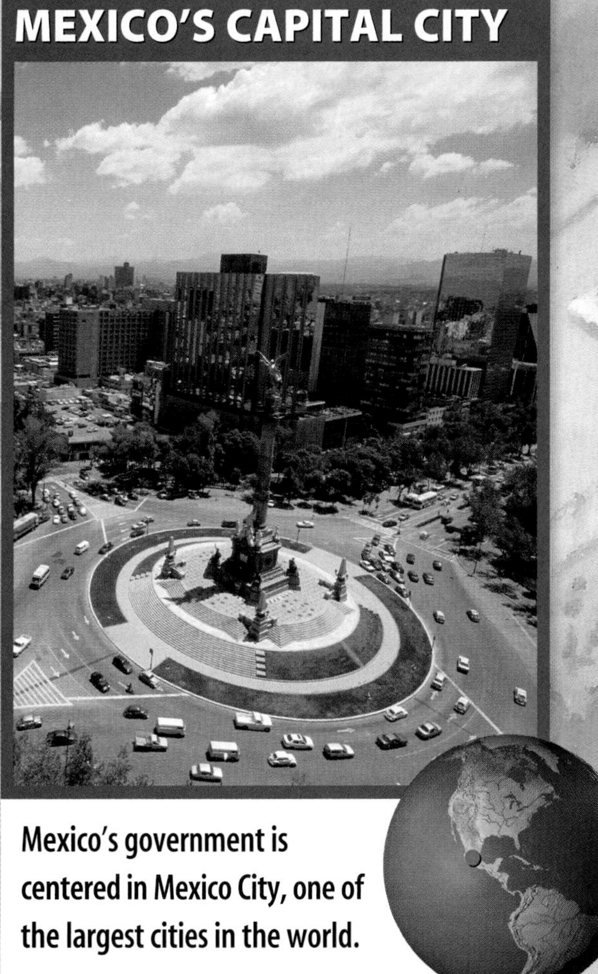

Mexico's government is centered in Mexico City, one of the largest cities in the world.

Foldables

Make this Foldable study guide, and use it to record what you learn about "How Government Works."

1. Fold a large sheet of paper into a shutter fold.
2. Draw a capitol building on the front, and label with the chapter title.
3. Write the titles of Lessons 1 and 2 on the inside of the shutter fold. Write the title of Lesson 3 on the back.

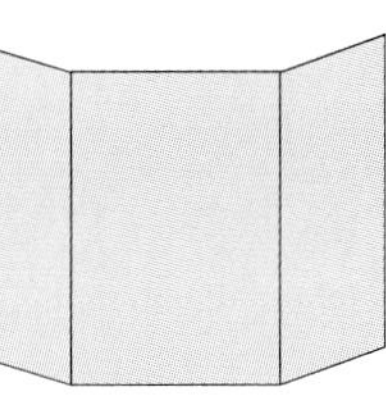

Lesson 1

Local Government

VOCABULARY

local government
mayor
city council
tax
capital
governor
capitol

READING STRATEGY

Use the **sequence** of events chart to show how the citizens of Jackson, Mississippi, got welcome signs for their community.

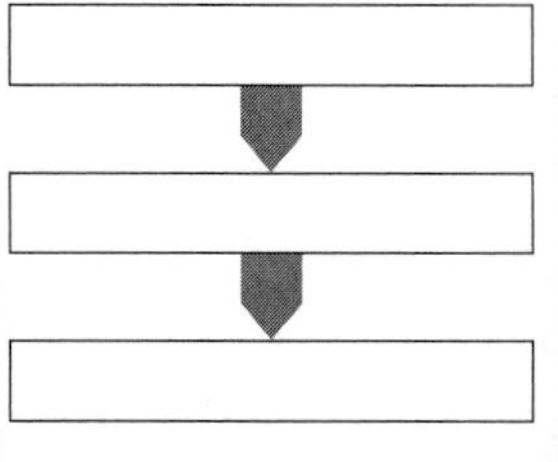

What does a local government do for a community?

Lesson Outline

- A Community Government
- Government in Action
- Community Services
- A Look at State Government

BUILD BACKGROUND

Who takes care of the parks, schools, and roads in your community? Who makes sure the streets are clean and the people safe? All of these jobs and many more are done by **local government**. Local government is the government in a community. It takes care of things that affect people's everyday lives.

A COMMUNITY GOVERNMENT

Communities in the United States have different types of local government. We are going to look at local government in Jackson, Mississippi. Many community governments in our country are set up like Jackson's.

Jackson's city government is led by the **mayor**. A mayor is the leader of city government. The people of a community vote for, or elect, their mayor. Harvey Johnson, Jr., was elected mayor of Jackson in 1997. He was elected again in 2001.

Being mayor is a big job. Mayor Johnson works to make sure that the community laws are obeyed. He thinks about city problems and works to fix them. He also makes speeches to tell people what is happening in the community.

Jackson, Mississippi

READING CHECK **What does a mayor do for a community?**

Mayor Harvey Johnson, Jr. (left), leads the city government in Jackson, Mississippi. He works at Jackson city hall (opposite).

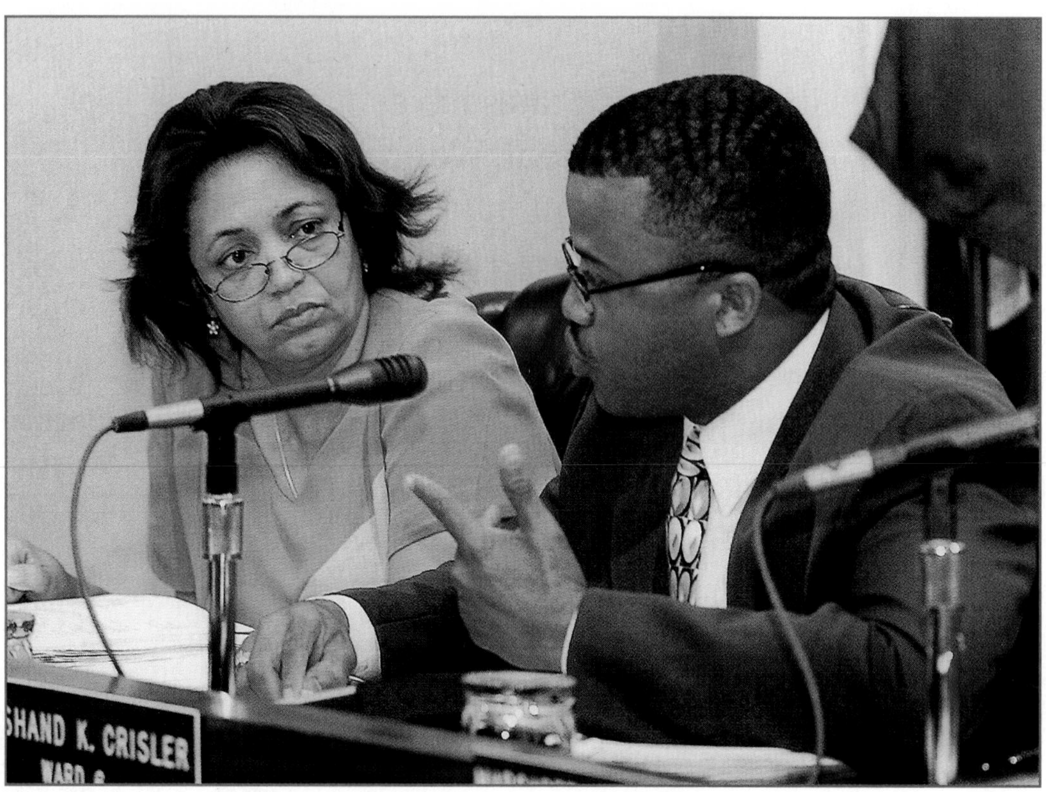

City council members make laws and decide what to spend on city services.

GOVERNMENT IN ACTION

Mayor Johnson does not run the city government by himself. He works with the **city council**. A city council is a group of elected people who make decisions and laws for a community. Many communities have city councils like the one in Jackson, Mississippi.

The mayor and the city council have meetings. At these meetings they discuss community needs. The community might need new schools, buses, or roads. The mayor and city council also meet with citizens to hear from them what the community needs.

Together the mayor and the city council decide how to meet these needs. They also decide how to pay for them. Then they make a city budget. The city budget guides the spending for Jackson's entire city government.

A Project for Jackson

People in the community take part in local government in many ways. They vote. They attend community meetings. They tell the mayor and the city council what they think. They even run for office.

Sometimes people in a community get an idea for a special project. For example, the people of Jackson wanted to have welcome signs to greet visitors to their community. The city council discussed the idea. They decided it was a good one. They hired a company to make and put up the signs. Now visitors to Jackson, Mississippi, are greeted with friendly signs welcoming them to the city.

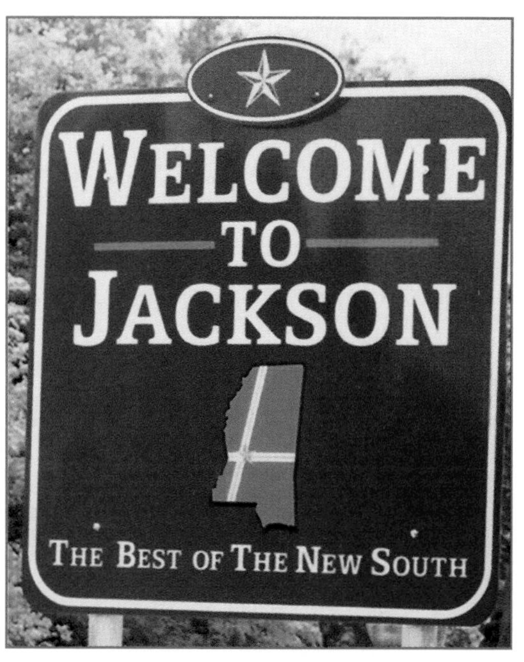

Signs now welcome visitors to Jackson (above). Taking care of city roads (below) is part of a community's budget.

What are some things that a city council does for its community?

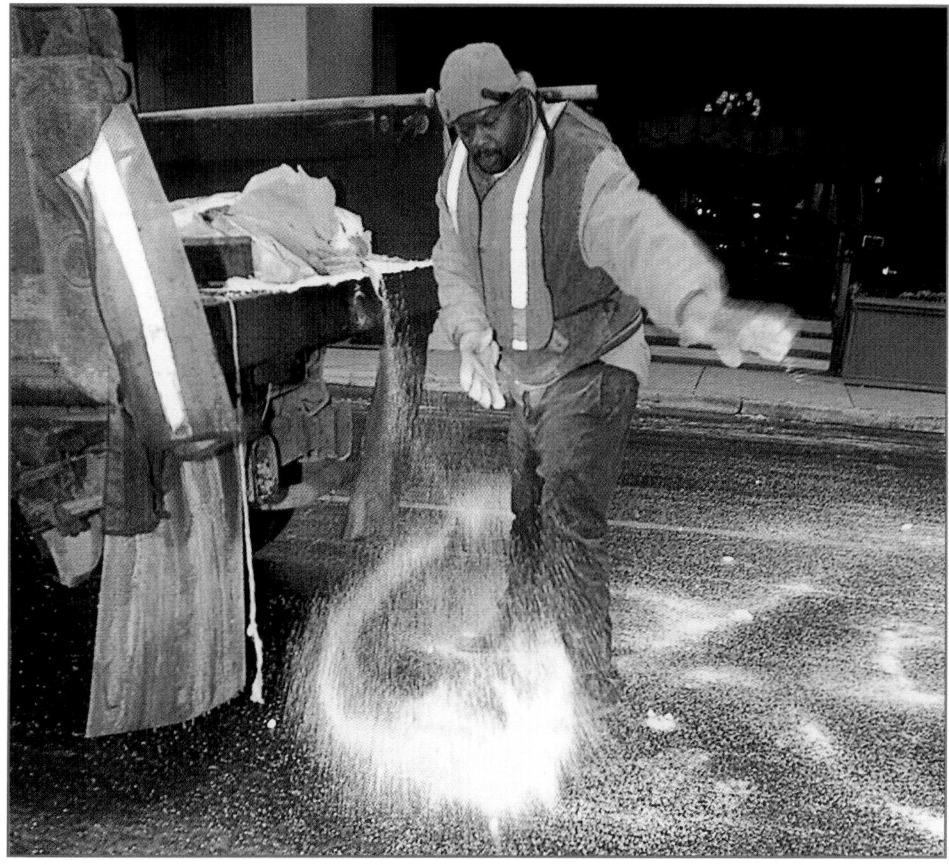

COMMUNITY SERVICES

Local governments provide many services for their communities. Jackson has a police department and a fire department. Jackson's government takes care of roads and parks. It also provides crossing guards at schools.

Where does the money come from? It comes from **taxes**. A tax is money that people pay to support their government. Tax money pays for the things a community needs. It also pays for jobs that city workers do.

Jackson's City Government

In Jackson the mayor and the city council are elected by citizens. They make decisions about the services the city provides. These services are paid for with **taxes**.

Mayor

Police Department

Fire Department

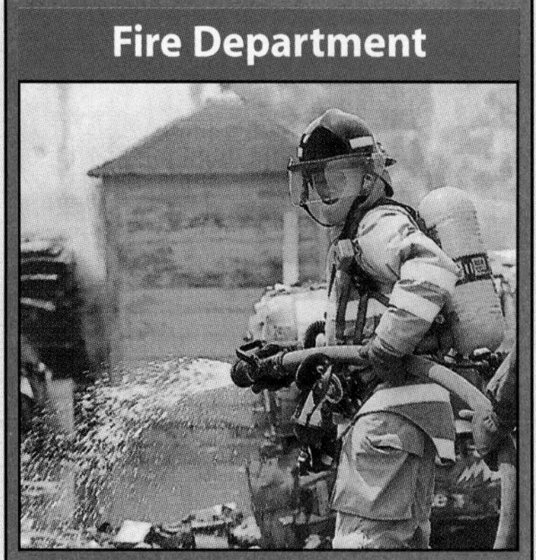

Parks and Recreation

Take a look at the chart. It shows how Jackson's government is set up. It also shows some of the services the city offers. What parts of Jackson's government keep people safe? What part is in charge of things that are fun for children? Is there a part of city government that guides how the city grows?

What services does Jackson provide for its citizens?

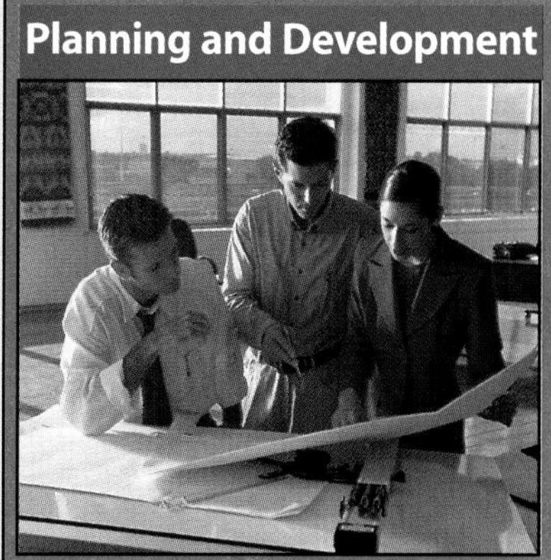

A LOOK AT STATE GOVERNMENT

States also have governments. State governments make decisions that affect people in the whole state, not just one community. In Mississippi the state government is in Jackson. That makes Jackson the **capital** of Mississippi. A capital is the place where the government of a state or country is located.

Mississippi's governor, Ronnie Musgrove (above), works in the state capitol building (below).

The state government makes important decisions for the state. These decisions affect all of the people in the state. The state government takes care of state highways. It makes laws to protect the state's environment. In fact, it makes all of the state's laws.

The person who is elected to lead the state government is the **governor**. He or she works in the state **capitol** building. A capitol is a building in which a state or national government works. Notice that the words *capital* and *capitol* are similar, but they mean different things.

READING CHECK **What does the state government do?**

PUTTING IT TOGETHER

Most communities in the United States have local governments. Local governments take care of many things important to people's daily lives. In many communities the people elect a mayor and a city council to run the local government. These officials work to meet the community's needs. They also work with people in state government. State and local governments work together to make our communities better places to live.

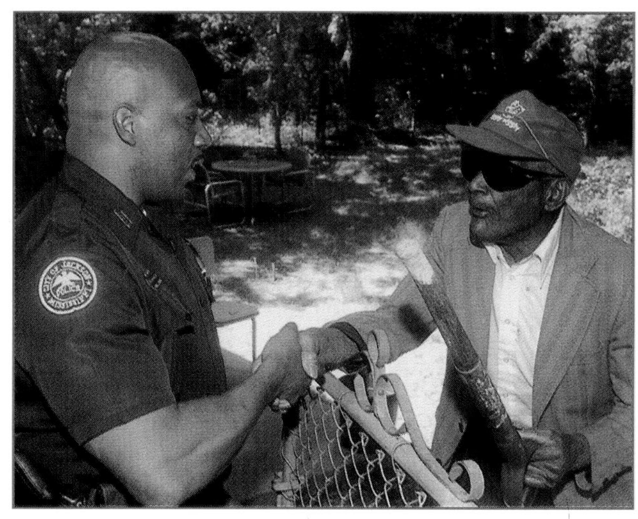

Citizens and city workers work together to make Jackson a better place.

Review and Assess

1. Write one sentence for each of the vocabulary terms.

   capital **capitol**
   city council **governor**
   mayor **tax**

2. How did Harvey Johnson, Jr., become the mayor of Jackson, Mississippi, in 1997 and in 2001?
3. Give examples of what a local government does for a community.
4. Identify three services provided by local **government**.
5. **Compare** the jobs of mayor and governor. How are they alike? How are they different?

Create a local government for your class. Elect a mayor and a city council. Decide what services your class needs. Write them down in a chart like the one on pages 224 to 225.

Write a letter to your city council. Describe a special project you would like to do. Explain why it is important.

Finding the Main Idea and Supporting Details

As you read, look for the **main idea** and **supporting details**. The main idea is what a paragraph or section is about. The details support or expand the main idea. Often, but not always, the main idea is stated directly in the first sentence of the paragraph. Keeping track of the main idea and supporting details will help you remember what you read.

VOCABULARY

main idea

supporting details

LEARN THE SKILL

Read the paragraph below. Then follow the steps to find the main idea and supporting details.

> Mrs. Johnson wanted to turn an empty lot on her street into a baseball field that the whole community could use. She talked to her friends about the idea. She wrote a letter to the city council, and everyone signed it. One year later, after many meetings, a lot of talking, and even more letter writing, the community did get a baseball field!

1. **Ask yourself, "What is this paragraph about?"** It is about trying to turn an empty lot into a baseball field.

2. **Look for the sentence that tells what the paragraph is about. That is the main idea.** In this paragraph the main idea is the first sentence.
3. **Look for facts that tell more about the main idea. Those are the supporting details.** In this paragraph the supporting details are all the facts that come after the first sentence.

TRYING THE SKILL

Read the paragraph below. Then answer the questions.

> Mr. Stuart's class is putting on a class play. Students got to choose what job they wanted to do. Four students wrote the play. Six students are acting in it. Five students are working on making the costumes and the stage set. Three students are making posters and programs for the play.

1. What is the paragraph about?
2. What sentence states the main idea of the paragraph?
3. What are two supporting details?

EXTEND THE SKILL

Write a paragraph on a topic of your choice. You could write about what you like to do on the weekend, or you could write about a special time you remember. After you have written your paragraph, use the steps you have learned.

- What is the main idea of your paragraph? Is it clear?
- List the details in your paragraph that support the main idea. Should you add other details to support your main idea?

Our Country's Government

VOCABULARY

President

Congress

Supreme Court

monument

PEOPLE

Alexander Hamilton

George Washington

Pierre L'Enfant

Benjamin Banneker

John Adams

Abigail Adams

READING STRATEGY

Copy the diagram. In the bar write a **main idea** about our national government. In the boxes write **supporting details.**

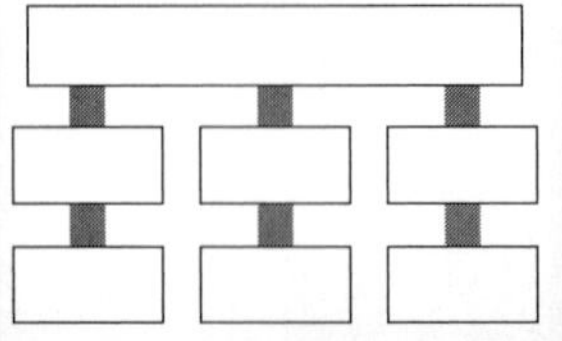

What is special about Washington, D.C.?

Lesson Outline

- A Special City
- Building a Capital
- Washington Today

BUILD BACKGROUND

Washington, D.C., is our country's capital. It is where our country's government is located. Some of our country's most important history has happened here. Many of our country's most important leaders have lived here. In this lesson you will find out what makes Washington, D.C., such a special place.

A SPECIAL CITY

Washington, D.C., is a special city. Unlike most cities, it was built to be a capital city. Today many important leaders work and live in Washington, D.C. One important leader is our **President**. The President is the leader of our country. The President lives in the White House. The President is elected by United States citizens every four years. The President makes sure our country's laws are followed.

The President works with the people in **Congress**. Congress is the part of our government that makes laws. Members of Congress are also elected by the people. Together Congress and the President make important decisions for our entire country.

Washington, D.C.

READING CHECK What does Congress do?

President George W. Bush (below) works with **Congress** (bottom) to make our country's laws.

BUILDING A CAPITAL

How did Washington, D.C., become our country's capital? In 1783 our country's capital was in **Philadelphia, Pennsylvania**. Many people did not want the country's capital to be in one state. Where should it go?

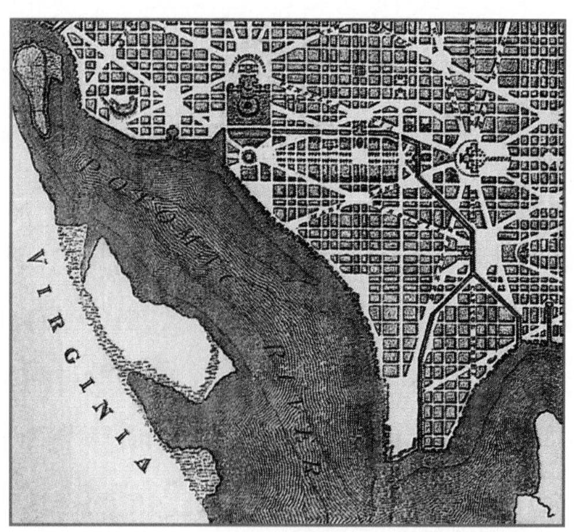

L'Enfant's plan for Washington, D.C. (above), left room for big parks and wide streets. George Washington watches the building of the White House (below).

Alexander Hamilton, one of our country's early leaders, had an idea. What if the capital was built on land that did not belong to one state? After searching for many months, President **George Washington**, our country's first President, chose a spot along the Potomac River. The spot was located between the states to the south and the states to the north. Maryland and Virginia each gave up land to create the capital.

Getting Started

President Washington hired **Pierre L'Enfant** to lay out the new city. L'Enfant was a planner and builder from France. He had come to America in 1777 to help our country win its freedom. L'Enfant drew up plans for the capital. He knew that one day Washington, D.C., would be a great city. That is why his plan called for wide streets and big parks.

BUILDING THE FIRST WHITE HOUSE
WASHINGTON D.C. 1798

Unfortunately, L'Enfant had trouble working with the other people who were building the capital. After one of many fights, L'Enfant left in anger. He took his plans with him. Luckily, **Benjamin Banneker**, an African American inventor, had worked closely with L'Enfant. He was able to remember the plans and draw them again.

The new capital was named after George Washington. The first building to be built was the White House. President **John Adams** and First Lady **Abigail Adams** were the first people to live in the White House. Read what President Adams wrote the day after he moved in.

Benjamin Banneker helped plan Washington, D.C.

***excerpt from* a letter by John Adams**

—November 2, 1800

I pray heaven to **bestow** the best of blessings on this house, and all that shall **hereafter inhabit** it. May none but honest and wise men ever rule under its roof.

What two things did John Adams think were important in a President?

bestow: give
hereafter: from now on
inhabit: live in

Why was the land near the Potomac chosen to be our nation's capital?

DATAGRAPHIC

How Our Government Works

Our government is made up of three parts, or branches. Look at the charts to learn more about how our country's government works.

Our Country's Government

Congress

Members of Congress meet in the Capitol building (above). They make our laws. Congress has two parts: the House of Representatives and the Senate.

President

The President lives and works in the White House (above). The President makes sure that our country's laws are carried out.

Supreme Court

The **Supreme Court** is made up of nine judges. They make sure our laws are fair. They meet in the Supreme Court Building (above).

Members of Congress (Selected States)

Congress has two parts, or "houses." The Senate has 100 members, 2 for each state. The House of Representatives has 345 members. States with more people get more representatives. The pictograph below shows the number of people in Congress for California, Florida, and Vermont.

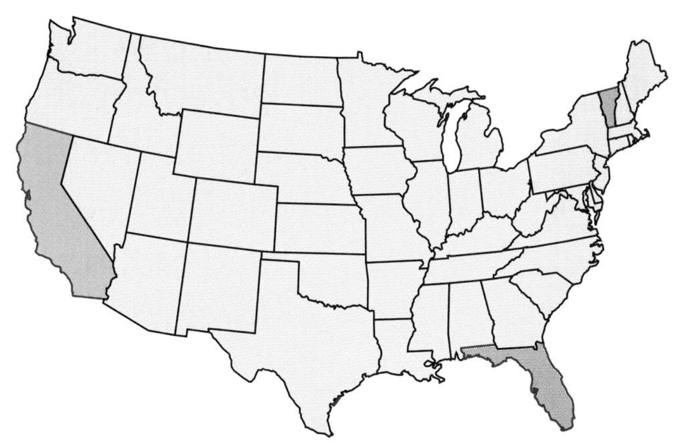

State	Senate	House of Representatives
California		
Florida		
Vermont		

Questions

1. Which part of our government makes sure that our laws are fair?
2. Which state shown on the pictograph sends the most members to the House of Representatives?
3. In what building does the President work? What is the President's main job?

Visit our website at **www.mhschool.com** *to learn more.*

WASHINGTON TODAY

If President George Washington could see Washington, D.C., today, he would be very surprised. The city has grown, and so has the government. Today more than 500,000 people live in Washington, D.C. Millions more people live just outside it. Tens of thousands of people in and around Washington, D.C., have jobs working for our country's government.

Every year people from around our country and the world visit our country's capital. They visit the **monuments** that remind them of our country's past. A monument is a building or statue made to honor a person or an event. Visitors come to see the city's museums. They also come to learn about our country's government.

How has Washington, D.C., changed?

The Washington Monument (left), the National Gallery of Art (below), and the Washington Zoo (right) are three places visitors enjoy.

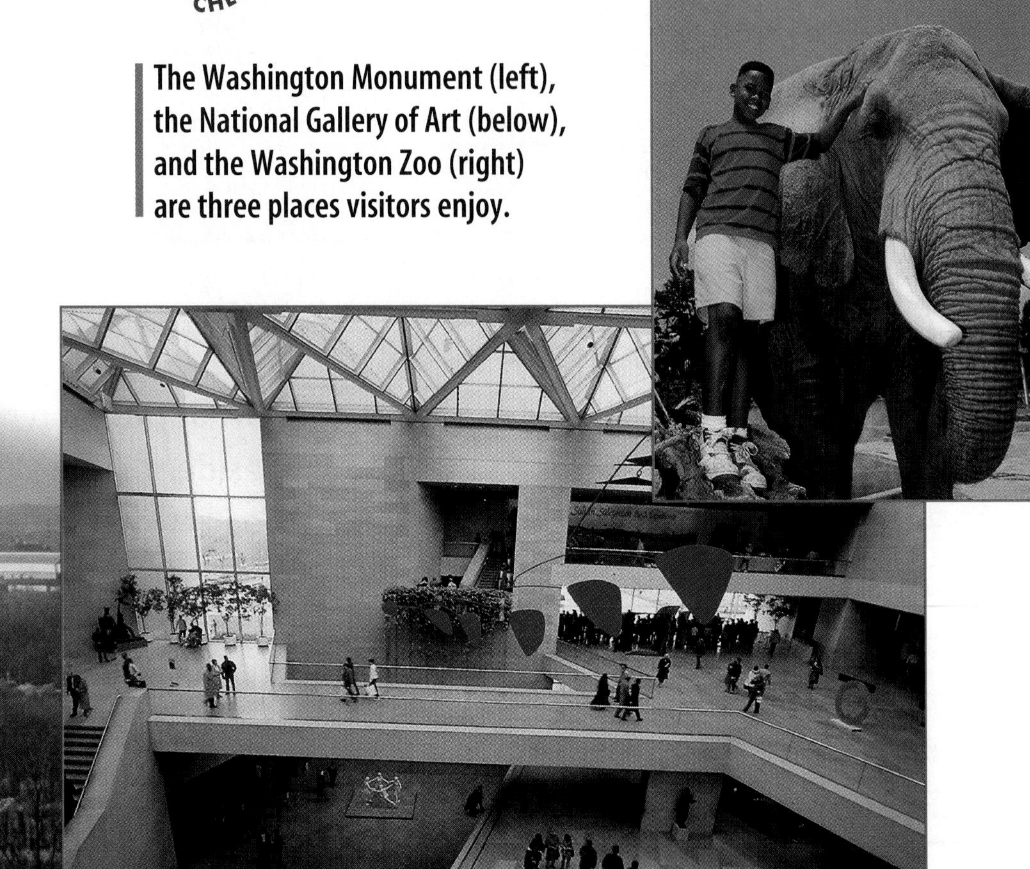

PUTTING IT TOGETHER

Over 200 years ago President George Washington helped choose the land that became our country's capital. Today Washington, D.C., is a special city. It is home to the three branches of our government. Visitors from around the world visit to see reminders of our past. Visitors also come to learn about our country's government.

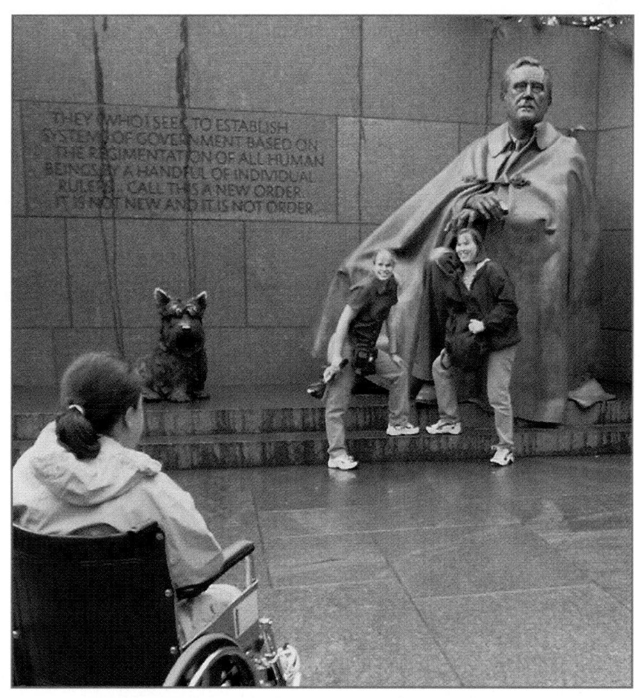

This monument honors Franklin Delano Roosevelt. He served more than 12 years as President.

Review and Assess

1. Write one sentence for each of the vocabulary words.

   Congress **monument**
   President

2. Where does the President live?
3. What is special about Washington, D.C.?
4. What are the three branches of our country's **government**?
5. What is the **main idea** of this lesson? What are two supporting details?

Suppose you are hired to make a plan for a capital city. What would you need to have? Draw your plan. Show roads, parks, buildings, and anything else you think is important.

Write about a monument you would like to create. Describe why you would build the monument. Tell how you would build it. Draw a picture to show what it would look like.

Using Grid Maps

Suppose you and your family went on a trip. One way to find your way around is to use a grid map. A grid map has a grid, or set of lines that cross to form boxes. Grid maps help us to quickly and easily find places on the map.

VOCABULARY

grid map

index

LEARN THE SKILL

Look at the map below. Then follow the steps to use the grid map.

1. **Read the map title.**
   Look at the title to see what the map shows. This map shows the Mall in Washington, D.C.

2. **Look at the lines, letters, and numbers on the map.**
   Grid maps have two sets of lines that make boxes. Rows are lettered from top to bottom. Columns are numbered from left to right.

3. **Look at the index for the name of the place you want to locate.**
   An **index** is an alphabetical list that tells you where information can be found. For a grid map the letters and numbers in the index tell you in which grid boxes you will find places.

Washington, D.C.: The Mall

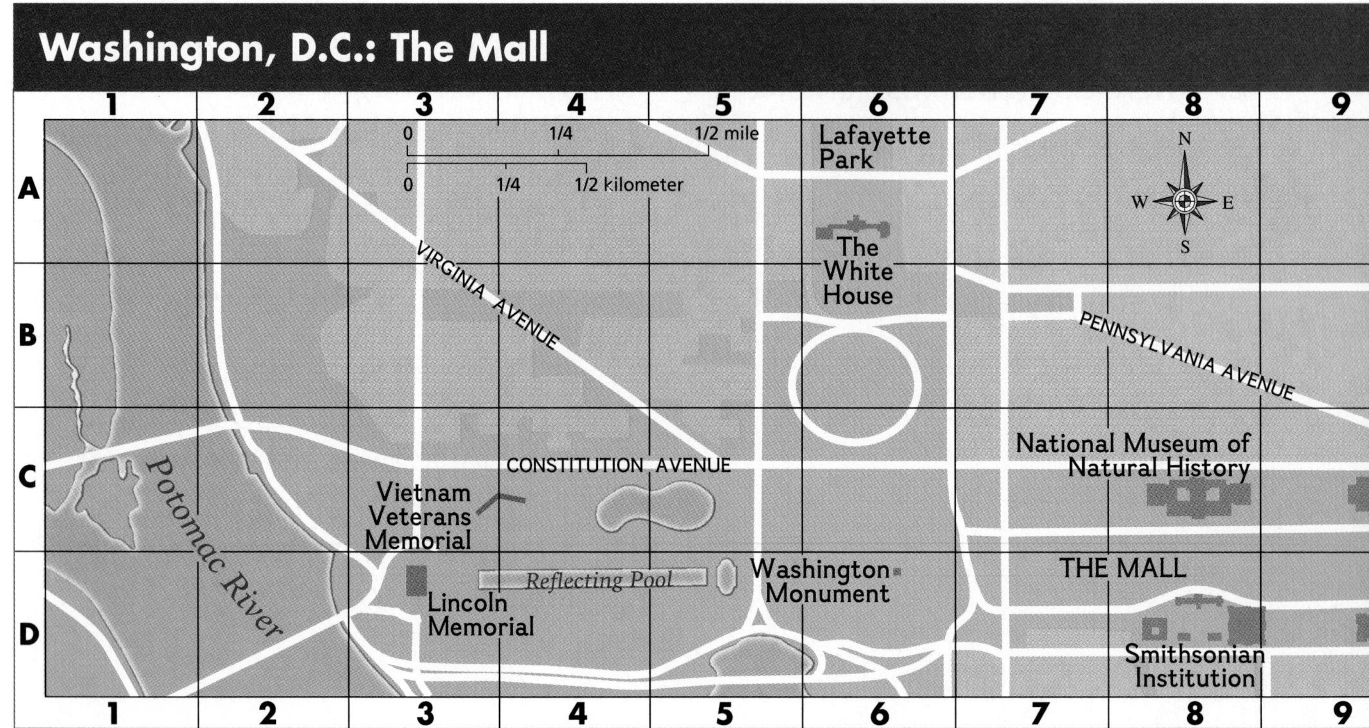

4. **Find a place on the map by using the letter and number of its grid box.**
   To find the Washington Monument, slide your finger down the left side of the map to the row marked *D*. Then move your finger across the map to the column numbered 6. Now you know where to go.

TRY THE SKILL

Look at the map to answer the questions.

1. In which grid box is the Lincoln Memorial?
2. What place of interest is found in both C9 and C10?
3. If you walked from the Washington Monument to the Lincoln Memorial, in what direction would you be going?
4. Use the map scale to find the distance from Union Station to the Supreme Court.

EXTEND THE SKILL

Mastering grid maps can help you understand latitude and longitude. Latitude and longitude are ways of measuring distance on Earth from fixed points. These points are part of what's called a global grid. Turn to page R10 to see a map that uses latitude and longitude.

NATIONAL GEOGRAPHIC

10 11 12 13
A
B
C
D
Union Station
National Gallery of Art
CONSTITUTION AVENUE
Supreme Court
Capitol
National Air and Space Museum
INDEPENDENCE AVENUE
Library of Congress

INDEX

Capitol	C12–D12
Lafayette Park	A6
Library of Congress	D13
Lincoln Memorial	D3
National Air and Space Museum	D9–D10
National Gallery of Art	C9–C10
National Museum of Natural History	C8
Smithsonian Institution	D8
Supreme Court	C13
Union Station	A12
Vietnam Veterans Memorial	C3–C4
Washington Monument	D6
White House	A6

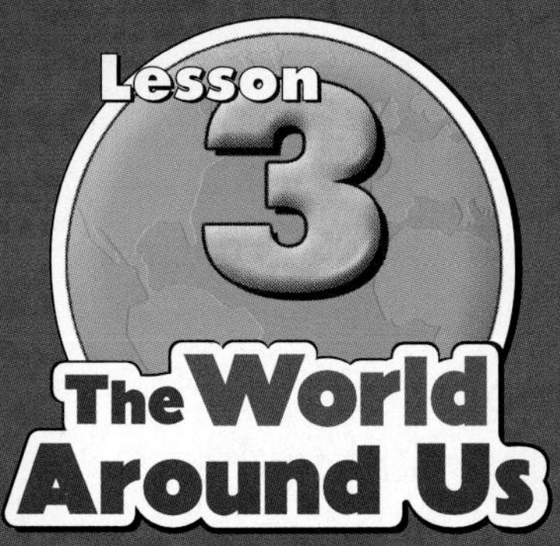

Mexico's Capital City

VOCABULARY

empire

What is life like in Mexico's capital city?

Lesson Outline

- A Historic City
- Governing Mexico
- Life in Mexico City

READING STRATEGY

Use a word web to **summarize.** Write "Mexico City" in the center. Write key features of the city in the other circles.

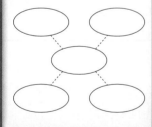

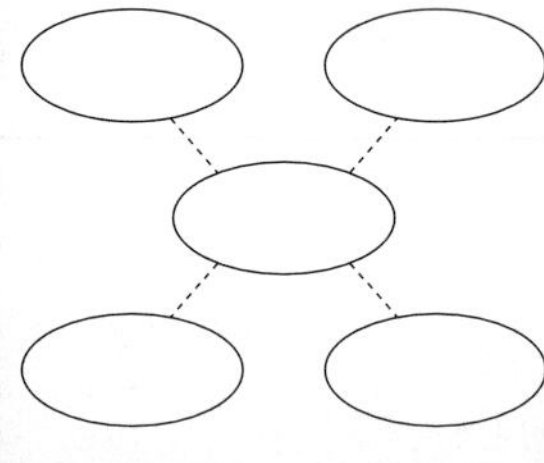

BUILD BACKGROUND

Mexico is our neighbor to the south. It has a long history and a rich culture. It also has a government that is similar to our country's government. Mexico's capital is Mexico City. Mexico City is the oldest city in all of the Americas. It also has more people than almost any other city in the world!

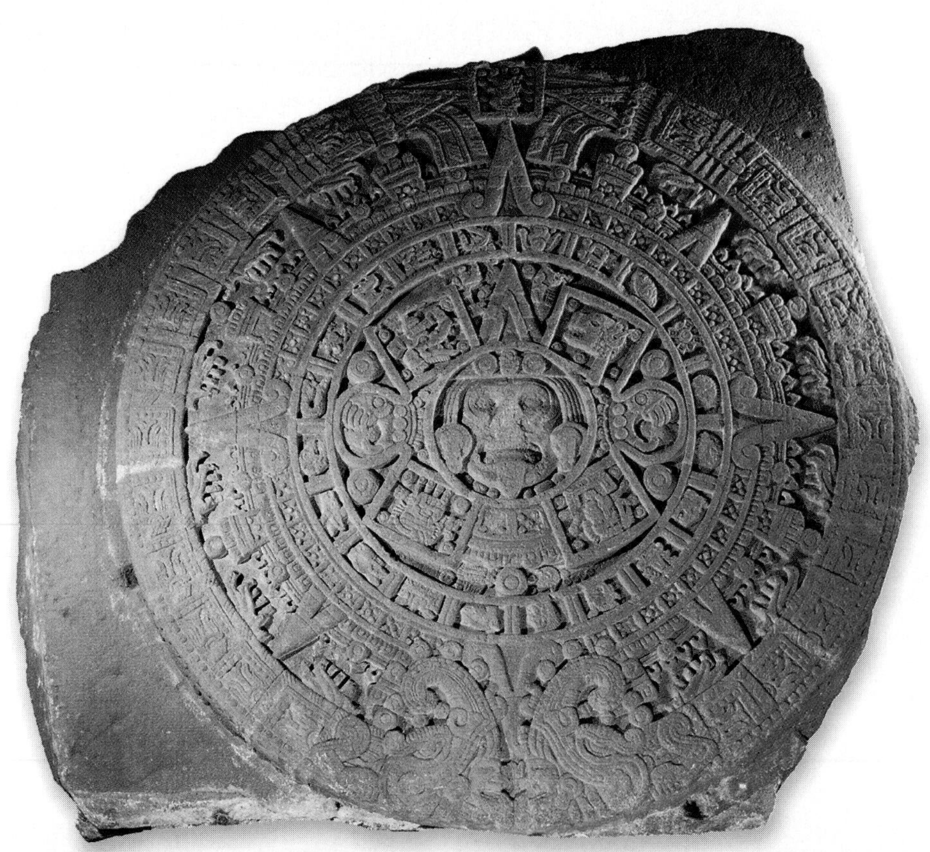

A HISTORIC CITY

Mexico City has a long history. It was founded about 675 years ago. At that time it was called Tenochtitlán (te noch tee TLAHN). It was the capital of the Aztec Indian **empire**. An empire is a group of lands and peoples governed by one ruler.

In 1519 Spanish explorers came to Tenochtitlán. The Spanish were amazed by the city's size, beauty, and wealth.

Today Mexico City is an exciting mix of old and new. Buildings from the time of the Spanish explorers stand side by side with modern buildings.

Mexico City blends ancient (opposite page) and modern (above).

HISTORY MYSTERY

Who is buried in Pyramid of the Moon?

Centuries before the Aztec, another ancient Indian culture ruled Mexico. This group built the first pyramids at Teotihuacan (tay oh tee wuh KAHN), which later became an Aztec city. In 1998 scientists found the skeleton of a man who was buried more than 1,800 years ago in the pyramid. Was he a priest? We still do not know for sure.

Who do you think might have been buried in a pyramid like the ones at Teotihuacan?

Who lived in what is now Mexico City before the Spanish arrived?

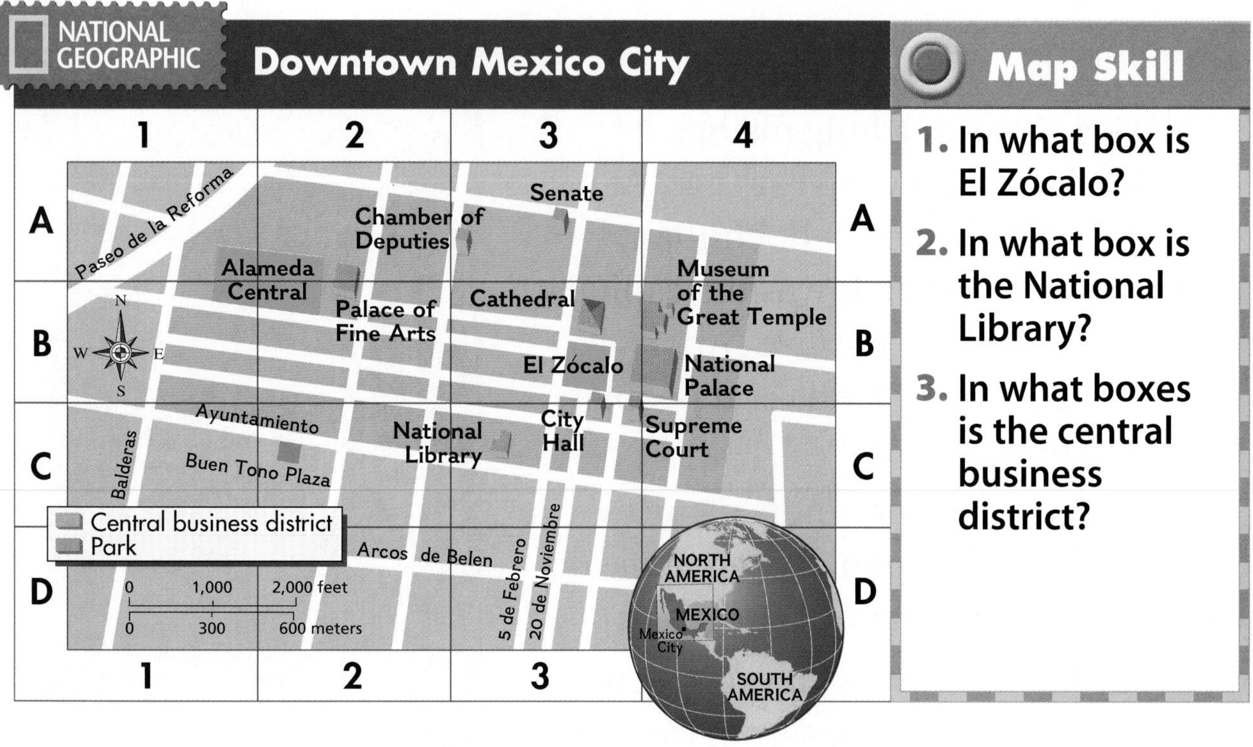

Map Skill

1. In what box is El Zócalo?
2. In what box is the National Library?
3. In what boxes is the central business district?

GOVERNING MEXICO

Mexico and the United States have many things in common. Both countries were colonies of other countries. The United States won its freedom from Britain in 1781. Mexico won its freedom from Spain in 1821.

As in the United States, citizens in Mexico elect a congress and a president. Mexico's congress has two "houses." One is called the Senate. The other is called the Chamber of Deputies. The Chamber of Deputies is a lot like our House of Representatives. In Mexico presidents serve one 6-year term.

Mexico has state and local governments, too. Mexico has 31 states. Like states in the United States, each Mexican state has its own governor and its own capital. Like Washington, D.C., Mexico City is not part of any state. It has its own local government led by a mayor.

Mexico's president works in the National Palace.

The Capital City

The mayor of Mexico City has a big job. More than 20 million people live in Mexico City. That is more than in almost any other city in the world. Mexico City is still growing fast.

The city's size has created some problems. The subways and buses are very crowded. Traffic often moves very slowly. Air pollution is a big problem. The local and national governments in Mexico City are working to solve these problems.

What are three ways the governments of Mexico and the United States are alike?

Vicente Fox (below) was elected president of Mexico in 2000. The Monument to Independence (right) celebrates Mexico's freedom from Spain.

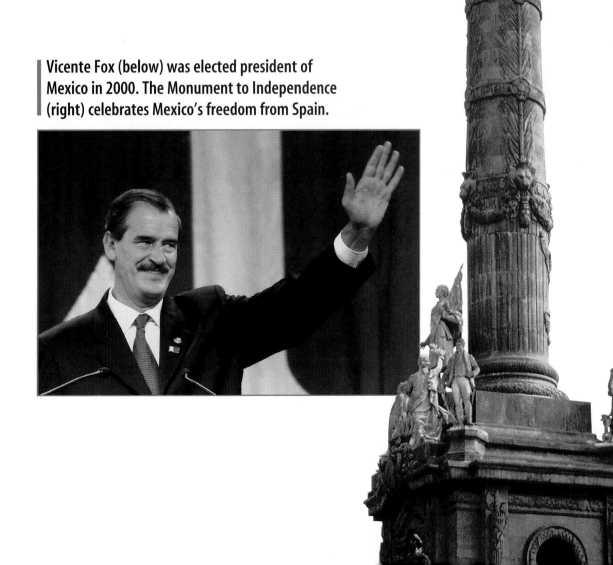

LIFE IN MEXICO CITY

Mexico City is an exciting place to live. The Zócalo (ZOH kah loh), or main square, is at the city's center. There you will find important government buildings. The National Palace runs along one whole side of the square. It is where the president works. Near the Zócalo is the Ballet Folklórico. The Ballet Folklórico is known around the world for its dances.

Another popular place to visit in Mexico City is Chapultepec (cha POOL tuh pek) Park. The park has a zoo, gardens, and a lake with rowboats. It also has a famous museum with beautiful Aztec sculptures. Families come to Chapultepec Park to picnic and to play soccer and other sports.

READING CHECK **What are some exciting things to do in Mexico City today?**

The Zócalo (below) is the busy center of Mexico City. The Ballet Folklórico (above) is world famous.

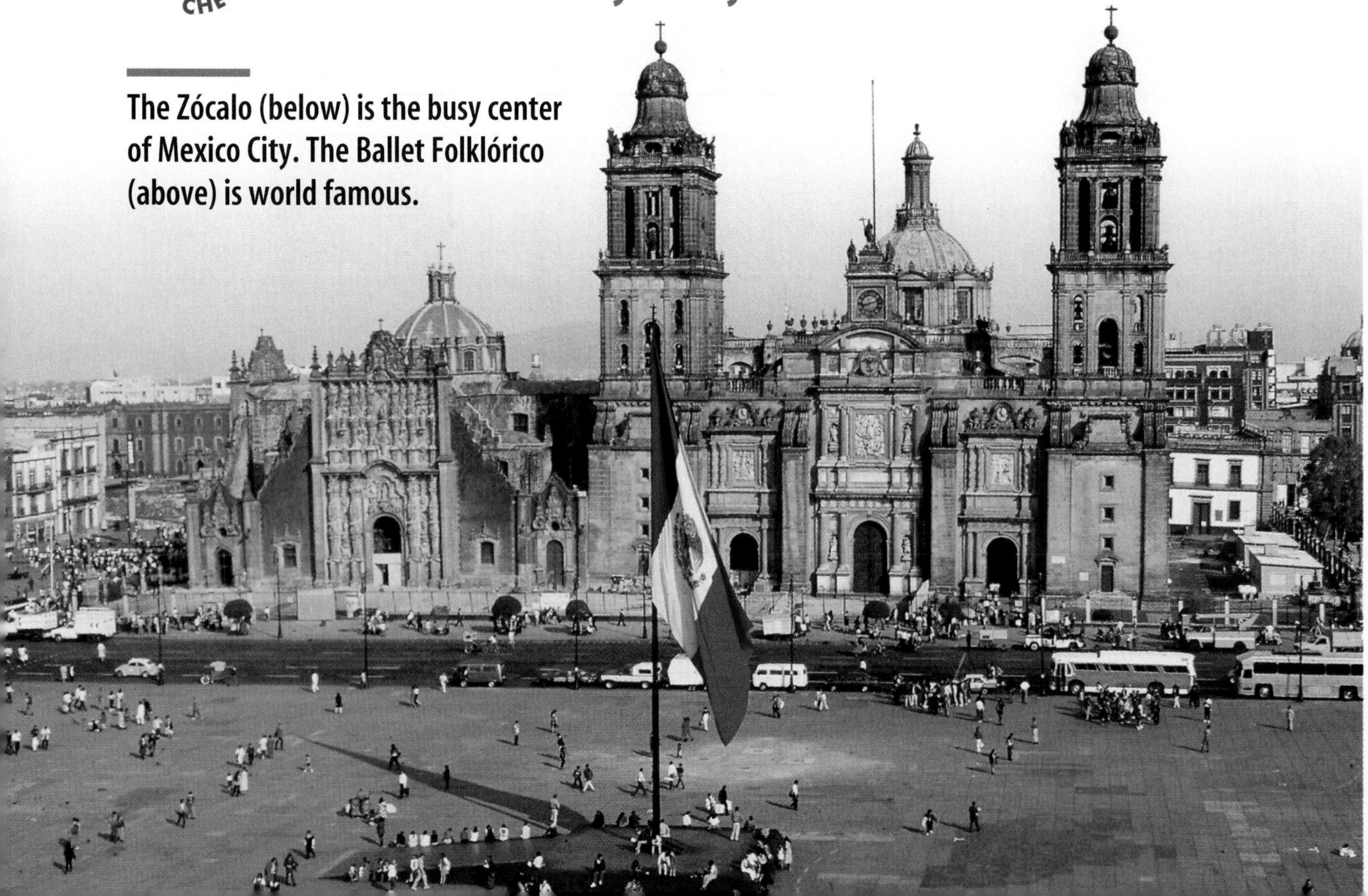

PUTTING IT TOGETHER

Mexico and the United States have many things in common. The governments of both countries are elected by the people. They both have a president, a congress, and a supreme court. Like Washington, D.C., Mexico City is an exciting place. Each city is home to its country's national government. Each city has many things for visitors to see and do.

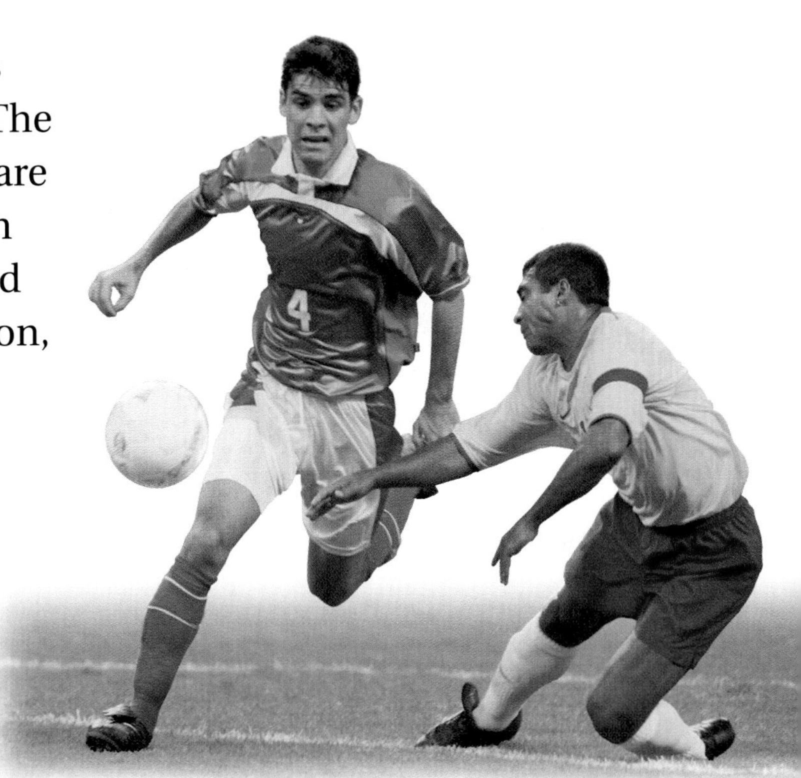

Soccer is one of Mexico's favorite sports.

Review and Assess

1. Write one sentence for the vocabulary word.

   empire

2. What is the capital of Mexico?
3. What is life like in Mexico City today?
4. What are some ways you can see Mexico City's **history** in the city today?
5. What is the **main idea** of page 244?

Make a chart comparing Mexico City and Washington, D.C. Write the two cities at the top of your page, and draw a line down the middle. How are the cities similar? How are they different?

Write a postcard as though you are visiting Mexico City. Tell your friend some of the things you saw and did.

Chapter 8 REVIEW

VOCABULARY REVIEW

Number a sheet of paper from 1 to 3. Beside each number write the word from the list below that matches the description.

empire **monument**

tax

1. A building or statue made to honor a person or an event
2. A group of lands and peoples governed by one ruler
3. Money that people pay to support their government

CHAPTER COMPREHENSION

4. How do government leaders in the United States get their jobs?
5. Identify the two parts that make up the United States Congress.
6. Write a paragraph describing two examples of past cultures that can still be found in Mexico City today.

SKILL REVIEW

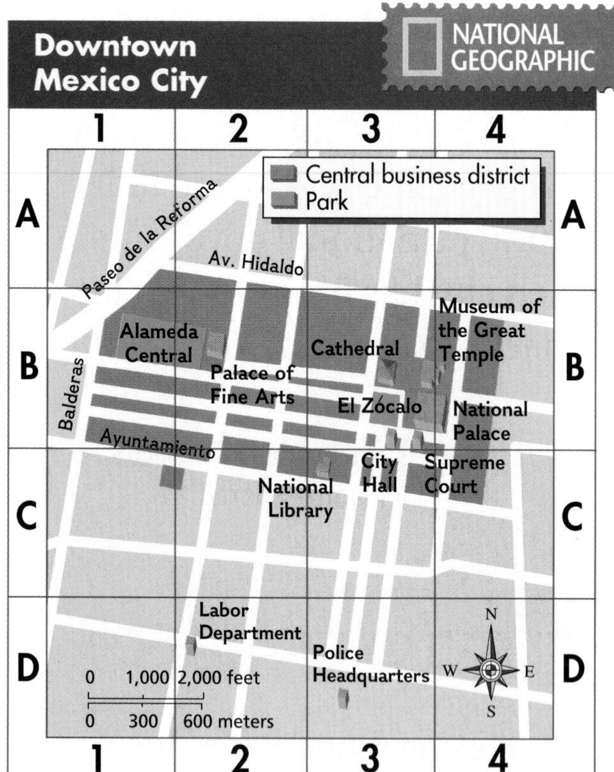

7. **Geography Skill** In which part of this grid map is Police Headquarters?
8. **Geography Skill** How many sections, or squares, are there in this grid map?
9. **Reading/Thinking Skill** Write a paragraph about a monument that you would like to see. Be sure to include a main idea and supporting details.

USING A BAR GRAPH

10. In which years did the House of Representatives have more representatives from New York than from California? In which years did it have more from California?

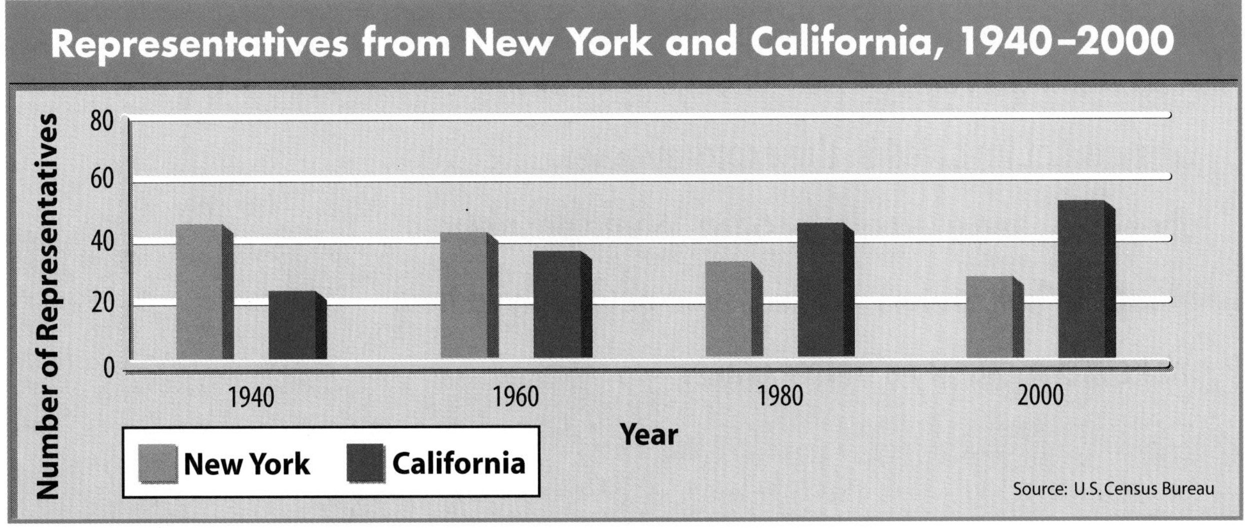

Activity

Writing About Government Plan a class government. List the things your class needs and the services it should have. Decide how your government will meet those needs and provide those services. Who will lead your government? What departments will take care of needs and services? Use your list to write a report explaining how your class government will work.

Use your Foldable to review what you have learned about local and national governments. Look at the front of your Foldable, and think about the roles of local and national governments. Find similarities between Mexico City and Washington, D.C. Review your notes on your Foldable to check your responses.

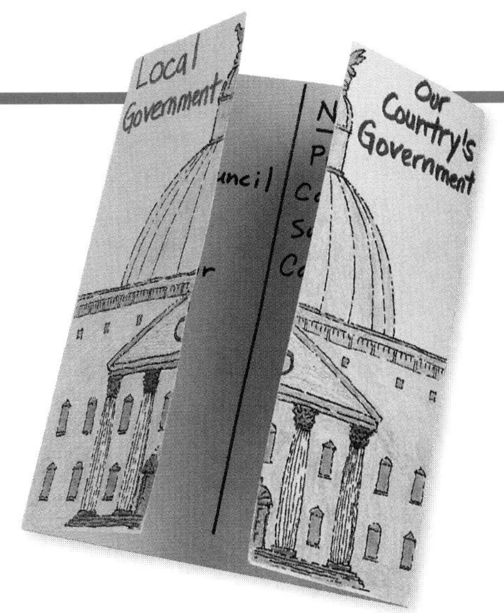

Chapter 9

THE Big IDEAS ABOUT...

Citizens in Action

Citizens get involved in their communities. They vote, obey laws, and even run for office. Some people join groups to help others. Citizens who get involved help make a community a better place.

GETTING INVOLVED

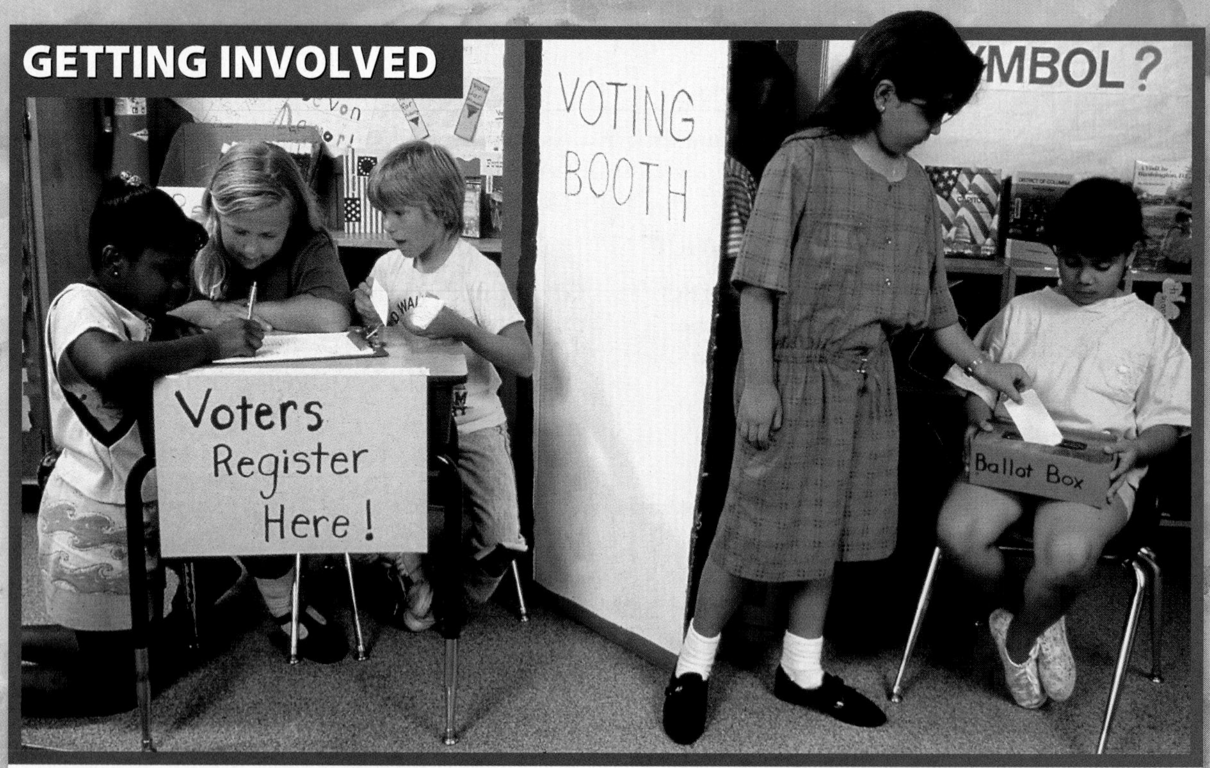

Voting is an important part of being a good citizen. Here third graders are voting in a class election.

HELPING OUT

Volunteer groups help people in many ways. This group helps people build homes.

Foldables

Make this Foldable study guide, and use it to record what you learn about "Citizens in Action."

1. Fold a sheet of paper like a hamburger. Then fold the hamburger in half once again.
2. Open and cut along the fold line on one side, forming two large tabs.
3. Write the titles of the lessons on the tabs. Illustrate the tabs of your Foldable.

Lesson 1

Getting Involved

VOCABULARY

common good

volunteer

Pledge of Allegiance

Why is it important to be a good citizen?

Lesson Outline

- Good Citizens
- Giving Something Back
- Sharing and Caring

READING STRATEGY

Copy the chart. In column one **predict** what you will learn about being a good citizen. In column two write what you learned.

BUILD BACKGROUND

Suppose you had a problem. Where would you go for help? You would probably go to your family first. Citizens in a community are like a family. If someone has a problem, there are people to turn to for help. Citizens who help each other help their communities. That is because communities work best when citizens work together.

GOOD CITIZENS

Do you throw trash in cans instead of on the street? If you do, you are acting for the **common good**. Acting for the common good means doing what is best for everyone. Putting trash in cans keeps streets clean. That is good for everyone. It is one way to be a good citizen.

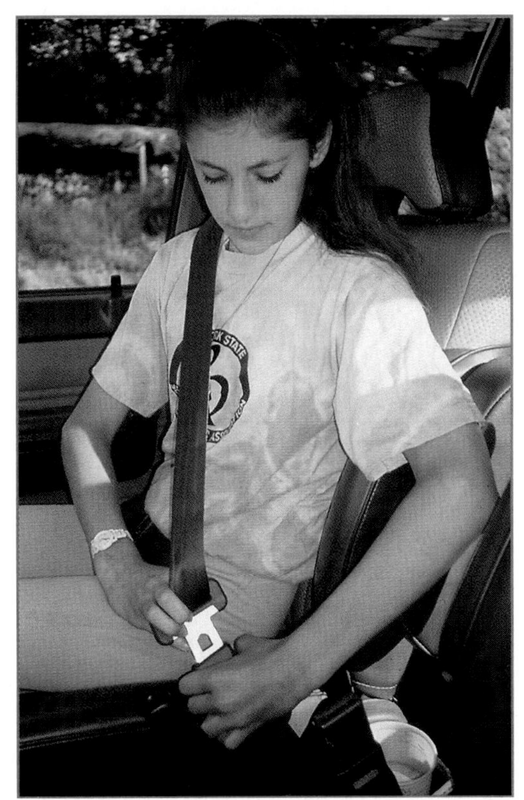

Helping out at a food bank (opposite page), obeying the law (above), and voting (below) are ways to be a good citizen.

There are many other ways to be a good citizen. One way is to obey laws. You may know that it is against the law to chain bikes to fire hydrants. That is because firefighters would not be able to open a hydrant if a fire broke out. Obeying this law protects everyone in the community.

Voting is another way to be a good citizen. People who vote care about what is best for their community and country. Getting involved is another way to be a good citizen. Keep reading to find out how two people got involved in their community.

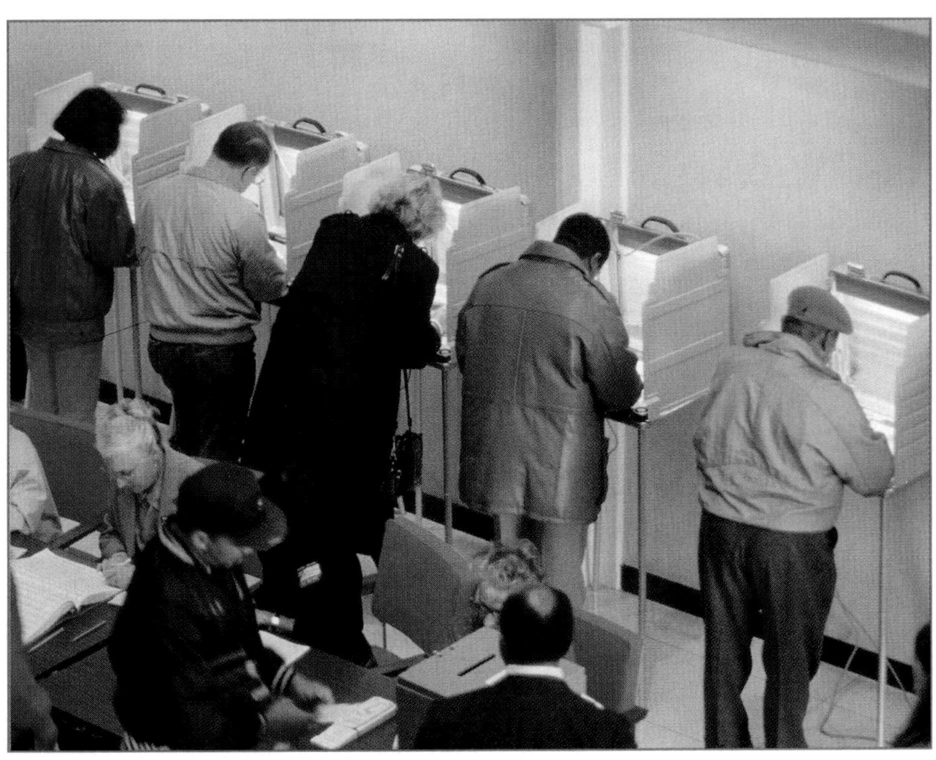

What are some ways to be a good citizen?

GIVING SOMETHING BACK

Dale Sherman lives in **Medina** (muh DIGH nuh), **Ohio**. He works as a **volunteer** teacher. A volunteer is a person who chooses to do a job without getting paid.

Dale Sherman is a **volunteer** teacher in his community.

Sherman helps people learn how to read. He had a hard time reading when he was growing up. That was back in the 1960s. Reading was still hard for Sherman even as an adult. Then volunteers in a program called Project Learn helped him learn to read better.

Today Sherman is a teacher at Project Learn. He helps other people learn to read. He also tells children that it is okay to speak out if they have learning problems. "When I was young, I did not feel good about myself," Sherman says. "Now I'm proud of who I am."

Exploring TECHNOLOGY

Walk at the Green, Not in Between!

Garrett Morgan gave something back to communities everywhere. He invented one of the first traffic lights. Morgan's traffic light made it safer for cars and for people crossing the street. His traffic light led to the green, yellow, and red lights we use today.

California State Senator Liz Figueroa talks with students from Independent Elementary School in Castro Valley, California.

Leading the Way

Some people serve their communities by getting involved in government. Liz Figueroa is a state senator in **Fremont, California** . Figueroa believes "it is important to get involved and help your community." As a state senator she works to improve schools. She also works to make sure that all sick people can see doctors even if they cannot pay for them.

Before becoming a senator, Figueroa ran a business that helped hurt workers get jobs. She also raised two children. She learned how hard it was for parents to work and to take care of their children at the same time. This helped her decide what laws to work for when she became a state senator.

What do Dale Sherman and Senator Figueroa have in common?

SHARING AND CARING

People are never too old or too young to help others. Take Katie Milton, for example. She lives in **Tampa, Florida**. When she was eight years old, she collected 50 children's books to give to a housing program in her community.

There are many things you can do to help your community. You can make get-well cards for people who are sick. You can help younger children with their homework. You can also collect toys, food, or clothes for people who need them.

Being a good citizen means caring about your community. It also means caring about our country. One way people show they care is by saying the **Pledge of Allegiance**. The Pledge of Allegiance is a promise to be loyal to our country.

Pledge of Allegiance

—first written by Francis Bellamy, 1892

I pledge **allegiance** to the flag of the United States of America and to the **Republic** for which it stands, one Nation under God, **indivisible**, with liberty and justice for all.

Which words in the Pledge of Allegiance describe the rights of United States citizens?

allegiance: loyalty
Republic: our country's government
indivisible: not to be broken

What are some things that good citizens care about?

PUTTING IT TOGETHER

There are many ways to be a good citizen. One way is to work for the common good of people in your community. That includes obeying laws, voting, volunteering, and serving in the government. Being a good citizen also means caring about your country. Working for the common good makes our country and your community strong.

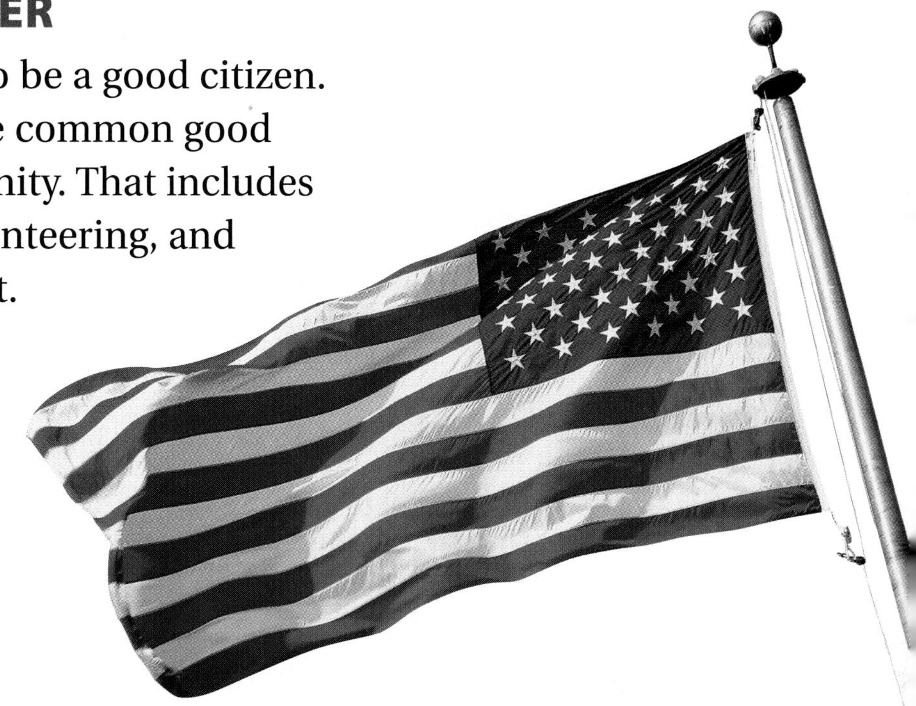

Review and Assess

1. Write one sentence for each of the vocabulary terms.

   common good **volunteer** **Pledge of Allegiance**

2. Why is obeying the law important in a community?
3. Analyze why it is important to be a good citizen. Find! out!
4. Why do some citizens get involved in **government**?
5. Review what you read about Dale Sherman on page 252. Then choose one paragraph, and write the **main idea**.

Activities

Make a two-column chart called "Good Citizenship." Label the first column "Obeying the Law." Label the second column "Being a Volunteer." List three examples in each column.

Write a story about someone you know who is a good citizen. What makes the person a good citizen?

BIOGRAPHY

Focus on Justice

Helen Keller

"Although the world is full of suffering, it is also full of the overcoming of it."

Helen Keller

Helen Keller overcame great hardship in her own life. She also spent her life helping others. She traveled to more than 35 countries. She gave speeches, wrote books, and raised money for people who needed help. She met many world leaders. There was even a movie made about her life. She did all this even though she was blind and deaf from the age of one and a half years old.

With the help of her teacher, Anne Sullivan, Helen learned to read and speak. In 1904 she became the first deaf and blind person to finish college. Helen kept on learning all her life.

THE LIFE OF HELEN KELLER

1880 | 1900 | 1920 | 1940 | 1960 | 1980

- **1880** Helen Keller is born in Tuscumbia, Alabama.
- **1887** Helen gets a new teacher, Anne Sullivan.
- **1903** Keller writes *The Story of My Life*.
- **1904** Keller graduates from Radcliffe College.
- **1924** Keller becomes spokesperson for the American Foundation for the Blind.
- **1968** Keller dies at 87.

Helen Keller meets with President Kennedy in 1961.

She learned that blindness was often caused by illnesses that could be treated. However, poor people did not have the money to buy the medicines they needed. Helen felt this was not right. She worked with the American Foundation for the Blind to raise money to help blind people around the world.

Helen believed strongly that all people are equal. As a blind person Helen had to work very hard to be treated fairly. That is one reason why she worked for justice for all people—African Americans, women, factory workers, and the poor. "Alone we can do so little," she said. "Together we can do so much."

Link to Today **Think of someone who is working for justice today. Write a report explaining what that person has in common with Helen Keller.**

Points of View

How can we have less conflict in school?

Name calling, teasing, kicking, and hitting are all different forms of conflict. People do not always agree on the best way to reduce conflict. Read and think about three different opinions on this issue. Then answer the questions that follow.

SINTHIA FRANCO
Whelan Elementary School
Lennox, California
Excerpt from an interview, 2001

"Some kids have a hard time controlling their anger. These kids need help. Special teachers might be able to show them how to control their anger. The other important thing is learning better ways to communicate."

A'LAYA MACKEY
Paul Robeson Academy
Detroit, Michigan
Excerpt from an interview, 2001

"If somebody starts pushing you, do not push back. Try talking. Find a teacher to help. Separate people who are fighting, sit them down, and ask questions about what happened."

JACOB MATTHEWS
Fred Olds Elementary School
Raleigh, North Carolina
Excerpt from an interview, 2001

"Kids should try to stay out of each other's personal space. There could be a school rule that kids have to stay an arm's length away from each other when they line up to go somewhere."

Thinking About the Points of View

1. What does Sinthia think could be done about fighting in school?
2. In what ways are A'laya's ideas similar to Sinthia's?
3. Do you agree with Jacob's idea? Why or why not?
4. What other points of view might people have on this issue?

Building Citizenship

Respect

All people are different. That is what makes each person special. Sometimes people do not respect these differences. That can lead to conflict. Discuss ways people can show more respect for each other.

Write About It!

Make a list of rules you think would help students get along at school. Share your list with the class.

T. A. L. K.

Talk about the problem.

Allow each person to speak.

Listen to what each person says.

Keep trying to solve the conflict.

Identifying Cause and Effect

Some events are connected in a special way. In the last lesson you read about Garrett Morgan. He invented one of the first traffic lights. That event led to safer streets for people and cars. His invention was a **cause**. A cause is something that makes another thing happen. Safer streets were an **effect** of Morgan's invention. An effect is something that happens as a result of something else. Identifying cause and effect is a useful skill. It can help you understand ways that events are connected.

VOCABULARY

cause
effect

LEARN THE SKILL

Read the sentences below. Then follow the steps for identifying cause and effect.

> Ted was thinking of running for class president. Since his friends thought he would do a good job, Ted decided to run.

1. **Look for clue words that can tell you how the events might be connected.**
   Clue words can often help you find that events are connected as causes or effects. *Because of, as a result of,* and *since* are some clue words that show a cause. *Since* is a clue word in the example above.
   So, therefore, and *as a result* are some clue words that show an effect.

2. **Identify the cause.**
   Ted's friends told him he would be a good class president. That is what caused him to run.

3. **Identify the effect.**
   Ted running for class president is the effect.

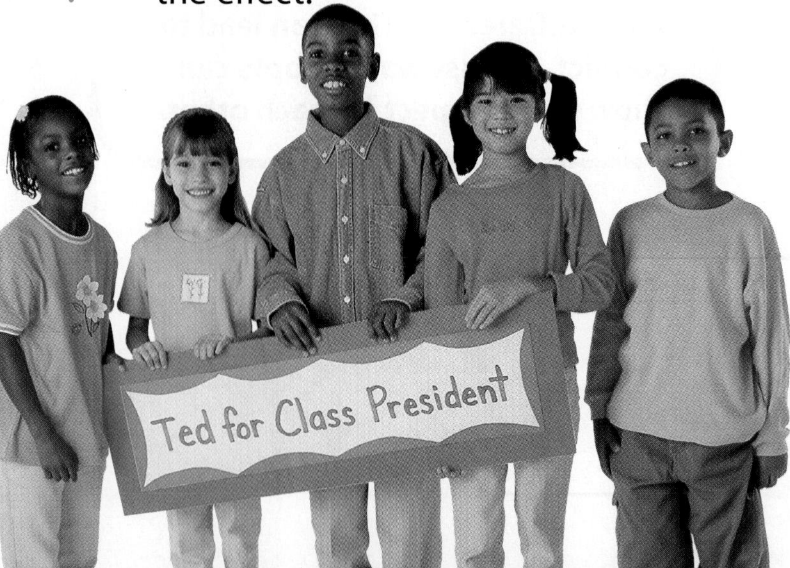

TRY THE SKILL

Read the paragraphs below. Then answer the questions.

> Kevin and Gina went outside to play in the snow. They saw their neighbor, Mrs. Johnson, shoveling snow from her driveway. Since the children saw Mrs. Johnson needed help, they changed their plans.
>
> They got two shovels and went to work on the snow pile. Finally, it was gone. As a result of their work, Mrs. Johnson was able to clear her driveway of snow much quicker.

1. Are there clue words in the paragraphs above that might help you identify a cause and an effect? What are they?
2. Which event in the first paragraph was the cause for Kevin and Gina changing their plans?
3. Which event in the second paragraph was the effect of the children's work?

EXTEND THE SKILL

Identifying cause and effect can help you understand how events in social studies are connected.

- Look back at Lesson 1.
- Identify three events that might be connected as causes and effects.
- Write three sentences that show how the events are connected. Use clue words, if possible.

Lesson 2

Helping Out

VOCABULARY

nonprofit

PEOPLE

Clara Barton

How do volunteer groups help communities?

Lesson Outline

- Building Homes
- Helping in Times of Need
- Doctors on Call

READING STRATEGY

Copy the diagram. Use it to show one **cause and effect** of a volunteer group discussed in this lesson.

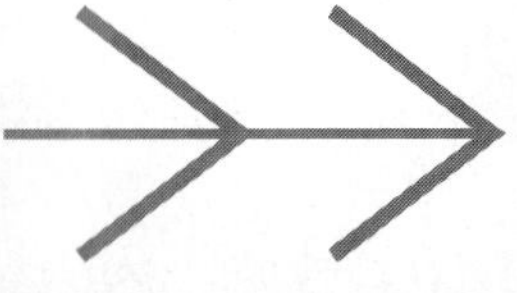

BUILD BACKGROUND

Sometimes people join together in groups to help other people. In our country there are many nonprofit groups that volunteers can join. A nonprofit group does not make money from the work it does. In this lesson you will read about some nonprofit groups that help people.

BUILDING HOMES

From 1977 to 1981 Jimmy Carter served as President of the United States. After he left office, he wanted to keep helping people. He joined a nonprofit group called Habitat for Humanity. Habitat helps families build homes for themselves. The families work with Habitat volunteers to build their homes.

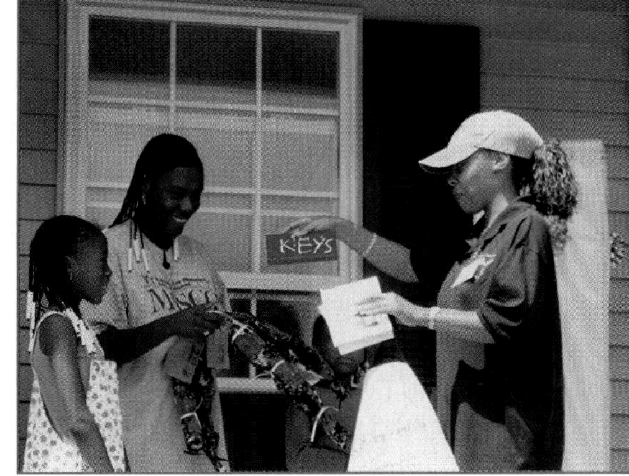

Jimmy Carter (top, second from the right) works with other Habitat for Humanity volunteers. A Habitat volunteer hands the keys to a new homeowner (above).

Beverley Smith built her family a home with help from Habitat. They had been living in an apartment. There were so many holes in the ceiling they sometimes used an umbrella indoors.

It was hard work building her home. Beverley knew it was worth it. Today Beverley Smith gives back to her community. She now helps other families build homes, too.

How does Habitat for Humanity help people help themselves?

HELPING IN TIMES OF NEED

The American Red Cross is another nonprofit group that helps people in communities. It was started in 1881 by **Clara Barton**. Barton worked as a nurse in the Civil War. After the war Barton learned about the International Red Cross. She decided to set up an American Red Cross. She wanted to help people both in wartime and in other times. Barton started working on the project in 1871. Ten years later she succeeded.

Today the American Red Cross helps communities during disasters. On September 11, 2001, four airplanes were hijacked from United States airports. Two of the planes flew into the World Trade Center towers in New York City. Both buildings were destroyed. Many people died. The American Red Cross helped many communities. It gave food and supplies to relief workers and victims' families. It also gave shelter to people who had lost their homes in the attack.

Clara Barton (top) founded the American Red Cross. Today the Red Cross works in communities to give everyday services and disaster relief (left, above, and opposite page).

Everyday Help

The American Red Cross also works every day to make communities better places. It teaches people how to prepare for emergencies. It gives lessons in first aid. It teaches children about water safety and trains lifeguards.

Red Cross volunteers work in homeless shelters. They collect food for people in need. They also bring meals to people who cannot leave their homes.

The Red Cross even has special programs that give children a chance to help. For example, you can visit a hospital to cheer up sick people. You can also write greeting cards to United States soldiers.

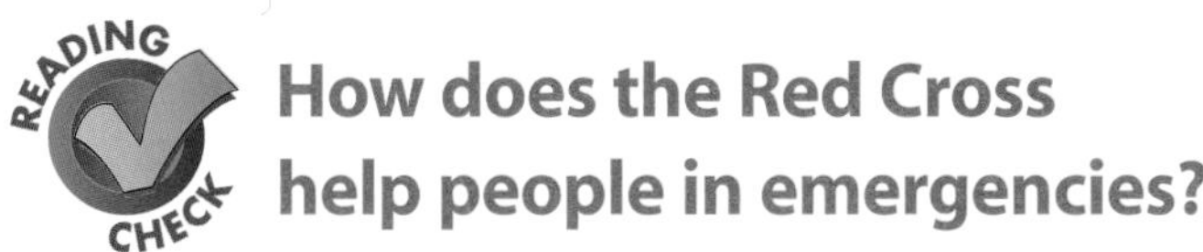

How does the Red Cross help people in emergencies?

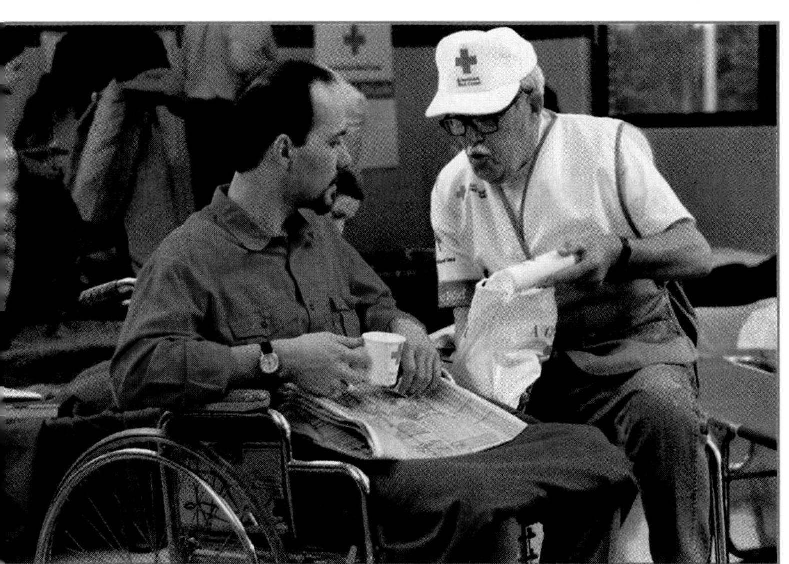

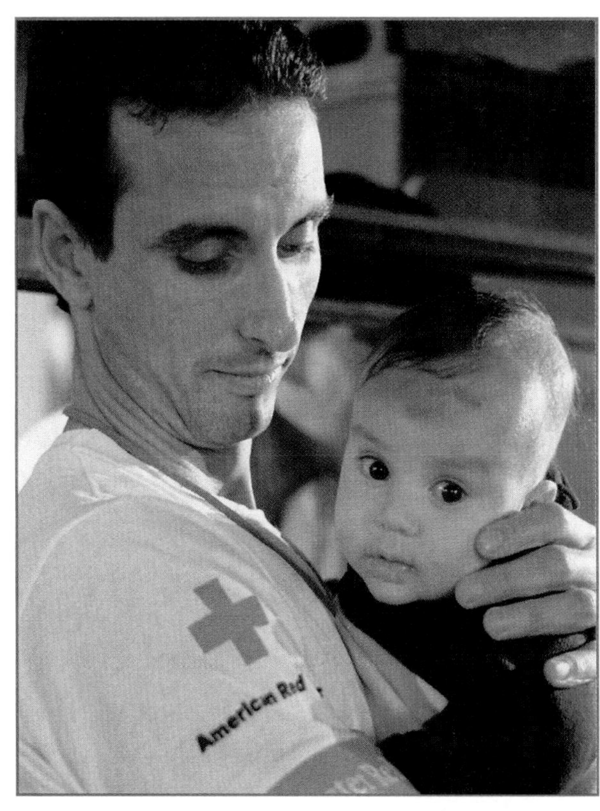

Exploring ECONOMICS

Every Little Bit Helps

Where do nonprofit groups get their money? Most of it comes from ordinary people who want to help.

In 2000 Americans gave over $152 billion. That is over $530 for every person in the United States.

Activity

If one person put aside one penny a day, it would add up to $3.65 by the end of the year. How much would it be if ten people did it? If everyone in your class did it?

DOCTORS ON CALL

Doctors Without Borders is a special kind of volunteer group. It brings together doctors, nurses, and other medical people from around the world. They help communities struck by war or natural disaster.

In 2001 an earthquake hit the country of **El Salvador** in Central America. About 1,000 people were badly hurt. Doctors Without Borders sent 85 volunteers from many countries to El Salvador. They provided medical care, tents, and clean water.

Doctors Without Borders helps people around the world (above and below).

Dr. Silvio Podda was one of the volunteers. He came to El Salvador from the United States. "You have to learn to adjust to the absence [lack] of basic needs [medical supplies]," he says. Dr. Podda did it because he wanted to help. With the help of people like Dr. Podda, El Salvador came back from the earthquake.

How did Doctors Without Borders help in El Salvador?

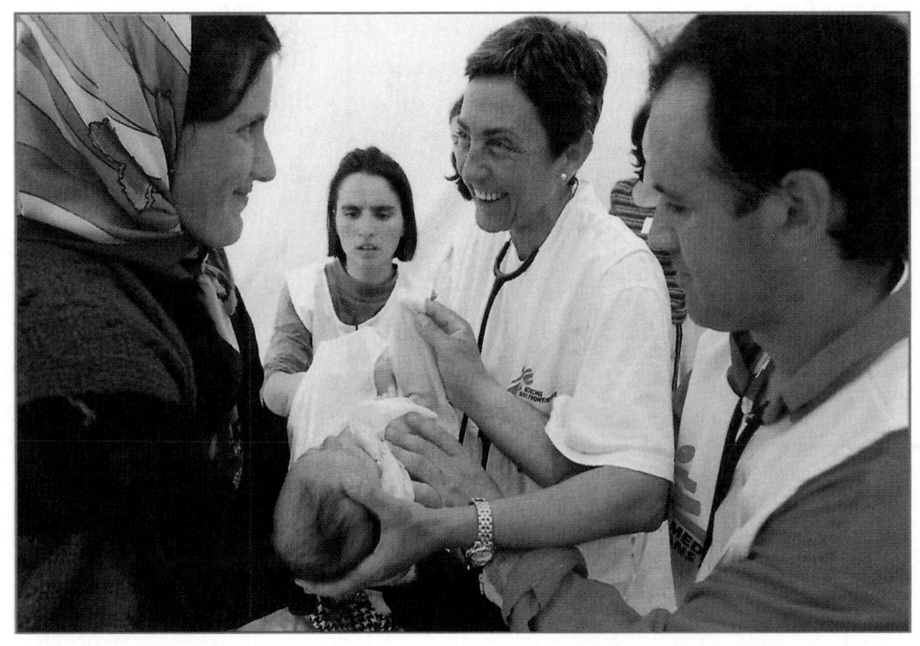

PUTTING IT TOGETHER

You have read about three groups that help people in communities. There are many other groups like them throughout the world. Each group helps people in different ways and in different places. However, all of these groups share the same goal: to work for the common good.

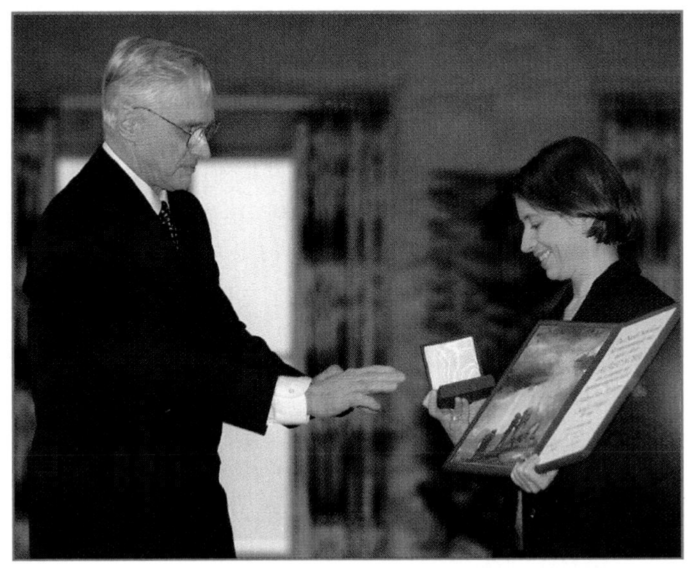

In 1999 Doctors Without Borders received a Nobel Peace Prize for its work.

Review and Assess

1. Write one sentence for the vocabulary word.
   nonprofit
2. What services does Doctors Without Borders provide?
3. Identify some of the ways in which volunteer groups help communities. Find out!
4. Explain why people who work for volunteer groups are good **citizens**.
5. What **caused** Doctors Without Borders volunteers to go to El Salvador in 2001?

Activities

Nonprofit groups like the Red Cross have symbols so that people can identify them. Use the library or the Internet to find the symbols of other groups, such as Habitat for Humanity and Doctors Without Borders. Make a poster showing the symbols and the groups they represent.

Write a letter to a nonprofit group discussed in this lesson. Thank its members for the work they do.

Chapter 9 REVIEW

VOCABULARY REVIEW

Number a sheet of paper from 1 to 3. Beside each number write the word or term from the list below that matches the description.

common good **nonprofit** **volunteer**

1. A person who chooses to do a job without getting paid
2. Something that is best for everyone
3. Something that is not done for profit, or money

CHAPTER COMPREHENSION

4. Explain why good citizens obey laws.
5. Identify two reasons for voting.
6. Write a sentence about an organization that works for the common good.

SKILL REVIEW

Read the sentences and answer the questions to practice the skill of identifying cause and effect.

> Cara's friend Nico failed his science test, so Cara volunteered to help him.
>
> Because Nico did well on his next test, he and Cara celebrated.

7. **Reading/Thinking Skill** In the first sentence, which event is the cause? Which event is the effect?
8. **Reading/Thinking Skill** In the second sentence, which event is the cause? Which event is the effect?
9. **Reading/Thinking Skill** Which signal words helped you identify the cause and effect in both sentences?

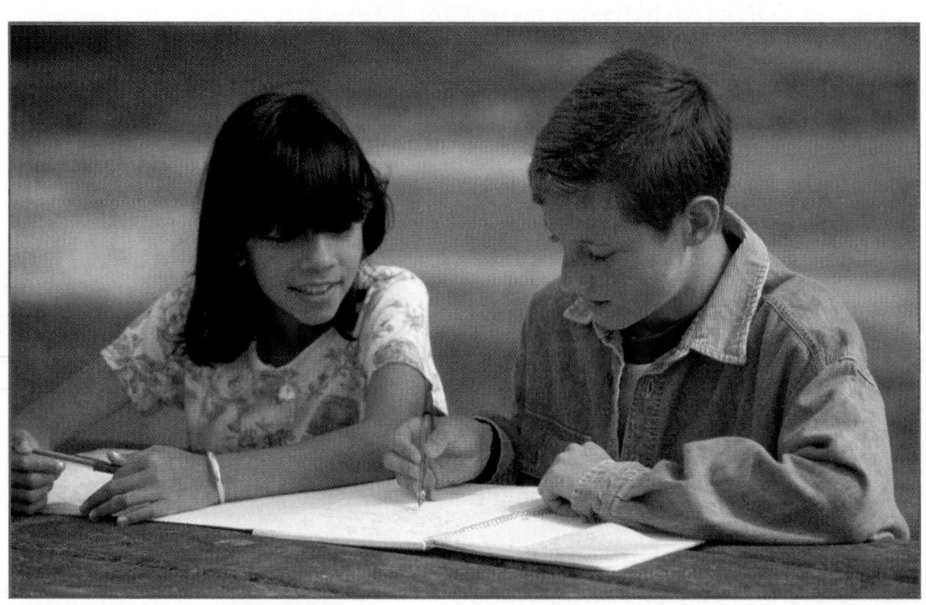

USING A CHART

10. Use the chart to identify two groups that help people in similar ways.

Nonprofit Group	What It Does
Habitat for Humanity	Helps people build homes
Red Cross	Helps during disasters
Doctors Without Borders	Gives medical care to communities around the world during disasters

Activity

Writing About Citizenship Suppose you were forming a volunteer group to help people in your community. Make a booklet describing your organization. Tell what purpose it would serve. Explain how it would work for the common good. Then share your booklet with your classmates. Find out how they feel about your ideas.

Use your Foldable to review what you have learned about citizens in action. As you look at the two sections of your Foldable, recall ways in which you can be a good citizen now and in the future. Discuss why it is a citizen's responsibility to be actively involved in the community and nation. Review your notes under the tabs of your Foldable to check your responses. Record any questions that you have, and discuss them with classmates or review the chapter to find answers.

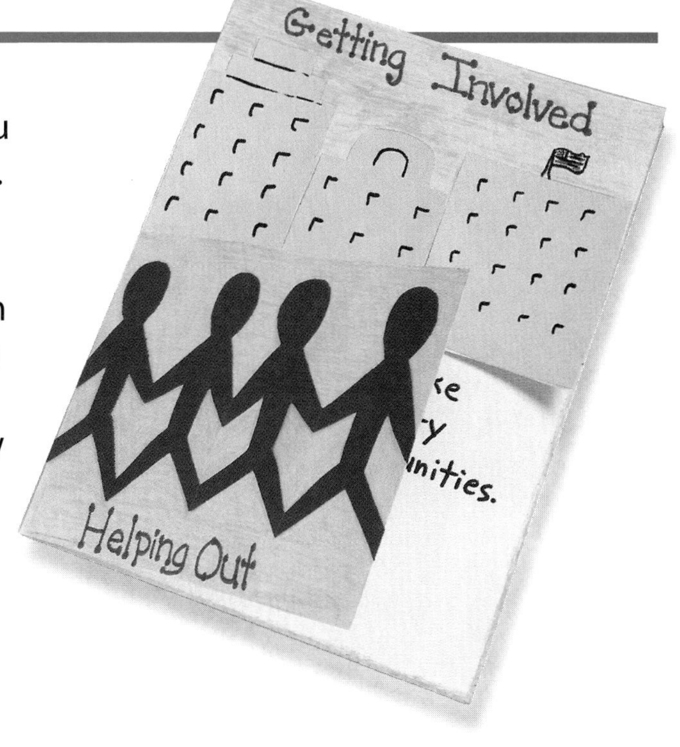

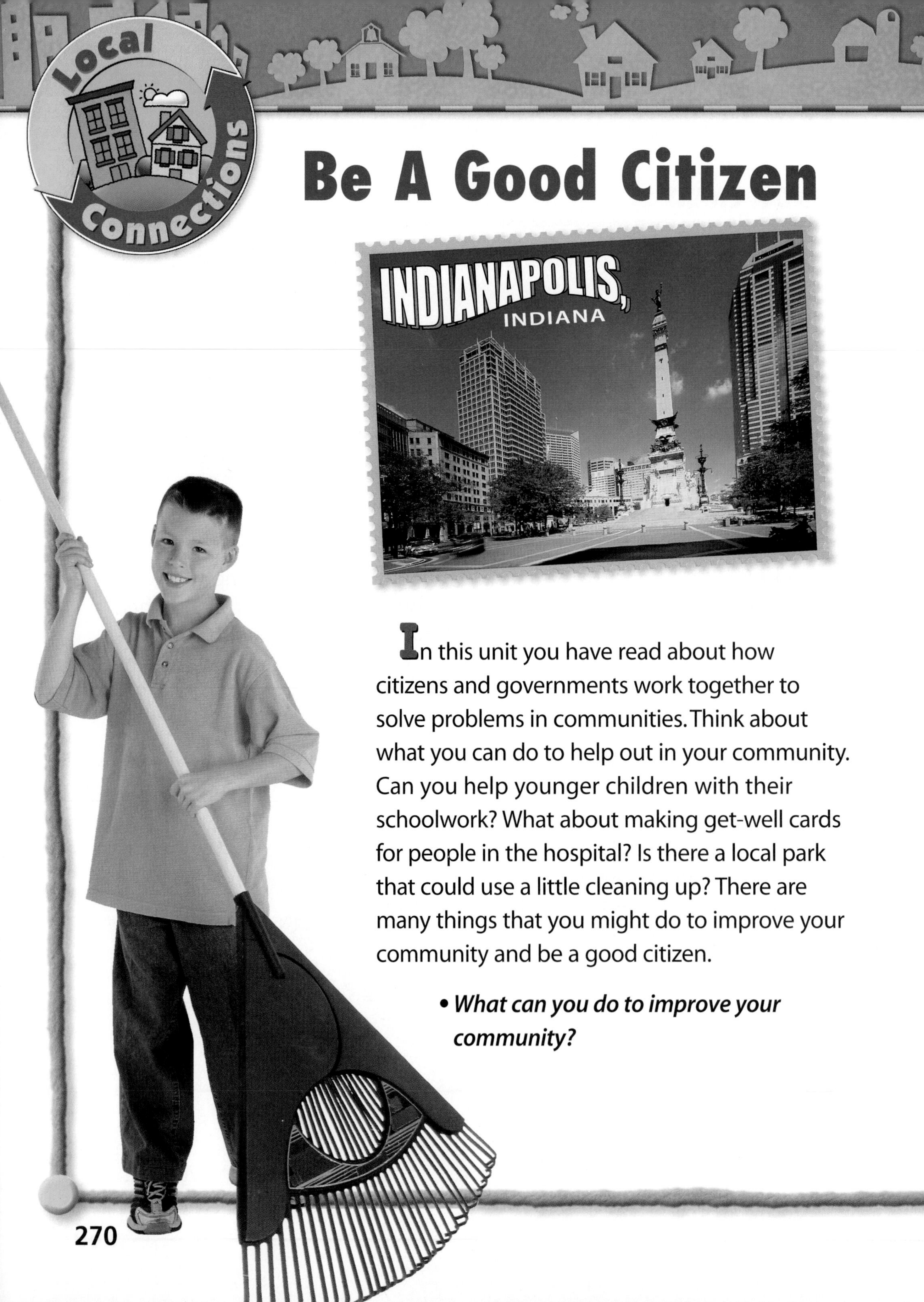

Be A Good Citizen

In this unit you have read about how citizens and governments work together to solve problems in communities. Think about what you can do to help out in your community. Can you help younger children with their schoolwork? What about making get-well cards for people in the hospital? Is there a local park that could use a little cleaning up? There are many things that you might do to improve your community and be a good citizen.

- ***What can you do to improve your community?***

Activity

Make an Action Plan

Materials
- oaktag or poster board
- markers or crayons
- paints, glitter, glue, or any other art material you like to decorate your poster

Step 1 Identify a problem in your community.

Step 2 Think of a solution to the problem. How can you help?

Step 3 Make a plan to solve the problem. Make a chart listing the things you need.

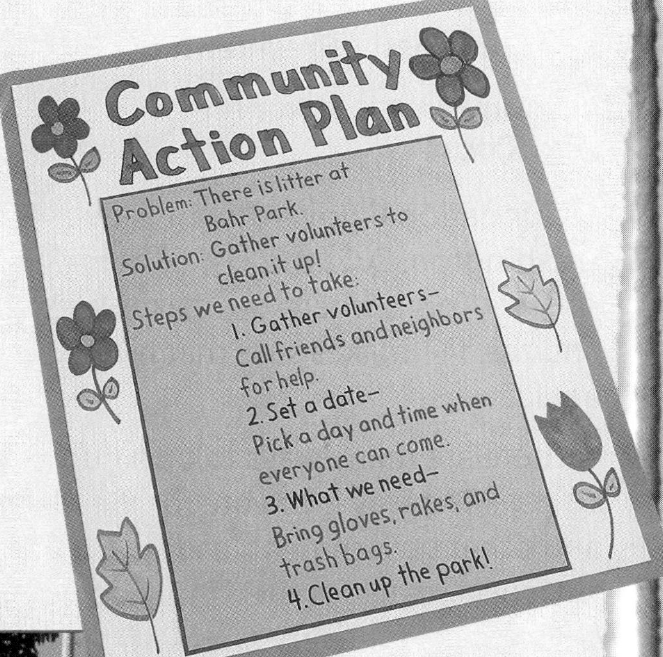

Community Action Plan
Problem: There is litter at Bahr Park.
Solution: Gather volunteers to clean it up!
Steps we need to take:
1. Gather volunteers– Call friends and neighbors for help.
2. Set a date– Pick a day and time when everyone can come.
3. What we need– Bring gloves, rakes, and trash bags.
4. Clean up the park!

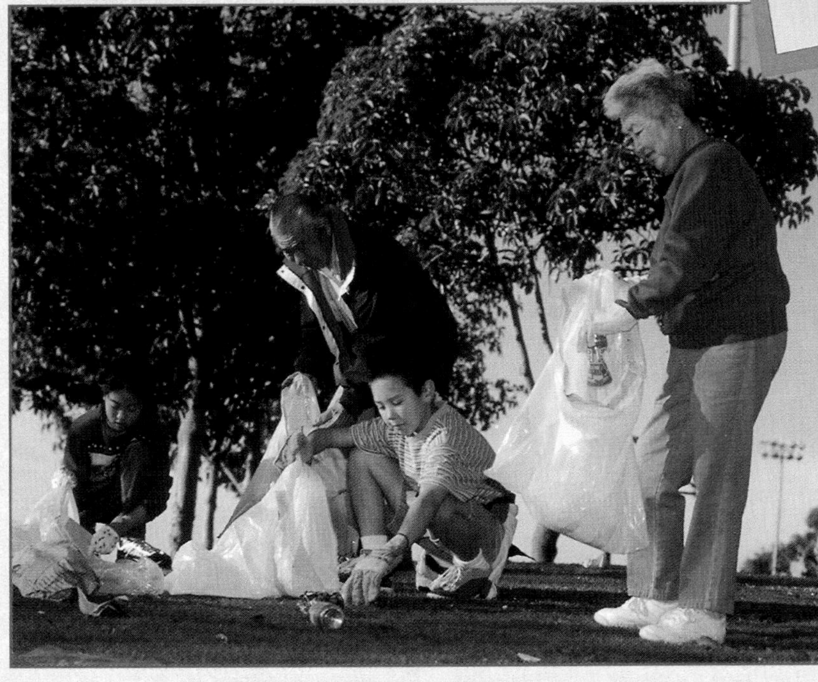

Step 4 Get to work! Follow the steps in your plan until the job is finished.

Unit 4 REVIEW

VOCABULARY REVIEW

Write the numbers 1 to 6 on a sheet of paper. Beside each number write the word or term that best completes the sentences in the paragraphs below.

capital	**common good**
Congress	**President**
Supreme Court	**volunteer**

Our national government is in Washington, D.C., the (1.) of our country. This is where (2.) makes laws and the (3.) makes sure that laws are fair.

There are many ways to be a good citizen. One way is to vote for the (4.) and other government leaders. Good citizens also act for the (5.) by doing what is best for everyone. Many citizens also help others without getting paid. A person who helps others without getting paid is a (6.).

TECHNOLOGY

To learn more about the people and places in this unit, visit www.mhschool.com and follow the links to Grade 3, Unit 4.

SKILL REVIEW

7. **Reading/Thinking Skill** Reread the first paragraph in the Vocabulary Review. Then identify the main idea and two of the supporting details.
8. **Reading/Thinking Skill** List three words or terms that show causes. List three words or terms that show effects.
9. **Geography Skill** Look at the grid map of the state of Georgia. In what box is the capital of Georgia? How do you know?
10. **Geography Skill** Where is the Okefenokee National Wildlife Refuge?

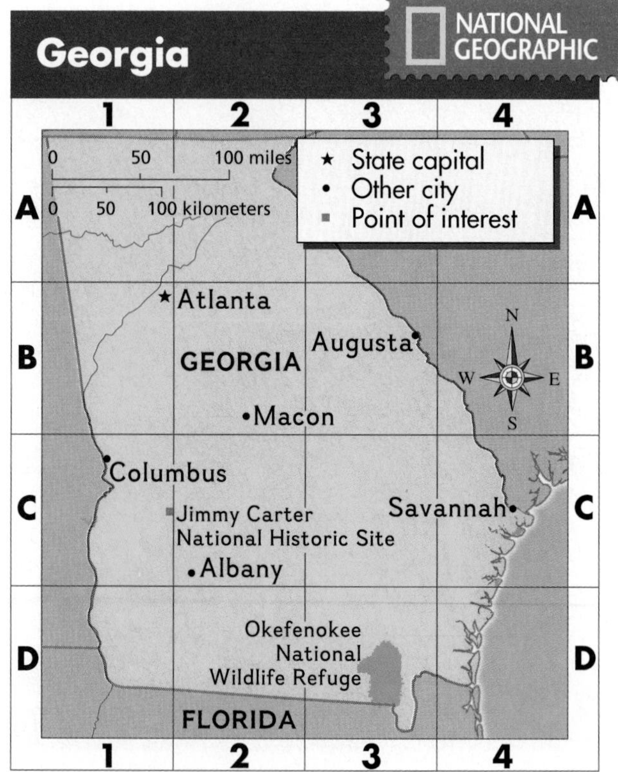

Read the passage and the questions that follow. Write the best answers on a piece of paper.

Every year people from around our country and the world visit Washington, D.C. They visit the monuments that remind them of our country's past. A monument is a building or statue made to honor a person or an event. Visitors come to see the city's museums. They also come to learn about our country's government.

1 What is the main idea of this paragraph?

- Every year people from around our country and the world visit Washington, D.C.
- People visit the monuments that remind them of our country's past.
- A monument is a building or statue made to honor a person or an event.
- Visitors come to see the city's museums.

2 Why do people visit Washington, D.C.?

- to see monuments
- to learn about our country's past
- to learn about our country's government
- all of the above

WRITING ACTIVITIES

Writing to Inform Write a short biography of someone you read about in this unit. Your biography should tell how that person worked for the common good.

Writing to Persuade Suppose you were one of our nation's leaders when they were trying to decide on a place for the capital of the United States. Write a speech telling where you think the capital should be and why.

Writing to Express Many people say the Pledge of Allegiance to show that they care about the United States. Write a pledge, poem, or song that shows how you feel about your country.

My Very Own Room

Mi propio cuartito

Story by Amada Irma Pérez
Illustrations by Maya Christina Gonzalez

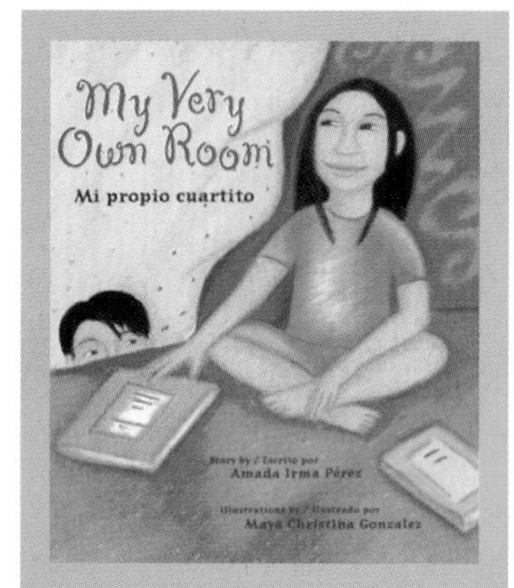

In this story a nine-year-old Mexican girl shares a room with her five brothers. She loves her brothers, but more than anything else, she wants a room of her own.

I tiptoed around our tiny, two bedroom house. I peeked behind the curtain that my mother had made from flour sacks to separate our living room from the storage closet.

"Aha! This is it! This could be my room." I imagined it with my own bed, table, and a lamp—a place where I could read the books I loved, write in my diary, and dream.

I sat down among the boxes. My mother must have heard me because she came in from the kitchen.

"Mama, it's perfect," I said, and I told her my idea.

"Ay, *mijita,* you do not understand. We are storing my sister's sewing machine and your uncle's garden tools. Someday they will need their things to make a better living in this country. And there's the furniture and old clothes," she said. Slowly she shook her head.

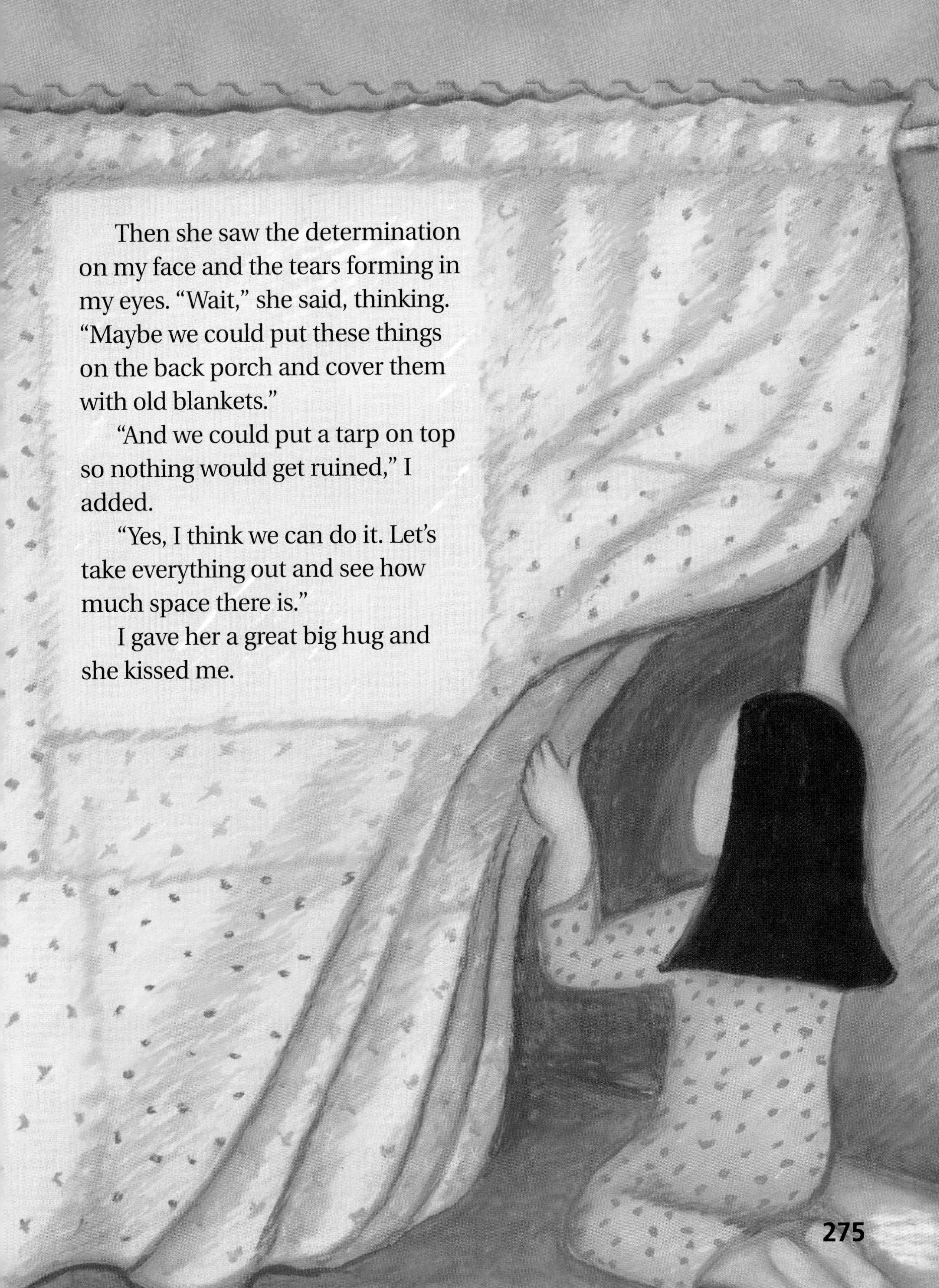

Then she saw the determination on my face and the tears forming in my eyes. “Wait,” she said, thinking. “Maybe we could put these things on the back porch and cover them with old blankets.”

“And we could put a tarp on top so nothing would get ruined,” I added.

“Yes, I think we can do it. Let’s take everything out and see how much space there is.”

I gave her a great big hug and she kissed me.

After breakfast we started pushing the old furniture out to the back porch. Everyone helped. We were like a mighty team of powerful ants.

We carried furniture, tools, and machines. We dragged bulging bags of old clothes and toys. We pulled boxes of treasures and overflowing junk. Finally, everything was out except for a few cans of leftover paint from the one time we had painted the house.

Each can had just a tiny bit of paint inside. There was pink and blue and white, but not nearly enough of any one color to paint the room.

"I have an idea," I said to my brothers. "Let's mix them!" Hector and Sergio helped me pour one can into another and we watched the colors swirl together. A new color began to appear, a little like purple and much stronger than pink. Magenta!

We painted and painted until we ran out of paint.

A little later Tio Pancho arrived with my new bed tied to the roof of his car. I ran out and hugged him. Papa helped him carry the bed in and carefully ease it into place.

My brothers jumped up and down and everybody clapped. Then Raul moved an empty wooden crate over to my new bed and stood it on end to make a bedside table for a lamp.

Then I lay on my new bed and stared at the ceiling, thinking. Something was still missing, the most important thing....

Books!

The next day I went to our public library and rushed home with my arms full of books, six to be exact. It was my lucky number, because there were six children in my family.

That evening, I turned on my lamp and read and read. My two littlest brothers, Mario and Victor, stood in the doorway holding back the flour-sack curtain. I invited them in. They cuddled up on my new bed and I read them a story. Then we said goodnight and they went back to their room.

I felt like the luckiest, happiest little girl in the whole world. Everyone in our family had helped to make my wish come true. Before I could even turn out the light, I fell asleep peacefully under a blanket of books—in my very own room.

Write About It!

Think about a time when someone helped you to get something you wanted. How did it make you feel? Write a paragraph explaining what you wanted, why you wanted it, and how someone helped you.

Many Cultures, One Country

What cultures make up our communities?

The cultures of people from around the world shape American communities.

Explore more about communities and culture at our Web site
www.mhschool.com

Chapter 10

THE Big IDEAS ABOUT...

People and Culture

In the United States people of many cultures share music, holidays, stories, and art. Culture is an important part of our lives. It shapes our communities and our country.

OUR COUNTRY'S PEOPLE

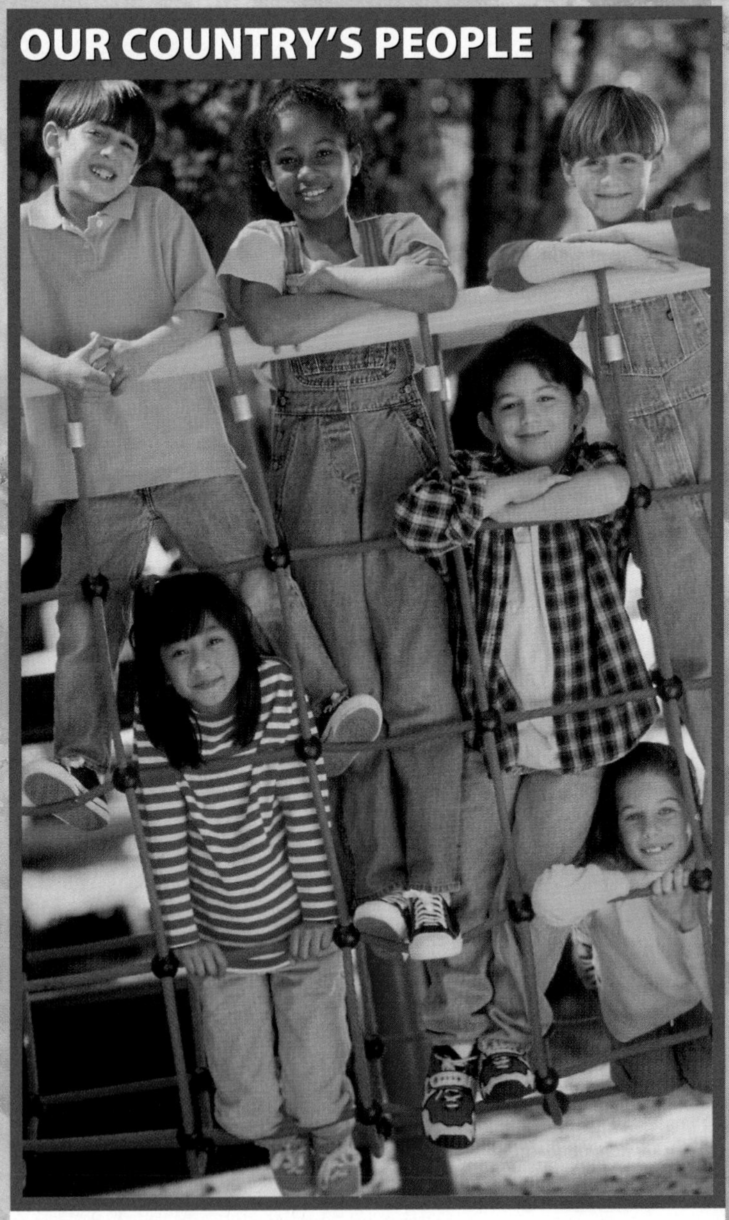

The United States is made up of people from many countries. We share each other's cultures. Together we form a strong and unified country.

SHARING CULTURE THROUGH STORIES

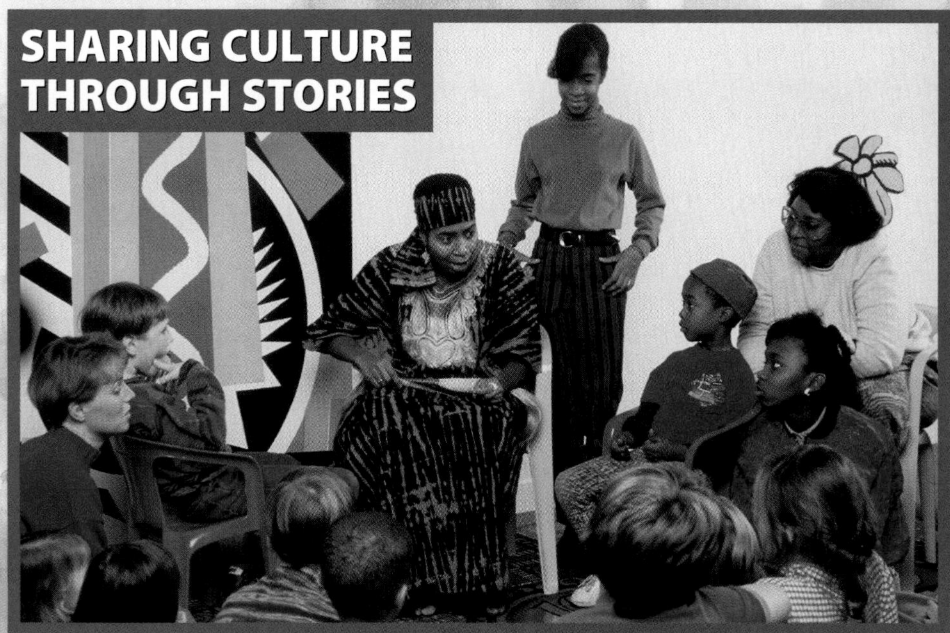

Stories are a way we share our cultures and learn about different cultures.

ARTISTS IN THE COMMUNITY

Artists show the world around them with paintings, photographs, and books. Diego Rivera's paintings often show scenes from Mexico's history.

Foldables

Use your Foldable to record what you learn about "People and Culture."

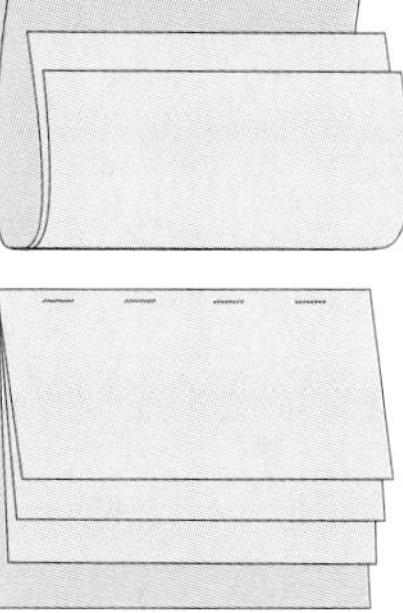

1. Place two sheets of paper one inch apart, forming a one-inch tab across the top.
2. Roll the bottom of the two sheets up to make three tabs the same size. Fold and staple.
3. Write the title of the chapter on the large tab and the lesson titles on the smaller tabs.

Lesson 1

Our Country's People

VOCABULARY

heritage

READING STRATEGY

How are Americans alike and different? Use the diagram to write a **main idea** and **supporting details.**

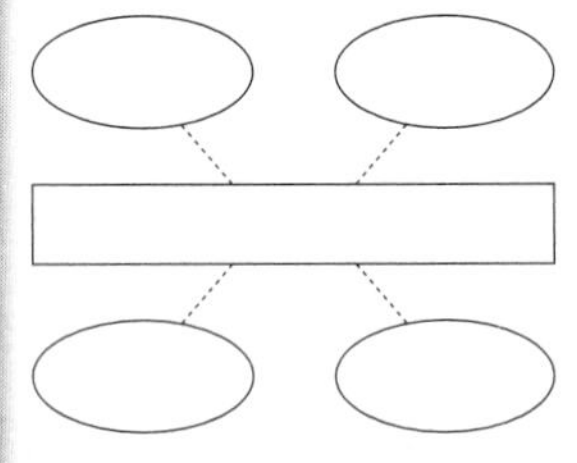

What makes Americans both alike and different?

Lesson Outline

- Sharing Cultures
- Coming to America
- Americans Share Beliefs

BUILD BACKGROUND

The United States is home to people from around the world. Here we learn about and enjoy each other's cultures. The mixture of many cultures is one thing that makes our country the special place it is.

In the United States people of many cultures come together to share their traditions and **heritages** with others.

SHARING CULTURES

Many communities in the United States are made up of people from different places and countries. Each group of people has its own special culture. Culture is the way of life for a group of people. It includes language, art, music, food, holidays, and customs. You may have eaten food or heard music from another country's culture. For example, spaghetti comes from Italian culture. Raga music comes from India's culture. Can you think of other examples?

As Americans we share and respect the cultures of all the people who make up our country. People often pass their cultural **heritage** on to others. Heritage is something handed down from earlier generations or from the past. Traditions are a part of heritage.

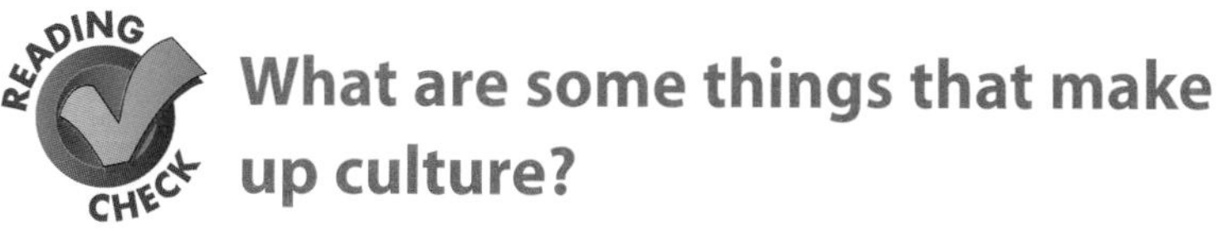

What are some things that make up culture?

COMING TO AMERICA

In Chapter 4 you read about the immigrants who came to America over a hundred years ago. Every year people still come from other countries to live in the United States.

These new Americans are like the immigrants who came here in the early 1900s. They want to find freedom and a better way of life. Parents want to live and work here. They want their children to get a good education. Like the earlier immigrants, our new neighbors bring their own cultures and heritages with them.

Look at the Datagraphic on page 287. It shows how immigration changed from 1900 to 1998.

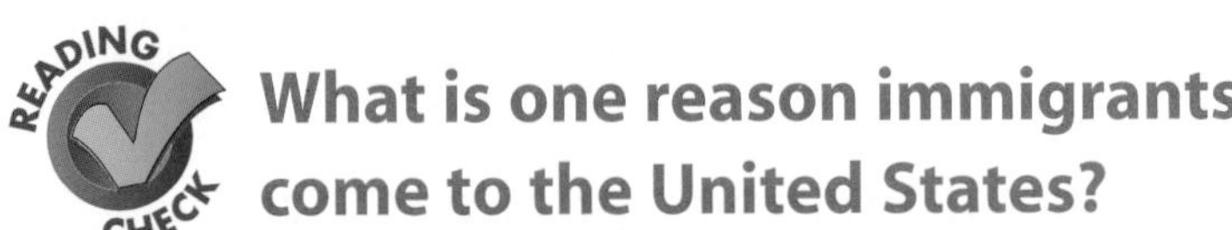

What is one reason immigrants come to the United States?

When immigrants become citizens, they pledge allegiance to the United States.

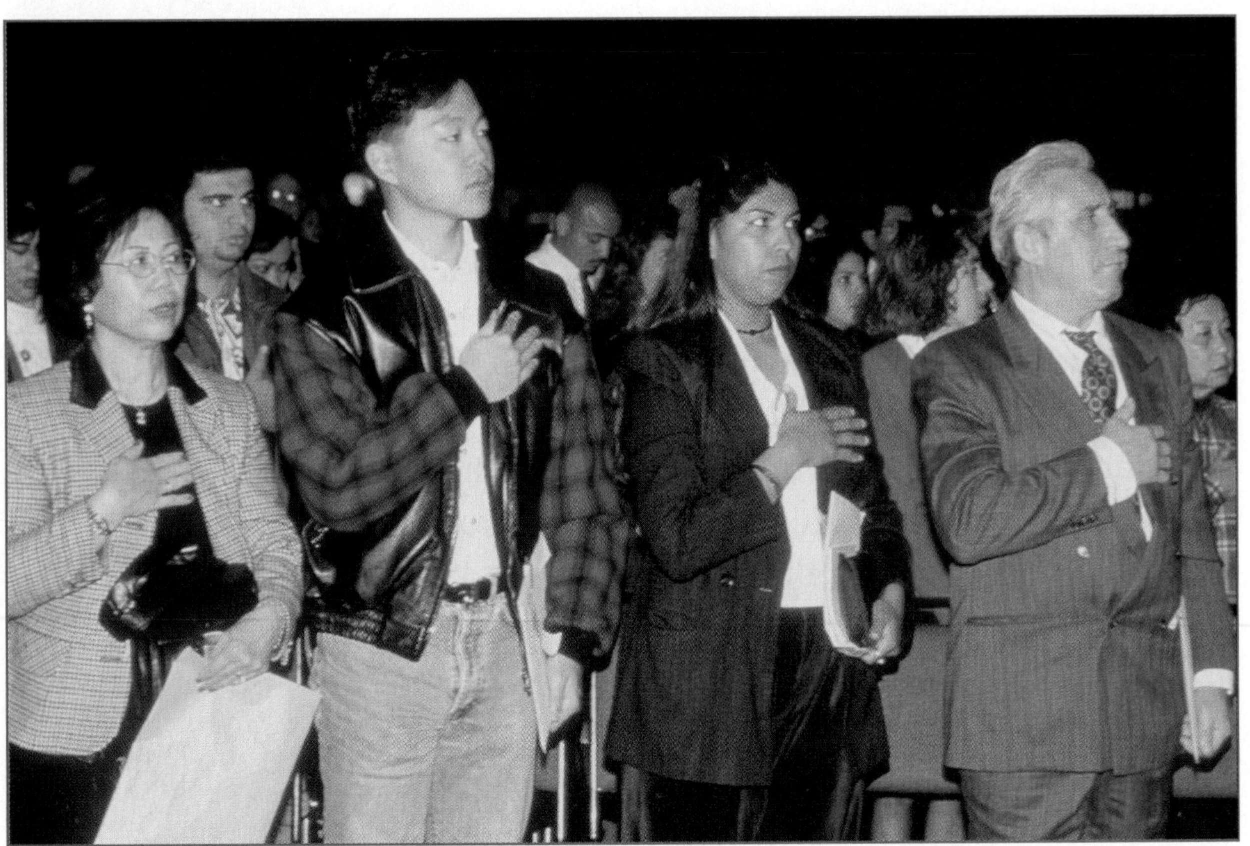

DATAGRAPHIC

Immigrants Then and Now

The two graphs show the top five countries of birth for immigrants to the United States in 1900 and in 1998. Study the information, and answer the questions below.

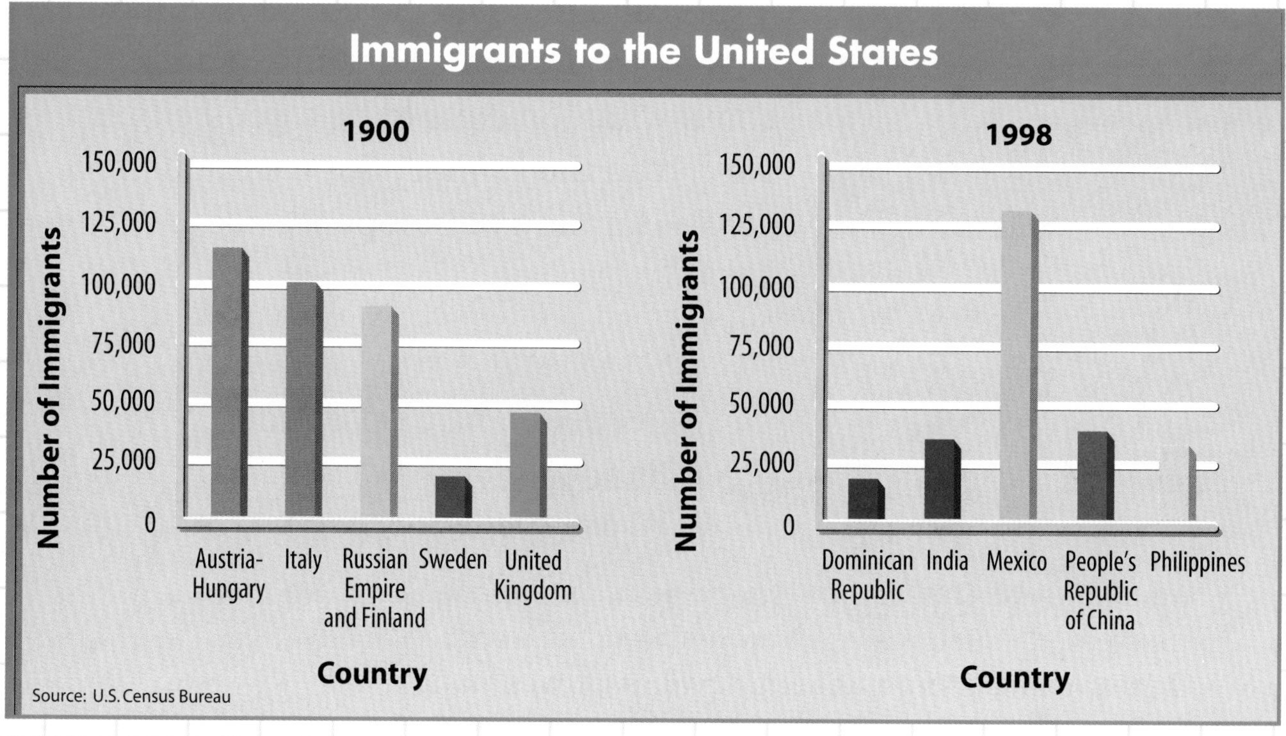

Questions

1. What was the top country of birth for immigrants to the United States in 1900?
2. What part of the world did most immigrants come from in 1998?
3. What is the source of the information shown on these graphs?

To learn more, visit our website at
www.mhschool.com

AMERICANS SHARE BELIEFS

Americans come from many cultures. Yet all Americans share some beliefs. We believe in being honest and fair with each other. We believe everyone deserves an equal chance to succeed. We also believe in working to make our communities better. We treat each other with respect.

Americans have many rights as citizens. We also know that we have many responsibilities. Our government is based on a belief in good citizenship. Think about what it means to be a good citizen. Then read the Primary Source quote from the Declaration of Independence.

***quote from* "The Declaration of Independence"**
— Thomas Jefferson, July 4, 1776

We hold these truths to be **self-evident**, that all men are created equal; that they are **endowed** by their Creator with certain **unalienable rights**; that among these are life, liberty, and the pursuit of happiness.

What are the beliefs described in this quotation?

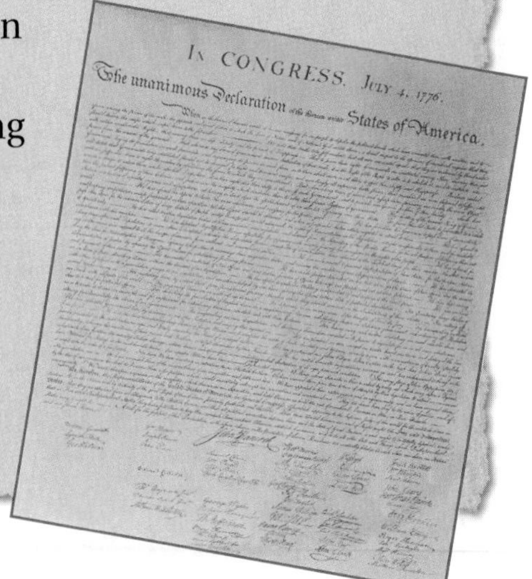
IN CONGRESS. July 4, 1776.
The unanimous Declaration of the thirteen united States of America.

self-evident: easily seen or understood
endowed: given
unalienable rights: freedoms that cannot be taken away

What is one belief that Americans share?

PUTTING IT TOGETHER

The United States is made up of people from many countries. Each group of people brings its own culture and heritage. As Americans we share in the cultures of many groups of people. We also share important beliefs about what it means to be an American citizen.

Review and Assess

1. Write a sentence for the vocabulary word.

   heritage

2. What are some beliefs that Americans share?
3. What makes Americans both alike and different from each other?
4. How do people from different countries pass on their **cultural** heritage?
5. What is one **effect** of immigrants coming to the United States?

Look at the two graphs on page 287. On a copy of a world map, identify the five countries where most immigrants came from in 1900. Draw red lines linking these countries to the United States. Then identify the five countries where most immigrants came from in 1998. Draw blue lines to link these countries to the United States.

Suppose you have a friend in another country who is about to move to your community. **Write** a letter to him or her explaining what life is like in your community.

Understanding Hemispheres

Earth is a **sphere**. A sphere is round, like a ball. A globe, which is a model of Earth, is also a sphere. If you look at a globe, you can see only half of it at a time. If you could look at Earth, you would see only half of it at a time. The part of Earth or the globe that you see is a **hemisphere**. A hemisphere is half of a sphere. *Hemi* means "half."

VOCABULARY

sphere
hemisphere
equator

LEARN THE SKILL

Geographers divide Earth in two ways—from side to side and from top to bottom. This means that we divide Earth into four halves, or hemispheres.

1. **The maps below show the Western and Eastern Hemispheres.**
   In which hemisphere is Australia? In which hemisphere is South America and North America?

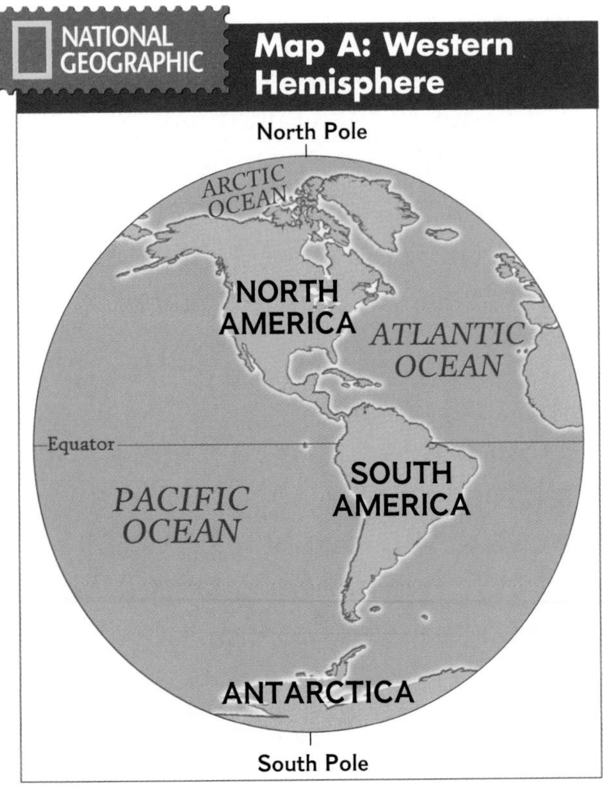

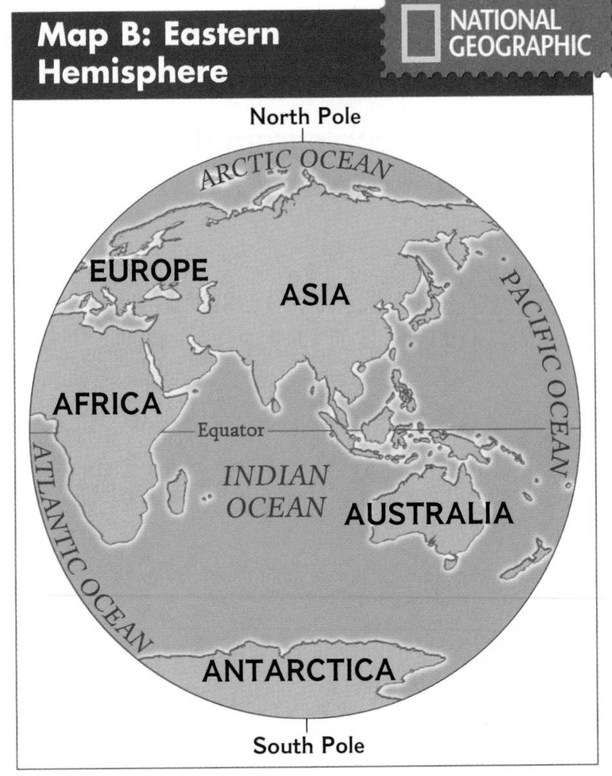

2. **The maps on page 291 show the Northern and Southern Hemispheres.**
   In which hemisphere is North America?

3. **The equator is an imaginary line around Earth. It divides the Northern and Southern Hemispheres.**
   In which hemisphere is the North Pole? In which hemisphere is the South Pole?

TRY THE SKILL

Look at the maps to answer the questions.

1. Name the four hemispheres.
2. In what three hemispheres is Europe?
3. The equator crosses which continents?

EXTEND THE SKILL

Find the countries below on a globe. Name the hemisphere in which each country is located.

- Mexico
- Brazil
- Australia
- Italy
- China
- Tanzania

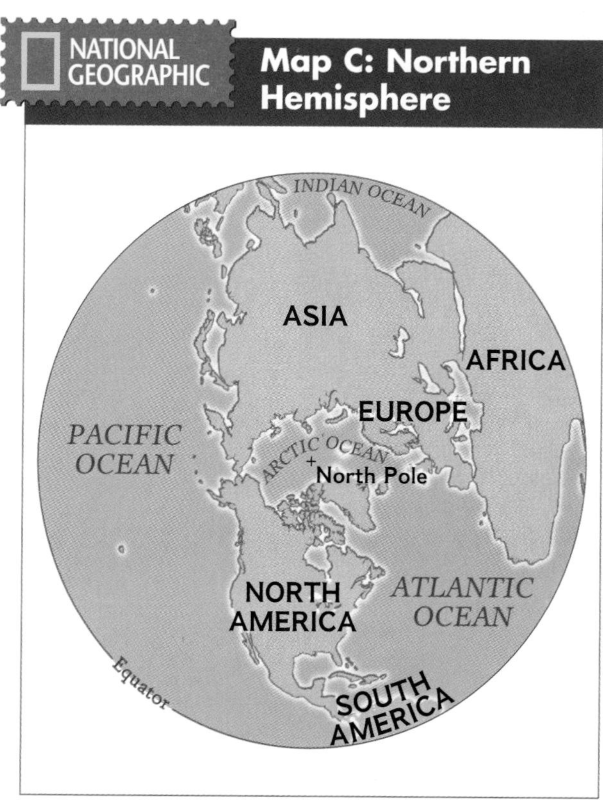

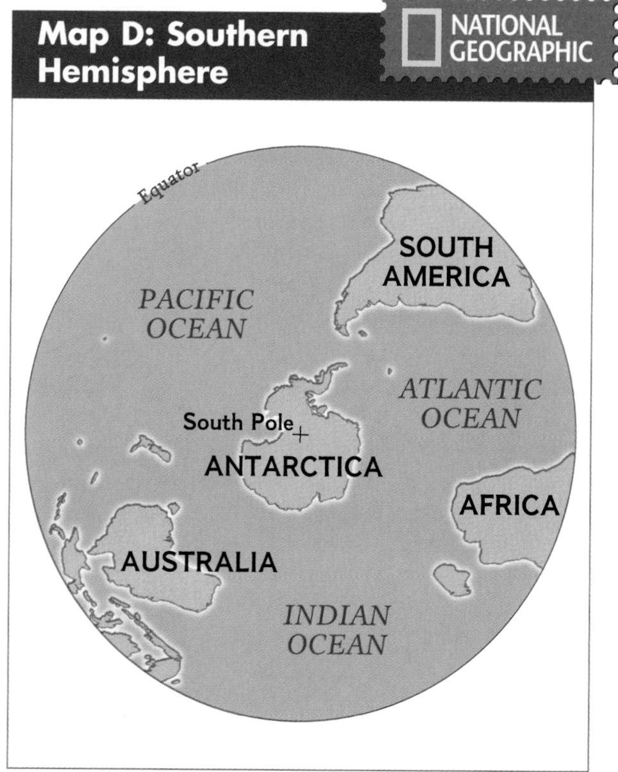

Sharing Culture Through Stories

VOCABULARY

hero

myth

legend

PEOPLE

Harriet Tubman

David Crockett

READING STRATEGY

Copy the diagram. Use it to show one **cause** and **effect** of telling stories about heroes.

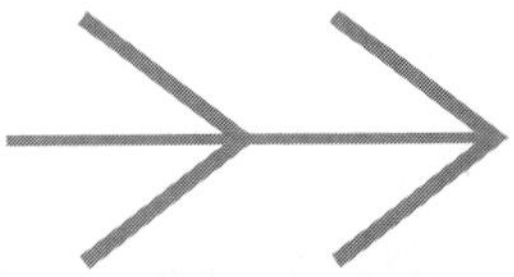

How do stories about heroes shape our culture?

Lesson Outline

- Communities Have Heroes
- Historical Heroes
- American Legends
- Sharing Fact and Legend

BUILD BACKGROUND

Reading and listening to stories is one way we share our culture with other people. Often these stories are about people who have helped to shape the culture of their community, state, or country. In this lesson you will read about some stories that are important in the culture of the United States.

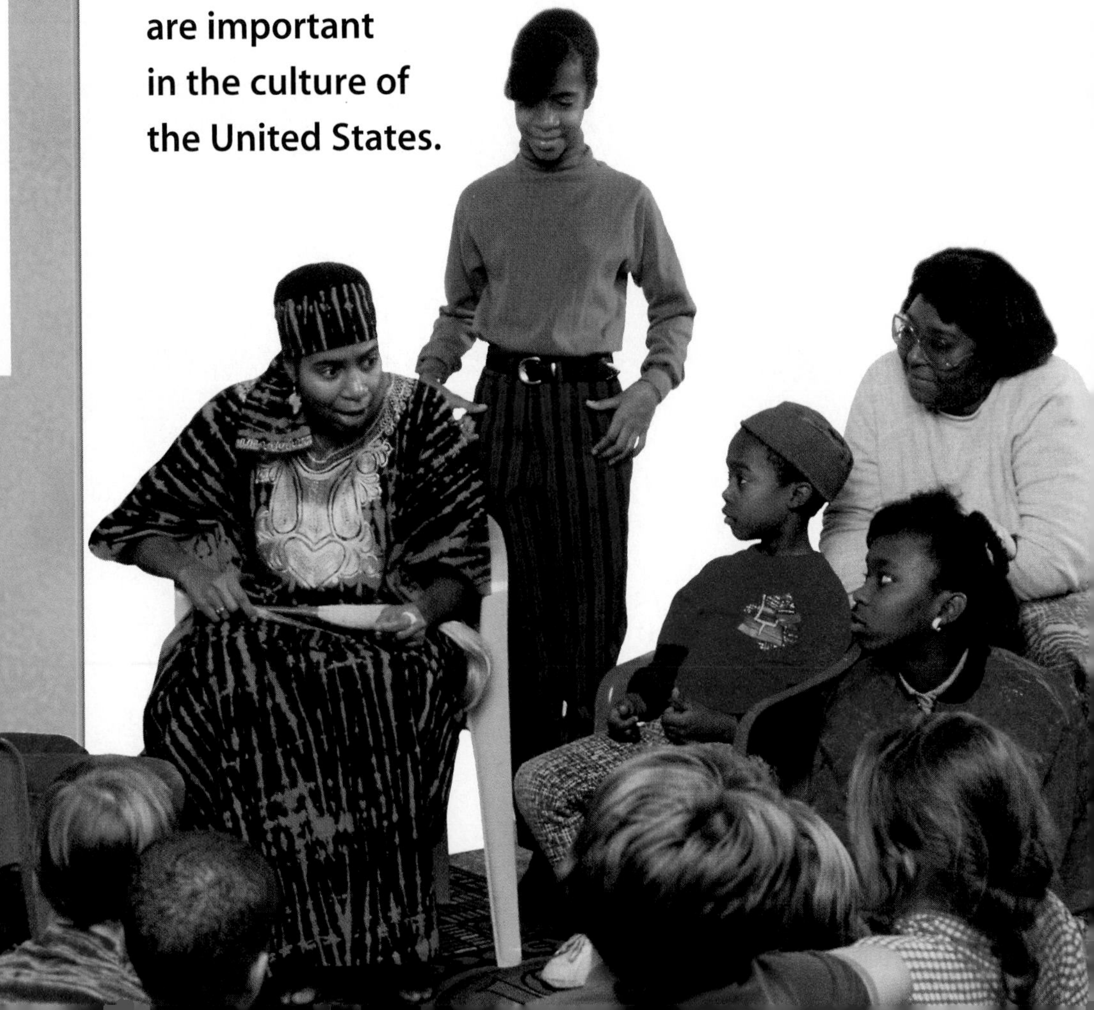

COMMUNITIES HAVE HEROES

A **hero** is someone who is looked up to because of his or her qualities or achievements. For centuries people in different communities have told stories about their heroes. The stories were one way for a group of people to pass on its heritage. They also helped people understand important ideas or beliefs. These stories were part of their culture.

Ancient Greek vases (left) often showed heroes. Athena (below) is a goddess in ancient Greek **myths**.

In Ancient Greece people told stories about real-life heroes, such as soldiers or athletes. The Greeks also told special stories called **myths**. A myth is a story that tells about a belief of a group of people. It may try to explain a custom or why something happens in nature.

One Greek myth told how the city of Athens got its name. The myth said that two gods made gifts to the city. The god who gave the most useful gift would win the city. The goddess Athena gave an olive tree. Olives and olive oil come from olive trees. Both were very useful. The city was named for Athena. The myth showed how Athenians liked to think of themselves as people who valued useful things.

Why do people tell stories about heroes?

HISTORICAL HEROES

Many of the people we admire today are real-life heroes who did amazing things in the past. **Harriet Tubman** is one such hero. Tubman was born enslaved in the South. In 1849 she escaped to freedom. For many years after her escape, Tubman risked her life helping others to freedom. She guided over three hundred people along the Underground Railroad. This was not a real railroad. It was a group of people who helped enslaved people escape along secret routes to the North or to Canada.

Harriet Tubman became the most famous "conductor" on the Underground Railroad. Today we remember Tubman for what she did to help others. Her story makes us think about what she stood for—courage and a belief in freedom.

Harriet Tubman (above) is an American hero. She helped enslaved people escape to freedom using hiding places (left) along the Underground Railroad.

Frontier Hero

David Crockett was another real-life American hero. He is known as a leader, a scout, a hunter, and a storyteller. Crockett was born in 1786. He grew up with his family on the Tennessee frontier. He had little money or education. Still, he became a success. He served in the army. He was elected to state office. He even served in the United States Congress. Later he helped Texans fight for their freedom from Mexico. Crockett died at the Battle of The Alamo in 1836.

After his death Crockett's life became a **legend**. A legend is a story passed down through the years that many people believe, but which is not entirely true. Stories about Crockett's adventures grew. Books and plays were written about him. People loved hearing about Crockett's courage and independence. Today David Crockett is remembered as both an important historical figure and a legend of the American frontier.

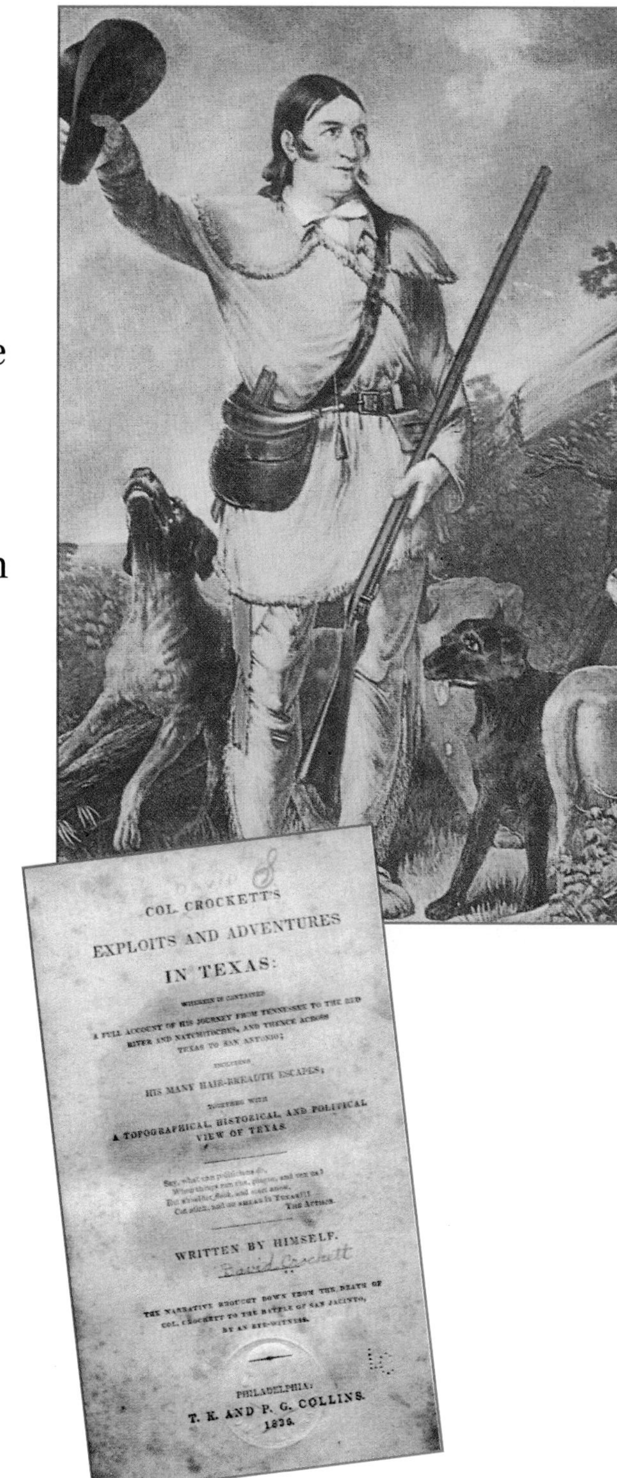

COL. CROCKETT'S
EXPLOITS AND ADVENTURES
IN TEXAS:
A FULL ACCOUNT OF HIS JOURNEY FROM TENNESSEE TO THE RED RIVER AND NATCHITOCHES, AND THENCE ACROSS TEXAS TO SAN ANTONIO;
HIS MANY HAIR-BREADTH ESCAPES;
A TOPOGRAPHICAL, HISTORICAL, AND POLITICAL VIEW OF TEXAS.
WRITTEN BY HIMSELF.
David Crockett
PHILADELPHIA:
T. K. AND P. G. COLLINS.
1836.

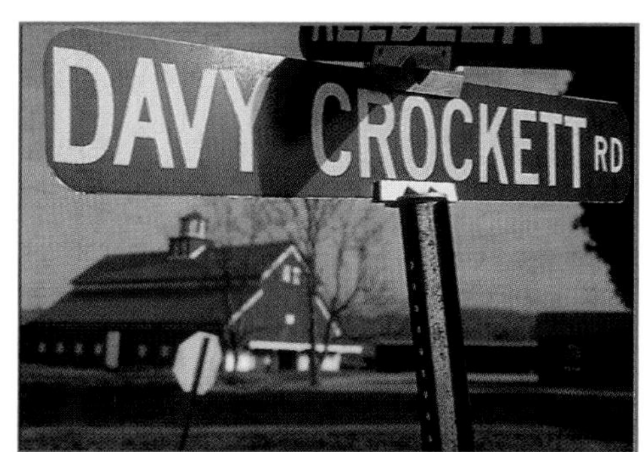

David "Davy" Crockett (top) became a **legend** for helping people. He wrote his life story (above). Today streets are named for him (left).

READING CHECK **What made Harriet Tubman and David Crockett heroes?**

AMERICAN LEGENDS

Our country has many legends about heroes who were not real people. One of the most famous of these make-believe heroes is Paul Bunyan. Bunyan was a lumberjack. A lumberjack is someone who cuts down trees and saws them into boards.

Paul Bunyan is famous for his great strength and size. Stories say he was more than 50 feet tall! His blue ox, Babe, was the size of a mountain. In the stories the two friends created many of our country's landforms. In one story Paul and Babe dug some ponds to get drinking water. When they finished, they had made the Great Lakes. In another story the two friends went west. As Paul walked, he dragged his ax. The ax made a deep ditch that turned into the Grand Canyon.

Stories about Paul Bunyan were first told by real-life lumberjacks around their campfires. Today we still laugh at the stories about Paul Bunyan and Babe. We admire his strength, hard work, and ability to solve any problem.

A statue of Paul Bunyan stands in Brainerd, Minnesota (above). In one story Bunyan and Babe make the Grand Canyon (right).

The Legend of Pecos Bill

Pecos Bill is one of our country's favorite make-believe cowboy heroes. People enjoy stories about his courage and strength. In the legend Pecos Bill was born in east Texas. When his pioneer family moved, he fell out of their wagon near the Pecos River. Coyotes raised Bill. He grew to be the biggest and toughest cowboy in the West.

People say Bill was the first cowboy to sing cowboy songs, wear spurs on his boots, and lasso animals. His ranch was so big that it covered all of New Mexico. One story says he was so strong that he once roped a railroad train! Yet another story says that Bill and his wife, Slue-Foot Sue, rode down the Rio Grande on a catfish as big as a whale!

In one story Pecos Bill and Slue-Foot Sue ride down the Rio Grande on a catfish (top). Today books still pass on the story of Pecos Bill (above).

What do the stories of Paul Bunyan and Pecos Bill have in common?

SHARING FACT AND LEGEND

With many American heroes, some of what we read is fact and some is legend. By sharing both kinds of stories, we share our beliefs and values. We use the stories as a guide for the way people should act. One famous American hero we share stories about is our first President, George Washington.

George Washington was our first President. He is also an American hero.

Washington's actions made him a hero to many Americans. When we share stories about Washington, we hope that others will try to be like him. What lesson can we learn from the legend below?

excerpt from **The Life of Washington**
— by Mason Weems, 1809

"George," said his father, "do you know who killed that beautiful little cherry-tree yonder in the garden?". . . He bravely called out, "I can't tell a lie, Pa; you know I can't tell a lie. I did cut it with my hatchet." . . . "Run to my arms, you dearest boy," cried his father. . . . Such an act of heroism [telling the truth] in my son is more worth than a thousand trees."

What does this story say about the kind of person George Washington was? Why was his father so proud of him?

What is one reason that there are legends about real people?

PUTTING IT TOGETHER

People in communities enjoy telling stories about heroes. Sometimes we tell true stories. Sometimes we tell myths and legends. All of these stories make us think about our heroes' good deeds. They show us actions and beliefs that are important to our community and our country. Reading and listening to these stories is an important way to share our culture.

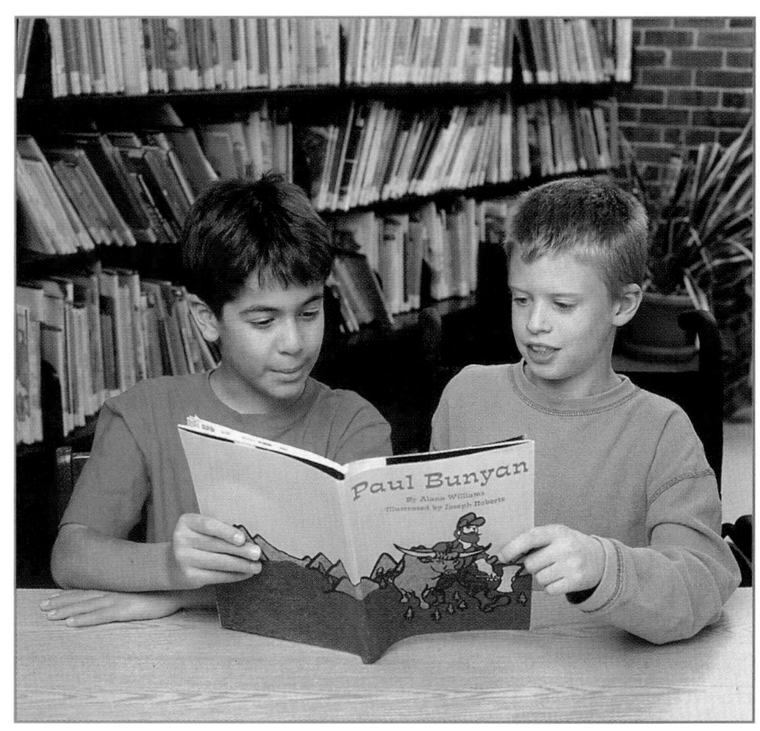

Review and Assess

1. Write one sentence for each of the vocabulary words.

   hero **legend**
   myth

2. How did Harriet Tubman help enslaved people?
3. Explain how stories about heroes shape our culture.
4. Think about the different heroes you read about in this lesson. List three things about them that are important in American **culture**.
5. **Summarize** the story of one of the American legends you read about in this lesson.

Read a biography of a real-life person you admire. Present a report about that person's life to your class. For your presentation you could dress up as your hero or tell his or her story using puppets.

Write a myth or legend about one of your heroes.

Using Parts of a Source

Books are important sources of information. Books have special parts that help you find the information you want. Learning how to use the different parts of a book will help you learn better and faster.

VOCABULARY

table of contents
glossary
index
keyword

LEARN THE SKILL

The numbered list below tells about some of the parts of a book.

1. **Table of Contents**
   A **table of contents** lists the parts of a book and tells the page on which each begins. It is found in the front of the book.

2. **Glossary**
   A **glossary** is an alphabetical list of difficult words and their meanings. It may also tell how to pronounce the words. A glossary is found in the back of the book. If you need to know the meaning of a word that is not listed in the glossary, you should use a dictionary.

CONTENTS

GLOSSARY

hero • legislature

hero A person you look up to because of his or her personal qualities or achievements.
history The story or record of what has happened in the past.

I

independence Freedom from others.

K

kin A person's whole family; relatives.
knowhow The knowledge of how to do something.

L

legacy A part of our past that we value in our lives today.
legend A story passed down through the years that many people believe, but which is not entirely true.

3. **Index**
An **index** is an alphabetical list of people, places, events, and other subjects that are mentioned in a book. It gives the pages where each is discussed. An index is found in the back of the book.

TRY THE SKILL

1. Look at the table of contents on page 300. On what pages can you read about Daniel Boone blazing trails?

2. Look at the glossary on page 300. What does *kin* mean?

3. Look at the index below. On what pages can you find information about David Crockett on the frontier and in the army?

INDEX

EXTEND THE SKILL

Suppose you wanted to learn more about heroes of the Old West. You could use a computer to do a **keyword** search on the Internet. A keyword is a word you use to find other information.

Think of a subject that interests you. Then find a search engine that you like. A search engine is a computer program that uses keywords to find information on the Internet. List three words or terms that you would use to do a keyword search.

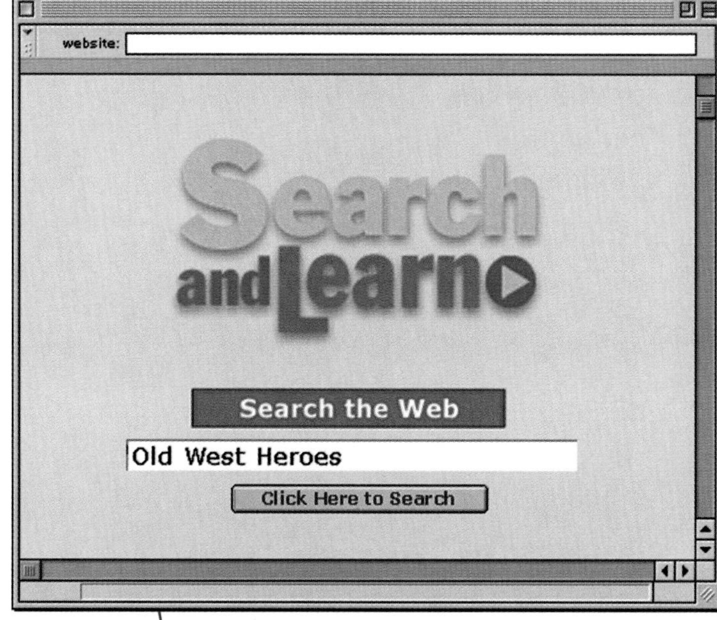

Artists in the Community

VOCABULARY

museum

daguerreotype

mural

PEOPLE

Mark Twain

Louis Daguerre

Berenice Abbott

Charles Harris

Diego Rivera

READING STRATEGY

Use the diagram to **compare** and **contrast** two artists discussed in this lesson. Show how they are alike and different.

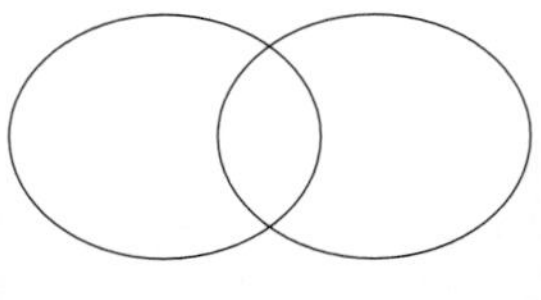

How do artists shape the culture of their communities?

Lesson Outline

- A City Honors Mark Twain
- Looking at Our Communities
- Painting History

BUILD BACKGROUND

Who is your favorite writer? How does he or she make you feel about the world? Writers and artists create stories and pictures that describe our world in special ways. Their work is important. It shapes and changes the cultural heritage of our communities.

A CITY HONORS MARK TWAIN

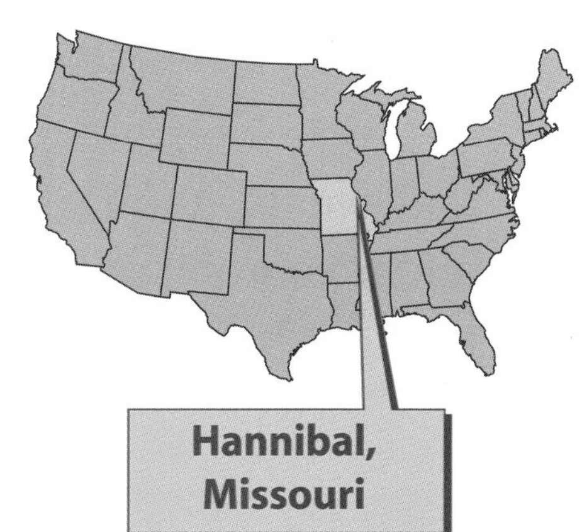

One famous American writer, **Mark Twain**, was born in **Hannibal, Missouri**, in 1835. Hannibal is a city in northeast Missouri. It is on the Mississippi River. Mark Twain used Hannibal as the setting of some of his books, including *The Adventures of Tom Sawyer.*

The community of Hannibal is very proud of Mark Twain. Much of the downtown area still looks the way it did when he was a boy. His childhood home is a **museum**. A museum is a building where works of art, science, or history are placed for people to see.

Every July Hannibal honors Mark Twain with a special celebration, "National Tom Sawyer Days." It includes a fence-painting contest based on a scene in *The Adventures of Tom Sawyer.*

How do people in Hannibal honor Mark Twain?

Mark Twain (above) wrote many books. The "Tom and Becky Look-Alike Contest" in Hannibal (left) recalls one of Twain's most famous books, *The Adventures of Tom Sawyer.* So does the "Fence-Painting Contest" (opposite page).

LOOKING AT OUR COMMUNITIES

Artists look for new ways to show people and events. About 1837 the French artist and inventor **Louis Daguerre** invented a type of photograph called a **daguerreotype** (duh GAYR uh tighp). This was an image made on a thin sheet of copper that was coated with silver. The sheet was placed in a camera, the way we use film today. Daguerreotypes made pictures that were clear and detailed.

Photography helped people around the world to learn about each other in a new way. Before photography artists drew or painted scenes. Now artists can make an instant record of people, places, and events. How do photos help you see and remember special people or events?

Louis Daguerre (above) invented a type of photography. Berenice Abbott (below) took many pictures of New York City (right).

Charles Harris (right) photographed African American life in Pittsburgh (above).

Seeing America Through Pictures

When photography was invented, cities were changing and growing. Many artists wanted to record those changes. **Berenice Abbott** was an American photographer. She took many photos of New York City in the 1930s.

Artists across America took pictures of their communities. **Charles Harris** was a photographer in Pittsburgh, Pennsylvania. He took thousands of photographs of the African American community there. These photos show what life was like in Pittsburgh in the 1900s.

Many artists have created special photos of American life. Their pictures are another way of sharing our culture.

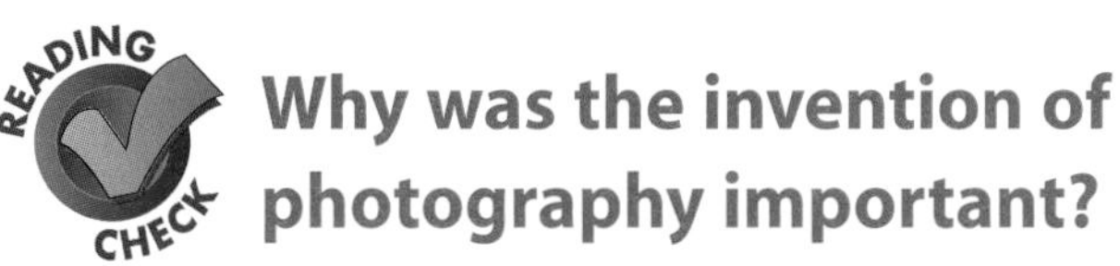

Why was the invention of photography important?

Exploring TECHNOLOGY

Changes in Cameras

Cameras have come a long way since their invention in the early 1800s. The first cameras made photographs on silver plates. Then people learned to take pictures using film.

The newest cameras are digital. They use no film at all. How does this work? First you take a picture, just as you would with a regular camera. The image is changed inside the camera into tiny bits of colored light. The picture bits are stored in the camera's memory. Digital cameras also let you view the photos you take. If you do not like a photo, you can press the "delete" button. The picture will be erased.

Rivera painted this mural (above) in San Francisco, California in 1931. Paintings by Rivera and his wife, the artist Frida Kahlo (below), hang in museums around the world.

PAINTING HISTORY

Diego Rivera was a famous Mexican artist. He painted many **murals** in Mexico and the United States. A mural is a large picture that is painted on a wall or ceiling. Rivera liked to paint murals in public buildings. That way people could see and enjoy his work. Many of his murals showed scenes from Mexican history. His murals brought Mexican history to life for the people of his country.

Rivera also painted murals that showed people in everyday life. He wanted the people looking at his paintings to see others like themselves. He felt that would help people to see that their lives are important. Rivera's work led other artists to paint murals, too. He encouraged both Mexicans and Americans to be proud of their cultural heritages.

READING CHECK **How did Diego Rivera share the culture of his country?**

PUTTING IT TOGETHER

Writers, photographers, and artists have shaped the culture of communities in America and around the world. By looking at the works of these artists, we better understand how our culture changes and grows. Artists are important people in our communities. They help us share our culture in different ways.

Review and Assess

1. Write one sentence for each of the vocabulary words.

   daguerreotype **mural**
   museum

2. How do the people of Hannibal, Missouri, celebrate the life of Mark Twain?

3. How do writers and artists shape the culture of their communities?

4. How might an artist's **cultural** heritage affect the artistic work that he or she does?

5. Describe how photography **affected** the way we could learn about other cultures.

Suppose you are an artist planning a mural. Make a list of things you might include to show what your community is like. Choose one thing from your list, and draw it on a piece of paper.

Write a description of one of the paintings or photographs in this lesson. Explain how you feel about the work of art. Share your description with the class.

BIOGRAPHY

Focus on Respect

Maya Lin

"The creative process isn't about sitting at a desk and waiting for it to hit you. . . . Artwork is very much research, reading, and then letting it sift through your head."

As a child Maya Lin always liked making things. She spent hours making pottery at the art school where her father was a teacher. It was not too long after that that she helped create one of America's most famous public monuments.

Maya Lin was a college student at Yale University in 1981. She entered a contest to design the Vietnam Veterans Memorial in Washington, D.C. Vietnam is a country in Southeast Asia. The United States fought in a war there from 1964 to 1973.

Maya Lin designed the Vietnam Veterans Memorial (opposite page, bottom).

THE LIFE OF MAYA LIN

1960 | 1970 | 1980 | 1990 | 2000

1959
Maya Lin is born in Athens, Ohio.

1982
Maya Lin's Vietnam Veterans Memorial opens in Washington, D.C.

1989
Maya Lin's Civil Rights Memorial opens in Montgomery, Alabama.

1993
Maya Lin completes work on the Museum of African Art in New York City.

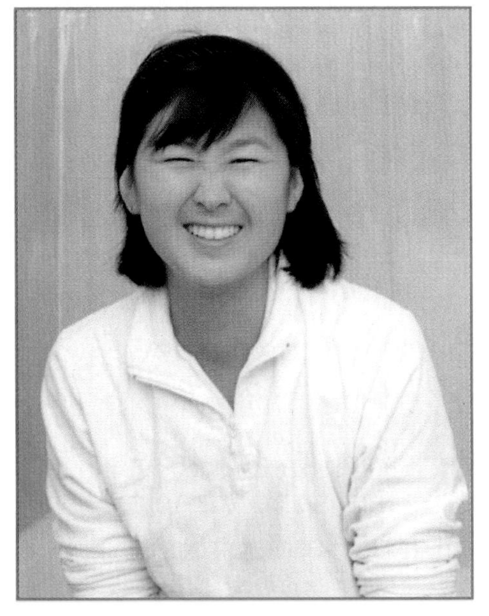

Maya Lin's design was chosen over 1,400 other designs. Her memorial has two walls in the shape of a "V." The walls list all of the names of the United States men and women who died or are missing from the war. Each year thousands of people visit the Vietnam Veterans Memorial. The monument is an important way we remember the Americans who died in Vietnam.

Other communities have hired Lin to design monuments as well. For example, she designed the Civil Rights Monument in Montgomery, Alabama. Today Lin works as both a sculptor and an architect. She continues to shape the culture of communities throughout the United States.

Link to Today **Think about someone in your community or our country whom you would like to honor. Make a drawing for a monument to that person.**

Chapter 10 REVIEW

VOCABULARY REVIEW

Number a sheet of paper from 1 to 3. Beside each number write the word from the list below that best matches the definition.

heritage **legend**

museum

1. A building where works of art, science, or history are placed for people to see
2. A story passed down through the years that many people believe, but which is not entirely true
3. Something handed down from earlier generations or from the past, such as traditions

CHAPTER COMPREHENSION

4. What is one basic belief that all Americans share?
5. Compare and contrast the stories you read about George Washington and David Crockett.
6. Write the name of one artist, and explain how he or she shaped the way we look at a community.

SKILL REVIEW

7. **Study Skill** If you wanted to find the definition of *hemisphere* in your Social Studies textbook, in what part of the book would you look?
8. **Geography Skill** What hemisphere is shown below?
9. **Geography Skill** What imaginary line divides the Northern Hemisphere and the Southern Hemisphere?

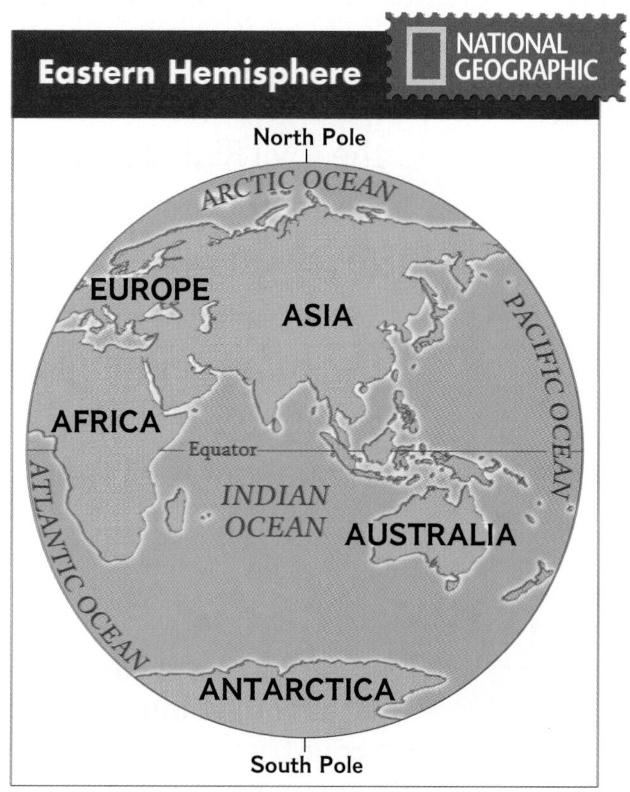

USING A CHART

10. Use the chart to explain what David Crockett and George Washington have in common.

	Legend	Real-Life	Both
Pecos Bill	✓		
David Crockett	✓	✓	✓
Paul Bunyan	✓		
George Washington	✓	✓	✓
Harriet Tubman		✓	

Activity

Writing About Culture Suppose you are designing a museum to show the culture of your community. Write a description of some of the stories, photographs, or paintings that you would include.

Using the Foldables Use your Foldable to review what you have learned about the importance of people and their cultures to our nation and its communities. As you look at the front of your Foldable, think about what you learned about the ways people share their culture with others. Review your notes under the tabs of your Foldable to check your responses.

Chapter 11

THE Big IDEAS ABOUT...

Communities and Culture

People celebrate their culture and history in many different ways. Through music, dance, art, and festivals, people around the world say who they are and what is important to them.

COMMUNITY CELEBRATIONS

People in communities celebrate their culture, as at this St. Patrick's Day parade in Savannah, Georgia.

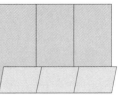

A VISIT TO NEW ORLEANS

New Orleans, Louisiana, is famous for its music, food, and festivals. People come from all over to share in the city's culture.

CULTURE IN GHANA

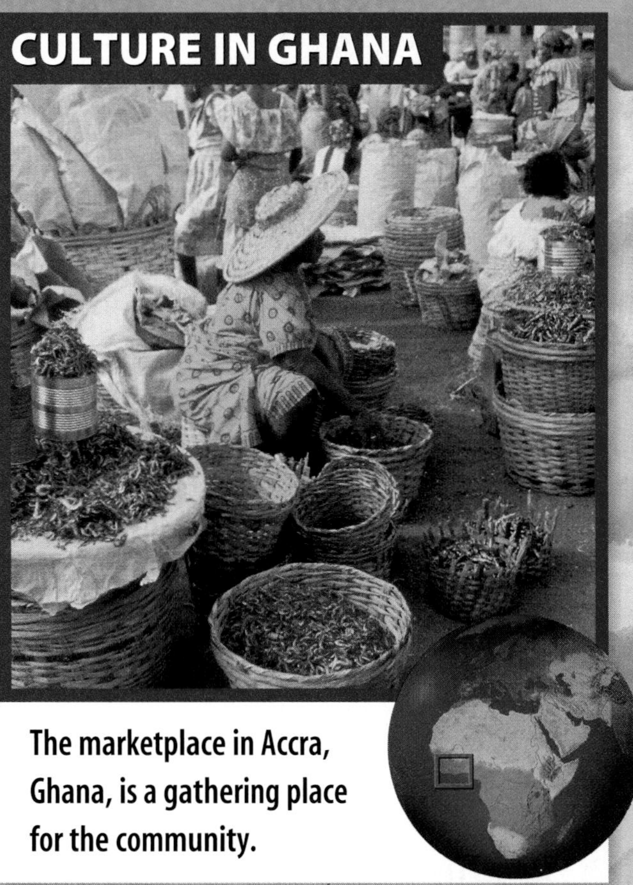

The marketplace in Accra, Ghana, is a gathering place for the community.

Foldables

Make this Foldable study guide, and use it to record what you learn about "Communities and Culture."

1. Fold an $8\frac{1}{2}$" x 11" piece of paper into thirds. Open and fold up a 2" tab along the long edge of the paper.
2. Glue the ends to form three pockets.
3. Write the lesson titles on the three pockets. Write and sketch what you learn on note cards, and place them in the pockets.

Lesson 1

Community Celebrations

VOCABULARY

ancestor

holiday

festival

PEOPLE

Casimir Pulaski

READING STRATEGY

Copy the diagram. Then write a main idea and supporting details about holidays.

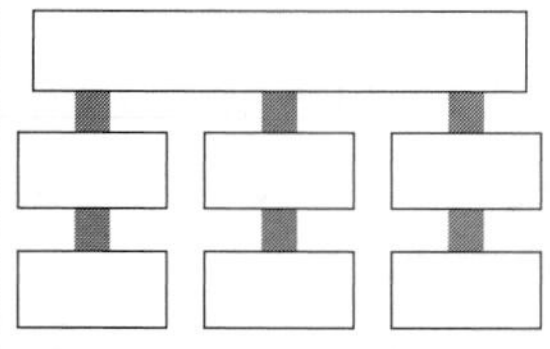

Why are celebrations important to communities?

Lesson Outline

- Special Days and Special People
- A Polish Hero in America
- Juneteenth
- Community Birthdays
- Remembering Important Times
- Celebrating America

BUILD BACKGROUND

People around the world find different ways to celebrate their culture and history. Let us look at how people in some communities in our country celebrate special times and special people.

SPECIAL DAYS AND SPECIAL PEOPLE

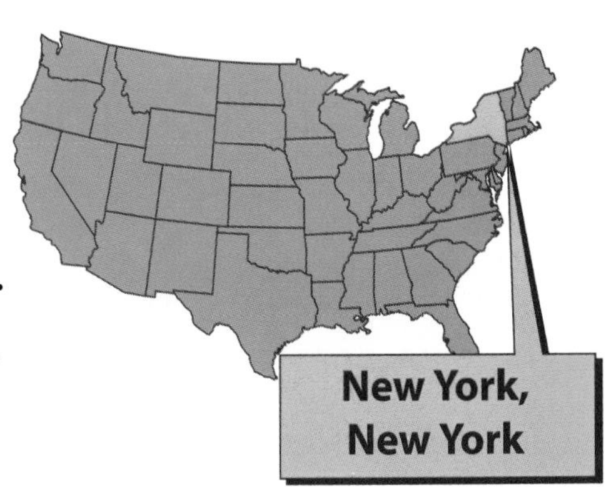

Gung Hay Fat Choy! You can hear those words during Chinese New Year's celebrations. It means "Happy and Rich New Year" in Chinese.

On New Year's Eve, Chinese American families enjoy a special dinner together. Each of the tasty foods they eat has a special meaning. Long noodles stand for a long life. Sweet dumplings mean you will find happiness. This is also a time for families and friends to visit one another. Children get gifts of money in red envelopes. The color red stands for good luck and happiness.

Why are children's gifts put in red envelopes during Chinese New Year celebrations?

In New York's Chinatown people watch lion dancers on parade (opposite). Children receive money in red envelopes—called *Lai-See*—to celebrate the New Year (below).

On Pulaski Day Polish Americans in Chicago, Illinois (right), recall Casimir Pulaski (below).

A POLISH HERO IN AMERICA

In Chicago, Illinois, many people's **ancestors** came from Poland. Ancestors are the people in your family who came before you and your parents. That includes your grandparents and the people who came before them.

Polish Americans are proud of their Polish heritage. In Chicago one way Polish Americans celebrate that heritage is by honoring **Casimir Pulaski** (KA zee meer puh LAS kee). Pulaski was a Polish army general. He came to America in 1777 to help our country win its freedom from Great Britain. He died fighting in 1779.

In Chicago the first Monday in March is Pulaski Day. It is a state **holiday**. A holiday is a day on which people or events are honored. On Pulaski Day people celebrate Polish culture. They eat Polish foods, such as a stuffed dumpling called pierogi (puh ROH gee) and a sausage called kielbasa (kil BAH suh). They also dance to the sounds of polka music played on an accordion.

Why do people in the United States honor Casimir Pulaski?

JUNETEENTH

On June 19, 1865, news reached Galveston, Texas, that the Civil War had ended. Enslaved African Americans in Texas were now free. Felix Haywood was one of the many people who got their freedom that day. "Everyone was singing. We [were] all walking on golden clouds," he remembered.

Ever since, African Americans from Texas have celebrated June 19, or Juneteenth for short. In 1980 Juneteenth became a state holiday in Texas. **Houston, Texas**, has one of the biggest Juneteenth celebrations. There are parades and barbecues. There are also concerts with many different kinds of music. Juneteenth celebrations in Texas and elsewhere also include art shows, live performances, and other celebrations of African American culture.

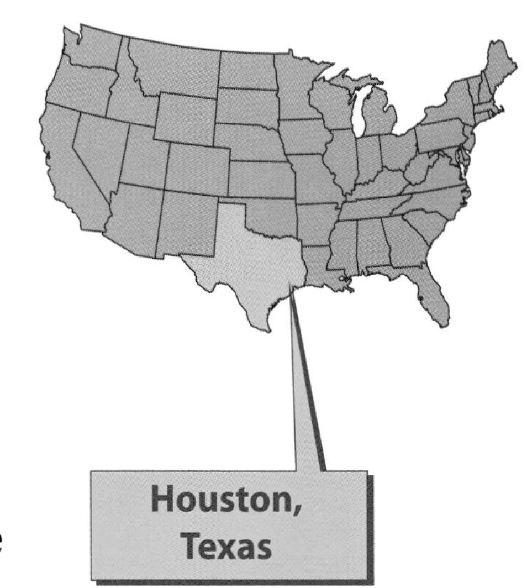

READING CHECK Why do people celebrate Juneteenth?

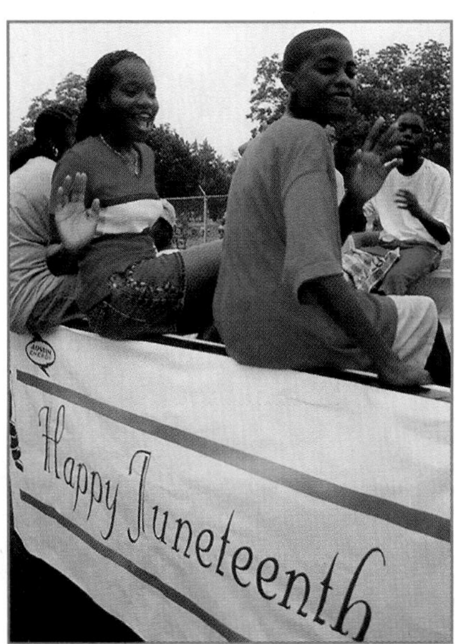

Parades (above) and family picnics (below) are two ways people celebrate Juneteenth.

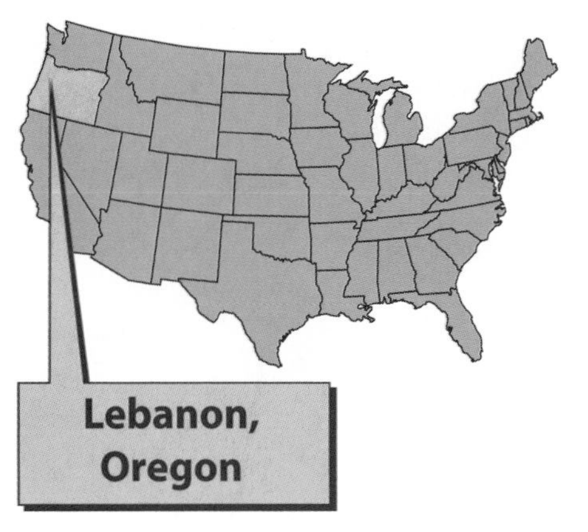

COMMUNITY BIRTHDAYS

Happy Birthday, **Lebanon, Oregon**! That is what you might say to the people in Lebanon each August. Lebanon was founded, or started, in 1847. Every year since 1914 the community has had a Founders Day celebration. Many communities across the United States also have Founders Day celebrations.

Founders Day in Lebanon, Oregon, is a time for fun and for remembering the past. Townspeople make quilts (above).

People in Lebanon, Oregon, make Founders Day a time to honor the hard work and courage of the community's early settlers. People practice pioneer skills, such as spinning and quilt making. There is a contest with a prize for the most beautiful quilt. It is also a time to have fun. People enjoy music, games, contests, and food. There are tours of old homes. The Lebanon Squarecirclers hold a big square dance.

READING CHECK **How does the community of Lebanon, Oregon, celebrate its founding?**

REMEMBERING IMPORTANT TIMES

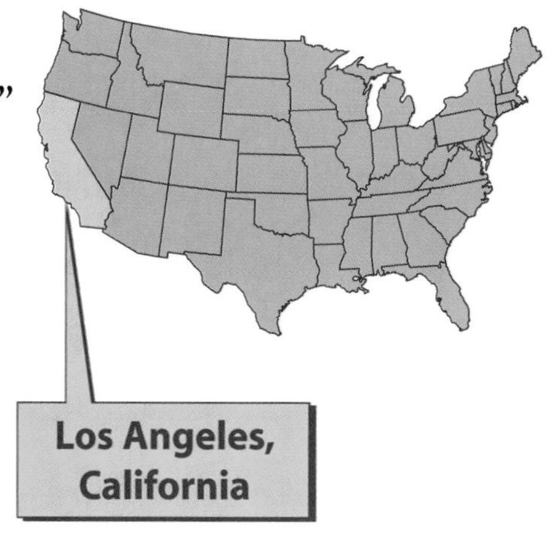

Cinco de Mayo is Spanish for the "Fifth of May." About 150 years ago, on May 5, 1862, a small Mexican army beat a French army twice its size. The Mexican people were proud of their army's bravery and success. Today many communities in the United States celebrate Cinco de Mayo. It is a way for Mexican Americans to celebrate their heritage and share it with others.

In **Los Angeles, California**, about 750,000 people attend this fiesta, or **festival**. A festival is a celebration. Mariachi (mahr ee AH chee) bands play music. Children dress in costumes and perform folk dances. Mexican foods are served. Leticia Quezada, president of the Mexican Cultural Institute, says, "We [come] together as a family to celebrate and remember our history."

How do Mexican Americans share their heritage during Cinco de Mayo?

Music and dance are big parts of the Cinco de Mayo **festival** in Los Angeles.

CELEBRATING AMERICA

Independence Day—Fourth of July—is celebrated with community parades (above and below).

Communities across the United States celebrate Independence Day, or the Fourth of July. On this date in 1776, the Declaration of Independence was signed. The declaration explained why the American colonies wanted to be free from British rule.

On July 4 every community in our country celebrates the same thing—our country's freedom. Each community, though, celebrates in its own way. In Washington, D.C., people gather to hear a public reading of the declaration. In Ennis, Montana, citizens attend a rodeo. In Kenwood, California, the town has a friendly pillow-fighting championship.

In almost every community there are fireworks, parades, music, and food. It is a time for friends and families to get together and celebrate America!

READING CHECK **What is one way that most communities celebrate Independence Day?**

PUTTING IT TOGETHER

Celebrations are a way that communities honor their history and their culture. The entire country celebrates some events, such as the Fourth of July, our country's birthday. Celebrations bring people in communities together. Celebrations are also a way for us to learn about each other's culture.

Review and Assess

1. Write one sentence for each of the vocabulary words.

   ancestor **festival**
   holiday

2. What event does Juneteenth celebrate?
3. How are celebrations important to communities?
4. How does the Cinco de Mayo festival bring people together?
5. **Compare and contrast** how different communities celebrate the Fourth of July.

Plan a celebration that would bring together the people in your community. Your celebration can be for a special person or event, or anything else you like. Share your plan with your classmates.

Write a two-paragraph report describing how you and your community celebrate the Fourth of July.

Making Decisions

A **decision** is a choice about what to do. You make many decisions every day. Some decisions, such as choosing between walking or riding your bicycle to school, are easy and not very important. Other decisions, such as choosing how to spend money you have saved, are harder and more important. In making important decisions, you need to think about your goals. You also need to think about the likely result of each choice.

VOCABULARY

decision

LEARN THE SKILL

Follow these steps as a guide to help you make good decisions.

1. **Set a goal that is important to you.**
   Felicia wants to learn about Juneteenth. Her goal is to find out more about it.

2. **Identify the different choices you have.**
   Felicia must make a decision about what to do on Saturday afternoon. She could go to the library, she could attend a Juneteenth celebration, or she could do research on the Internet. These are her choices.

3. **Think about the possible results of each choice.**
   If Felicia goes to the library, she can read a book about Juneteenth. She can also learn about the holiday using the Internet. The celebration, though, is held only once each year. If she misses it, she will have to wait another year.

4. **Select the best choice to meet your goal. Check your decision with your parents, a teacher, or another adult.**
   Felicia decides to attend the Juneteenth celebration. That way she can learn firsthand about the holiday from people who know about it. This choice will best help her meet her goal of learning more about Juneteenth. Her mother agreed, and the two went to the Juneteenth celebration together.

TRY THE SKILL

James wants a new scooter. He has been saving most of his allowance for almost a year, and now he has enough money. One week before he plans to buy the scooter, though, James's friends invite him to an amusement park. It will cost the same amount of money as the scooter. James has a decision to make.

1. What goal is important to James?
2. What are three possible choices James could make for his savings?
3. Describe the probable results of each choice James has.
4. How can making decisions help you to better understand goals and choices?

EXTEND THE SKILL

Suppose you are in charge of planning your family vacation. You may travel to any place in the United States, but you can only go to one place. What is your goal for this vacation? What choices do you have? Where will you decide to go?

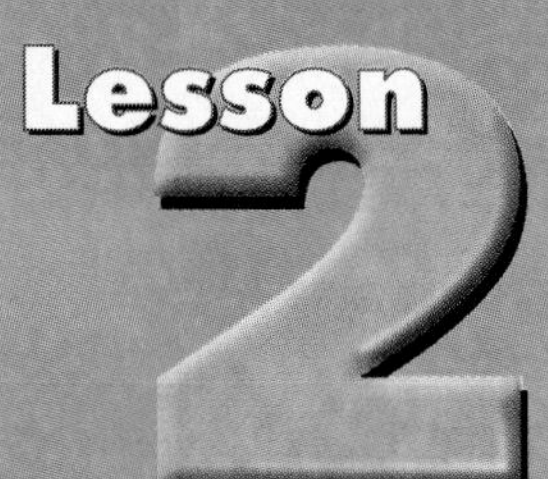

A Visit to New Orleans

VOCABULARY

jazz

Cajun

zydeco

Mardi Gras

PEOPLE

Andrew Jackson

Louis Armstrong

READING STRATEGY

Copy the chart. In separate columns write the steps for making decisions. Then decide how you would spend one day in New Orleans.

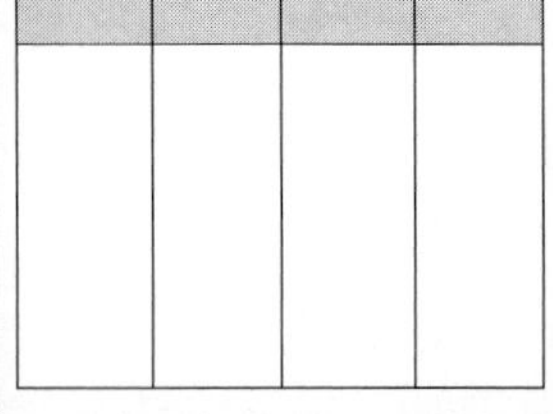

What is the culture of New Orleans?

Lesson Outline

- A Community Grows
- Sounds of the City
- What's Cooking in New Orleans?
- Mardi Gras

BUILD BACKGROUND

On a hot summer day, you are sitting by a river eating a spicy stew. You can hear the sounds of a band playing nearby. Where are you? It must be New Orleans, Louisiana! New Orleans is known around the world for its music, food, and celebrations.

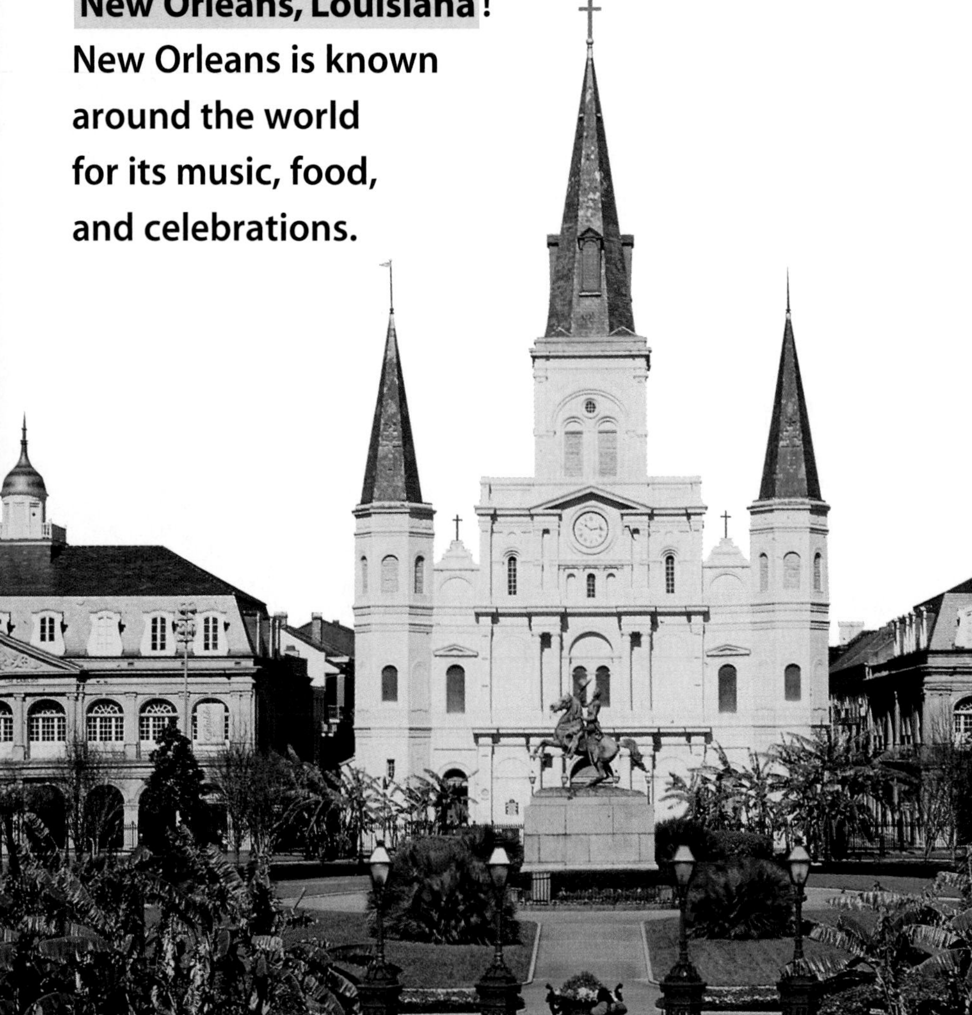

Many buildings in New Orleans (opposite page and left) look like buildings in France.

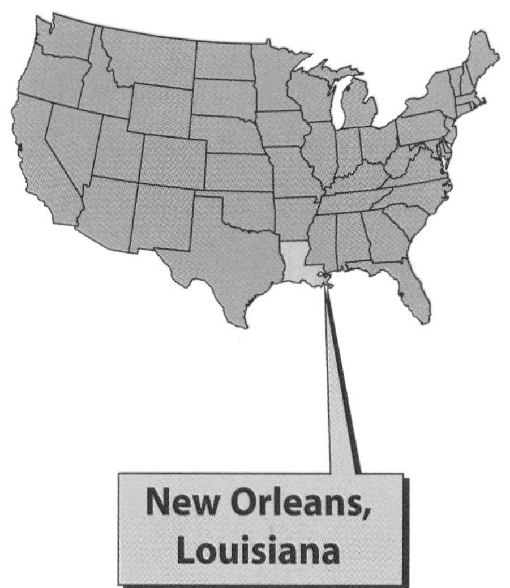

A COMMUNITY GROWS

New Orleans is a community with a special culture. This culture is a mixture of the cultures of the many groups of people who have called New Orleans home.

Native Americans were the first people to live in the area. In the 1700s settlers began to arrive from France. In 1802 the United States bought land including New Orleans from France for $15 million. This was called the Louisiana Purchase.

The French heritage can still be seen in New Orleans. The oldest part of the city is called the French Quarter. The buildings here look like buildings in France.

In 1812 the United States and Great Britain went to war. The British attacked New Orleans. United States troops, led by General **Andrew Jackson**, won the Battle of New Orleans. Today a statue of Andrew Jackson stands in the city.

How did New Orleans become part of the United States?

SOUNDS OF THE CITY

Music is an important part of the city's culture. You can hear it everywhere in New Orleans. You can hear it in clubs, churches, and concert halls. You can even hear it on the street.

Jazz is one kind of music you will hear in New Orleans. Jazz is a kind of music that grew from traditional African rhythms and the melodies of African American spirituals, work songs, and blues. Jazz music was invented in New Orleans in the early 1900s.

Today people come from all over the world to listen to jazz music in New Orleans. Every year the city celebrates jazz at the New Orleans Jazz and Heritage Festival.

A very popular jazz musician was born in New Orleans. His name was **Louis Armstrong**. He played the trumpet and sang. His music was heard on records, on TV, and in the movies. He helped to spread jazz all over the world. New Orleans remembers this important artist. There is a park in the city named for him.

In New Orleans **jazz** can be heard in the streets (left) and at the Jazz and Heritage Festival (top). Louis Armstrong (above) helped spread jazz music.

New Forms of Music

Jazz is not the only music you can hear in New Orleans. You can also hear **Cajun** (KAY juhn) music. This music takes its name from the Cajun people. Cajuns were French Canadians who came to Louisiana in the 1700s. They came from Acadia (now Nova Scotia) and called themselves Acadians (uh KAY dee uhnz). Later this was shortened to Cajun. Many Cajun songs have French words. They are played on fiddles, guitars, and accordions.

Cajun music is popular at the Festivals Acadiens in Lafayette, Louisiana (above). The Chenier brothers, Clifton (below) and Cleveland (bottom), play **zydeco** music.

Another kind of music from New Orleans is called **zydeco** (ZIGH duh koh). Zydeco was created by Creole people. Many Creoles are French-speaking African Americans. Zydeco songs often have French words. The music mixes African rhythms, blues, and jazz. Zydeco bands often have a guitar, an accordion, and a washboard.

READING CHECK **What are three kinds of music created in New Orleans?**

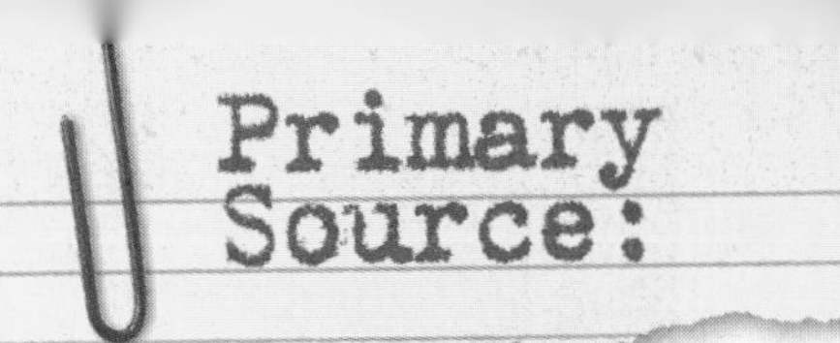
Primary
Source:

On the Bayou

—words and music by Hank Williams, 1952

This song tells about tastes and sounds of life on the bayous of southern Louisiana. A bayou is a small, slow-moving body of water.

Chorus
C
G7
JAM - BA - LA-YA and a craw - fish pie and fil - let gum - bo
C
'Cause to - night I'm gon - na see my ma cher a - mi - o
G7
Pick gui - tar, fill fruit jar and be gay - o
C
Son of a gun, we'll have big fun on the bay - ou.

What three foods are mentioned in this song?

---

ma cher amio: my dear friend

WHAT'S COOKING IN NEW ORLEANS?

Food is another important part of the culture of New Orleans. Like the city's music, its food comes from people of many different backgrounds.

A sweet treat from people of French background is called a beignet (bayn YAY). A beignet is a small, round sugar doughnut. People in New Orleans often sit in cafés eating beignets.

One of the most popular Creole dishes is called gumbo. It is a stew made with seafood, chicken, rice, and a green vegetable called okra. The name *gumbo* comes from an African word for "okra."

Many Cajun people like to put hot sauce on their food. This makes the food extra spicy. Hot sauce is made from chili peppers. Be careful when you eat a chili pepper. It may be small, but it can make your mouth burn!

Chefs like Emeril Lagasse (above) have made New Orleans cooking famous. People in the city like to start the day with coffee and a beignet (below).

READING CHECK **What are some foods important to the culture of New Orleans?**

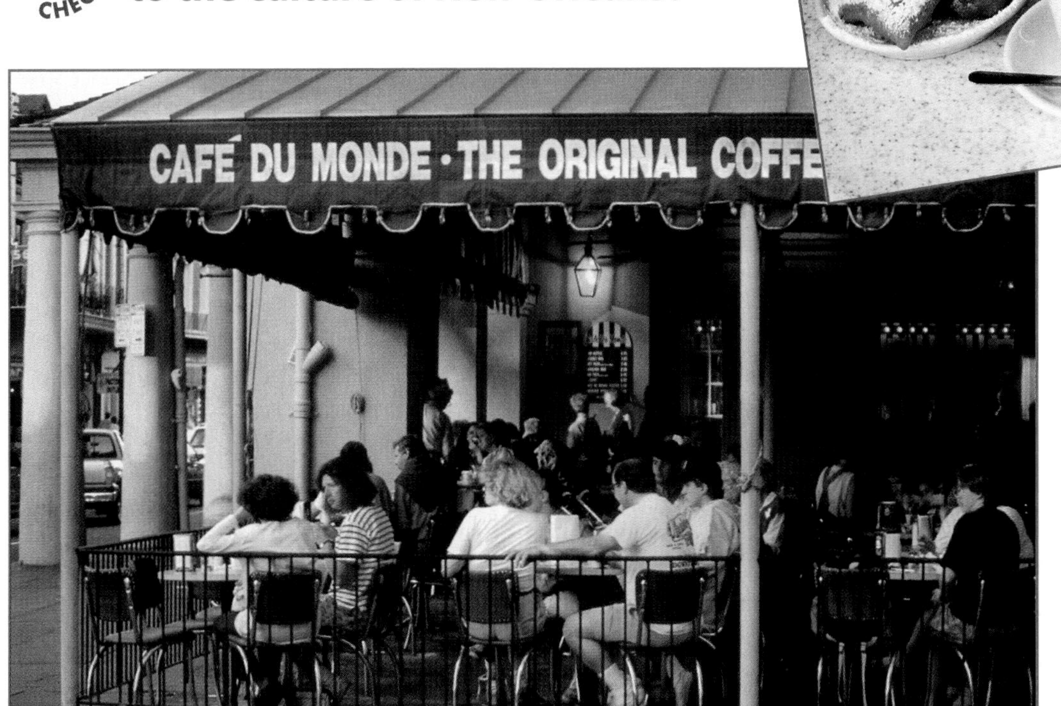

MARDI GRAS

Each winter New Orleans has a big festival called **Mardi Gras** (MAHR dee GRAH). People from the city's many different cultures work together to create one big community celebration. There is music, food, dancing, costumes, and parades. The fun begins on January 6. It can last for weeks!

During Mardi Gras people dress in costumes (above), ride on floats (below), and throw coins and beads to the crowds.

Parades are held every day during Mardi Gras. More than a million people line the streets to watch. Many people dress in colorful costumes and masks. Special clubs, called krewes, work all year to build the giant floats for the parades.

French settlers first celebrated Mardi Gras in Louisiana in the 1700s. The name means "Fat Tuesday" in French. The festival ends on the Tuesday before Lent. In the Christian religion, Lent is a 40-day time of fasting and doing good deeds.

Who were the first people to celebrate Mardi Gras?

PUTTING IT TOGETHER

New Orleans is a community with a special history and culture. The people of New Orleans have created their own kinds of music and food, and even their own kinds of celebrations. The culture of New Orleans has been shaped by people from many different backgrounds.

Communities around the world have their own cultures. Next you will find out about the culture of a community outside of the United States.

Exploring
ECONOMICS

The Cost of Mardi Gras Floats

Mardi Gras floats are beautiful—and expensive! Each float is decorated to show a theme. One float may cost anywhere from $25,000 to $850,000!

Make a model Mardi Gras float. Find a shoe box or a wagon to use as the float. Think of a theme. Now get creative! Decorate your float using beads, balloons, and colored paper.

Review and Assess

1. Write one sentence for each of the vocabulary terms.
   Cajun **jazz**
   Mardi Gras
2. Where is New Orleans located?
3. Find! Out! What is the culture of New Orleans like? Give three examples of culture in the city.
4. What community celebration is part of New Orleans **culture**?
5. **Summarize** how people from different backgrounds have helped to shape the culture of New Orleans.

The Cajun people originally came from Acadia, now known as Nova Scotia. Find out where Nova Scotia is. Draw a map showing the route a ship might have taken to get from Nova Scotia to Louisiana.

Write a paragraph describing a song or music style. You might describe Cajun or jazz music, or some other music that you like.

Being a Good Citizen
Adding Art to a City

A few years ago people driving down the main road into Athens, Ohio, barely noticed the 8-foot wall they passed on the way. Now they do. Some people even stop to take a closer look. That is because a colorful mural, or painting, covers the wall.

About 15 volunteers, ages 11 to 17, made the mural. They were helped by Rural Action, a community group in Ohio. The mural is one of nine murals in the area created by young people working with local artists.

"We made our community better."

Laura Zielinski

Work on the Athens mural began in the spring of 2000. Volunteers met weekly with artist Lisa Trocchia to plan the mural. They talked about their community and shared ideas about growing up there. She listened and made drawings.

"Athens has a lot of brick buildings, so we put bricks in," said Trocchia. "The area is very green and beautiful, so the group wanted green in the mural." In the center they put a mirror made of tiny pieces of glass. "People can look in and see themselves," said Laura Zielinski. "Each time they do, they see something different."

Once they had a plan for their mural, the group went to the city council for approval. When painting began in July, local businesses helped with free art supplies. By October the mural was finished. "We were proud of what we did," said Zielinski. "We made our community better."

Be a Good Citizen

Making Connections

- **What are some places in your community where people can see works of art?**

Talk About It!

- **Murals like the one in Athens are often called "public art." Why do you think many communities like to have public art?**

Acting on It

In the Classroom

Make a mural for your school. What pictures of people and places will you put in it? What objects will you include?

Culture in Ghana

VOCABULARY

kente

READING STRATEGY

To learn more about Ghana, would you decide to read a book, rent a video, or go to Ghana? Fill out the chart, and follow the steps for **making decisions.**

What are examples of the culture of Ghana?

Lesson Outline

- Welcome to Ghana
- Crafts, Food, and More
- Music and Dance

BUILD BACKGROUND

Have you ever wondered what life might be like if you lived in another country? Cultures can be very different in different communities around the world. In this lesson we will explore culture in Ghana. Ghana is a country in Africa.

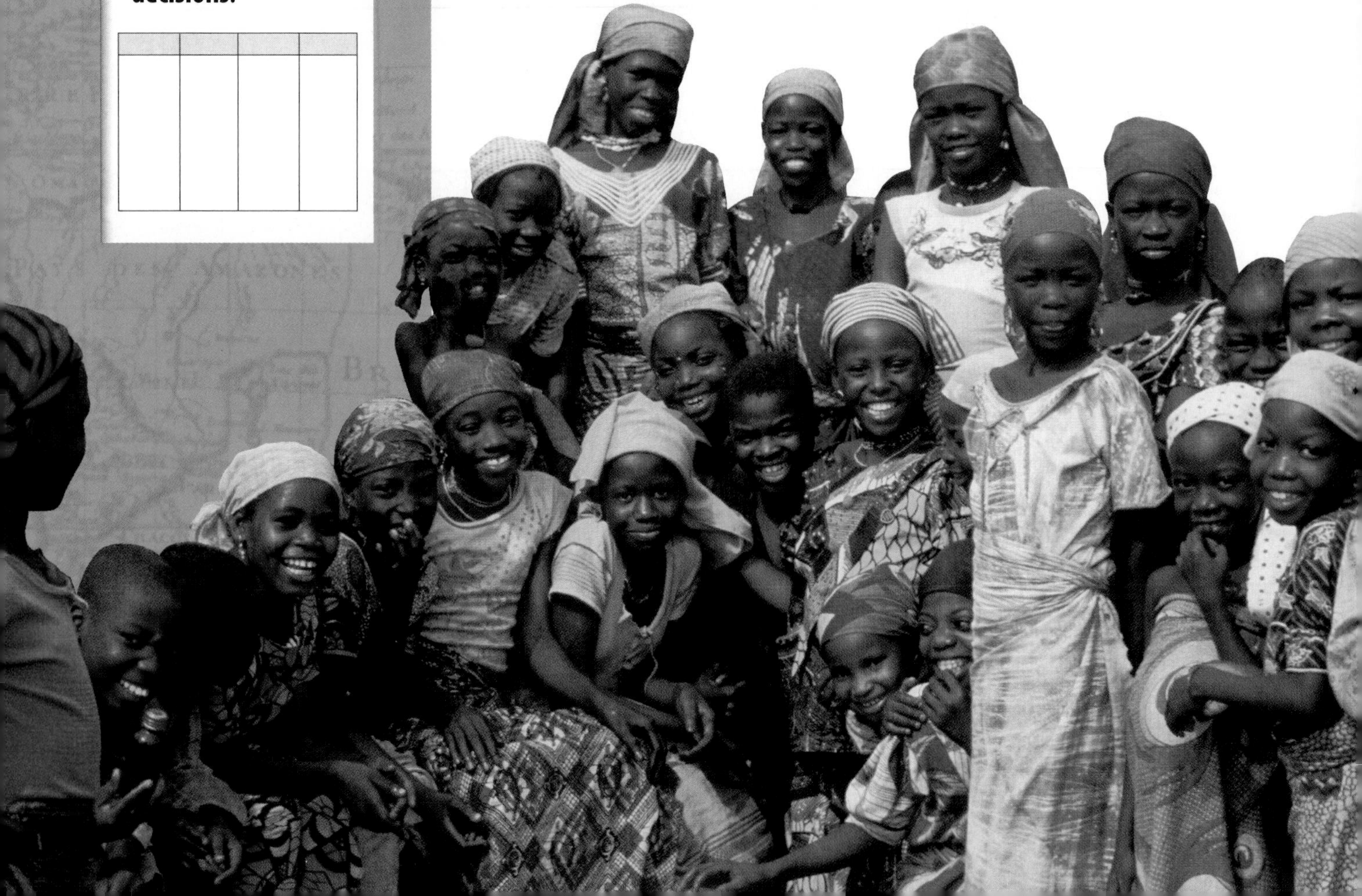

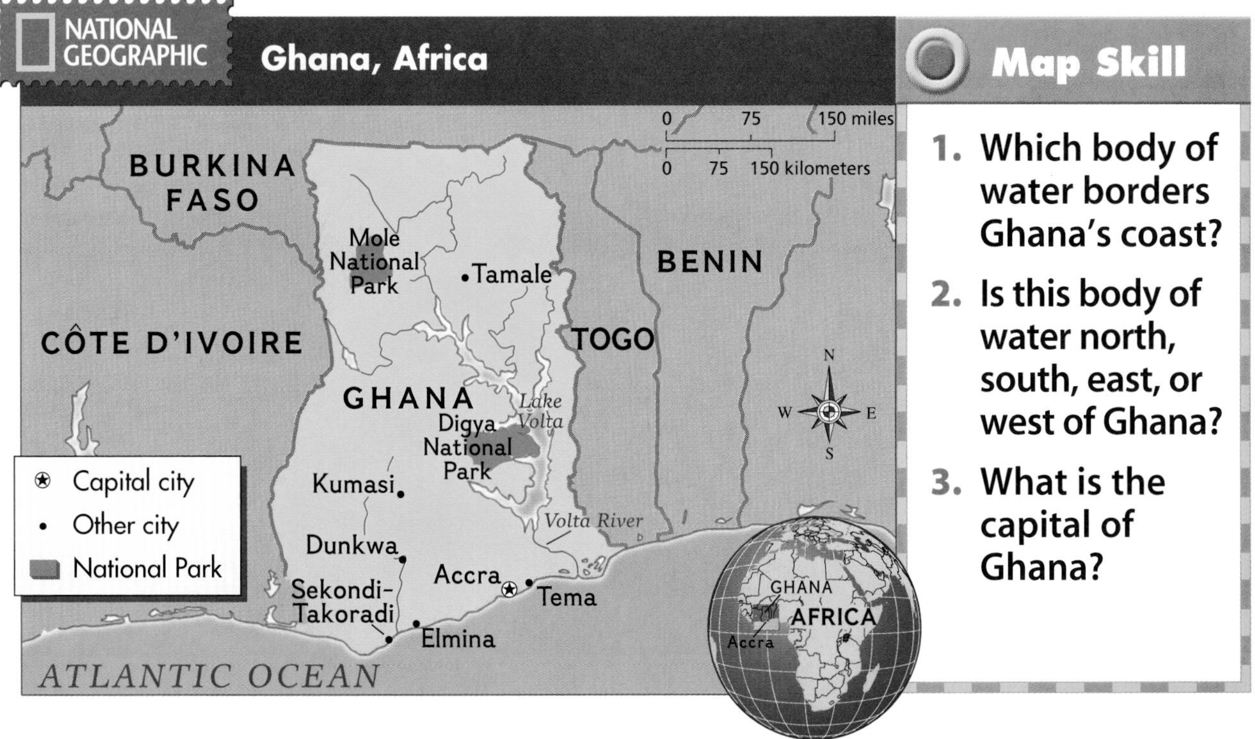

Map Skill

1. Which body of water borders Ghana's coast?
2. Is this body of water north, south, east, or west of Ghana?
3. What is the capital of Ghana?

WELCOME TO GHANA

Ghana is a place with many different cultures. That is because there are so many groups of people who live there. You can hear more than 35 different languages spoken in Ghana!

The national language of Ghana is English. This is because Ghana, like the United States, was a colony of Great Britain. Ghana became an independent country in 1957.

Look at the map. Ghana is located in West Africa. It is in the Northern Hemisphere. The capital of Ghana is Accra. A capital is the place where the government is located. Accra has a population of almost two million people. It is the largest city in Ghana.

What is special about the country of Ghana?

Downtown Accra has modern buildings and sculptures.

CRAFTS, FOOD, AND MORE

Many shoppers come to Accra's marketplace (above). Craftspeople (below) still make **kente** cloths (bottom) by hand.

If you lived in Ghana, you would likely visit the Accra marketplace. People from all over the country meet there to trade goods and be together. It has more than four thousand different booths. People sell fruits, vegetables, fish, crafts, furniture, **kente** (KEN tay) cloths, and more.

Kente are colorful woven cloths that are worn during special times. Kente is more than just cloth. The patterns and symbols have special meanings. For example, one pattern is called "one person does not rule a nation." The Ashanti people who make kente believe that all people must come to an agreement. Kente cloth shows the culture and history of the Ashanti people.

The Land of Festivals

With so many different groups of people in Ghana, you can find a festival going on somewhere almost every week! Music, dancing, and eating make the festivals lively and fun. Festivals are important to the people of Ghana. They are held to honor ancestors, leaders, and communities.

One festival, in the city of Elmina, celebrates the beginning of the fishing season. A parade honors the local leaders. Singers, dancers, and stilt walkers perform in the parade. Another festival celebrates Ghana's freedom from Great Britain. It brings together different groups of people from all over Ghana. It includes storytelling, theater, and traditional dances.

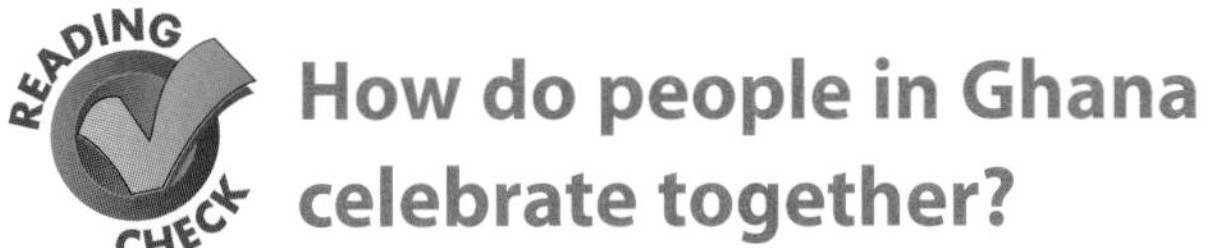

How do people in Ghana celebrate together?

Parades (below) and singing (above) mark Ghana's independence day celebration in Accra.

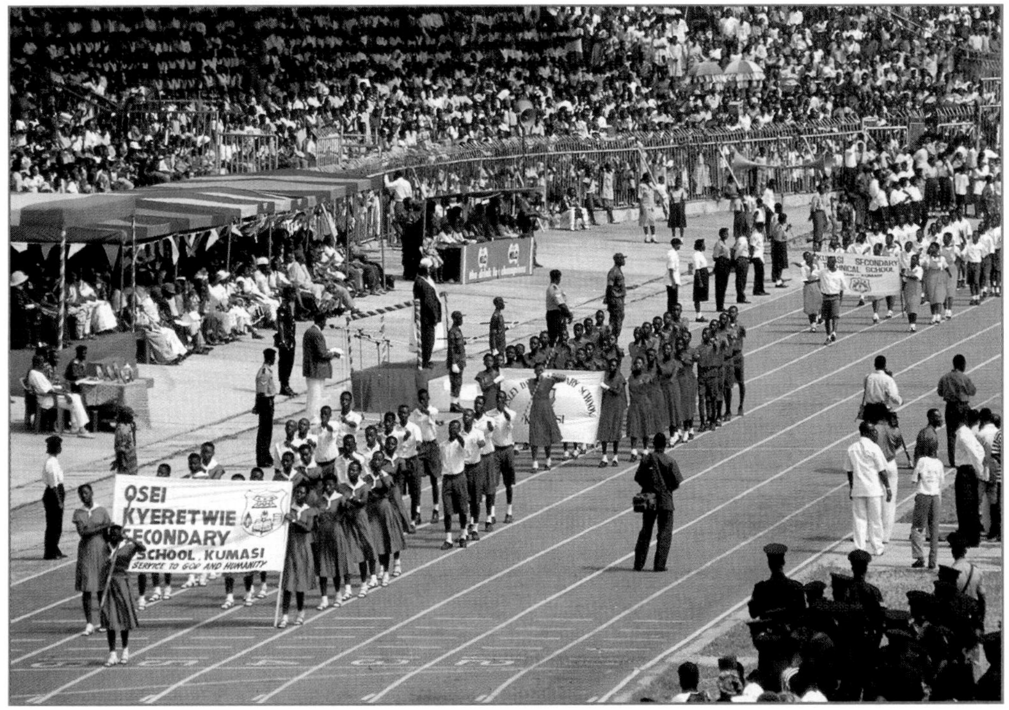

MUSIC AND DANCE

Music and dance have been important parts of Ghana's culture for many hundreds of years. In the 1920s musicians in Accra created a new type of music called "Highlife." It mixed African rhythms with instruments from Europe and America. Traditional Ghanian music also remains very popular today.

The drum is the most common instrument in Ghana. It is most popular in the southern part of the country. The kpanlogo (pan LOH goh) is a drum that was created in Ghana. It is played with sticks. A musician plays several kpanlogo drums at one time. Kpanlogos are often played at celebrations. Then people join in the music by dancing. These dances can last for up to three hours without stopping!

Kpanlogos (above) are a type of drum made in Ghana. This drummer (below) plays kpanlogos. Music and dance performances often take place in Ghana's National Theatre (bottom).

READING CHECK What is a kpanlogo?

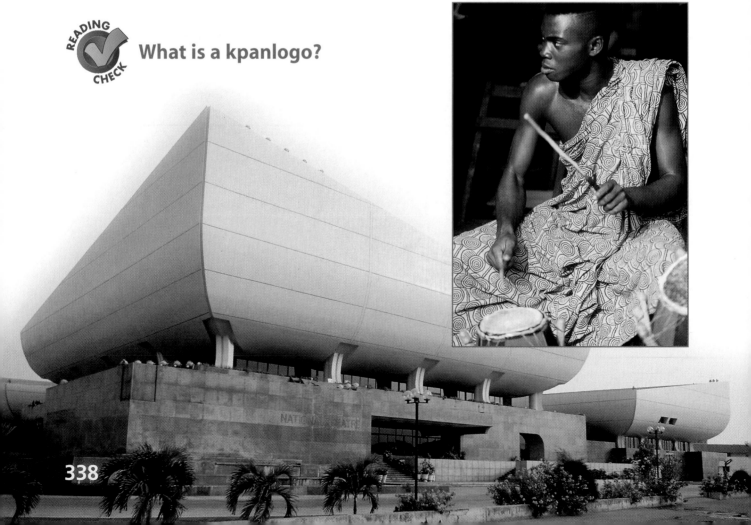

PUTTING IT TOGETHER

Culture in Ghana includes beautiful crafts, delicious foods, and festivals that people enjoy throughout the year.

Communities all around the world are special. Each has its own geography, history, and culture. All of the communities together make up one world that we all share.

Review and Assess

1. Write one sentence for the vocabulary word.

   kente

2. What kinds of activities can you see at festivals in Ghana?
3. Give three examples of culture in Ghana.
4. Why are festival celebrations an important part of Ghana's **culture**?
5. **Compare and contrast** festival celebrations in Ghana and the Unites States.

Copy and complete the chart below. Put one example in each box.

	My Community	Accra
Celebration		
Food		
Music		

Suppose you had a friend in Ghana. **Write** a letter asking about something you would like to learn more about in Ghana.

Chapter 11 REVIEW

VOCABULARY REVIEW

Number a sheet of paper from 1 to 3. Beside each number write the word from the list below that matches the description.

ancestor **kente**

zydeco

1. A kind of music that was created by Creole people
2. A person in your family who came before you
3. Colorful woven cloths used for clothing and decoration

CHAPTER COMPREHENSION

4. Why do communities across the United States celebrate Independence Day?
5. Explain why you might see French-style buildings and hear French words if you were in New Orleans.
6. Why is the marketplace in Accra important to the people of Ghana?

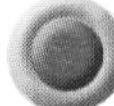

SKILL REVIEW

Read the paragraph, and answer the questions to practice the skill of making decisions.

Paul is going to ride his bike in the Fourth of July parade. He wants his bike to look special. He could buy decorations, but they would be expensive. He could paint his bike red, white, and blue, but then it would always be those colors. He could make paper streamers and an American flag to put on his bike.

7. **Reading/Thinking Skill** What goal does Paul have?
8. **Reading/Thinking Skill** Identify his choices and the results of each one.
9. **Reading/Thinking Skill** What decision does Paul make?

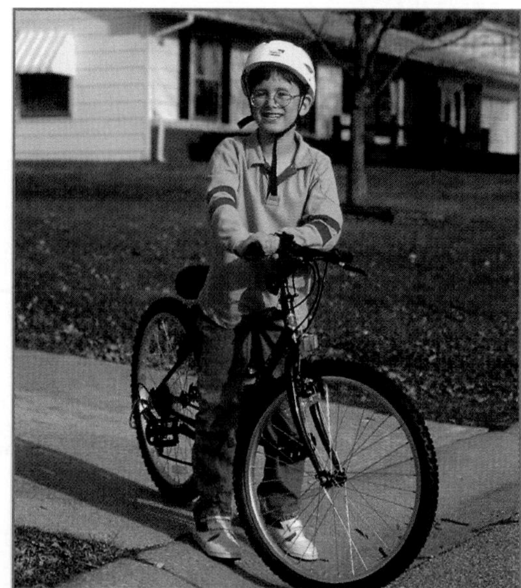

USING A CHART

10. Use the chart to answer the question. The chart shows how people share their cultures by celebrating important times. Which special day is celebrated all over our country?

Holiday	Celebrates	Place
Juneteenth	Enslaved people in Texas learned they were free.	Texas
Fourth of July	Declaration of Independence was signed.	United States
Founders Day	Community of Lebanon was founded.	Lebanon, Oregon
Cinco de Mayo	Small Mexican army defeated large French army.	Los Angeles, California

Writing About Culture Find out about a community celebration some place in the world. What is being celebrated? How do people there celebrate? What do they do? Use what you learn to make an invitation to the celebration. You can decorate your invitation with colorful photos or drawings.

Use your Foldable to review what you have learned about communities and cultures near and far. As you look at the lesson titles on the front of your Foldable pockets, mentally review what you learned in each lesson. Look at your notes and visuals in each pocket to check your memory and responses. Record any questions that you have and discuss them with classmates or review the chapter to find answers.

Local Connections

Sharing Cultures

In this unit you have read about people sharing their different cultures in communities. One of the things that make each culture special is food!

Henry lives in Arlington, Virginia. His class held a food festival celebrating different cultures. The students worked in groups to choose a culture they were interested in learning more about. On the day of the festival, they brought in the ingredients to make special dishes. Each group made its own dish. Everyone enjoyed the food festival!

- ***What would you share with your class?***

Activity

Hold a Classroom Festival

Materials
- recipe
- ingredients
- bowl or dish

Step 1 Work with a group to choose a culture you want to learn more about.

Step 2 Find a recipe at the library or on the Internet. Gather the ingredients.

Step 3 Bring in ingredients. Work together to make your foods in the school kitchen or cafeteria. Your teacher can help you.

Step 4 On the day of the festival, share your dish with the class. Enjoy!

VOCABULARY REVIEW

Number a sheet of paper from 1 to 6. Read the definition of each underlined word. Write **T** if the definition is true and **F** if it is false. If it is false, write a sentence correctly defining the word.

1. An ancestor is a story that has been passed down through the years, which many people believe but which may not be true.
2. Zydeco is a kind of music created by Creole people.
3. French Canadians who came to Louisiana in the 1700s are called kente.
4. Heritage is the arts, beliefs, and customs that make up a way of life for a group of people.
5. A mural is a large picture that is painted on a wall or ceiling.
6. A hero is a person in your family who came before you.

TECHNOLOGY

To learn more about the people and places in this unit, visit www.mhschool.com and follow the links to Grade 3, Unit 5.

SKILL REVIEW

7. **Study Skill** In which part of your Social Studies book would you look to find out if David Crockett is mentioned?
8. **Reading/Thinking Skill** What is a decision? What are the steps you should follow to come to a good decision?
9. **Geography Skill** Which hemisphere does the map show?
10. **Geography Skill** What continents are completely in that hemisphere? What continents are partly in that hemisphere? What continents are not in that hemisphere?

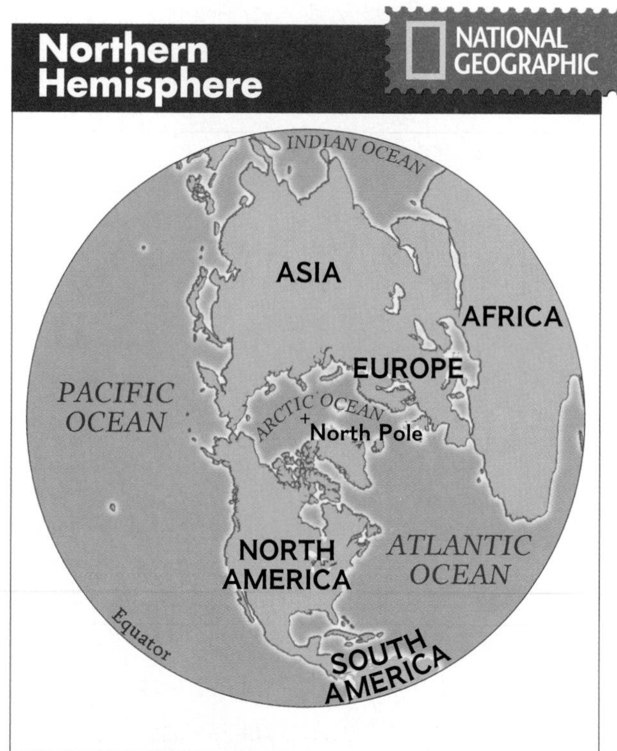

Read the passage and the questions that follow. Write the best answers on a piece of paper.

If you lived in Ghana, you would visit the Accra marketplace. People from all over the country meet there to trade goods and be together. It has more than four thousand different booths. People sell fruits, vegetables, fish, crafts, furniture, kente cloths, and more.

Kente is more than just cloth. It shows the culture and history of the Ashanti people. The patterns and symbols on the cloth have special meanings. For example, one pattern is called "one person does not rule a nation." The Ashanti people who make kente believe that all people must come to an agreement.

1 A cloth maker in Ghana wants to sell his kente cloth. What do you think he will do?

- Keep the cloth at home until a buyer calls him
- Sell the cloth at the marketplace in Accra
- Open a cloth store
- Advertise his cloth in the newspaper

2 Which of these is an opinion in this story?

- The Accra marketplace is in Ghana.
- The Ashanti people make kente.
- Kente cloths show the history of the Ashanti people.
- Kente cloth is beautiful.

WRITING ACTIVITIES

Writing to Inform Choose an artist or musician you read about in the unit. Make a list of questions about that person. Then do research to find the answers. Write your questions and answers in the form of an interview.

Writing to Express Suppose you just attended one of the festivals described in this unit. Write a journal entry about your day.

Writing to Persuade Suppose the people in your community have decided to create a mural. All citizens have been asked for ideas about what the mural should show. Write a letter to the mayor explaining your idea and why it should be chosen.

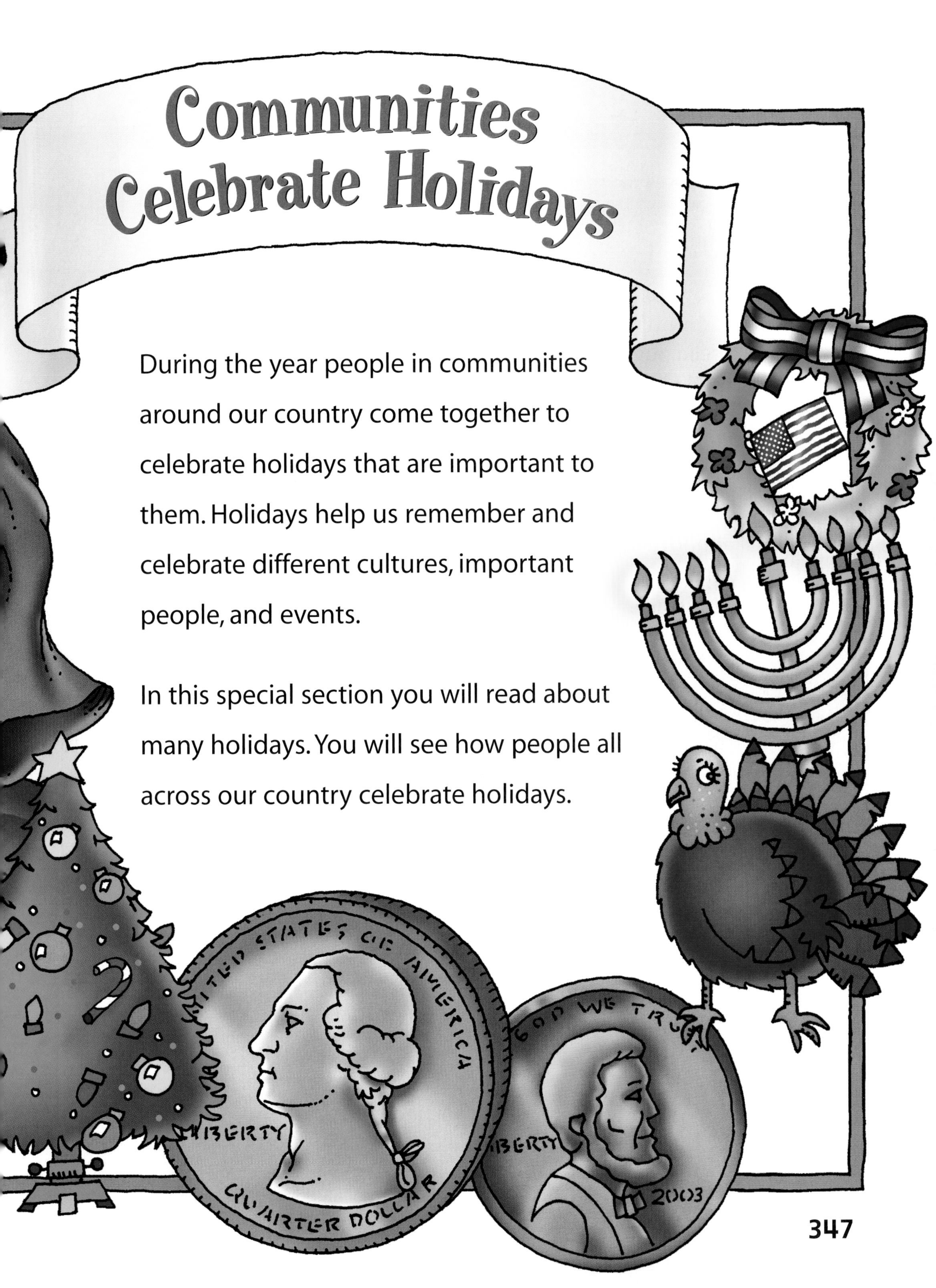

Communities Celebrate Holidays

During the year people in communities around our country come together to celebrate holidays that are important to them. Holidays help us remember and celebrate different cultures, important people, and events.

In this special section you will read about many holidays. You will see how people all across our country celebrate holidays.

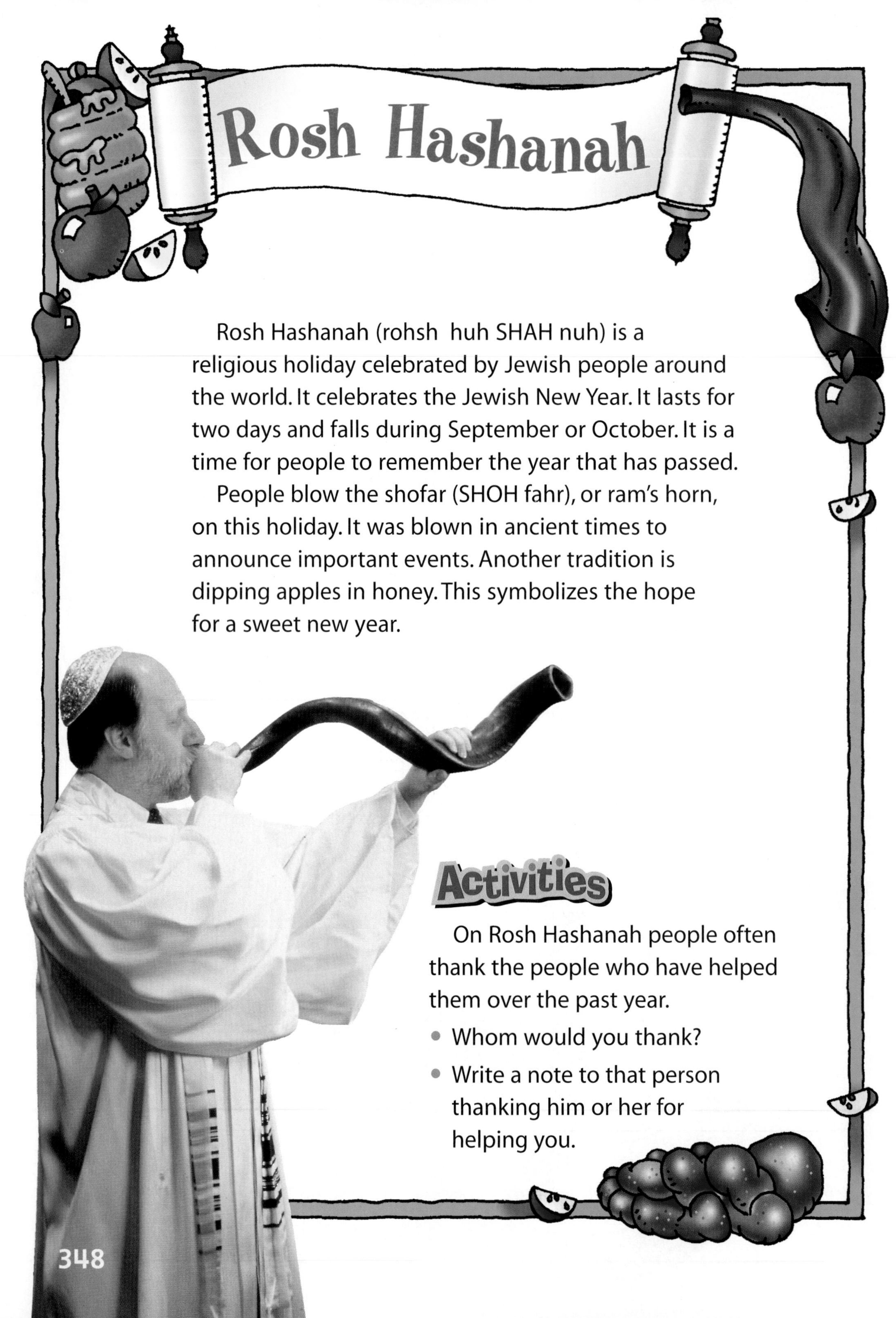

Rosh Hashanah

Rosh Hashanah (rohsh huh SHAH nuh) is a religious holiday celebrated by Jewish people around the world. It celebrates the Jewish New Year. It lasts for two days and falls during September or October. It is a time for people to remember the year that has passed.

People blow the shofar (SHOH fahr), or ram's horn, on this holiday. It was blown in ancient times to announce important events. Another tradition is dipping apples in honey. This symbolizes the hope for a sweet new year.

Activities

On Rosh Hashanah people often thank the people who have helped them over the past year.

- Whom would you thank?
- Write a note to that person thanking him or her for helping you.

Eid al-Fitr

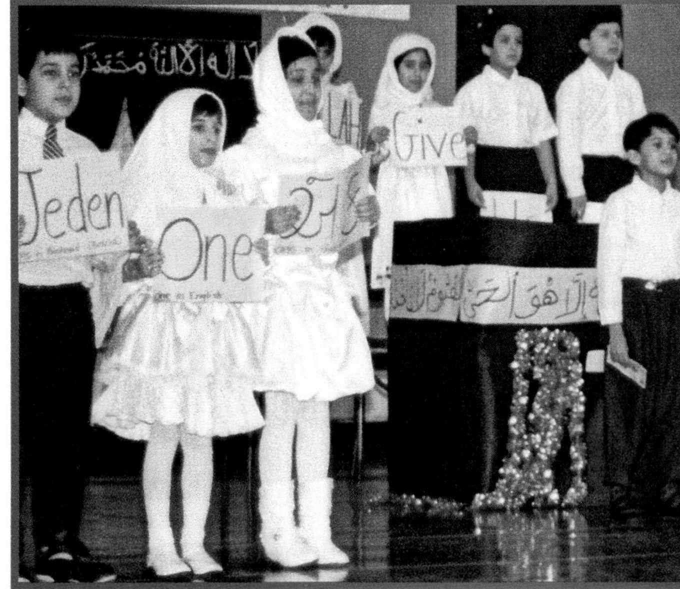

People in Muslim communities around the world celebrate a religious holiday called Eid al-Fitr (EED AHL FIT er), which means the "Festival of Fast-Breaking." Eid al-Fitr takes place every year after the end of a month that Muslims call Ramadan (RAM uh dahn). During Ramadan, Muslims fast, or do not eat, during the day. They also do good deeds and study their holy book, the Quran.

On the first day of Eid al-Fitr, families and friends celebrate with an early-morning prayer. Children dress in new clothes and receive presents. Families share a special meal. Sweet foods made with dates and honey are favorite treats—and a great way to break the fast!

Activities

- Do a good deed for someone today.
- Write a paragraph describing your good deed. How did it make the other person feel?

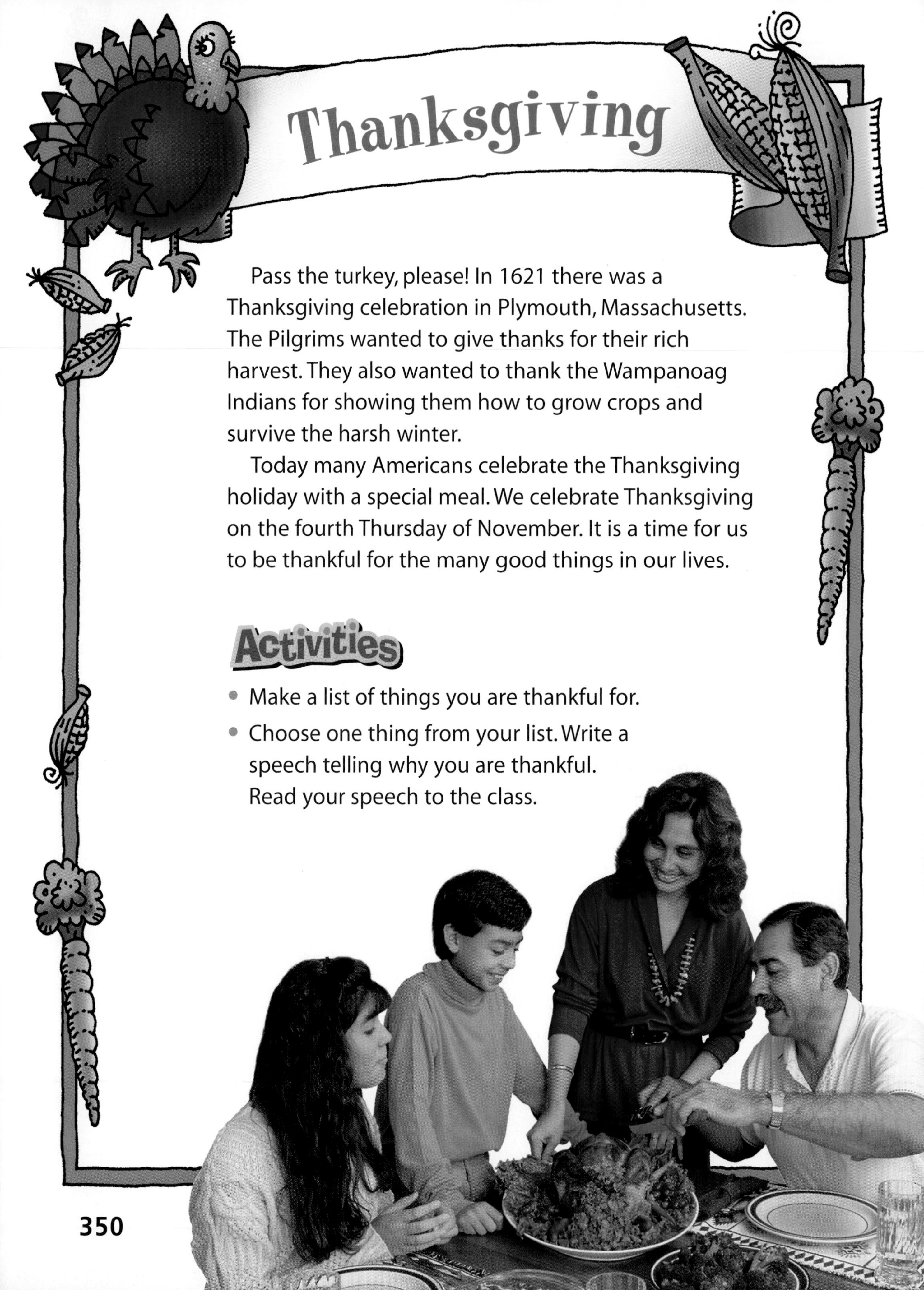

Thanksgiving

Pass the turkey, please! In 1621 there was a Thanksgiving celebration in Plymouth, Massachusetts. The Pilgrims wanted to give thanks for their rich harvest. They also wanted to thank the Wampanoag Indians for showing them how to grow crops and survive the harsh winter.

Today many Americans celebrate the Thanksgiving holiday with a special meal. We celebrate Thanksgiving on the fourth Thursday of November. It is a time for us to be thankful for the many good things in our lives.

Activities

- Make a list of things you are thankful for.
- Choose one thing from your list. Write a speech telling why you are thankful. Read your speech to the class.

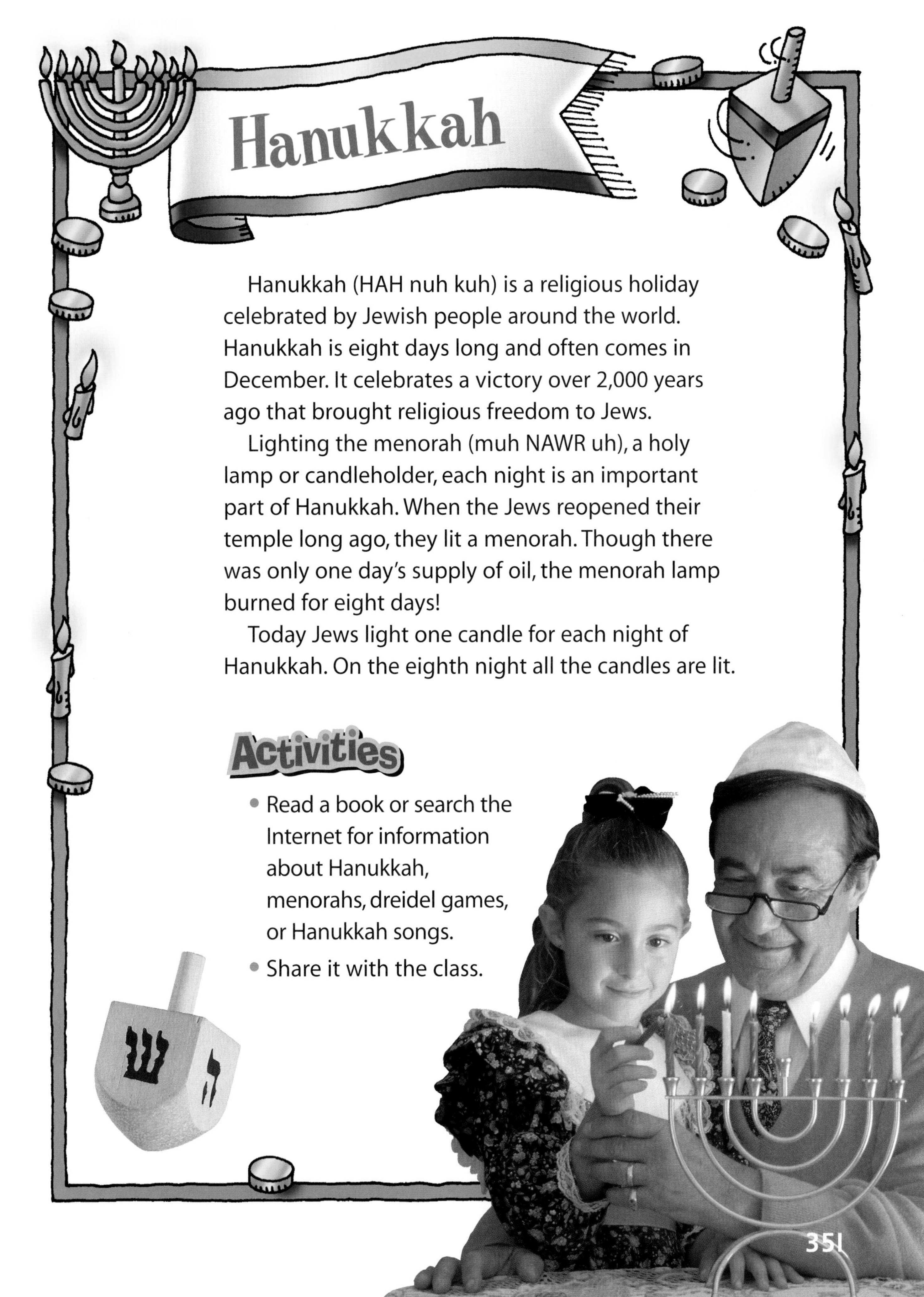

Hanukkah

Hanukkah (HAH nuh kuh) is a religious holiday celebrated by Jewish people around the world. Hanukkah is eight days long and often comes in December. It celebrates a victory over 2,000 years ago that brought religious freedom to Jews.

Lighting the menorah (muh NAWR uh), a holy lamp or candleholder, each night is an important part of Hanukkah. When the Jews reopened their temple long ago, they lit a menorah. Though there was only one day's supply of oil, the menorah lamp burned for eight days!

Today Jews light one candle for each night of Hanukkah. On the eighth night all the candles are lit.

Activities

- Read a book or search the Internet for information about Hanukkah, menorahs, dreidel games, or Hanukkah songs.
- Share it with the class.

Christmas

Christmas is a religious holiday that is celebrated by Christian people around the world. Christmas celebrates the birth of Jesus Christ. Christmas happens on December 25.

On Christmas Day people gather around the Christmas tree. They give each other gifts. Some people like to celebrate the holiday by singing Christmas carols. In some communities you will see streets lit up with Christmas lights. You might even join in a Christmas carol sing-along.

Activities

People say "Merry Christmas" in many languages.

- Make a Christmas card that says "Merry Christmas" in another language.
- Here are some ways people say "Merry Christmas" in other countries.
  France—Joyeux Noël
  Italy—Buon Natale
  Peru—Feliz Navidad
  Sweden—God Jul
  Philippines—Maligayang Pasko

Kwanzaa

Kwanzaa (KWAHN zuh) is a special holiday that is celebrated by many African Americans today. The name *Kwanzaa* comes from the African language of Swahili (swah HEE lee). It means "first fruits." Kwanzaa is a time for people to celebrate their heritage. It also honors important beliefs, such as helping others.

Kwanzaa lasts for seven days, from December 26 to January 1. People gather each night of this week to celebrate and share food. They also light candles on the kinara (kee NAH rah), a candleholder. Symbols of Kwanzaa are placed on a straw mat. One symbol is an ear of corn. One ear is placed on the mat for each child in the family.

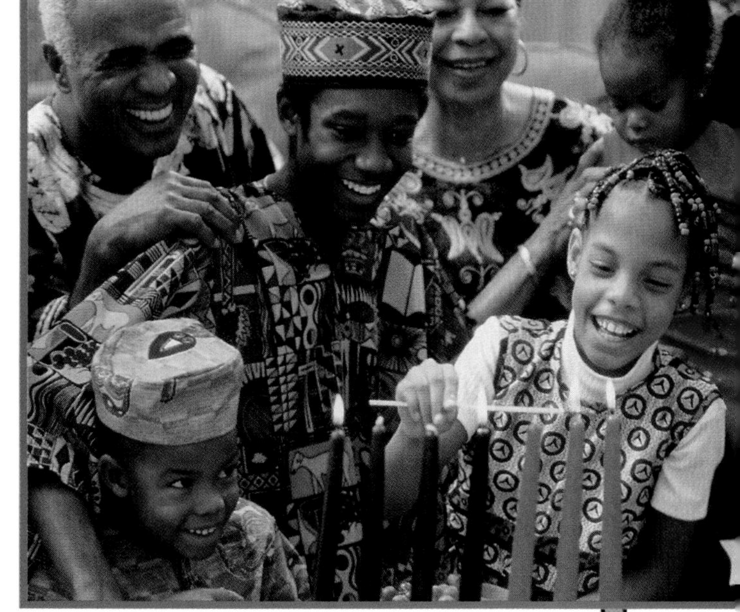

Activities

On January 1 people come together for a big feast. Before they share food, they often read poems.

- Write a poem about helping others, and read it to a partner.

Martin Luther King, Jr., Day

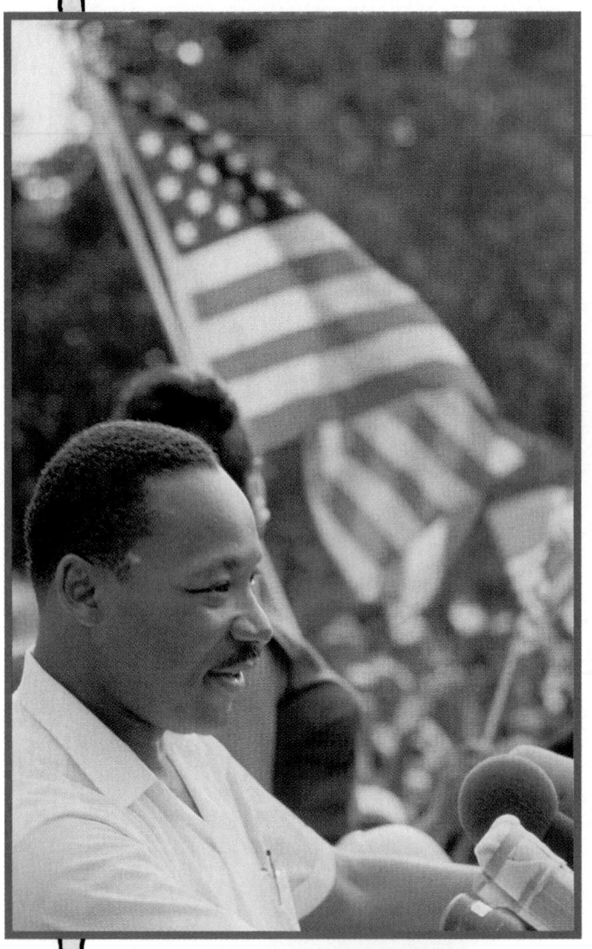

Dr. Martin Luther King, Jr., was born in Atlanta, Georgia, on January 15, 1929. During the 1950s and 1960s, he worked to make sure people of all backgrounds were treated fairly. In 1963 he made an important speech in Washington, D.C. He said, "I have a dream that my four children will one day live in a nation where they will not be judged by the color of their skin."

Dr. King was killed in 1968. His birthday later became a holiday. It is celebrated on the third Monday in January. Today many people honor this day by working together for their communities. In this way they are working to make Dr. King's dream come true.

Activities

Dr. Martin Luther King, Jr., had a dream that one day Americans of all backgrounds could live together as friends.

- Write about something that you wish for that would help the world.

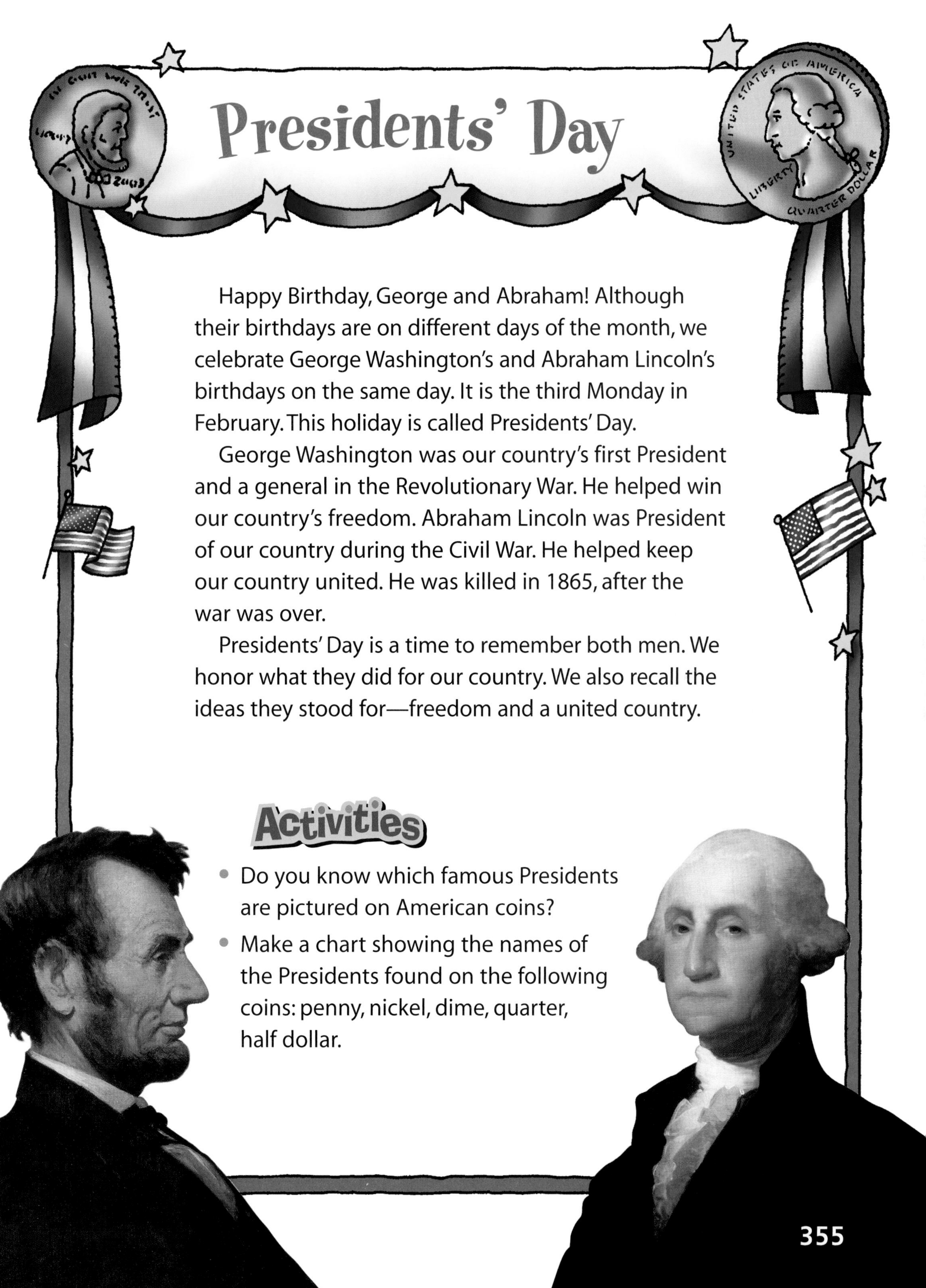

Presidents' Day

Happy Birthday, George and Abraham! Although their birthdays are on different days of the month, we celebrate George Washington's and Abraham Lincoln's birthdays on the same day. It is the third Monday in February. This holiday is called Presidents' Day.

George Washington was our country's first President and a general in the Revolutionary War. He helped win our country's freedom. Abraham Lincoln was President of our country during the Civil War. He helped keep our country united. He was killed in 1865, after the war was over.

Presidents' Day is a time to remember both men. We honor what they did for our country. We also recall the ideas they stood for—freedom and a united country.

Activities

- Do you know which famous Presidents are pictured on American coins?
- Make a chart showing the names of the Presidents found on the following coins: penny, nickel, dime, quarter, half dollar.

Saint Patrick's Day

On March 17 people in communities around the world celebrate Saint Patrick's Day. Saint Patrick was born over 1,600 years ago. He taught people in Ireland about Christianity and set up many schools and churches.

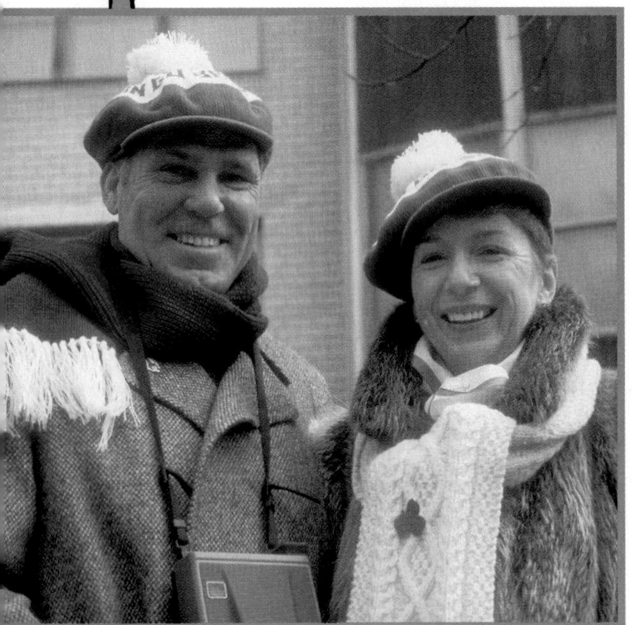

This holiday has become a day to celebrate the Irish culture. You may hear people playing Irish folk songs or see people dancing traditional Irish step dances.

On Saint Patrick's Day people often wear green clothes and paint shamrocks on windows. A shamrock is a three-leaf clover. It is used as a symbol for the Irish.

Activities

- Find out where and when the first Saint Patrick's Day Parade was held. You can look it up on the Internet or in the library.
- Make a Saint Patrick's Day poster.

Cinco de Mayo

Have you ever heard someone say, "Viva la libertad!" (vee VAH LAH LEE bir tahd)? It means "Long live liberty" in Spanish. In some communities you can hear these words during a holiday called Cinco de Mayo (SEEN koh DAY MIGH yoh). This holiday celebrates a Mexican victory over a much larger French army on May 5, 1862. The Mexicans fought because they wanted liberty, or freedom, from France.

Cinco de Mayo means "Fifth of May" in Spanish. On this day Mexicans and Mexican Americans celebrate with parades, dancing, mariachi music, and Mexican foods.

Activities

You read that Cinco de Mayo means "Fifth of May" in Spanish.

- Find out how to say the numbers one through five in Spanish.
- Recite the numbers one through five in Spanish forward and backward.

Memorial Day

On the last Monday in May, we celebrate Memorial Day. The holiday used to be called Decoration Day because people would decorate the graves of soldiers who had lost their lives in war. Memorial Day began as a day to remember those killed during the Civil War. Today we honor all soldiers who have died for our country.

People celebrate Memorial Day in different ways. Families place flags and flowers at the graves of relatives who died in wars. Many communities remember our soldiers with a parade. Often a lone bugler will play "Taps," the song for fallen soldiers. How is Memorial Day celebrated in your community?

Activities

- Design a patriotic poster celebrating Memorial Day.
- Hang it in your classroom to remember the Americans who lost their lives in war.

Independence Day

Summer is a special time across our country. For many people, summer fun starts only after a very well known holiday. Independence Day marks the celebration of our country's birthday: July 4, 1776. It reminds us of our country's declaration of independence from England.

How do you like to celebrate Independence Day? If your town is like many across the country, you might enjoy a fireworks display!

Activities

Do you know what the colors of our flag stand for? Red stands for courage. White stands for purity. Blue is for loyalty.

- Make a flag for your classroom. What colors will you use? What will they stand for?
- Will your classroom flag have stars? How many?

Reference Section

The Reference Section has many parts, each with a different type of information. Use this section to look up people, places, and events as you study.

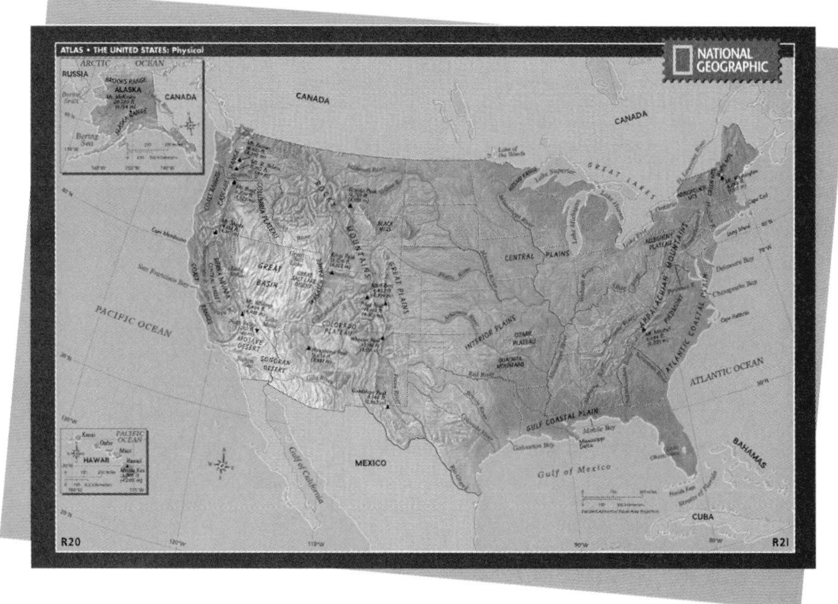

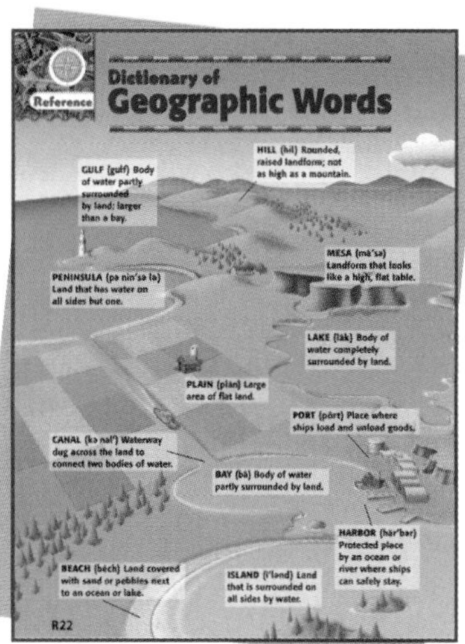

Martin Luther King, Jr.

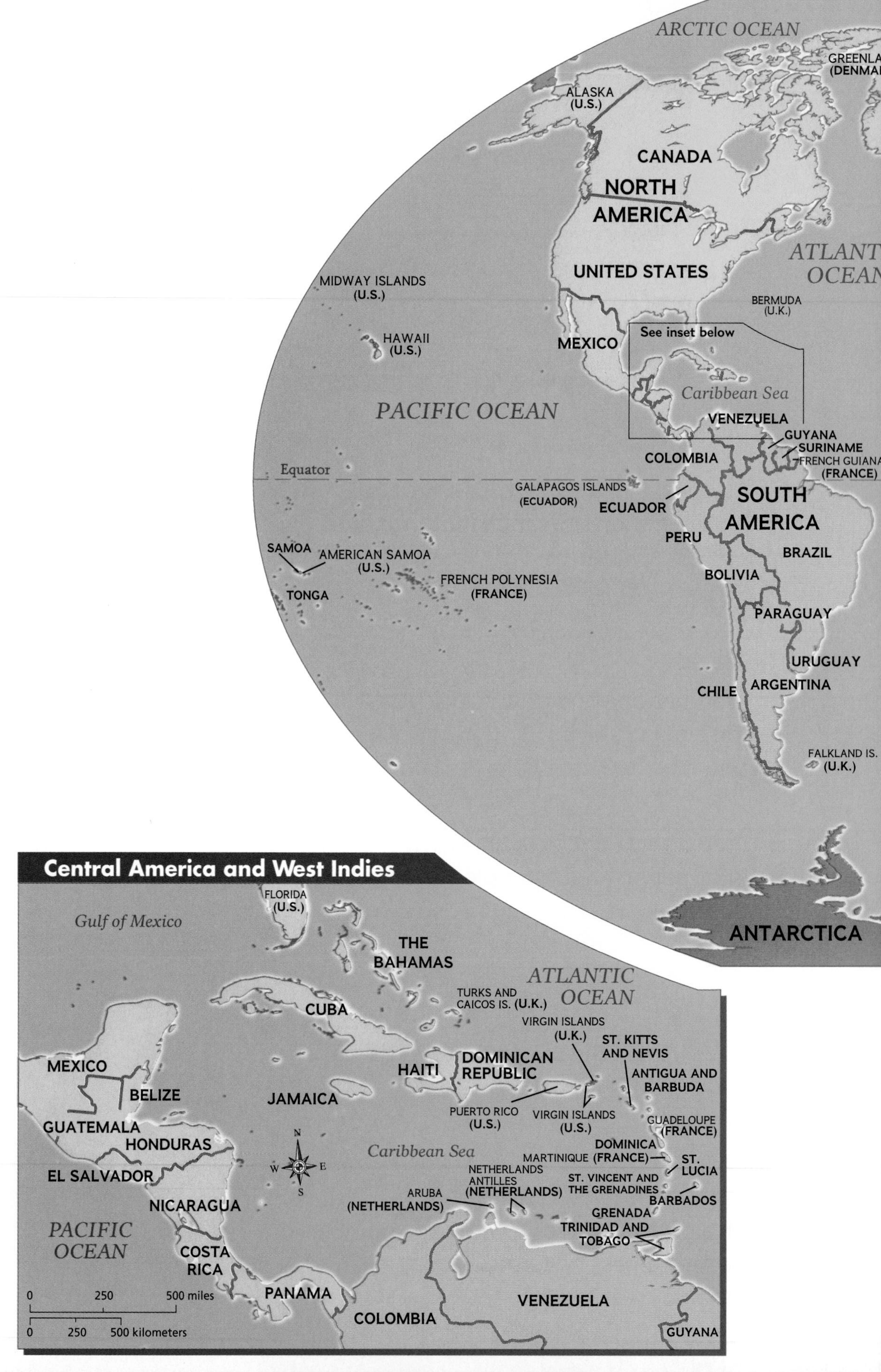
ARCTIC OCEAN
GREENLAND (DENMARK)
ALASKA (U.S.)
CANADA
NORTH AMERICA
ATLANTIC OCEAN
UNITED STATES
MIDWAY ISLANDS (U.S.)
BERMUDA (U.K.)
HAWAII (U.S.)
MEXICO
See inset below
Caribbean Sea
PACIFIC OCEAN
VENEZUELA
GUYANA
SURINAME
FRENCH GUIANA (FRANCE)
COLOMBIA
Equator
GALAPAGOS ISLANDS (ECUADOR)
ECUADOR
SOUTH AMERICA
PERU
SAMOA
AMERICAN SAMOA (U.S.)
BRAZIL
FRENCH POLYNESIA (FRANCE)
BOLIVIA
TONGA
PARAGUAY
URUGUAY
CHILE
ARGENTINA
FALKLAND IS. (U.K.)
ANTARCTICA
Central America and West Indies
FLORIDA (U.S.)
Gulf of Mexico
THE BAHAMAS
ATLANTIC OCEAN
TURKS AND CAICOS IS. (U.K.)
CUBA
VIRGIN ISLANDS (U.K.)
ST. KITTS AND NEVIS
DOMINICAN REPUBLIC
MEXICO
HAITI
ANTIGUA AND BARBUDA
BELIZE
JAMAICA
PUERTO RICO (U.S.)
VIRGIN ISLANDS (U.S.)
GUADELOUPE (FRANCE)
GUATEMALA
HONDURAS
Caribbean Sea
DOMINICA
MARTINIQUE (FRANCE)
ST. LUCIA
EL SALVADOR
NETHERLANDS ANTILLES (NETHERLANDS)
ST. VINCENT AND THE GRENADINES
ARUBA (NETHERLANDS)
BARBADOS
NICARAGUA
GRENADA
PACIFIC OCEAN
TRINIDAD AND TOBAGO
COSTA RICA
0 250 500 miles
0 250 500 kilometers
PANAMA
VENEZUELA
COLOMBIA
GUYANA
N
S
E
W

SPITSBERGEN (NORWAY)
SVALARD IS. (NORWAY)
ICELAND
See inset below
North Sea
EUROPE
RUSSIA
ASIA
KAZAKHSTAN
MONGOLIA
UZBEKISTAN
KRGYZSTAN
GEORGIA
ARMENIA
TURKMENISTAN
TAJIKISTAN
TURKEY
AZERBAIJAN
CHINA
NORTH KOREA
SOUTH KOREA
JAPAN
TUNISIA
LEBANON
SYRIA
ISRAEL
IRAQ
JORDAN
AFGHANISTAN
IRAN
PAKISTAN
BHUTAN
NEPAL
PACIFIC OCEAN
MOROCCO
ALGERIA
LIBYA
EGYPT
KUWAIT
QATAR
SAUDI ARABIA
UNITED ARAB EMIRATES
INDIA
MYANMAR (BURMA)
BANGLADESH
TAIWAN
WAKE ISLAND (U.S.)
NORTHERN MARIANA IS. (U.S.)
MARSHALL IS.
OMAN
LAOS
MALI
NIGER
CHAD
ERITREA
YEMEN
THAILAND
VIETNAM
CAMBODIA
PHILIPPINES
SUDAN
DJIBOUTI
BURKINA FASO
BENIN
GUINEA
AFRICA
NIGERIA
ETHIOPIA
SRI LANKA
GUAM (U.S.)
FEDERATED STATES OF MICRONESIA
LIBERIA
CENTRAL AFRICAN REP.
TOGO
GHANA
CAMEROON
BRUNEI
PALAU
MALAYSIA
UGANDA
SOMALIA
MALDIVES
Equator
KIRIBATI
KENYA
GABON
RWANDA
CONGO
BURUNDI
DEM. REP. OF THE CONGO
INDONESIA
PAPUA NEW GUINEA
TANZANIA
SEYCHELLES
INDIAN OCEAN
SOLOMON ISLANDS
EAST TIMOR
ANGOLA
TUVALU
ATLANTIC OCEAN
ZAMBIA
MALAWI
MOZAMBIQUE
VANUATU
MADAGASCAR
MAURITIUS
FIJI
NAMIBIA
ZIMBABWE
BOTSWANA
NEW CALEDONIA (FRANCE)
AUSTRALIA
SWAZILAND
SOUTH AFRICA
LESOTHO
N
W
E
S
0 1,000 2,000 miles
0 1,000 2,000 kilometers
Winkel Tripel Projection
NEW ZEALAND
ANTARCTICA
Europe
FINLAND
NORWAY
North Sea
SWEDEN
ESTONIA
UNITED KINGDOM
DENMARK
LATVIA
RUSSIA
IRELAND
Baltic Sea
LITHUANIA
RUSSIA
NETHERLANDS
BELARUS
POLAND
ATLANTIC OCEAN
BELGIUM
GERMANY
CZECH REPUBLIC
LUXEMBOURG
UKRAINE
LIECHTENSTEIN
SLOVAKIA
FRANCE
AUSTRIA
MOLDOVA
SWITZERLAND
HUNGARY
SLOVENIA
ROMANIA
CROATIA
MONACO
BOSNIA AND HERZEGOVINA
SERBIA and MONTENEGRO
Black Sea
GEORGIA
PORTUGAL
ANDORRA
CORSICA (FR.)
BULGARIA
SPAIN
ITALY
BALEARIC IS. (SP.)
MACEDONIA
TURKEY
SARDINIA (IT.)
ALBANIA
GREECE
ASIA
GIBRALTAR (U.K.)
Mediterranean Sea
SICILY (IT.)
0 250 500 miles
0 250 500 kilometers
MALTA
SYRIA
CYPRUS
LEBANON
CRETE (GR.)

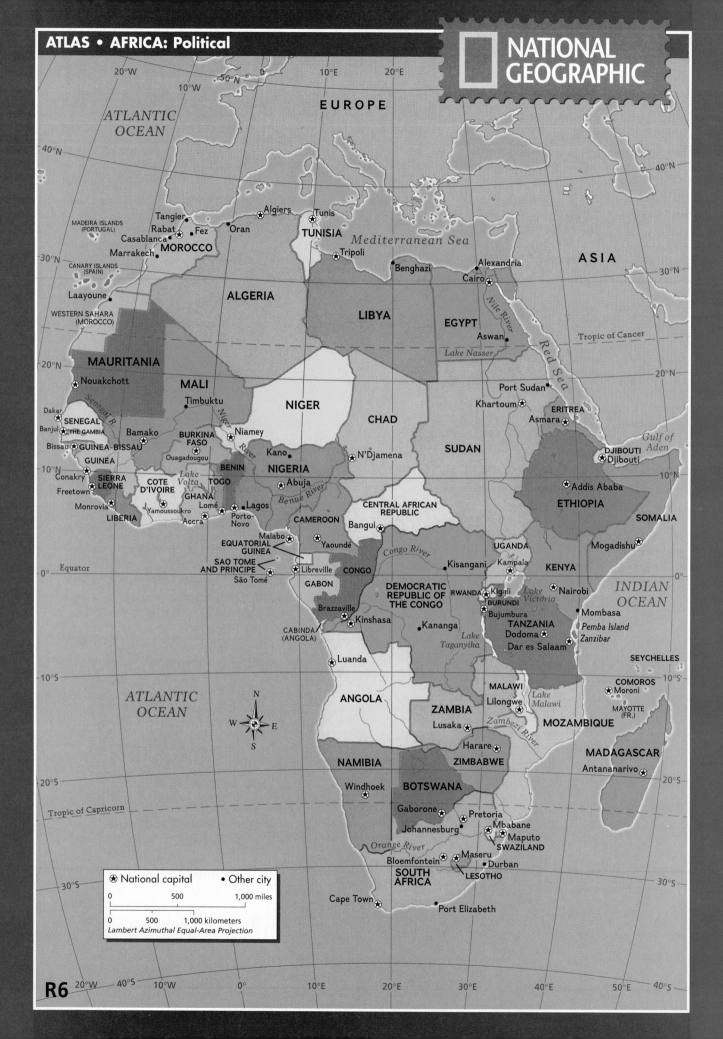

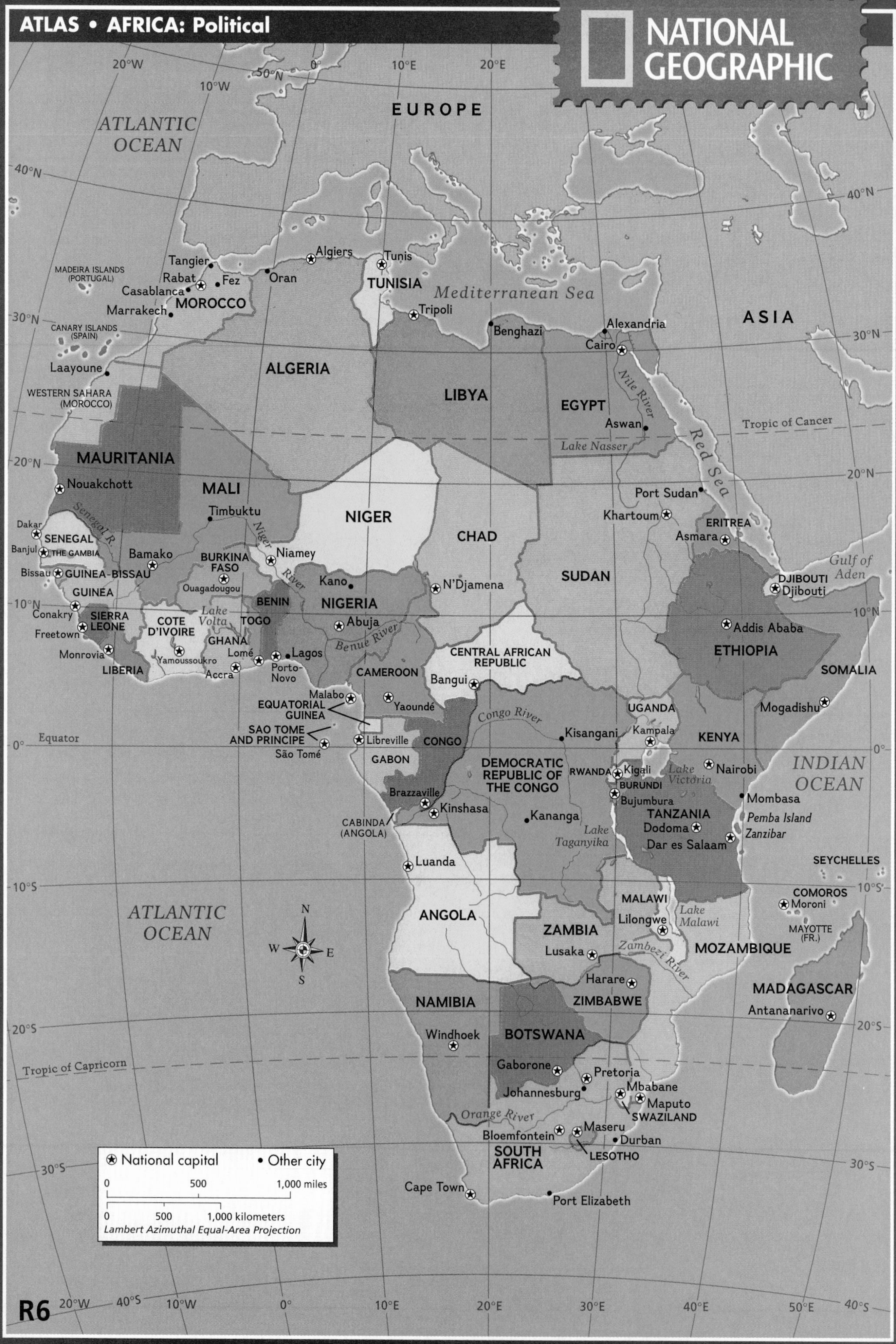
NATIONAL GEOGRAPHIC
EUROPE
ATLANTIC OCEAN
ASIA
Mediterranean Sea
MADEIRA ISLANDS (PORTUGAL)
CANARY ISLANDS (SPAIN)
Tangier
Rabat
Fez
Casablanca
Marrakech
MOROCCO
Algiers
Oran
Tunis
TUNISIA
Tripoli
Benghazi
Alexandria
Cairo
Laayoune
WESTERN SAHARA (MOROCCO)
ALGERIA
LIBYA
EGYPT
Nile River
Aswan
Lake Nasser
Red Sea
Tropic of Cancer
MAURITANIA
Nouakchott
MALI
Timbuktu
NIGER
CHAD
SUDAN
Port Sudan
Khartoum
ERITREA
Asmara
Gulf of Aden
DJIBOUTI
Djibouti
Dakar
SENEGAL
Senegal R.
Banjul
THE GAMBIA
Bissau
GUINEA-BISSAU
Bamako
BURKINA FASO
Ouagadougou
Niamey
Niger River
GUINEA
Conakry
SIERRA LEONE
Freetown
Monrovia
LIBERIA
COTE D'IVOIRE
Yamoussoukro
Lake Volta
GHANA
Accra
TOGO
Lomé
BENIN
Porto-Novo
Lagos
Kano
NIGERIA
Abuja
Benue River
N'Djamena
CAMEROON
Yaoundé
CENTRAL AFRICAN REPUBLIC
Bangui
ETHIOPIA
Addis Ababa
SOMALIA
Mogadishu
Malabo
EQUATORIAL GUINEA
SAO TOME AND PRINCIPE
São Tomé
Libreville
GABON
CONGO
Congo River
Brazzaville
Kinshasa
CABINDA (ANGOLA)
Equator
DEMOCRATIC REPUBLIC OF THE CONGO
Kisangani
Kananga
UGANDA
Kampala
KENYA
Nairobi
Mombasa
RWANDA
Kigali
BURUNDI
Bujumbura
Lake Victoria
TANZANIA
Dodoma
Dar es Salaam
Lake Taganyika
Pemba Island
Zanzibar
INDIAN OCEAN
SEYCHELLES
COMOROS
Moroni
MAYOTTE (FR.)
Luanda
ANGOLA
ZAMBIA
Lusaka
MALAWI
Lilongwe
Lake Malawi
Zambezi River
MOZAMBIQUE
Harare
ZIMBABWE
MADAGASCAR
Antananarivo
NAMIBIA
Windhoek
BOTSWANA
Gaborone
Pretoria
Johannesburg
Mbabane
Maputo
SWAZILAND
Tropic of Capricorn
Orange River
Bloemfontein
Maseru
LESOTHO
Durban
SOUTH AFRICA
Cape Town
Port Elizabeth
N
S
E
W
National capital
Other city
0 500 1,000 miles
0 500 1,000 kilometers
Lambert Azimuthal Equal-Area Projection
20°W
10°W
0°
10°E
20°E
30°E
40°E
50°E
50°N
40°N
30°N
20°N
10°N
0°
10°S
20°S
30°S
40°S

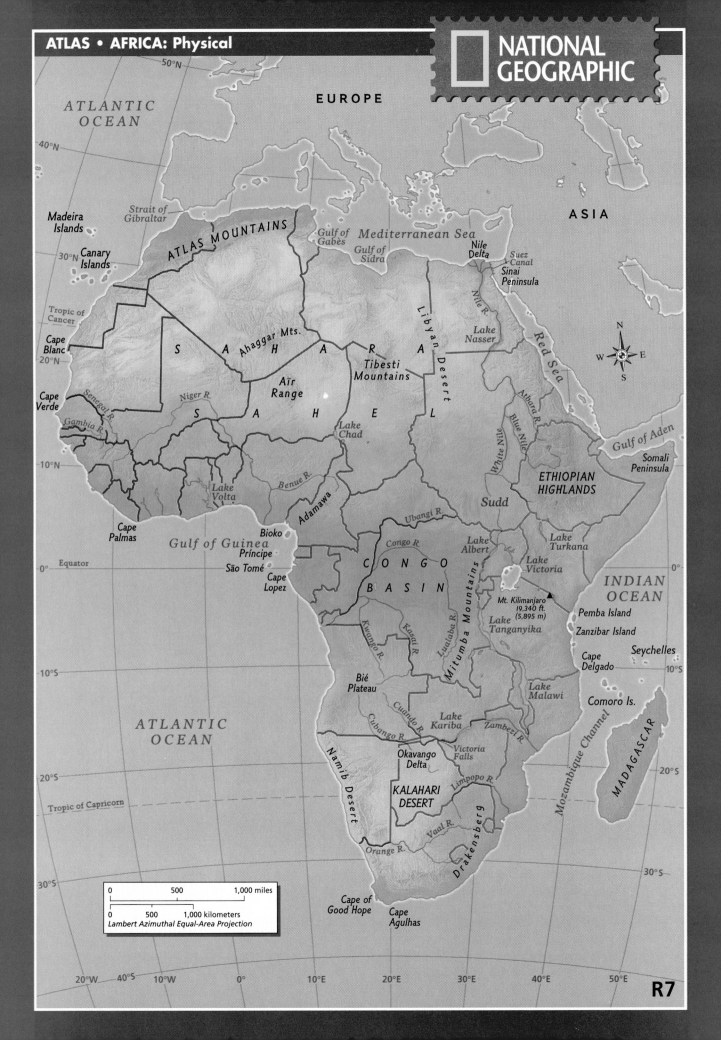

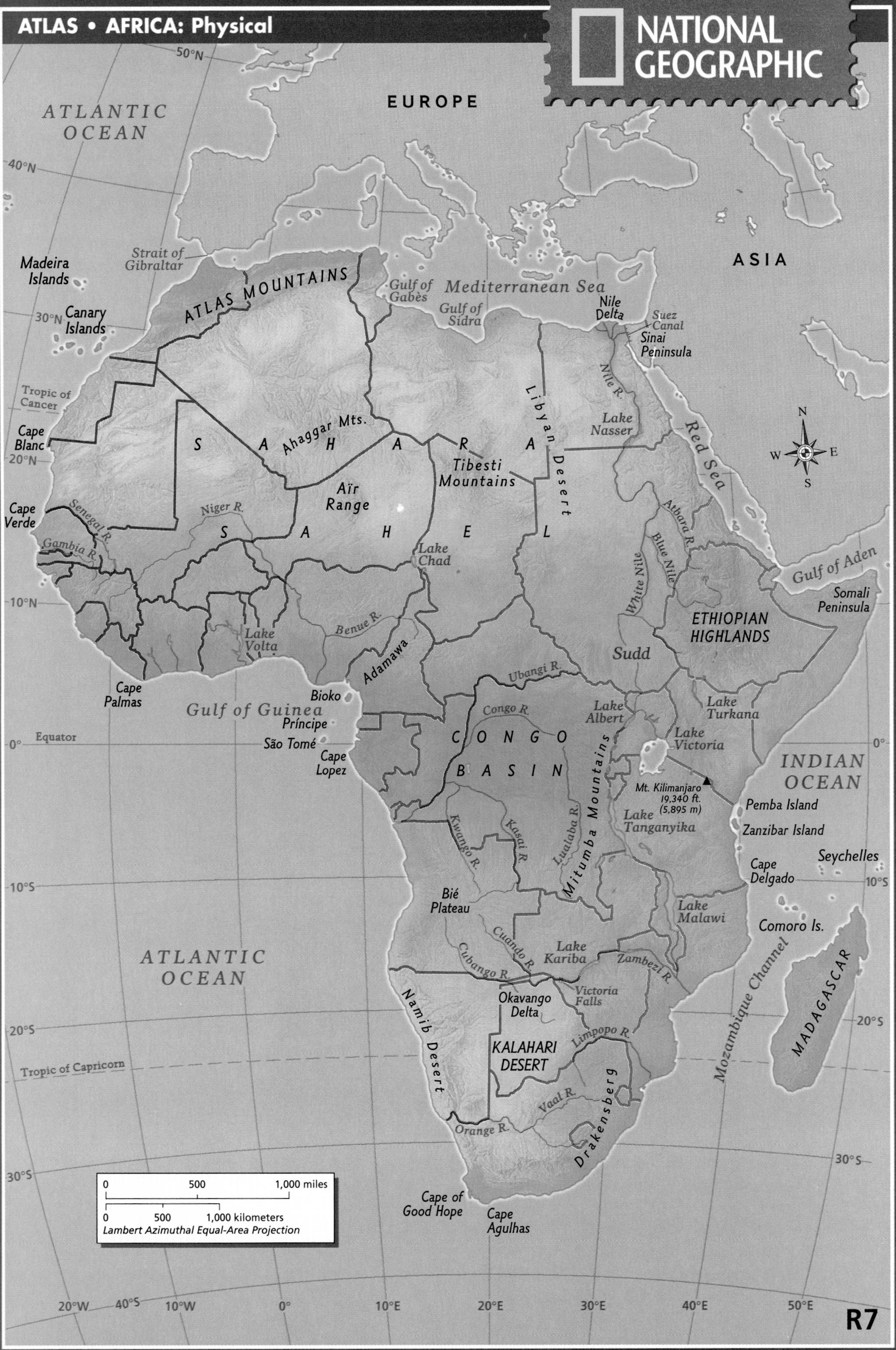
NATIONAL GEOGRAPHIC
EUROPE
ATLANTIC OCEAN
ASIA
Madeira Islands
Strait of Gibraltar
Canary Islands
ATLAS MOUNTAINS
Gulf of Gabès
Mediterranean Sea
Gulf of Sidra
Nile Delta
Suez Canal
Sinai Peninsula
Nile R.
Tropic of Cancer
Cape Blanc
Ahaggar Mts.
S A H A R A
Libyan Desert
Lake Nasser
Red Sea
Tibesti Mountains
Aïr Range
Cape Verde
Senegal R.
Niger R.
S A H E L
Gambia R.
Lake Chad
Atbara R.
Blue Nile
White Nile
Gulf of Aden
Somali Peninsula
ETHIOPIAN HIGHLANDS
Lake Volta
Benue R.
Adamawa
Sudd
Ubangi R.
Cape Palmas
Bioko
Gulf of Guinea
Príncipe
São Tomé
Equator
Cape Lopez
Congo R.
CONGO BASIN
Lake Albert
Lake Turkana
Lake Victoria
Mitumba Mountains
Mt. Kilimanjaro 19,340 ft. (5,895 m)
INDIAN OCEAN
Pemba Island
Zanzibar Island
Lake Tanganyika
Kwango R.
Kasai R.
Lualaba R.
Seychelles
Cape Delgado
Bié Plateau
Lake Malawi
Comoro Is.
ATLANTIC OCEAN
Cuando R.
Lake Kariba
Zambezi R.
Cubango R.
Namib Desert
Okavango Delta
Victoria Falls
Mozambique Channel
MADAGASCAR
KALAHARI DESERT
Limpopo R.
Tropic of Capricorn
Drakensberg
Vaal R.
Orange R.
Cape of Good Hope
Cape Agulhas
0 500 1,000 miles
0 500 1,000 kilometers
Lambert Azimuthal Equal-Area Projection
N
S
E
W
50°N
40°N
30°N
20°N
10°N
0°
10°S
20°S
30°S
40°S
20°W
10°W
0°
10°E
20°E
30°E
40°E
50°E

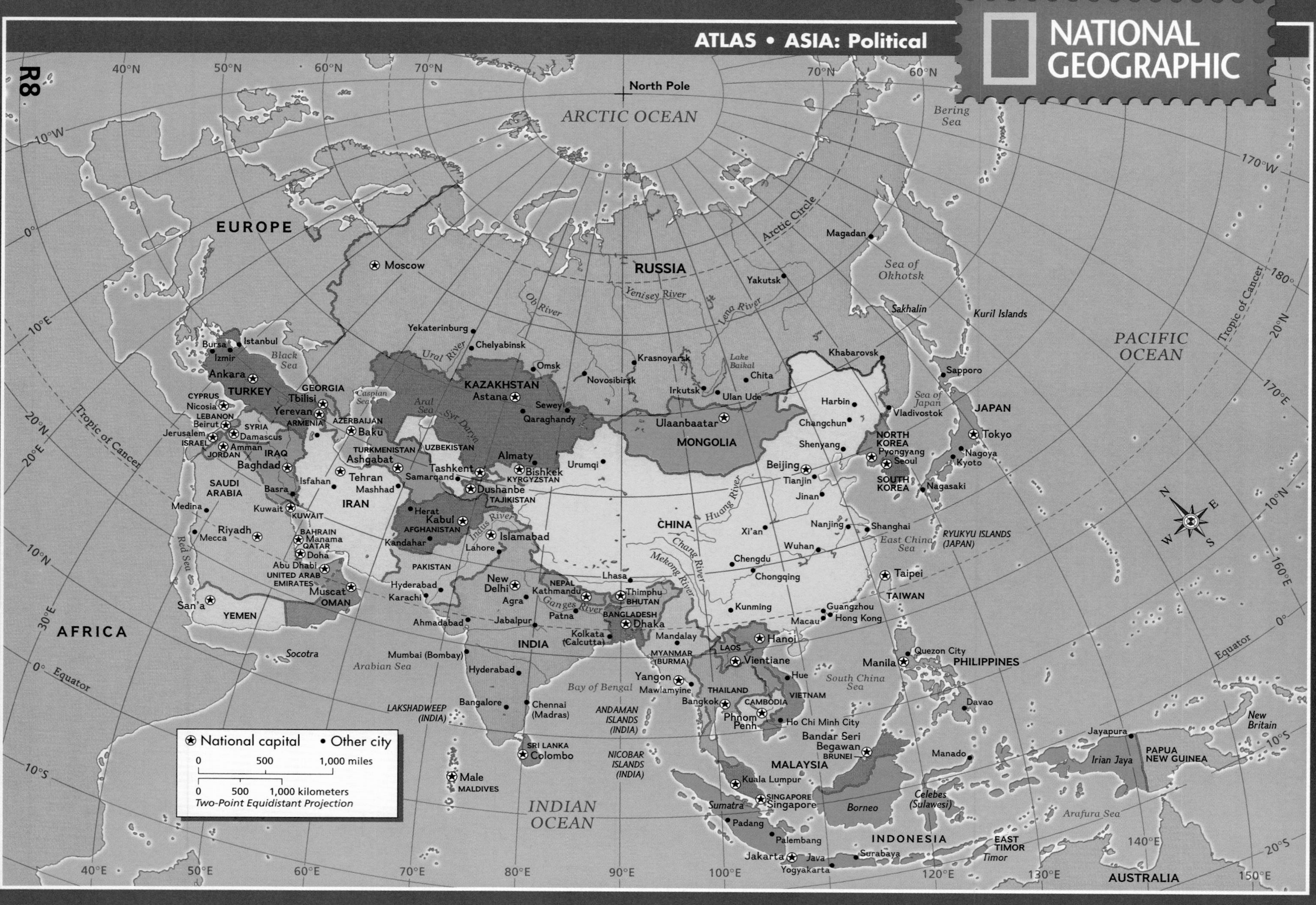
NATIONAL GEOGRAPHIC
North Pole
ARCTIC OCEAN
PACIFIC OCEAN
INDIAN OCEAN
EUROPE
AFRICA
RUSSIA
Moscow
Yekaterinburg
Chelyabinsk
Omsk
Novosibirsk
Krasnoyarsk
Irkutsk
Ulan Ude
Chita
Yakutsk
Magadan
Khabarovsk
Vladivostok
Ob River
Yenisey River
Lena River
Ural River
Lake Baikal
Arctic Circle
Bering Sea
Sea of Okhotsk
Sakhalin
Kuril Islands
Sea of Japan
JAPAN
Sapporo
Tokyo
Nagoya
Kyoto
Nagasaki
NORTH KOREA
Pyongyang
SOUTH KOREA
Seoul
MONGOLIA
Ulaanbaatar
CHINA
Harbin
Changchun
Shenyang
Beijing
Tianjin
Jinan
Nanjing
Shanghai
Wuhan
Xi'an
Chengdu
Chongqing
Kunming
Guangzhou
Hong Kong
Macau
Lhasa
Urumqi
Huang River
Chang River
Mekong River
East China Sea
RYUKYU ISLANDS (JAPAN)
TAIWAN
Taipei
KAZAKHSTAN
Astana
Semey
Qaraghandy
Almaty
Aral Sea
Syr Darya
Caspian Sea
Black Sea
UZBEKISTAN
Tashkent
Samarqand
TURKMENISTAN
Ashgabat
KYRGYZSTAN
Bishkek
TAJIKISTAN
Dushanbe
AFGHANISTAN
Kabul
Herat
Kandahar
PAKISTAN
Islamabad
Lahore
Hyderabad
Karachi
Indus River
IRAN
Tehran
Mashhad
Isfahan
TURKEY
Ankara
Istanbul
Bursa
Izmir
GEORGIA
Tbilisi
ARMENIA
Yerevan
AZERBAIJAN
Baku
CYPRUS
Nicosia
LEBANON
Beirut
SYRIA
Damascus
ISRAEL
Jerusalem
JORDAN
Amman
IRAQ
Baghdad
Basra
KUWAIT
Kuwait
SAUDI ARABIA
Riyadh
Medina
Mecca
BAHRAIN
Manama
QATAR
Doha
UNITED ARAB EMIRATES
Abu Dhabi
OMAN
Muscat
YEMEN
San'a
Socotra
Red Sea
Arabian Sea
INDIA
New Delhi
Agra
Jabalpur
Ahmadabad
Mumbai (Bombay)
Hyderabad
Bangalore
Chennai (Madras)
Kolkata (Calcutta)
Patna
Ganges River
NEPAL
Kathmandu
BHUTAN
Thimphu
BANGLADESH
Dhaka
LAKSHADWEEP (INDIA)
SRI LANKA
Colombo
Male
MALDIVES
Bay of Bengal
ANDAMAN ISLANDS (INDIA)
NICOBAR ISLANDS (INDIA)
MYANMAR (BURMA)
Mandalay
Yangon
Mawlamyine
THAILAND
Bangkok
LAOS
Vientiane
VIETNAM
Hanoi
Hue
Ho Chi Minh City
CAMBODIA
Phnom Penh
South China Sea
PHILIPPINES
Manila
Quezon City
Davao
MALAYSIA
Kuala Lumpur
BRUNEI
Bandar Seri Begawan
SINGAPORE
Singapore
INDONESIA
Sumatra
Padang
Palembang
Jakarta
Java
Yogyakarta
Surabaya
Borneo
Celebes (Sulawesi)
Manado
EAST TIMOR
Timor
Arafura Sea
Irian Jaya
Jayapura
PAPUA NEW GUINEA
New Britain
AUSTRALIA
Tropic of Cancer
Equator
National capital
Other city
0 500 1,000 miles
0 500 1,000 kilometers
Two-Point Equidistant Projection

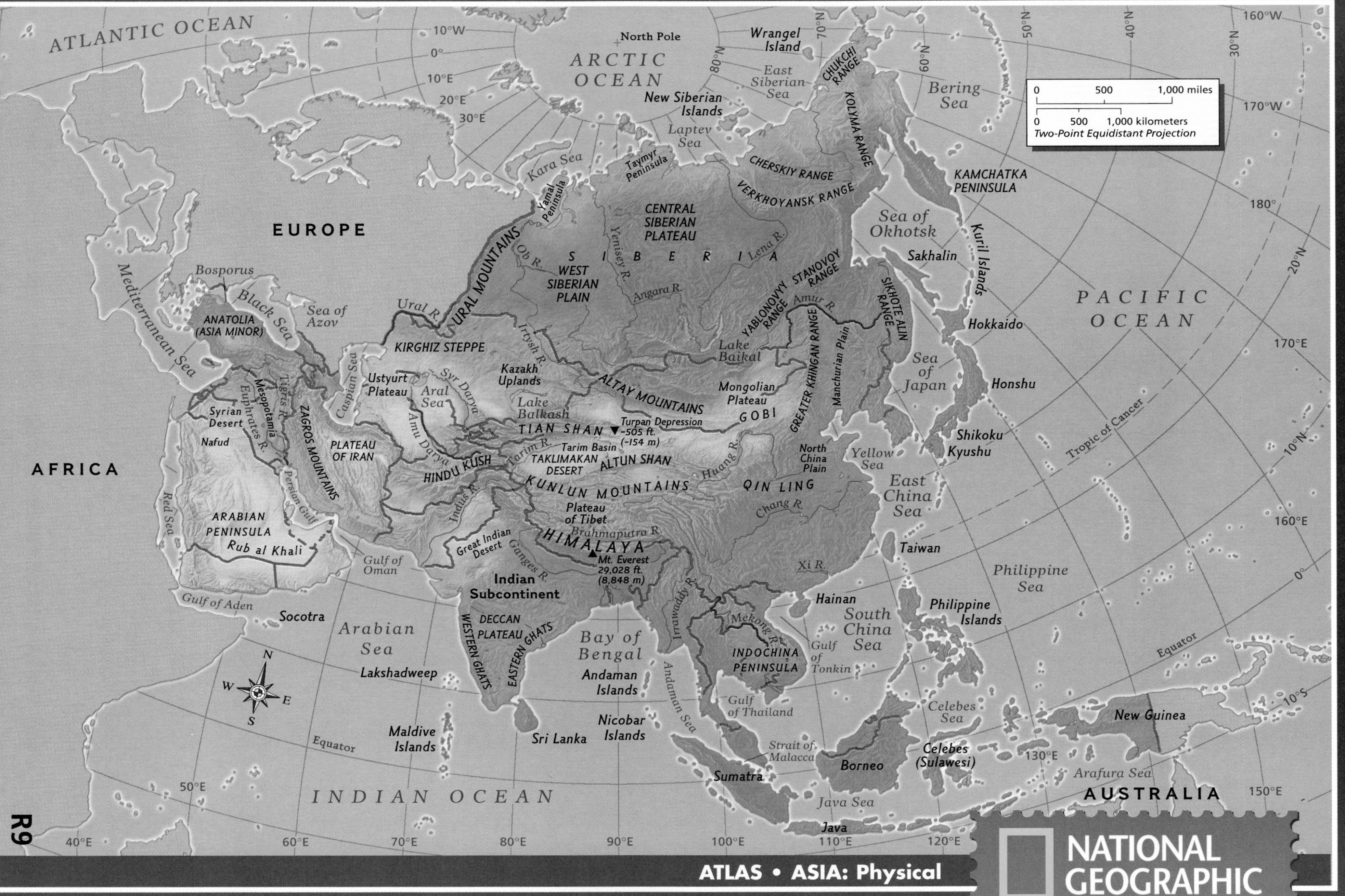

NATIONAL GEOGRAPHIC

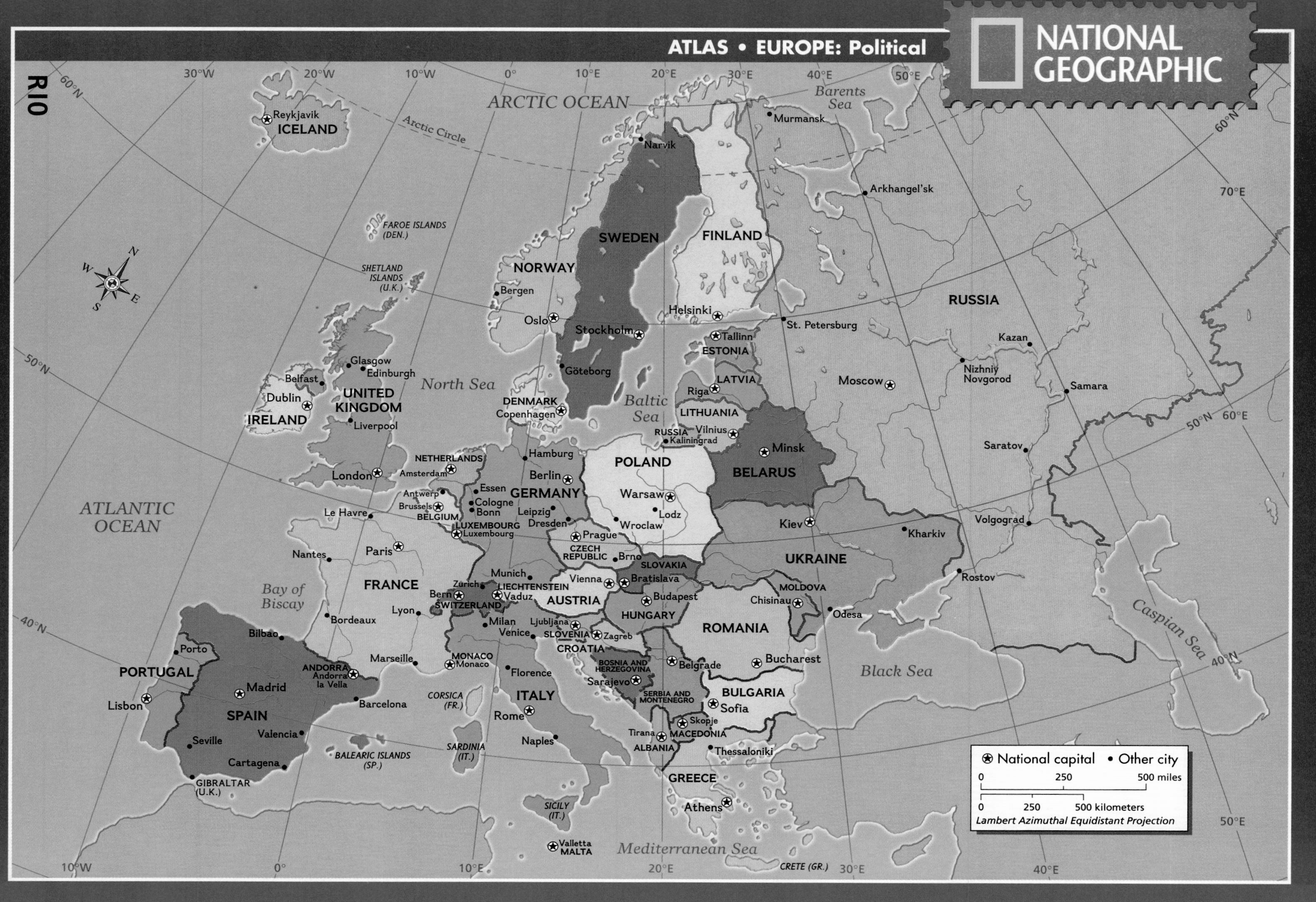
NATIONAL GEOGRAPHIC
ARCTIC OCEAN
Arctic Circle
Barents Sea
ATLANTIC OCEAN
North Sea
Baltic Sea
Bay of Biscay
Mediterranean Sea
Black Sea
Caspian Sea
ICELAND
Reykjavik
FAROE ISLANDS (DEN.)
SHETLAND ISLANDS (U.K.)
IRELAND
Dublin
Belfast
UNITED KINGDOM
Glasgow
Edinburgh
Liverpool
London
NORWAY
Bergen
Oslo
Narvik
SWEDEN
Stockholm
Göteborg
FINLAND
Helsinki
DENMARK
Copenhagen
ESTONIA
Tallinn
LATVIA
Riga
LITHUANIA
Vilnius
RUSSIA
Kaliningrad
Murmansk
Arkhangel'sk
St. Petersburg
Moscow
Nizhniy Novgorod
Kazan
Samara
Saratov
Volgograd
Rostov
BELARUS
Minsk
POLAND
Warsaw
Lodz
Wroclaw
NETHERLANDS
Amsterdam
BELGIUM
Antwerp
Brussels
LUXEMBOURG
Luxembourg
GERMANY
Hamburg
Berlin
Essen
Cologne
Bonn
Leipzig
Dresden
Munich
CZECH REPUBLIC
Prague
Brno
SLOVAKIA
Bratislava
AUSTRIA
Vienna
HUNGARY
Budapest
UKRAINE
Kiev
Kharkiv
Odesa
MOLDOVA
Chisinau
ROMANIA
Bucharest
FRANCE
Paris
Le Havre
Nantes
Bordeaux
Lyon
Marseille
SWITZERLAND
Zurich
Bern
LIECHTENSTEIN
Vaduz
MONACO
Monaco
ITALY
Milan
Venice
Florence
Rome
Naples
CORSICA (FR.)
SARDINIA (IT.)
SICILY (IT.)
MALTA
Valletta
SLOVENIA
Ljubljana
CROATIA
Zagreb
BOSNIA AND HERZEGOVINA
Sarajevo
SERBIA AND MONTENEGRO
Belgrade
MACEDONIA
Skopje
ALBANIA
Tirana
BULGARIA
Sofia
GREECE
Thessaloniki
Athens
CRETE (GR.)
PORTUGAL
Porto
Lisbon
SPAIN
Bilbao
Madrid
Valencia
Seville
Cartagena
Barcelona
ANDORRA
Andorra la Vella
BALEARIC ISLANDS (SP.)
GIBRALTAR (U.K.)
60°N
50°N
40°N
30°W
20°W
10°W
0°
10°E
20°E
30°E
40°E
50°E
60°E
70°E
N
E
S
W
National capital
Other city
0
250
500 miles
0
250
500 kilometers
Lambert Azimuthal Equidistant Projection

ATLAS • EUROPE: Physical

NATIONAL GEOGRAPHIC

Tropic of Cancer
Philippine Sea
NORTHERN MARIANA ISLANDS (U.S.)
Saipan
Guam (U.S.)
Hagatna
NORTH PACIFIC OCEAN
Wake Island (U.S.)
MARSHALL ISLANDS
Hawaii (U.S.)
Johnston Atoll (U.S.)
PALAU
Koror
Palikir
Majuro
FEDERATED STATES OF MICRONESIA
Kingman Reef (U.S.)
Palmyra Atoll (U.S.)
Howland Island (U.S.)
Tarawa
Baker Island (U.S.)
Equator
Yaren
NAURU
Jarvis Island (U.S.)
KIRIBATI
PAPUA NEW GUINEA
SOLOMON ISLANDS
TUVALU
Funafuti
Tokelau (N.Z.)
Marquesas Islands (Fr.)
Port Moresby
Honiara
Darwin
Coral Sea Islands Territory (Australia)
VANUATU
Wallis Island (Fr.)
FIJI ISLANDS
SAMOA
Apia
American Samoa (U.S.)
Pago Pago
Cook Islands (N.Z.)
Tahiti
Papeete
French Polynesia (Fr.)
Coral Sea
NEW CALEDONIA (Fr.)
Port-Vila
Suva
TONGA
Nukualofa
Noumea
Henderson Island (U.K.)
Tropic of Capricorn
Pitcairn Island (U.K.)
Ducie Island (U.K.)
AUSTRALIA
Brisbane
Norfolk Island (Australia)
Perth
Lord Howe Island (Australia)
Kermadec Islands (N.Z.)
Adelaide
Sydney
Canberra
Melbourne
Tasman Sea
Auckland
NEW ZEALAND
SOUTH PACIFIC OCEAN
Wellington
Christchurch
Chatham Islands (N.Z.)
INDIAN OCEAN

120°E 130°E 140°E 150°E 160°E 170°E 180° 170°W 160°W 150°W 140°W 130°W 120°W
20°N 10°N 0° 10°S 20°S 30°S 40°S 50°S

⊛ National capital • City
0 500 1,000 miles
0 500 1,000 kilometers
Mercator Projection

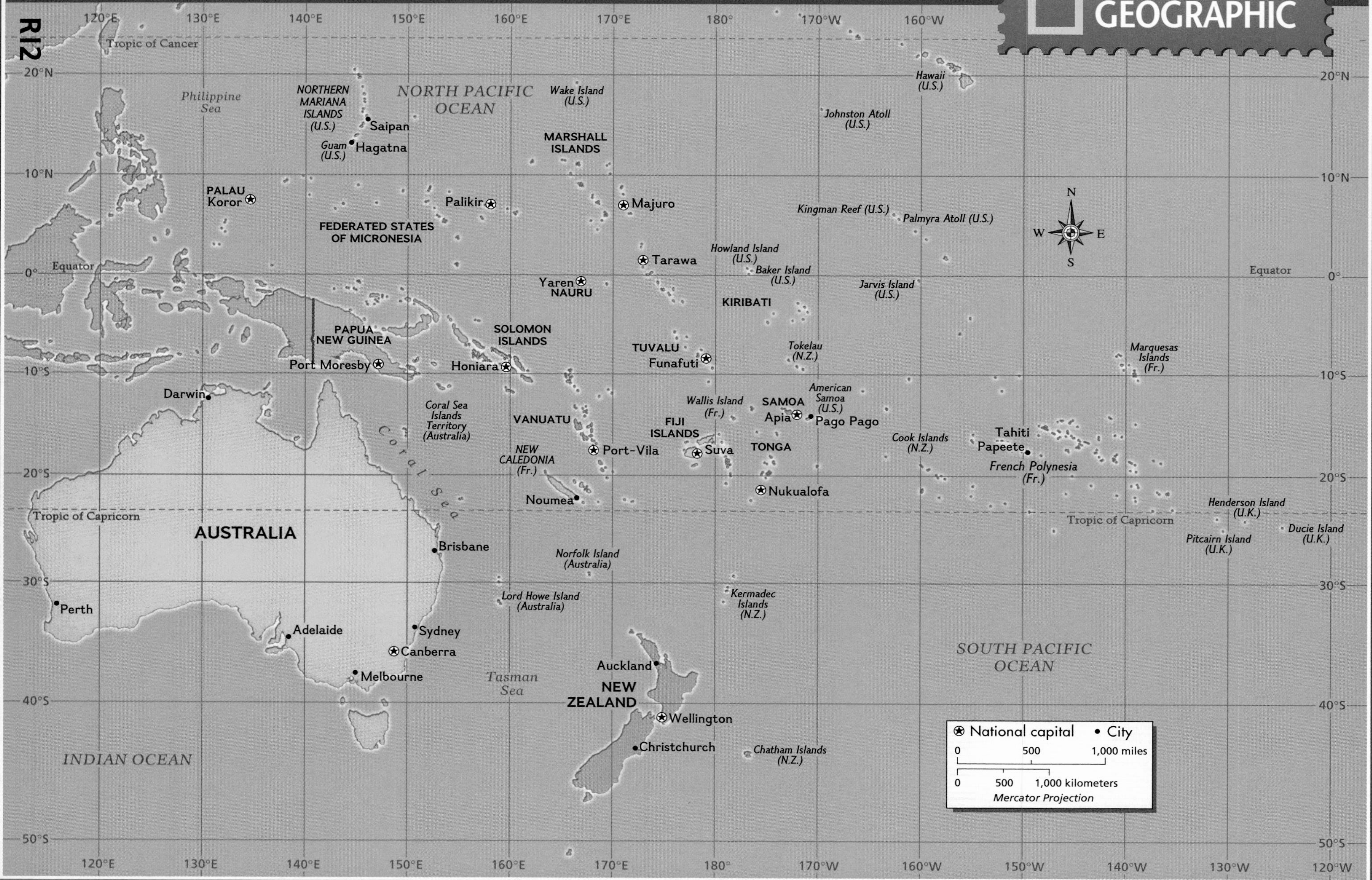

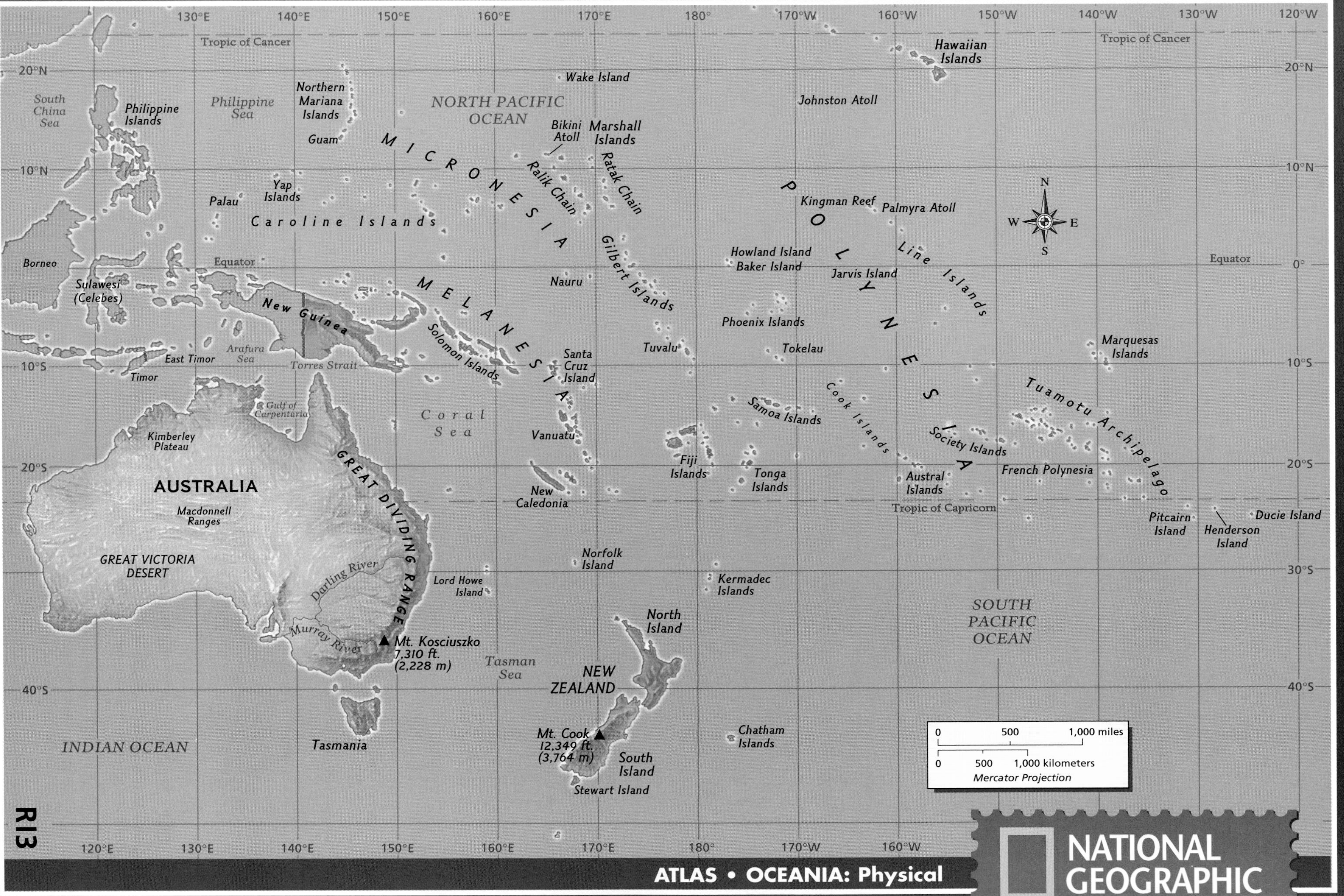
South China Sea
Philippine Islands
Philippine Sea
Northern Mariana Islands
Guam
NORTH PACIFIC OCEAN
Wake Island
Bikini Atoll
Marshall Islands
Ralik Chain
Ratak Chain
MICRONESIA
Palau
Yap Islands
Caroline Islands
Borneo
Sulawesi (Celebes)
Equator
Nauru
Gilbert Islands
MELANESIA
New Guinea
Solomon Islands
Santa Cruz Island
East Timor
Timor
Arafura Sea
Torres Strait
Gulf of Carpentaria
Coral Sea
Vanuatu
New Caledonia
Kimberley Plateau
AUSTRALIA
Macdonnell Ranges
GREAT VICTORIA DESERT
GREAT DIVIDING RANGE
Darling River
Murray River
Mt. Kosciuszko 7,310 ft. (2,228 m)
Lord Howe Island
Norfolk Island
Tasman Sea
NEW ZEALAND
North Island
South Island
Mt. Cook 12,349 ft. (3,764 m)
Stewart Island
Tasmania
INDIAN OCEAN
Hawaiian Islands
Johnston Atoll
Kingman Reef
Palmyra Atoll
POLYNESIA
Howland Island
Baker Island
Jarvis Island
Line Islands
Phoenix Islands
Tokelau
Tuvalu
Samoa Islands
Cook Islands
Fiji Islands
Tonga Islands
Kermadec Islands
Chatham Islands
Marquesas Islands
Tuamotu Archipelago
Society Islands
French Polynesia
Austral Islands
Tropic of Capricorn
Tropic of Cancer
Pitcairn Island
Henderson Island
Ducie Island
SOUTH PACIFIC OCEAN
N
S
E
W
0 500 1,000 miles
0 500 1,000 kilometers
Mercator Projection
NATIONAL GEOGRAPHIC

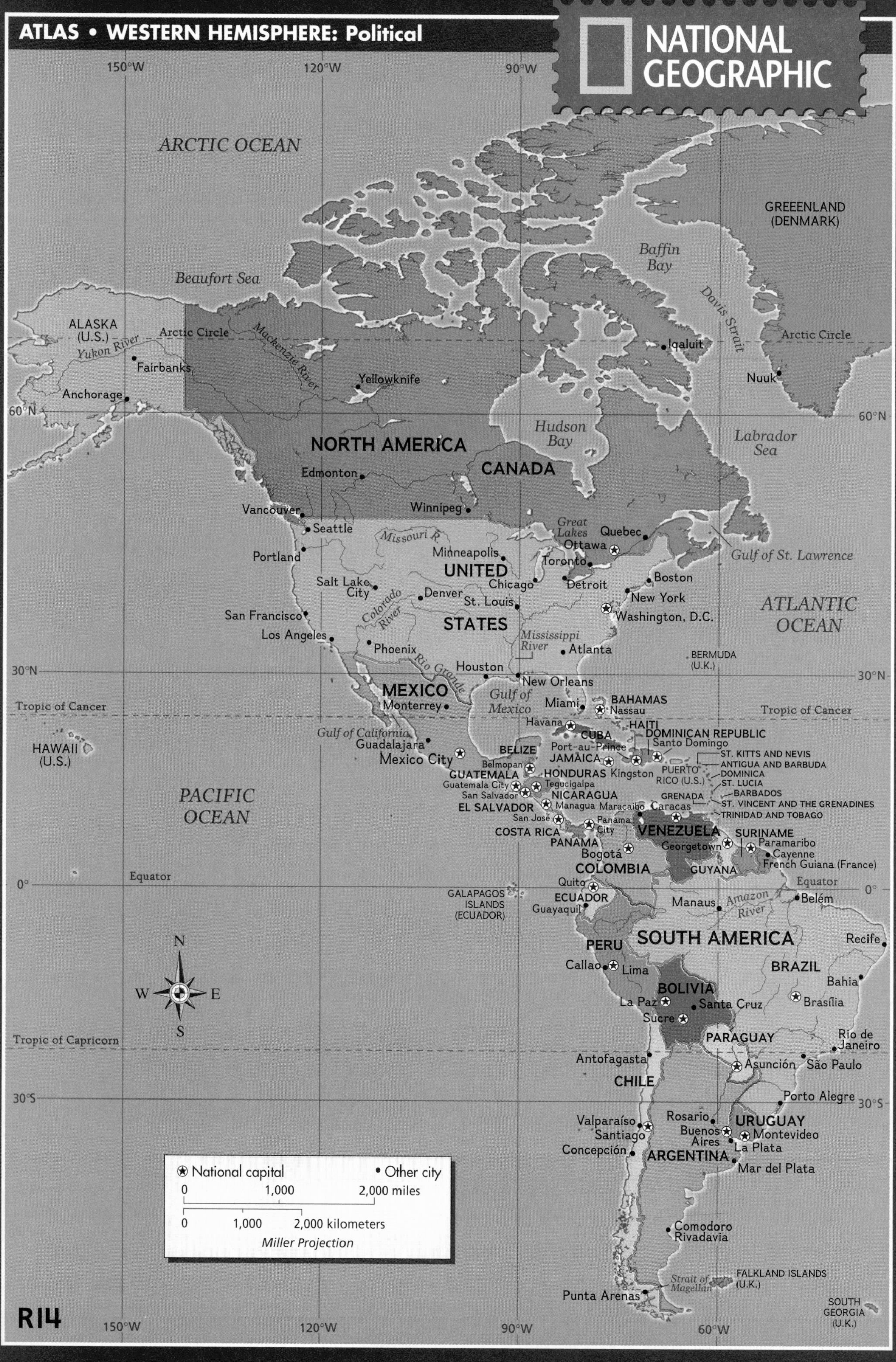
NATIONAL GEOGRAPHIC
150°W
120°W
90°W
60°W
60°N
30°N
0°
30°S
ARCTIC OCEAN
Beaufort Sea
ALASKA (U.S.)
Arctic Circle
Yukon River
Fairbanks
Anchorage
Mackenzie River
Yellowknife
Baffin Bay
Davis Strait
Iqaluit
GREEENLAND (DENMARK)
Nuuk
Hudson Bay
Labrador Sea
NORTH AMERICA
CANADA
Edmonton
Vancouver
Winnipeg
Seattle
Great Lakes
Quebec
Ottawa
Gulf of St. Lawrence
Missouri R.
Portland
Minneapolis
Toronto
UNITED STATES
Salt Lake City
Chicago
Detroit
Boston
New York
Denver
St. Louis
Washington, D.C.
ATLANTIC OCEAN
San Francisco
Colorado River
Los Angeles
Mississippi River
Phoenix
Atlanta
Rio Grande
Houston
BERMUDA (U.K.)
New Orleans
MEXICO
Gulf of Mexico
Monterrey
Miami
BAHAMAS
Nassau
Tropic of Cancer
Havana
CUBA
HAITI
DOMINICAN REPUBLIC
Gulf of California
Guadalajara
Santo Domingo
Port-au-Prince
HAWAII (U.S.)
Mexico City
BELIZE
JAMAICA
ST. KITTS AND NEVIS
ANTIGUA AND BARBUDA
Belmopan
Kingston
PUERTO RICO (U.S.)
DOMINICA
GUATEMALA
HONDURAS
ST. LUCIA
Guatemala City
Tegucigalpa
BARBADOS
San Salvador
NICARAGUA
GRENADA
PACIFIC OCEAN
EL SALVADOR
Managua
Maracaibo
Caracas
ST. VINCENT AND THE GRENADINES
TRINIDAD AND TOBAGO
San José
Panama City
COSTA RICA
VENEZUELA
SURINAME
PANAMA
Georgetown
Paramaribo
Cayenne
Bogotá
French Guiana (France)
COLOMBIA
GUYANA
Equator
Quito
GALAPAGOS ISLANDS (ECUADOR)
ECUADOR
Manaus
Amazon River
Belém
Guayaquil
SOUTH AMERICA
Recife
PERU
N
W
E
S
Callao
Lima
BRAZIL
BOLIVIA
Bahia
La Paz
Santa Cruz
Brasília
Sucre
Tropic of Capricorn
PARAGUAY
Rio de Janeiro
Antofagasta
Asunción
São Paulo
CHILE
Porto Alegre
Rosario
URUGUAY
Valparaíso
Buenos Aires
Montevideo
Santiago
La Plata
Concepción
ARGENTINA
Mar del Plata
National capital
Other city
0
1,000
2,000 miles
0
1,000
2,000 kilometers
Miller Projection
Comodoro Rivadavia
Strait of Magellan
FALKLAND ISLANDS (U.K.)
Punta Arenas
SOUTH GEORGIA (U.K.)

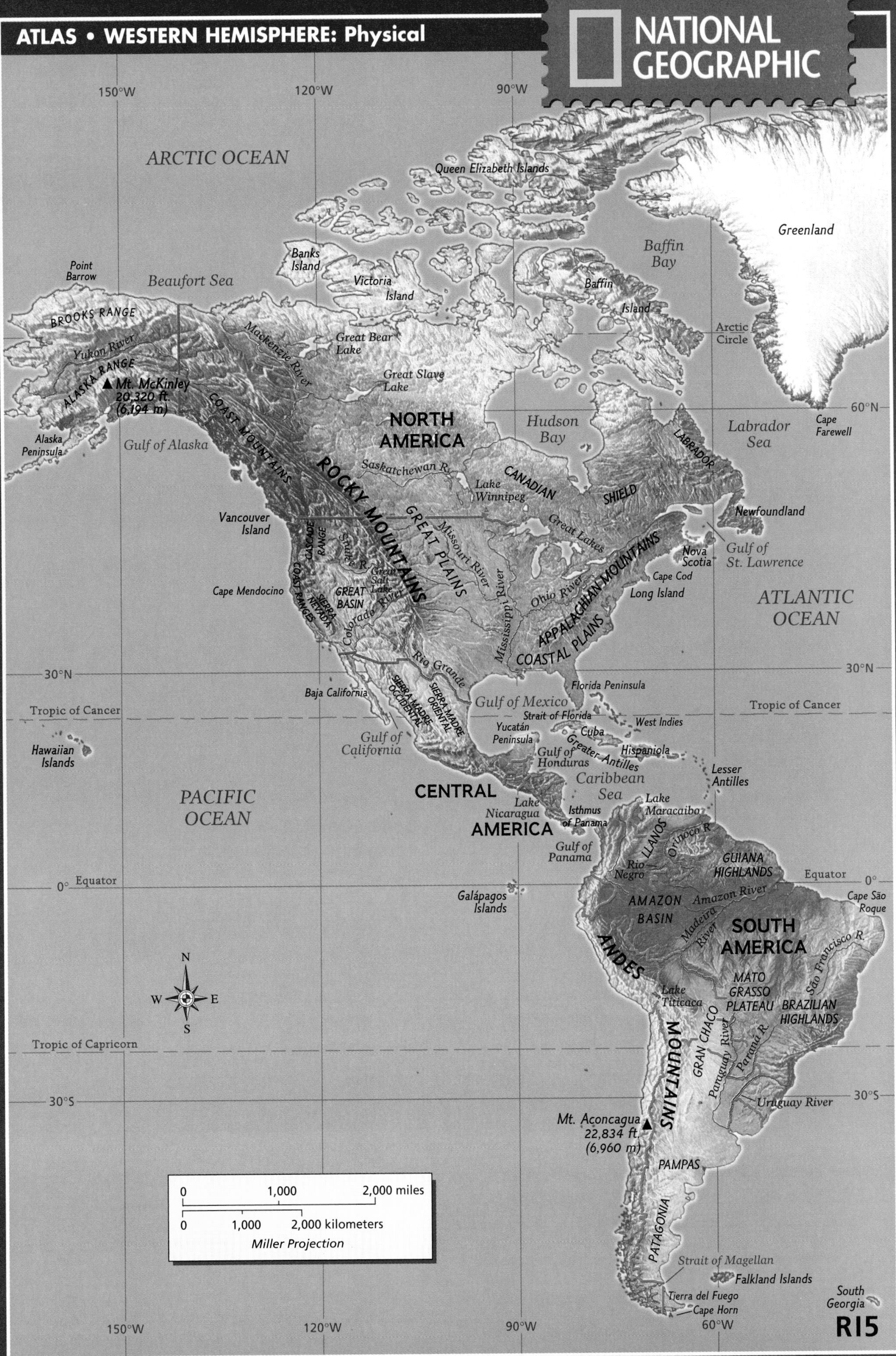
NATIONAL GEOGRAPHIC
ARCTIC OCEAN
Queen Elizabeth Islands
Greenland
Baffin Bay
Banks Island
Victoria Island
Baffin Island
Point Barrow
Beaufort Sea
BROOKS RANGE
Yukon River
Mackenzie River
Great Bear Lake
Great Slave Lake
Arctic Circle
ALASKA RANGE
Mt. McKinley
20,320 ft.
(6,194 m)
COAST MOUNTAINS
NORTH AMERICA
Hudson Bay
Labrador Sea
LABRADOR
Cape Farewell
Alaska Peninsula
Gulf of Alaska
ROCKY MOUNTAINS
Saskatchewan R.
Lake Winnipeg
CANADIAN
SHIELD
Newfoundland
Vancouver Island
CASCADE RANGE
Snake R.
GREAT PLAINS
Missouri River
Great Lakes
APPALACHIAN MOUNTAINS
Nova Scotia
Gulf of St. Lawrence
Cape Cod
Long Island
Cape Mendocino
COAST RANGES
SIERRA NEVADA
GREAT BASIN
Great Salt Lake
Colorado River
Mississippi River
Ohio River
ATLANTIC OCEAN
COASTAL PLAINS
Rio Grande
Baja California
SIERRA MADRE OCCIDENTAL
SIERRA MADRE ORIENTAL
Florida Peninsula
Gulf of Mexico
Strait of Florida
West Indies
Tropic of Cancer
Hawaiian Islands
Gulf of California
Yucatán Peninsula
Cuba
Gulf of Honduras
Greater Antilles
Hispaniola
Lesser Antilles
Caribbean Sea
PACIFIC OCEAN
CENTRAL AMERICA
Lake Nicaragua
Isthmus of Panama
Lake Maracaibo
Orinoco R.
LLANOS
Gulf of Panama
Rio Negro
GUIANA HIGHLANDS
Equator
Galápagos Islands
AMAZON BASIN
Amazon River
Cape São Roque
Madeira River
SOUTH AMERICA
São Francisco R.
ANDES
Lake Titicaca
MATO GRASSO PLATEAU
BRAZILIAN HIGHLANDS
GRAN CHACO
Paraguay River
Paraná R.
MOUNTAINS
Tropic of Capricorn
Uruguay River
Mt. Aconcagua
22,834 ft.
(6,960 m)
PAMPAS
PATAGONIA
Strait of Magellan
Falkland Islands
Tierra del Fuego
Cape Horn
South Georgia
N
W
E
S
150°W
120°W
90°W
60°W
60°N
30°N
0°
30°S
0
1,000
2,000 miles
0
1,000
2,000 kilometers
Miller Projection

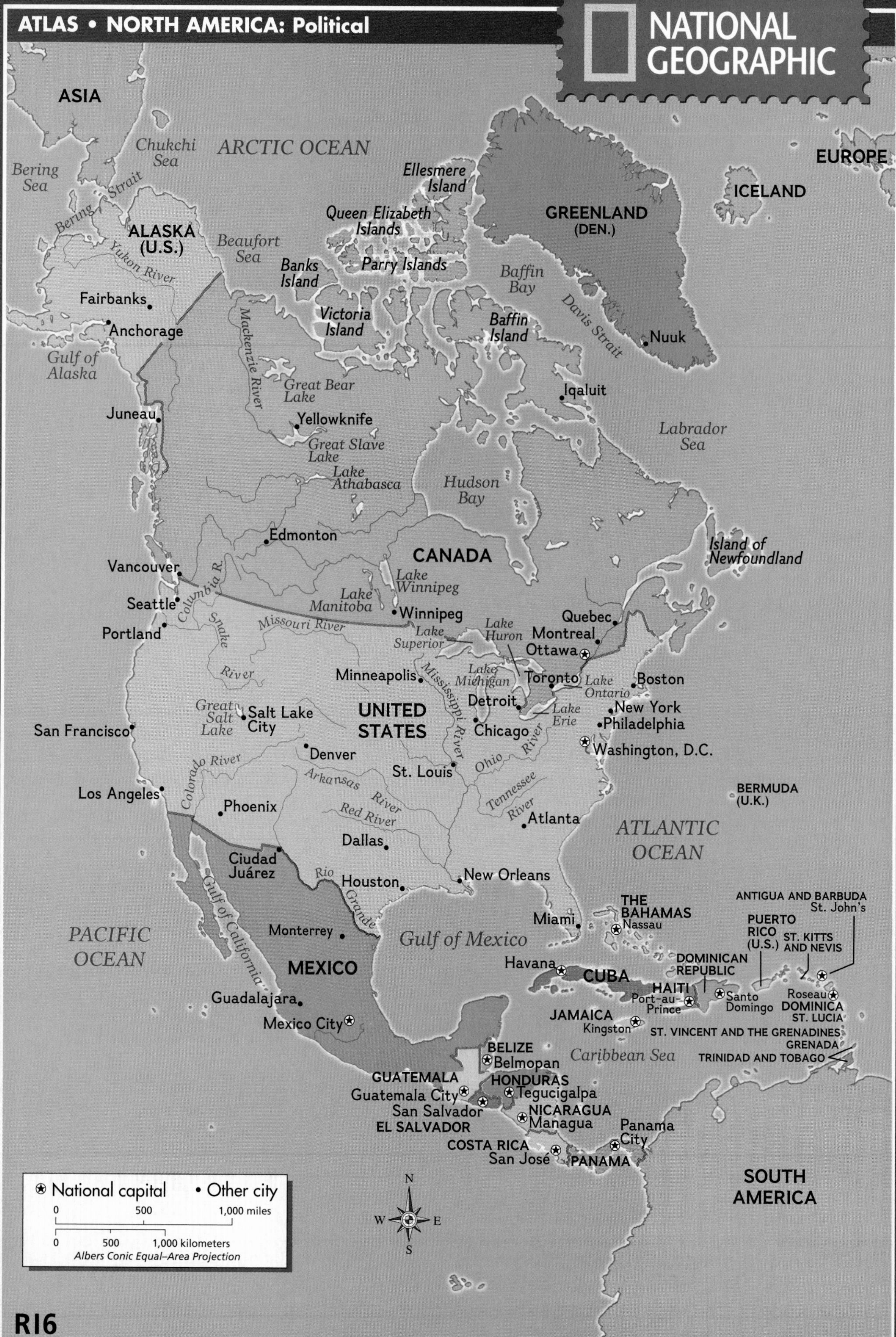
NATIONAL GEOGRAPHIC
ASIA
EUROPE
ICELAND
GREENLAND (DEN.)
ARCTIC OCEAN
Chukchi Sea
Bering Sea
Bering Strait
ALASKA (U.S.)
Beaufort Sea
Yukon River
Fairbanks
Anchorage
Gulf of Alaska
Juneau
Ellesmere Island
Queen Elizabeth Islands
Banks Island
Parry Islands
Victoria Island
Baffin Bay
Baffin Island
Davis Strait
Nuuk
Iqaluit
Mackenzie River
Great Bear Lake
Yellowknife
Great Slave Lake
Lake Athabasca
Hudson Bay
Labrador Sea
Edmonton
CANADA
Island of Newfoundland
Vancouver
Columbia R.
Lake Winnipeg
Lake Manitoba
Winnipeg
Seattle
Portland
Snake River
Missouri River
Lake Superior
Lake Huron
Quebec
Montreal
Ottawa
Lake Michigan
Minneapolis
Mississippi River
Toronto
Lake Ontario
Boston
Detroit
Lake Erie
New York
Philadelphia
Great Salt Lake
Salt Lake City
UNITED STATES
Chicago
San Francisco
Washington, D.C.
Denver
Colorado River
Ohio River
St. Louis
Arkansas River
Tennessee River
Los Angeles
Phoenix
Red River
Atlanta
BERMUDA (U.K.)
ATLANTIC OCEAN
Dallas
Ciudad Juárez
Rio Grande
Houston
New Orleans
Gulf of California
PACIFIC OCEAN
Monterrey
Gulf of Mexico
Miami
THE BAHAMAS
Nassau
ANTIGUA AND BARBUDA
St. John's
PUERTO RICO (U.S.)
ST. KITTS AND NEVIS
DOMINICAN REPUBLIC
Havana
CUBA
HAITI
Port-au-Prince
Santo Domingo
Roseau
DOMINICA
ST. LUCIA
MEXICO
Guadalajara
Mexico City
JAMAICA
Kingston
ST. VINCENT AND THE GRENADINES
GRENADA
TRINIDAD AND TOBAGO
BELIZE
Belmopan
Caribbean Sea
GUATEMALA
Guatemala City
HONDURAS
Tegucigalpa
San Salvador
EL SALVADOR
NICARAGUA
Managua
Panama City
COSTA RICA
San José
PANAMA
SOUTH AMERICA
National capital
Other city
0
500
1,000 miles
0
500
1,000 kilometers
Albers Conic Equal-Area Projection
N
S
E
W

NATIONAL GEOGRAPHIC

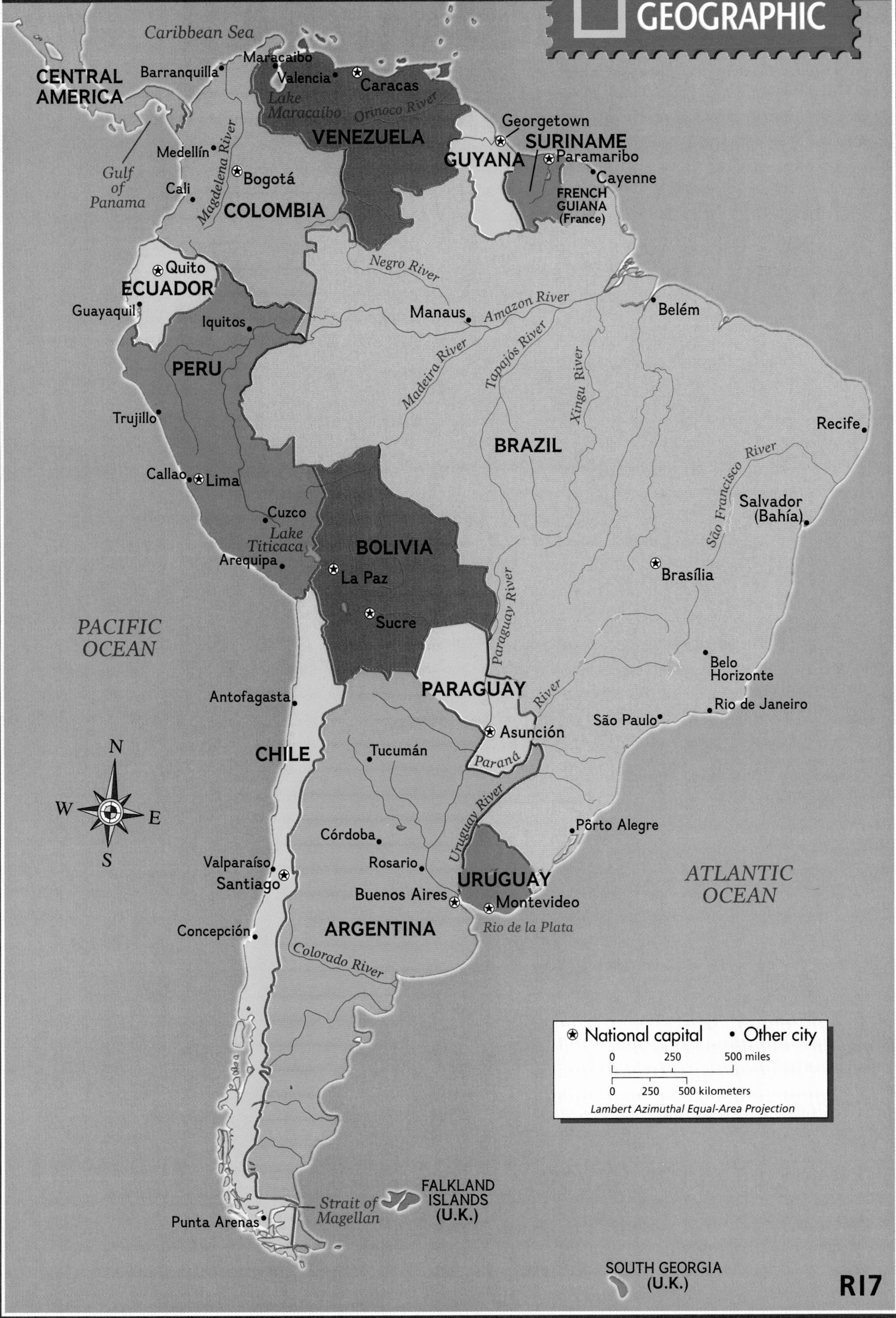

Caribbean Sea
CENTRAL AMERICA
Barranquilla
Maracaibo
Valencia
Caracas
Lake Maracaibo
Orinoco River
VENEZUELA
Georgetown
SURINAME
GUYANA
Paramaribo
Cayenne
FRENCH GUIANA (France)
Medellín
Magdalena River
Gulf of Panama
Bogotá
Cali
COLOMBIA
Negro River
Quito
ECUADOR
Guayaquil
Iquitos
Manaus
Amazon River
Belém
PERU
Madeira River
Tapajós River
Xingu River
Trujillo
BRAZIL
Recife
São Francisco River
Callao
Lima
Cuzco
Lake Titicaca
Arequipa
BOLIVIA
La Paz
Salvador (Bahía)
Brasília
Sucre
Paraguay River
PACIFIC OCEAN
Belo Horizonte
Antofagasta
PARAGUAY
River
Rio de Janeiro
São Paulo
Asunción
Tucumán
CHILE
Paraná
N
W
E
S
Uruguay River
Córdoba
Pôrto Alegre
Valparaíso
Rosario
URUGUAY
ATLANTIC OCEAN
Santiago
Buenos Aires
Montevideo
Río de la Plata
Concepción
ARGENTINA
Colorado River

National capital • Other city
0 250 500 miles
0 250 500 kilometers
Lambert Azimuthal Equal-Area Projection

Strait of Magellan
FALKLAND ISLANDS (U.K.)
Punta Arenas
SOUTH GEORGIA (U.K.)

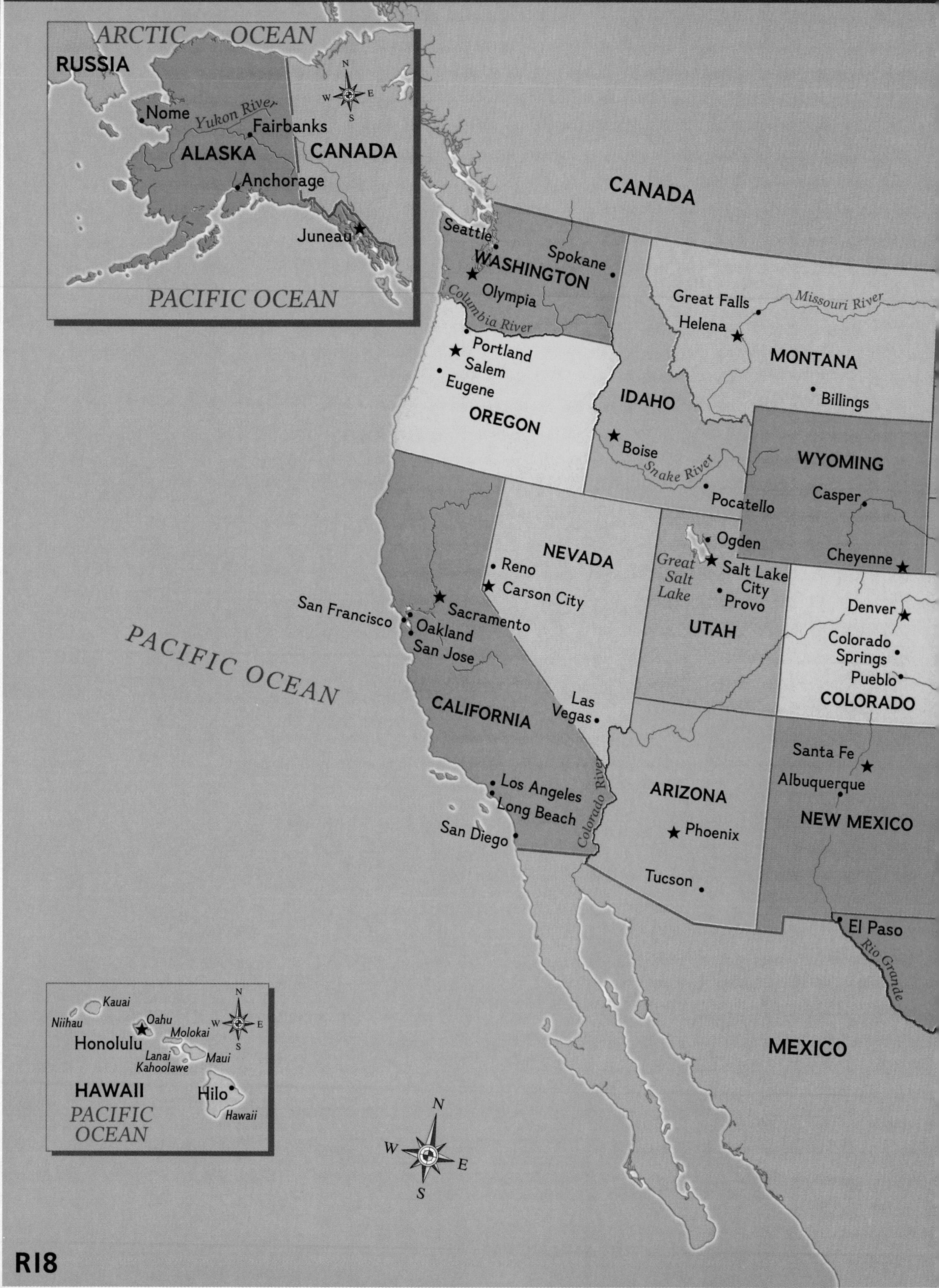

ARCTIC OCEAN
RUSSIA
Nome
Yukon River
Fairbanks
ALASKA
CANADA
Anchorage
Juneau
PACIFIC OCEAN

CANADA
Seattle
Spokane
WASHINGTON
Olympia
Columbia River
Portland
Salem
Eugene
OREGON
Great Falls
Missouri River
Helena
MONTANA
Billings
IDAHO
Boise
Snake River
Pocatello
WYOMING
Casper
Cheyenne
NEVADA
Reno
Carson City
Ogden
Great Salt Lake
Salt Lake City
Provo
UTAH
San Francisco
Oakland
San Jose
Sacramento
PACIFIC OCEAN
Denver
Colorado Springs
Pueblo
COLORADO
CALIFORNIA
Las Vegas
Santa Fe
Albuquerque
NEW MEXICO
Los Angeles
Long Beach
San Diego
Colorado River
ARIZONA
Phoenix
Tucson
El Paso
Rio Grande
MEXICO

Kauai
Niihau
Oahu
Molokai
Honolulu
Lanai
Kahoolawe
Maui
HAWAII
Hilo
Hawaii
PACIFIC OCEAN

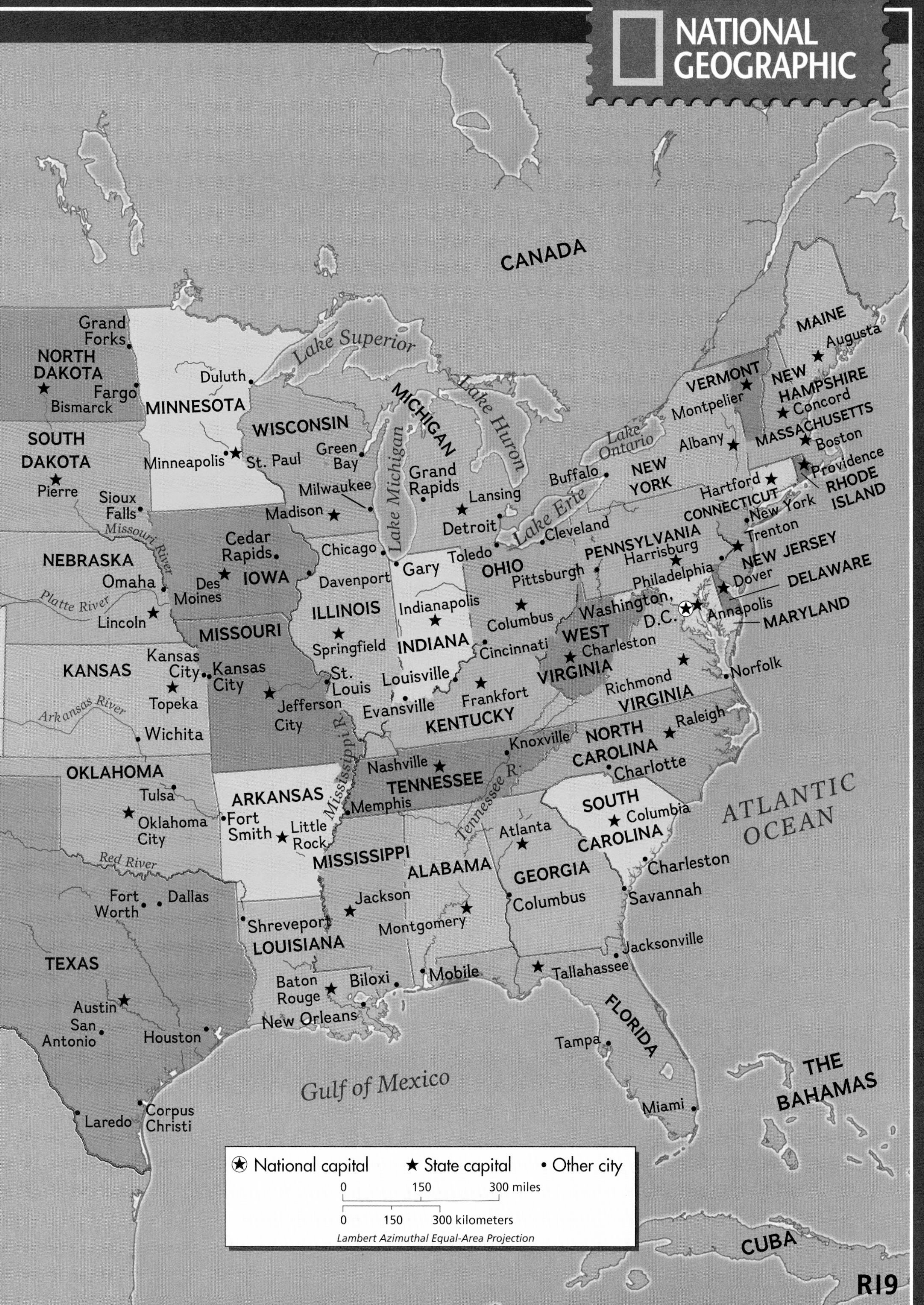

NATIONAL GEOGRAPHIC
CANADA
Lake Superior
Lake Michigan
Lake Huron
Lake Ontario
Lake Erie
NORTH DAKOTA
Grand Forks
Fargo
Bismarck
MINNESOTA
Duluth
Minneapolis
St. Paul
SOUTH DAKOTA
Pierre
Sioux Falls
WISCONSIN
Green Bay
Milwaukee
Madison
MICHIGAN
Grand Rapids
Lansing
Detroit
NEBRASKA
Omaha
Lincoln
Missouri River
Platte River
IOWA
Cedar Rapids
Des Moines
Davenport
Chicago
Gary
ILLINOIS
Springfield
INDIANA
Indianapolis
OHIO
Toledo
Cleveland
Columbus
Cincinnati
Pittsburgh
PENNSYLVANIA
Harrisburg
Philadelphia
NEW YORK
Buffalo
Albany
New York
VERMONT
Montpelier
NEW HAMPSHIRE
Concord
MAINE
Augusta
MASSACHUSETTS
Boston
Providence
RHODE ISLAND
CONNECTICUT
Hartford
NEW JERSEY
Trenton
DELAWARE
Dover
MARYLAND
Annapolis
Washington, D.C.
WEST VIRGINIA
Charleston
VIRGINIA
Richmond
Norfolk
KANSAS
Kansas City
Topeka
Wichita
Arkansas River
MISSOURI
Kansas City
Jefferson City
St. Louis
Louisville
Evansville
KENTUCKY
Frankfort
Knoxville
TENNESSEE
Nashville
Memphis
Tennessee R.
Mississippi R.
NORTH CAROLINA
Raleigh
Charlotte
SOUTH CAROLINA
Columbia
Charleston
OKLAHOMA
Tulsa
Oklahoma City
Red River
ARKANSAS
Fort Smith
Little Rock
MISSISSIPPI
Jackson
Biloxi
ALABAMA
Montgomery
Mobile
GEORGIA
Atlanta
Columbus
Savannah
TEXAS
Fort Worth
Dallas
Austin
San Antonio
Houston
Laredo
Corpus Christi
LOUISIANA
Shreveport
Baton Rouge
New Orleans
FLORIDA
Jacksonville
Tallahassee
Tampa
Miami
ATLANTIC OCEAN
Gulf of Mexico
THE BAHAMAS
CUBA
National capital
State capital
Other city
0
150
300 miles
0
150
300 kilometers
Lambert Azimuthal Equal-Area Projection

ARCTIC OCEAN
RUSSIA
BROOKS RANGE
ALASKA
Bering Srait
Mt. McKinley 20,320 ft. (6,194 m)
ALASKA RANGE
CANADA
Yukon River
60°N
Bering Sea
170°W
0 250 500 miles
0 250 500 kilometers
160°W 150°W 140°W

CANADA
Puget Sound
Mt. Rainier 14,410 ft. (4,392 m)
Mt. St. Helens 8,363 ft. (2,549 m)
Columbia R.
Missouri River
CASCADE RANGE
COAST RANGES
Mt. Hood 11,239 ft. (3,426 m)
COLUMBIA PLATEAU
ROCKY MOUNTAINS
Granite Peak 12,799 ft. (3,901 m)
Yellow R.
40°N
Snake River
BLACK HILLS
Mt. Shasta 14,162 ft. (4,317 m)
Cape Mendocino
Sacramento R.
SIERRA NEVADA
CENTRAL VALLEY
COAST RANGES
Great Salt Lake
GREAT BASIN
Lake Tahoe
GREAT SALT LAKE DESERT
WASATCH RANGE
Kings Peak 13,528 ft. (4,123 m)
GREAT PLAINS
San Francisco Bay
San Joaquin R.
Mt. Whitney 14,494 ft. (4,418 m)
Colorado River
Mt. Elbert 14,433 ft. (4,399 m)
Pikes Peak 14,110 ft. (4,301 m)
PACIFIC OCEAN
Lake Mead
Death Valley -282 ft. (-86 m)
COLORADO PLATEAU
MOJAVE DESERT
Wheeler Peak 13,161 ft. (4,011 m)
Humphreys Peak 12,633 ft. (3,851 m)
30°N
Salton Sea
SONORAN DESERT
Gila River
Pecos River
Guadalupe Peak 8,749 ft. (2,667 m)
130°W
Gulf of California
MEXICO

PACIFIC OCEAN
Kauai
Oahu
Maui
HAWAII
Hawaii
20°N
Mauna Kea 13,796 ft. (4,205 m)
0 100 200 miles
0 100 200 kilometers
160°W 155°W

20°N
120°W
110°W

NATIONAL GEOGRAPHIC
CANADA
Lake of the Woods
GREAT LAKES
Lake Superior
MESABI RANGE
Mississippi River
Lake Michigan
Lake Huron
St. Lawrence River
L. Ontario
Lake Erie
WHITE MTS.
Mt. Washington 6,288 ft. (1,917 m)
GREEN MTS.
ADIRONDACK MTS.
Cape Cod
Hudson R.
Susquehanna R.
Long Island
40°N
70°W
ALLEGHENY PLATEAU
APPALACHIAN MOUNTAINS
CENTRAL PLAINS
Missouri River
Platte River
Wabash River
Ohio River
Delaware Bay
Potomac R.
Chesapeake Bay
PIEDMONT
ATLANTIC COASTAL PLAIN
Cape Hatteras
Arkansas River
INTERIOR PLAINS
OZARK PLATEAU
Tennessee River
Mt. Mitchell 6,684 ft. (2,037 m)
OUACHITA MOUNTAINS
Mississippi River
Red River
Alabama River
Chattahoochee River
Savannah River
ATLANTIC OCEAN
30°N
Brazos River
Colorado River
GULF COASTAL PLAIN
Mobile Bay
Galveston Bay
Mississippi Delta
Lake Okeechobee
BAHAMAS
Rio Grande
Gulf of Mexico
0 150 300 miles
0 150 300 kilometers
Lambert Azimuthal Equal-Area Projection
Florida Keys
Straits of Florida
CUBA
90°W
80°W

Dictionary of Geographic Words

HILL (hil) Rounded, raised landform; not as high as a mountain.

GULF (gulf) Body of water partly surrounded by land; larger than a bay.

MESA (mā′sə) Landform that looks like a high, flat table.

PENINSULA (pə nin′sə lə) Land that has water on all sides but one.

LAKE (lāk) Body of water completely surrounded by land.

PLAIN (plān) Large area of flat land.

PORT (pôrt) Place where ships load and unload goods.

CANAL (kə nal′) Waterway dug across the land to connect two bodies of water.

BAY (bā) Body of water partly surrounded by land.

HARBOR (här′bər) Protected place by an ocean or river where ships can safely stay.

BEACH (bēch) Land covered with sand or pebbles next to an ocean or lake.

ISLAND (ī′lənd) Land that is surrounded on all sides by water.

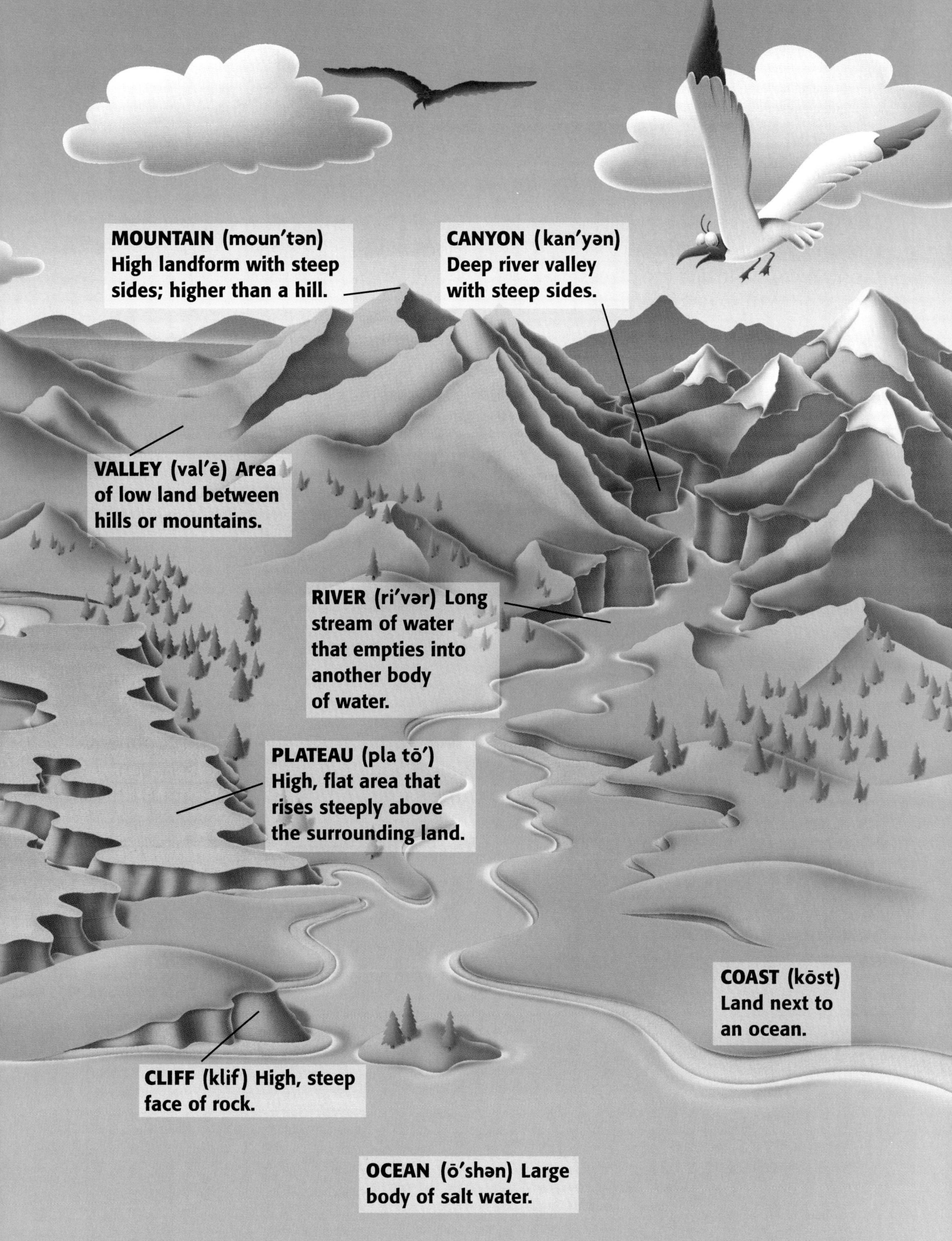
MOUNTAIN (moun′tən) High landform with steep sides; higher than a hill.
CANYON (kan′yən) Deep river valley with steep sides.
VALLEY (val′ē) Area of low land between hills or mountains.
RIVER (ri′vər) Long stream of water that empties into another body of water.
PLATEAU (pla tō′) High, flat area that rises steeply above the surrounding land.
COAST (kōst) Land next to an ocean.
CLIFF (klif) High, steep face of rock.
OCEAN (ō′shən) Large body of salt water.

Gazetteer

This Gazetteer is a geographical dictionary that will help you to pronounce and locate the places discussed in this book. The page numbers tell you where each place appears on a map (m.) or in the text (t.).

A

Accra (ə krä′) Capital of Ghana, a country in West Africa. (m. 335, t. 335)

Africa (af′ri kə) One of Earth's seven continents. (m. H10, t. 90)

Alamo, The (al′ə mō) A mission in San Antonio, Texas, where Mexican troops defeated Texan defenders in 1836. (m. 14, t. 13)

Alexandria (al ig zan′drē ə) A suburban community in Virginia, across the Potomac River from Washington, D.C. (m. 23, t. 23)

Antarctica (ant ärk′ti kə) A continent in the Southern Hemisphere. (m. H10)

Appalachian Mountains (ap ə lā′chē ən moun′tənz) A chain of mountains in eastern North America, stretching from Canada to Alabama. (m. 38)

Arctic Ocean (ärk′tik ō′shən) A large body of water located in the Northern Hemisphere. (m. H10)

Arkansas River (är′kən sô riv′ər) A river that begins in Colorado and flows southeast through Kansas, Oklahoma, and Arkansas into the Mississippi River. (m. 38)

Asia (ā′zhə) A continent in the Eastern and Northern Hemispheres. (m. H10)

Athens (ath′ənz) A Greek city named for the Greek goddess Athena. (t. 293)

Atlanta (at lan′tə) The capital and largest city in the state of Georgia. (m. 272)

Atlantic Ocean (at lan′tik ō′shən) A large body of salt water located to the east of North and South America. (m. H10, t. 33)

Australia (ôs trāl′yə) An island continent in the Southern Hemisphere between the Pacific and Indian Oceans. (m. H10)

B

Baton Rouge (bat′ən rüzh) The capital of Louisiana. (m. R19)

Beatrice (bē a′tris) A rural community in eastern Nebraska. (m. 21, t. 21)

pronunciation key

a	**at**	ī	**ice**	u	**up**	th	**th**in
ā	**ape**	îr	**pierce**	ū	**use**	<u>th</u>	**th**is
ä	**far**	o	**hot**	ü	**rule**	zh	mea**s**ure
âr	**care**	ō	**old**	ů	**pull**	ə	**a**bout, tak**e**n, penc**i**l, lem**o**n, circ**u**s
e	**end**	ô	**fork**	ûr	**turn**		
ē	**me**	oi	**oil**	hw	**wh**ite		
i	**it**	ou	**out**	ng	so**ng**		

Bodie (bō′dē) A California town that was once rich from its gold supply but is now a ghost town. (t. 44)

Boston (bôs′tən) The capital and largest city in Massachusetts. (t. 108)

C

Canada (kan′ə də) A very large country located in the northern part of North America, bordering the United States. (m. R16, t. 203)

Cape Cod (kāp kod) A peninsula in southeastern Massachusetts. (t. 33)

Capitol (kap′i təl) The building in Washington, D.C., where Congress meets. (m. 238, t. 234)

Cascade (kas kād′) A logging community in Idaho. (t. 42)

Central America (sen′trəl ə mer′i kə) A region between the Pacific Ocean and the Caribbean Sea. It is south of Mexico and part of the continent of North America. (m. R16, t. 266)

Chesapeake Bay (ches′ə pēk bā) A bay, partly enclosed by Maryland and Virginia, that flows into the Atlantic Ocean. (m. 38)

Chicago (shi kä′gō) A port city in northeastern Illinois. It is the largest city in the state. (m. 125, t. 125)

Coast Ranges (kōst rānj′əz) The mountain ranges along the Pacific Coast of North America. (m. 38)

Colorado Plateau (kol ə rad′ō pla tō′) A plateau found in New Mexico, Colorado, Arizona, and Utah. (m. 38, t. 32)

Colorado River (kol ə rad′ō riv′ər) A river in the southwestern United States, flowing from Colorado to the Gulf of California. (m. 38)

Columbia River (kə lum′bē ə riv′ər) A river in northwestern North America that begins in Canada and flows between Oregon and Washington into the Pacific Ocean. (m. 38)

D

Death Valley (deth val′ē) The lowest point in the Western Hemisphere. It is part of the Mojave Desert in California. (m. R20)

Denver (den′vər) The capital and largest city in the state of Colorado. (t. 28)

Detroit (di troit′) The largest city in Michigan. It is an important automobile manufacturing center. (m. 193, t. 193)

E

Eastern Hemisphere (ēs′tərn hem′i sfîr) The half of Earth east of the Atlantic Ocean that includes Europe, Africa, Asia, and Australia. (m. 290, t. 290)

El Salvador (el sal′və dôr) A country in western Central America. (m. R16, t. 266)

Ellis Island (el′is ī′lənd) A small island located near New York City. It was the first stop for millions of immigrants who came to the United States between 1892 and 1954. (t. 107)

England (ing′glənd) Part of the United Kingdom, an island country off the continent of Europe. (t. 96)

Equator (i kwā′tər) An imaginary line around the middle of Earth between the Northern Hemisphere and the Southern Hemisphere. (m. 290, t. 290)

Erie (îr′ē) A port city on Lake Erie in northwestern Pennsylvania. (m. 183, t. 183)

Europe (yůr′əp) One of Earth's seven continents, between Asia and the Atlantic Ocean. (m. H10, t. 84)

Everglades (ev′ər glādz) A large wetland in southern Florida that is a national park. It is home to many plants and animals. (t. 46)

G

Ghana (gä′nə) A country in West Africa. (m. 335, t. 335)

Grand Canyon (grand kan′yən) A huge canyon on the Colorado River in northwestern Arizona. (t. 296)

Grand Rapids (grand rap′idz) A city in southwest Michigan. (t. 34)

Great Basin (grāt bā′sin) A region in the western part of the United States that has no drainage to the Pacific Ocean. It includes most of Nevada and parts of California, Idaho, Utah, Wyoming, and Oregon. (m. 38)

Great Lakes (grāt lāks) A group of five large freshwater lakes in North America along the border between Canada and the United States. The Great Lakes are Lake Superior, Lake Michigan, Lake Huron, Lake Ontario, and Lake Erie. (m. 38)

Great Plains (grāt plānz) An area of flat land that stretches from North Dakota to Texas. (m. 38, t. 32)

Great Salt Lake (grāt sôlt lāk) A lake in northwestern Utah. The largest salt lake in North America. (m. 38)

Gulf of Mexico (gulf əv mek′si kō) A large body of water between the United States and Mexico. (m. 38)

H

Hannibal (han′ə bəl) A city on the Mississippi River in northeastern Missouri. It was the birthplace of author Mark Twain. (m. 303, t. 303)

Harlem (här′ləm) A neighborhood in New York City. (t. 118)

Houston (hyōō′stən) A city in southeastern Texas. (m. 317, t. 317)

I

Independence (in di pen′dəns) A community in Missouri that marked the beginning of the Oregon Trail in the 1840s. (m. 100, t. 100)

Indian Ocean (in′dē ən ō′shən) A large body of water located west of Africa. (m. H10)

Ine (ē′nā) A fishing village in Japan. (m. 53, t. 53)

J

Jackson (jak′sən) The capital and largest city in Mississippi. (m. 221, t. 221)

Jacksonville (jak′sən vil) A city in northeast Florida. (m. R19)

Jamestown (jāmz′toun) Settled in 1607, it was the first permanent English colony established in North America. (m. 87, t. 85)

Japan (jə pan′) A country of islands in the Pacific Ocean off the eastern coast of Asia. (m. 53, t. 53)

Jefferson City (jef′ər sən sit′ē) The capital of Missouri. (m. 39)

K

Kansas City (kan′zəs sit′ē) A city in western Missouri; the largest city in the state. (m. 39)

L

Lake Erie (lāk îr′ē) The most southern of the five Great Lakes. It is located on the border between Canada and the United States. (m. 38)

Lake Huron (lāk hyůr′ən) The second largest of the five Great Lakes. It is located on the border between Canada and the United States. (m. 38)

Lake Michigan (lāk mish′i gən) The third largest of the five Great Lakes. It is located between the states of Michigan and Wisconsin. (m. 38)

Lake Okeechobee (lāk ō kē chō′bē) A large lake in south-central Florida. (m. R21)

Lake Ontario (lāk on târ′ē ō) The smallest of the five Great Lakes. It is located on the border between Canada and the United States. (m. 38)

Lake Superior (lāk sə pîr′ē ər) The largest of the five Great Lakes. It is located on the border between Canada and the United States. (m. 38)

Largo (lär′gō) A town in western Florida. (m. 177, t. 176)

Little Rock (lit′əl rok) The capital and largest city in the state of Arkansas. (m. R19, t. 34)

Los Angeles (lôs an′jə ləs) A city in southwestern California. It is the largest city in the state. (m. 319, t. 319)

M

Mesa Verde (mā′sə vûr′dē) The ruins of an Anasazi community built into the side of a cliff and located in the southwestern part of the state of Colorado. (m. 83, t. 79)

Mesa Verde National Park (mā′sə vûr′dē nash′ə nəl pärk) A national park in the state of Colorado that was an Anasazi community long ago. (m. 83, t. 82)

Mexico (mek′si kō) A country in North America on the southern border of the United States. (m. R16, t. 203)

Mexico City (mek′si kō sit′ē) The capital and largest city in Mexico. (m. 242, t. 240)

Miami (mī am′ē) A port city in southeastern Florida. (m. R19)

Mississippi River (mis ə sip′ē riv′ər) A river in the central United States, flowing from Minnesota to the Gulf of Mexico. It is the longest river in the United States. (m. 38, t. 98)

pronunciation key

a **at**; ā **ape**; ä **far**; âr **care**; e **end**; ē **me**; i **it**; ī **ice**; îr **pierce**; o **hot**; ō **old**; ô **fork**; oi **oil**; ou **out**; u **up**; ū **use**; ü **rule**; ů **pull**; ûr **turn**; hw **white**; ng **song**; th **thin**; <u>th</u> **this**; zh **measure**; ə **a**bout, tak**e**n, penc**i**l, lem**o**n, circ**u**s

Missouri River (mi zůr′ē riv′ər) A large river flowing from Montana to the Mississippi River north of St. Louis. (m. 38)

Montgomery (mont gum′ə rē) The capital of Alabama. (m. 208)

N

Nashville (nash′vil) A city in central Tennessee. (m. R19)

New Orleans (nü ôr′lē ənz) The largest city in the state of Louisiana. It is an important Mississippi River port. (m. 325, t. 324)

New York City (nü yôrk sit′ē) The largest city in the United States, located in southeastern New York. (t. 107)

North America (nôrth ə mer′i kə) A continent in the Northern and Western Hemispheres. (m. H10, t. 74)

North Pole (nôrth pōl) The place farthest north on Earth. (m. 290)

Northern Hemisphere (nôr′t͟hərn hem′i sfîr) The half of Earth north of the equator. (m. 291)

O

Ohio River (ō hī′ō riv′ər) A river in the east-central United States, flowing from Pittsburgh, Pennsylvania, southwest into the Mississippi River. (m. 38)

Oregon Trail (ôr′i gən trāl) A route west used by pioneers in the 1840s. It stretched from Independence, Missouri, to northwestern Oregon. (m. 100, t. 100)

Outer Banks (ou′tər bangks) A chain of sandy islands along the North Carolina coast.

P

Pacific Ocean (pə sif′ik ō′shən) A large body of salt water bordering the west side of the United States. The Pacific Ocean is the largest ocean in the world. (m. H10, t. 33)

Pecos River (pā′kōs riv′ər) A river in New Mexico and Texas that runs into the Rio Grande. (t. 297)

Philadelphia (fil ə del′fē ə) A port city in southeastern Pennsylvania. It is the largest city in the state. (t. 232)

Phoenix (fē′niks) The capital and largest city in the state of Arizona. (t. 34)

Pittsburgh (pits′bûrg) A city in southwestern Pennsylvania. A leading center of iron making and steel making. (t. 305)

Platte River (plat riv′ər) A river flowing from central Nebraska into the Missouri River. (m. R19)

R

Richmond (rich′mənd) The capital of Virginia. (m. R19, t. 166)

Rio Grande (rē′ō grand) A river in southwestern North America, flowing from Colorado into the Gulf of Mexico. It forms part of the border between the United States and Mexico. (t. 297)

Rocky Mountains (rok′ē moun′tənz) The longest mountain range in North America. It stretches from Alaska into Mexico. (m. 38, t. 32)

S

San Antonio (san an tō′nē ō) A city in south-central Texas. (m. 14, t. 13)

San Antonio River (san an tō′nē ō riv′ər) A river in South Texas flowing southeast into the Gulf of Mexico. (m. 14, t. 15)

San Francisco (san frən sis′kō) A port city located in California along the Pacific Ocean. (m. 22, t. 22)

Sea of Japan (sē əv jə pan′) An arm of the North Pacific west of Japan. (m. 53, t. 53)

Sierra Nevada (sē er′ə nə vad′ə) A mountain range in eastern California. (m. 38)

Snake River (snāk riv′ər) A river in the northwestern United States that flows into the Columbia River. (m. 98)

South America (south ə mer′i kə) A continent in the Southern and Western Hemispheres. (m. H10)

South Pole (south pōl) The place farthest south on Earth. (m. 290)

Southern Hemisphere (su<u>th</u>′ərn hem′i sfîr) The half of Earth south of the equator. (m. 291)

St. Lawrence River (sānt lôr′əns riv′ər) A river in eastern North America between the United States and Canada, flowing from Lake Ontario into the Atlantic Ocean. (m. 98)

St. Louis (sānt lü′is) A city in western Missouri located near the joining of the Missouri River and the Mississippi River. (m. 98, t. 98)

T

Tallahassee (tal ə has′ē) The capital of Florida. (m. R19)

Tampa (tam′pə) A city in western Florida on Tampa Bay. (m. R19)

Tennessee River (ten ə sē′ riv′ər) A river that flows through Tennessee, Alabama, and Kentucky into the Ohio River. (m. 38)

Tenochtitlán (te noch tē tlän′) The capital of the ancient Aztec empire, on the site of present-day Mexico City. (t. 241)

W

Washington, D.C. (wô′shing tən) The capital city of the United States. (m. 230, t. 230)

Western Hemisphere (wes′tərn hem′i sfîr) The half of Earth that includes North and South America. (m. 290)

Wilderness Road (wil′dər nis rōd) An early road across the Appalachian Mountains, between western Virginia and eastern Kentucky. (t. 97)

pronunciation key

a **a**t; ā **a**pe; ä f**a**r; âr c**are**; e **e**nd; ē m**e**; i **i**t; ī **i**ce; îr p**ier**ce; o h**o**t; ō **o**ld; ô f**o**rk; oi **oi**l; ou **ou**t; u **u**p; ū **u**se; ü r**u**le; u̇ p**u**ll; ûr t**ur**n; hw **wh**ite; ng so**ng**; th **th**in; <u>th</u> **th**is; zh mea**s**ure; ə **a**bout, tak**e**n, penc**i**l, lem**o**n, circ**u**s

Biographical Dictionary

The Biographical Dictionary tells you about many of the people you have read about in this book. The Pronunciation Key helps you to say their names. The page numbers let you see where each person first appears in the text.

A

Abbott, Berenice (ab′ət, bâr ə nēs′), 1898–1991 Photographer best known for her photographs of New York City. (p. 305)

Adams, Abigail (ad′əmz), 1744–1818 Wife of President John Adams and mother of another President, John Quincy Adams. (p. 233)

Adams, John (ad′əmz), 1735–1826 The second President of the United States, 1797–1801. He was the first President to live in the White House. (p. 233)

Addams, Jane (ad′əmz), 1860–1935 An American social reformer, she opened the first settlement house, in Chicago in 1889. (p. 137)

pronunciation key

a	**a**t	ī	**i**ce	u	**u**p	th	**th**in
ā	**a**pe	îr	**pier**ce	ū	**u**se	<u>th</u>	**th**is
ä	f**a**r	o	h**o**t	ü	r**u**le	zh	mea**s**ure
âr	**car**e	ō	**o**ld	ů	p**u**ll	ə	**a**bout, tak**e**n, pen**c**il, lem**o**n, circ**u**s
e	**e**nd	ô	f**o**rk	ûr	**tur**n		
ē	m**e**	oi	**oi**l	hw	**wh**ite		
i	**i**t	ou	**ou**t	ng	so**ng**		

Armstrong, Louis (ärm′strông, lü′ē), 1901–1971 A jazz musician born in New Orleans, Louisiana. (p. 326)

B

Banneker, Benjamin (ban′i kər), 1731–1806 A surveyor who helped to draw plans for designing the city of Washington, D.C., in 1791. (p. 233)

Barton, Clara (bär′tən), 1821–1912 Founder of the American Red Cross Society. (p. 264)

Bell, Alexander Graham (bel, al ig zan′dər grā′əm), 1847–1922 Inventor who built the first working telephone, in 1876. (p. 132)

Boone, Daniel (bün), 1734–1820 American pioneer who played a big part in the exploration and settlement of Kentucky. (p. 97)

Bush, George W. (bůsh), 1946– Elected forty-third President of the United States in 2000 in one of the closest elections in U.S. history. (p. 231)

C

Clark, William (klärk), 1770–1838 Explorer, along with Meriwether Lewis, of the West and Northwest from 1804 to 1806. (p. 98)

Columbus, Christopher (kə lum′bəs), 1451–1506 Italian sea captain and explorer who reached the Americas in 1492. (p. 84)

Crockett, David (kräk′ət), 1786–1836 American frontiersman and government leader. He died at The Alamo and became a legend. (p. 295)

D

Daguerre, Louis (də gâr′), 1789–1851 French inventor of the daguerreotype (də gâr′ə tīp), which was an early form of photography. (p. 304)

Douglas, Marjory Stoneman (dug′ləs), 1890–1998 Environmental activist who helped create the Everglades National Park. (p. 46)

Drew, Charles (drü), 1904–1950 A scientist who invented a way to preserve blood. (p. 138)

E

Edison, Thomas (ed′ə sən), 1847–1931 American inventor of more than 1,000 inventions, including the light bulb and motion-picture cameras. (p. 127)

F

Ford, Henry (fôrd), 1863–1947 Maker of the Model T car, in 1908. He made his cars so that many people could afford them. (p. 194)

Franklin, Benjamin (fran′klən), 1706–1790 American colonial leader, writer, and scientist. (p. 171)

H

Harris, Charles (har′is), 1908–1988 Photographer best known for showing African American life in Pittsburgh, Pennsylvania. (p. 305)

J

Jackson, Andrew (jak′sən), 1767–1845 The seventh President of the United States, 1829–1837. He helped defeat British soldiers in New Orleans, Louisiana. (p. 325)

Jenney, William Le Baron (jen′ē), 1832–1907 American architect and engineer. He built the first skyscraper, the Home Insurance Company Building, in 1885. (p. 127)

K

Keller, Helen (kel′ər), 1880–1968 Blind and deaf since childhood, she became a world-famous writer and speaker about treating all people fairly. (p. 256)

King, Martin Luther, Jr. (king), 1929–1968 Leader who worked to make laws fair for all people. (p. 118)

L

Lawrence, Jacob (lôr′əns), 1917–2000 Artist best known for making a series of paintings about the Great Migration in 1941. (p. 117)

L′Enfant, Pierre (län fän′, pē′yâr), 1754–1825 Builder who drew up the plans for Washington, D.C., in 1791. (p. 232)

Lewis, Meriwether (lü′is), 1774–1809 Explorer, along with William Clark, of the American West and Northwest between 1804 and 1806. (p. 98)

Lin, Maya (lin, mī′ə), 1959– Architect and sculptor best known for designing the Vietnam Veterans Memorial in Washington, D.C. (p. 308)

Lincoln, Abraham (ling′kən), 1809–1865 The sixteenth President of the United States, 1861–1865. He led the country during the Civil War and ended slavery. (p. 115)

M

McCormick, Cyrus (mə kôr′mək, sī′rus), 1809–1884 Inventor of a mechanical reaper for harvesting grain. (p. 185)

O

Otis, Elisha (ō′təs, e lī′shə), 1811–1861 Inventor of an automatic safety clamp in 1852 that led to the first safe elevators. (p. 126)

P

Pasteur, Louis (pas tûr′), 1822–1895 French scientist who invented the process of pasteurization to make foods safer. (p. 138)

Pocahontas (pō kə hon′təs), 1595?–1617 Daughter of Chief Powhatan, she married an English settler named John Rolfe. (p. 89)

Powhatan (pou ə tan′), 1550?–1618 Chief of the Powhatan, he helped the English colony of Jamestown to survive. (p. 86)

Pulaski, Casimir (pə las′kē, ka′zē mîr), 1747–1779 Polish army general who fought and died in the American Revolutionary War. (p. 316)

R

Rivera, Diego (ri vâr′ə), 1886–1957 A Mexican artist best known for painting murals. (p. 306)

Rolfe, John (rälf), 1582–1622 Leader of Jamestown colony who grew a new kind of tobacco that sold for a lot of money. (p. 89)

S

Sacagawea (sak ə jə wē'ə), 1787?–1812 Native American translator and guide for Lewis and Clark's journey. (p. 99)

Salk, Jonas (sôlk), 1914–1995 American doctor and scientist who developed the first vaccine against a dangerous disease called polio. (p. 138)

Smith, John (smith), 1580?–1631 English colonial leader who helped the Jamestown, Virginia, settlement to survive during hard times. (p. 86)

T

Tubman, Harriet (tub'mən), 1820–1913 Famous "conductor" on the Underground Railroad. (p. 294)

Twain, Mark (twān), 1835–1910 Famous American author of many books, including *The Adventures of Tom Sawyer.* He was born in Hannibal, Missouri. (p. 303)

W

Walker, Maggie Lena (wô'kər), 1867–1934 First woman to be president of a bank in the United States. (p. 166)

Washington, George (wô'shing tən), 1732–1799 The first President of the United States, 1789–1797. He led the American army during the War for Independence. (p. 96)

Glossary

This Glossary will help you to pronounce and understand the meanings of the vocabulary in this book. The page number at the end of the definition tells where the word first appears.

A

adapt (ə dapt′) To change in order to make useful. We **adapt** to cold weather by wearing warm clothes. (p. 34)

agriculture (ag′ri kul chər) The business of growing crops and raising farm animals. Farmers are an important part of **agriculture**. (p. 184)

ancestor (an′ses tər) An early member of a person's family. In Ghana, Africa, many festivals are held to honor people's **ancestors**. (p. 316)

ancient (ān′shənt) Having to do with times long ago. The remains of the buildings at Mesa Verde are **ancient**. (p. 74)

assembly line (ə sem′blē līn) A line of workers and machines used for putting together a product in a factory. Many goods are made on **assembly lines**. (p. 194)

B

bay (bā) A part of an ocean or lake that is partly surrounded by land. The waves are always calmer in the **bay** than they are out at sea. (p. 85)

budget (buj′it) A plan for using your money. Karen's **budget** includes money for pizza on Wednesday. (p. 171)

C

Cajun (kā′jən) Word describing French settlers who left Canada for Louisiana, and their music. **Cajun** music is lively and is usually played on the fiddle, guitar, and accordion. (p. 327)

canyon (kan′yən) A deep valley with very high, steep sides. You can hike all the way down the Grand **Canyon**. (p. 78)

pronunciation key

a	**a**t	ī	**i**ce	u	**u**p	th	**th**in
ā	**a**pe	îr	p**ier**ce	ū	**u**se	<u>th</u>	**th**is
ä	f**a**r	o	h**o**t	ü	r**u**le	zh	mea**s**ure
âr	**car**e	ō	**o**ld	u̇	p**u**ll	ə	**a**bout, tak**e**n,
e	**e**nd	ô	f**o**rk	ûr	t**ur**n		penc**i**l, lem**o**n,
ē	m**e**	oi	**oi**l	hw	**wh**ite		circ**u**s
i	**i**t	ou	**ou**t	ng	so**ng**		

capital (kap′i təl) The location of a state's or country's government. Washington, D.C., is the **capital** of our country. (p. 226)

capitol (kap′i təl) The building in which the state or national government meets. The state's **capitol** building is located downtown. (p. 226)

century (sen′chə rē) One hundred years. Life was very different a **century** ago. (p. 96)

citizen (sit′ə zən) A person who lives in a community and has certain rights and responsibilities. Each **citizen** in our town has the right to vote for the mayor. (p. 15)

city council (sit′ē koun′səl) A group of elected officials who make decisions and laws for a community. The **city council** meets every week. (p. 222)

Civil War (siv′əl wôr) The war between the Northern and Southern states that lasted from 1861 to 1865. After the **Civil War** slavery was ended. (p. 115)

cliff (klif) The steep face of a rock. The Anasazi lived in homes built on **cliffs**. (p. 79)

climate (klī′mit) A place's weather over a long period of time. The **climate** in Florida is hot. (p. 34)

coast (kōst) Land next to the ocean. There are many beaches along the **coast**. (p. 53)

colonist (kol′ə nist) A person who lives in a colony. The Jamestown **colonists** had a very hard winter. (p. 86)

colony (kol′ə nē) A place that is ruled by another country. Before the United States was its own country, it was a **colony** of Great Britain. (p. 85)

combine (kom′bīn) A farm machine that harvests grain. I saw Tina riding the **combine** on the farm. (p. 184)

common good (kom′ən gu̇d) What is best for everyone. He wants to find a job that serves the **common good**. (p. 251)

community (kə mū′ni tē) A place where people live, work, and play. Jane's **community** has beautiful gardens. (p. 12)

Congress (kong′gris) The part of the United States government that makes laws. **Congress** makes the laws of our country. (p. 231)

construction (kən struk′shən) The act of building something. There is a lot of **construction** taking place in the downtown area. (p. 14)

consumer (kən sü′mər) A person who buys goods and services. **Consumers** buy all sorts of products. (p. 163)

culture (kul′chər) A way of life shared by a group of people, including art, music, food, and stories. Cajun music is an important part of Cajun **culture**. (p. 75)

D

daguerreotype (də gâr′ə tīp) A type of photograph made on a thin sheet of copper that was coated with silver. Emma found a **daguerreotype** photo in her family's basement. (p. 304)

database (dā′tə bās) A computer program that holds lots of similar information. We searched the **database** for names of immigrants. (p. 111)

demand (di mand′) The number of people who want the goods that are in supply. Tickets to the ball game were in great **demand** this season. (p. 186)

desert (dez′ərt) A hot, dry area where little rain falls. Temperatures are very high in the **desert**. (p. 78)

domestic trade (də mes′tik trād) Trade within one country. When people in Michigan buy wheat grown in Kansas, they are part of **domestic trade**. (p. 203)

E

economy (i kon′ə mē) The making and consuming of goods and services. Our country's **economy** needs people to buy and sell products. (p. 164)

elevator (el′ə vā tər) A small room that can be raised or lowered to carry people and things from one floor to another in a building. It is much easier to take the **elevator** than it is to walk up 11 floors! (p. 126)

empire (em′pīr) A group of lands and peoples governed by one ruler. The Aztec **empire** was located in what is now Mexico. (p. 241)

employee (em ploi′ē) A person who works for a person or business. There are ten **employees** in that toy store. (p. 162)

environment (en vī′rən mənt) The air, water, land, and all the living things around us. People are working to protect the **environment** and its many natural resources. (p. 44)

expenses (ek spen′siz) Things that money is spent on. A new seat for his bicycle was one of John's **expenses** this month. (p. 162)

export (ek spôrt′) To sell goods to another country. The United States **exports** computers to many countries all over the world. (p. 203)

F

factory (fak′tə rē) A place where things are manufactured. Many of the products we use are made in **factories**. (p. 193)

fertilizer (fûr′tə lī zər) A substance added to soil to make it better for growing crops. Tiffany put **fertilizer** on the garden yesterday. (p. 184)

festival (fes′tə vəl) A celebration. On Cinco de Mayo many communities have a **festival**. (p. 319)

frontier (frun tîr′) The far edge of a country where people are just beginning to settle. Daniel Boone explored the **frontier.** (p. 97)

G

geography (jē og′rə fē) The study of Earth and the way people, plants, and animals use it. Studying **geography** helps people learn about the land and water in their community. (p. 31)

global marketplace (glō′ bəl mär′kit plās) When countries trade with each other, they are taking part in the global marketplace. The United States is part of the **global marketplace.** (p. 206)

goods (gu̇dz) Things that people make or grow. The shop sells **goods.** (p. 161)

governor (guv′ər nər) The person who is elected to be in charge of the state government. The **governor** will sign the education bill into law. (p. 226)

Great Migration (grāt mī grā′shən) The journey of thousands of African Americans from the South to the North in the early 1900s. Helen's great-grandmother moved to Chicago during the **Great Migration.** (p. 114)

H

harvest (här′vist) When the ripe crops are ready to be gathered. This year's corn **harvest** was very good. (p. 183)

heritage (her′i tij) Something handed down from earlier generations or from the past, such as a tradition. Stories and dances are part of Native Americans' **heritage.** (p. 285)

hero (hîr′ō) A person you look up to because of his or her personal qualities or achievements. People look up to **heroes** for their bravery. (p. 293)

holiday (hol′i dā) A day on which people or events are honored. The Fourth of July is a **holiday** throughout the United States. (p. 316)

I

immigrant (im′i grənt) A person who comes to live in another country. **Immigrants** came to this country from all over the world. (p. 107)

import (im pôrt′) To buy goods made or grown in another country. The United States **imports** cars from Japan. (p. 203)

income (in′kum) The money you earn. The **income** from Joe's job was used to buy a tractor for the family. (p. 171)

interest (in′trist) An amount of money that a bank pays you for borrowing your money, or you pay a bank if you borrow money. Jennifer paid **interest** on her loan from the bank. (p. 173)

pronunciation key

a **a**t; ā **a**pe; ä f**a**r; âr c**are**; e **e**nd; ē m**e**; i **i**t; ī **i**ce; îr p**ier**ce; o h**o**t; ō **o**ld; ô f**o**rk; oi **oi**l; ou **ou**t; u **u**p; ū **u**se; ü r**u**le; u̇ p**u**ll; ûr t**ur**n; hw **wh**ite; ng so**ng**; th **th**in; t͟h **th**is; zh mea**s**ure; ə **a**bout, tak**e**n, penc**i**l, lem**o**n, circ**u**s

international trade (in tər nash′ə nəl trād) Trade between people in different countries. **International trade** is important to most countries around the world. (p. 203)

Internet (in′tər net) A computer network that connects people all over the world. You can do research on the **Internet**. (p. 185)

invention (in ven′shən) A thing that has been made for the first time. The automobile was a very important **invention**. (p. 126)

island (ī′lənd) A body of land that is completely surrounded by water and is smaller than a continent. Hawaii is a very beautiful **island**. (p. 53)

J

jazz (jaz) Lively music that was invented in New Orleans. Louis Armstrong was an early musician who played **jazz** music. (p. 326)

K

kente (ken′tā) A beautifully woven, colorful cloth made in Ghana. You can buy beautiful **kente** cloth at the market. (p. 336)

L

landform (land′fôrm) The shape of the surface of the land. You can see many **landforms** when you fly in an airplane. (p. 32)

legend (lej′ənd) A story passed down through the years that many people believe, but which is not entirely true. The adventures of Davy Crockett became **legends**. (p. 295)

local government (lō′ kəl guv′ərn mənt) A group of people who run a community. **Local governments** are often led by a mayor. (p. 220)

M

manufacturing (man yə fak′chər ing) The business of making things. People who work in **manufacturing** make things such as cars, books, and toys. (p. 192)

Mardi Gras (mär′dē grä) A French phrase meaning Fat Tuesday that is also the name of a festival in New Orleans. Linda went to New Orleans during the **Mardi Gras** festival. (p. 330)

marketplace (mär′kit plās) A place where people sell things and buy things they want or need. They went to the town **marketplace** on Tuesday. (p. 206)

mayor (mā′ər) The head of the local government elected by the community. All citizens may vote for the **mayor** of their community. (p. 221)

mesa (mā′sə) A landform that looks like a high, flat table. Anasazi Indians often built communities on **mesas**. (p. 78)

migration (mī grā′shən) Moving from one part of the country to another. There was a **migration** of people from the South to the North after the Civil War. (p. 114)

mineral (min′ər əl) A thing found in the earth that is not a plant or an animal. Coal and diamonds are both **minerals**. (p. 41)

monument (mon′yə mənt) A building or statue made in memory of a person or event. The Washington **Monument** honors the first President of our country. (p. 236)

mural (myůr′əl) A large picture that is painted on a wall or ceiling. Mrs. Smith's art class painted a **mural** on the schoolyard wall. (p. 306)

museum (mū zē′əm) A building where objects of art, science, or history are displayed for people to see. We saw beautiful paintings and sculpture at the **museum**. (p. 303)

myth (mith) A story that tells about a belief of a group of people. It may try to explain a custom or why something happens in nature. The Greek **myths** are full of battles and adventures. (p. 293)

N

natural resource (nach′ər əl rē′sôrs) A thing found in nature that people use. Water is a very important **natural resource**. (p. 41)

nonprofit (non prof′it) Not for profit, or money. Red Cross volunteers work for a **nonprofit** organization. (p. 262)

nonrenewable resource (non ri nü′ə bəl rē′sôrs) A thing found in nature that cannot be replaced. Minerals are **nonrenewable resources**. (p. 42)

P

pasteurization (pas chə rī zā′shən) The use of heat to stop germs from growing in food. **Pasteurization** has made milk safer to drink. (p. 138)

peninsula (pə nin′sə lə) Land that has water on three sides. Most of Florida is a **peninsula**. (p. 53)

pioneer (pī ə nîr′) The first of a group of people to settle in an area. **Pioneers** followed along the paths made by explorers and settled new lands. (p. 97)

plain (plān) A large area of flat land. Long ago many buffalo lived on the **plains** of our country. (p. 32)

pronunciation key

a **at**; ā **ape**; ä **far**; âr **care**; e **end**; ē **me**; i **it**; ī **ice**; îr **pierce**; o **hot**; ō **old**; ô **fork**; oi **oil**; ou **out**; u **up**; ū **use**; ü **rule**; ů **pull**; ûr **turn**; hw **white**; ng **song**; th **thin**; th **this**; zh **measure**; ə **about**, **taken**, **pencil**, **lemon**, **circus**

plateau (pla tō′) A large area of flat land that is raised high above the land around it. Ann hiked up to the top of the **plateau.** (p. 32)

Pledge of Allegiance (plej uv ə lē′jəns) The promise to be loyal to our country. We say the **Pledge of Allegiance** during assembly. (p. 254)

preserve (pri zûrv′) To store something so that it can be used later. A refrigerator helps to **preserve** food for many days. (p. 138)

President (prez′i dənt) The leader of our country. The **President** will make a speech tonight. (p. 231)

producer (prə dü′sər) A person, company, or thing that makes or creates something. Farmers and carmakers are two kinds of **producers**. (p. 162)

profit (prof′it) The amount of money left after all the costs have been paid. The bake sale made a good **profit** for the school. (p. 162)

R

recycle (rē sī′kəl) To use something over again. We **recycle** cans and bottles. (p. 44)

renewable resource (ri nü′ə bəl rē′sôrs) A thing found in nature that can be replaced. Water is a **renewable resource**. (p. 42)

rural (rür′əl) A place of farms or open country. Jessie grew up on a farm in a **rural** community. (p. 21)

S

scarcity (skâr′si tē) A shortage. There was a **scarcity** of sandbags during the flood. (p. 186)

services (sûr′vis əz) People or businesses that provide something people need or want. A website provides a **service** by giving information. (p. 161)

skyscraper (skī′skrā pər) A very tall building. The Empire State Building is one of the world's most famous **skyscrapers**. (p. 124)

slavery (slā′və rē) The practice of one person owning another. Colonists brought **slavery** to Jamestown. (p. 90)

suburb (sub′ûrb) A community that is near a city. People who live in **suburbs** often work in nearby cities. (p. 23)

supply (sə plī′) The amount of goods available at any time. The **supply** of scooters was very high this past year. (p. 186)

Supreme Court (sə prēm′ kôrt) The part of the U.S. government that makes sure laws are fair. There are nine judges on the **Supreme Court**. (p. 234)

T

tax (taks) Money that people pay to support their government. Citizens pay **taxes** for schools and other important things. (p. 224)

technology (tek nol′ə jē) The use of skills, ideas, and tools to meet people's needs. Computers and cell phones are part of modern-day **technology**. (p. 78)

trade (trād) The buying and selling of goods and services. Countries around the world **trade** many kinds of goods with each other. (p. 202)

transcontinental (trans kon tə nen′təl) Something that stretches across the continent. You can go from one coast of the country to the other on the **transcontinental** railroad. (p. 102)

transportation (trans pər tā′shən) A way of getting from one place to another. Cars, buses, and trains are all forms of **transportation**. (p. 23)

U

urban (ûr′bən) A city and its surrounding areas. Many people in **urban** communities live in tall apartment buildings. (p. 22)

V

vaccine (vak sēn′) A liquid that contains the dead or weakened germs of a certain disease. **Vaccines** have helped to cure many diseases. (p. 138)

volunteer (vol ən tîr′) A person who chooses to do something without getting paid. Marion works as a **volunteer** at the community park on Saturdays. (p. 252)

W

wildlife (wīld′līf) Animals and plants that live in an area. Alligators and panthers are some of the **wildlife** in Florida. (p. 54)

Z

zydeco (zī′də kō) Creole music from Louisiana. You can hear **zydeco** music in New Orleans. (p. 327)

pronunciation key

a **a**t; ā **a**pe; ä f**a**r; âr c**are**; e **e**nd; ē m**e**; i **i**t; ī **i**ce; îr p**ier**ce; o h**o**t; ō **o**ld; ô f**o**rk; oi **oi**l; ou **ou**t; u **u**p; ū **u**se; ü r**u**le; ů p**u**ll; ûr t**ur**n; hw **wh**ite; ng so**ng**; th **th**in; th **th**is; zh mea**s**ure; ə **a**bout, tak**e**n, penc**i**l, lem**o**n, circ**u**s

Index

This index lists many topics that appear in the book, along with the pages on which they are found. Page numbers after an *m* refer you to a map and after a *p* refer you to photographs or artwork.

A

B

C

Credits

Cover Design: The Mazer Corporation

Maps: National Geographic.; Ortelious Design, Inc.: A2–A16

Illustration Credits: Robert Barrett: 114, 116. Ken Bowser: 48, 49, 346, 348, 349, 350, 351, 352, 353, 354, 355, 356, 358, 359. Renee Daily: 77. Bob Dorsey: 2, 4, 6, 214. Mary Haverfield: 36, 366. Adam Hook: 61. Robert Korta: 141. Joe LeMonnier: 46, 80, 120, 156, 198, 234, 266, 296, 324, 360, 386. Diana Magnuson: 296, 297. Stephen Marchesi: 76. MMSD: 201, 315. Susan Moore: 81, 104. Taia Morley: 14, 335. Greg Newbold: A4, b. ©Leah Palmer: A4, t.r. Linda Pierce: 262. Jane Shasky: 43, 91. Steve Stankiewicz: 129, 190, 191, 197, 273. Val Paul Taylor: 17, 81, 96, 104, 105, 140, 206, 217, 241, 312. Bryon Thompson: 205, 343. Elizabeth Wolf: 10, 24, 28, 72, 94, 122, 158, 180, 218, 248, 282, 312. Portraits in Biographical Dictionary by Randy Hamblin, Mike Joroszko & Margaret Sanfilippo: pp. R30–R35. [TX version: ©Walter Stuart: A9. Doug Horne: A13.]

Chart/Graph Credits: Design 5 Creatives: 27, 37, 43, 49, 50, 51, 59, 60, 82, 93, 110, 146, 172, 173, 177, 179, 186, 188, 202, 204, 205, 209, 210, 224, 225, 234, 235, 247, 259, 269, 270, 287, 292, 300, 301, 303, 323, 328, 333, 341, 342, 343, 351, 364, 365, 372, 391, 402, 416, 417.

Photography Credits: All photographs are by Macmillan/McGraw-Hill School Division (MMH) and David Mager for MMH, except as noted below:

Cover, i: John Lawrence/Stone; Corel. A1-16: bdr. PhotoLink/Photo Disc. A1: clockwise from t.l.: ©Michael Krasowitz/FPG International; ©Jerry Tobias/Corbis; ©Simon Wilkinson/The Image Bank; ©Elyse Lewin Studio Inc./The Image Bank; ©LWA-Dann Tardif/Corbis Stock Market; ©Ghislain & Marie David de Lossy/The Image Bank; b.r. ©AJA Productions/The Image Bank; ©Ross Whitaker/The Image Bank; b.l. ©Vicky Kasala/The Image Bank; ©Vicky Kasala/The Image Bank; ©LWA-Dann Tardif/Corbis Stock Market; c. ©Elyse Lewin Studio Inc./The Image Bank. A2: b.r. ©Joseph Sohm/Corbis, t.r. ©Michal Bryant/Woodfin Camp and Associates. A3: t.r. ©Joseph Sohm; Visions of America/Corbis, b.l. ©National Archives. A4: m.l. ©Joseph Sohm/Corbis. A5: b.r. ©Ken Karp/MMH, t.r. ©Joseph Sohm; Visions of America/Corbis. A6: b. ©Ken Karp/MMH, m.r. ©Michelle D. Bridwell/PhotoEdit, t.r. ©National Archives. A6-7: ©Jim Cummins/FPG. A7: ©Ken Karp/MMH. A8: b.r. ©Bettmann/Corbis, bg. ©The Granger Collection. A9: ©Bettmann/Corbis. A10: b. ©Thomas Winz/Panoramic Images, t. ©David L. Brown. A11: b.l. ©Tracy Knauer 1979/Photo Researchers, Inc., b.r. ©Richard Sisk/Panoramic Images, t.l. ©Elsa Peterson 1989/Stock Boston, t.r. ©Jim Tuten/Earth Scenes. A12: t.r. ©Tommy Thompson/Black Star Publishing/PictureQuest, m.r. ©Lloyd Sutton/Masterfile, m.t.r. ©John Elk III/Stock Boston; bg. ©2000 Universal/Dreamworks. A13: ©Donald Dietz/Stock Boston. A14: bg. ©Albert J. Copley/Visuals Unlimited, t.r. ©Phyllis Picardi/Stock Boston. A15: bg. ©Bob Rowan; Progressive Images/Corbis, t.l. ©Judy Gelles/Stock Boston. A16: ©Robert Karpa/Masterfile. [TX version: A1: Row 1: l. to r. © Bob Daemmrich Photography, Inc.; ©Superstock; ©Max Spitzenberger/Bob Daemmrich Photography, Inc.; ©Bob Daemmrich Photography, Inc.; ©John Bova/Photo Researchers, Inc., ©Bob Daemmrich Photography, Inc.; ©Bob Daemmrich Photography, Inc.; ©Superstock; Row 2: l. to r. ©Max Spitzenberger/Bob Daemmrich Photography, Inc.; ©Jeff Lepore/Photo Researchers, Inc.; ©Bob Daemmrich Photography, Inc.; ©Jeff Lepore/Photo Researchers, Inc.; ©John Bova/Photo Researchers, Inc.; ©Bob Daemmrich Photography, Inc.; ©Jeff Lepore/Photo Researchers, Inc.; ©John Bova/Photo Researchers, Inc.; ©Bob Daemmrich Photography, Inc.; ©Max Spitzenberger/Bob Daemmrich Photography, Inc.; Row 3: l. to r. ©Bob Daemmrich Photography, Inc.; ©Bob Daemmrich Photo, Inc.; ©John Bova/Photo Researchers, Inc.; ©Bob Daemmrich Photography, Inc.; ©Max Spitzenberger/Bob Daemmrich Photography, Inc.; ©John Bova/Photo Researchers, Inc.; ©Bob Daemmrich Photography, Inc.; ©Bob Daemmrich Photography, Inc.; ©Walter Bibikow/Folio, Inc.; ©Gregory T. Martin/Superstock; Row 4: l. to r. ©Bob Daemmrich Photo, Inc.; ©Bob Daemmrich Photography, Inc.; ©Jeff Lepore/Photo Researchers, Inc.; ©Walter Bibikow/Folio, Inc.; ©Superstock; ©Bob Daemmrich Photography, Inc.; ©Walter Bibikow/Folio, Inc.; ©Max Spitzenberger/Bob Daemmrich Photography, Inc.; ©Jeff Lepore/Photo Researchers, Inc.; ©Bob Daemmrich Photo, Inc.; Row 5: l. to r. ©Jeff Lepore/Photo Researchers, Inc.; ©Max Spitzenberger/Bob Daemmrich Photography, Inc.; ©Bob Daemmrich Photography, Inc.; ©Superstock; ©Gregory T. Martin/Superstock; ©Jeff Lepore/Photo Researchers, Inc.; ©Gregory T. Martin/Superstock; ©Bob Daemmrich Photography, Inc., ©John Bova/Photo Researchers, Inc.; Row 6: l. to r. ©Superstock; ©John Bova/Photo Researchers, Inc.; ©Gregory T. Martin/Superstock; ©Max Spitzenberger/Bob Daemmrich Photography, Inc.; ©Bob Daemmrich Photo, Inc.; ©Bob Daemmrich Photography, Inc.; ©Walter Bibikow/Folio, Inc.; ©Max Spitzenberger/Bob Daemmrich Photography, Inc.; Row 7: l. to r. ©Jeff Lepore/Photo Researchers, Inc.; ©Walter Bibikow/Folio, Inc.; ©Bob Daemmrich Photography, Inc.; ©Bob Daemmrich Photo, Inc.; ©Jeff Lepore/Photo Researchers, Inc.; ©Max Spitzenberger/Bob Daemmrich Photography, Inc.; ©John Bova/Photo Researchers, Inc.; ©Walter Bibikow/Folio, Inc.; ©Jeff Lepore/Photo Researchers, Inc.; Row 8: l. to r. ©Gregory T. Martin/Superstock; ©Bob Daemmrich Photo, Inc.; ©Max Spitzenberger/Bob Daemmrich Photography, Inc.; ©Superstock; ©Bob Daemmrich Photography, Inc.; ©Jeff Lepore/Photo Researchers, Inc.; ©Bob Daemmrich Photography, Inc.; ©Superstock; ©Max Spitzenberger/Bob Daemmrich Photography, Inc.; ©Bob Daemmrich Photo, Inc.; Row 9: l. to r. ©Bob Daemmrich Photo; ©Bob Daemmrich/The Image Works; ©Richard Sisk/Panoramic Images; ©Bob Daemmrich Photo; ©Bob Daemmrich/The Image Works; ©Richard Sisk/Panoramic Images; ©Bob Daemmrich Photo; ©Bob Daemmrich/The Image Works; ©Richard Sisk/Panoramic Images; ©Bob Daemmrich Photo; Row 10: l. to r. ©Cathy & Gordon ILLG/Earth Scenes; ©Charles W. Mann/Photo Researchers, Inc.; ©Ron Jautz/Folio, Inc.; ©Cathy & Gordon ILLG/Earth Scenes; ©Conrad Zobel/Corbis; ©Bob Daemmrich Photo; ©Charles W. Mann/Photo Researchers, Inc.; ©Conrad Zobel/Corbis; ©Jeff Greenberg/Folio, Inc.; ©Cathy & Gordon ILLG/Earth Scenes; Row 11: l. to r. ©Superstock; ©Jeff Greenberg/Folio, Inc.; ©Mary Steinbacher/PhotoEdit; ©Charles W. Mann/Photo Researchers, Inc.; ©Ron Jautz/Folio, Inc.; ©Cathy & Gordon ILLG/Earth Scenes; ©Jeff Greenberg/Folio, Inc.; ©Superstock; ©Ron Jautz/Folio, Inc.; ©Charles W. Mann/Photo Researchers, Inc.; Row 12: l. to r. ©Ron Jautz/Folio, Inc.; ©Conrad Zobel/Corbis; ©Cathy & Gordon ILLG/Earth Scenes; ©Superstock; ©Jeff Greenberg/Folio, Inc.; ©Mary Steinbacher/PhotoEdit; ©Charles W. Mann/Photo Researchers, Inc.; ©Conrad Zobel/Corbis; ©Mary Steinbacher/PhotoEdit; ©Jeff Greenberg/Folio, Inc., m.m. ©Bob Daemmrich/The Image Works. A2: b.r. ©Joseph Sohm/Corbis; t.r. ©Michal Bryant/Woodfin Camp and Associates. A3: t.r. ©Joseph Sohm; Visions of America/Corbis; b.l. ©National Archives. A4: m.l. ©Joseph Sohm/Corbis. A5: b.r. ©Ken Karp/MMH; t.r. ©Joseph Sohm; Visions of America/Corbis. A6: b. ©Ken Karp/MMH; m.r.©Michelle D. Bridwell/PhotoEdit; t.r. ©National Archives. A6-7: ©Jim Cummins/FPG. A7: r. ©Ken Karp/MMH; b.r.Superstock. A8: m.r. Giraudon/Art Resource, NY; b.m. ©Ted Hooper/Folio, Inc.; b.l. ©Bettmann/Corbis; m.l. ©Kal Muller/Woodfin Camp/PictureQuest, ©Tom & Pat Leeson/Photo Reseachers, Inc.; t.m. Gilcrease Museum, Tulsa; t.r. ©Joel Salcido/Daemmrich Photo Associates. A9: t.m.r. Leo Touchet/Woodfin Camp & Associates; t.l. Superstock; t.r. Harry Cabluck/Associated Press; m. Bettmann/Corbis; m.r. Claudio Cruz/Associated Press; b.m.l. Don Troiani; b.l. Brown Brothers; b.m. Superstock; b.m.r. ©Bettmann Archives/Corbis; b.r. ©Jeffrey MacMillan/Folio, Inc; m.l. ©Bettmann/Corbis. A10: bg. ©David Matherly/Visuals Unlimited; c. ©William Boyce/Corbis; b.r. ©Warren Faidley/Weathersock. A12: m.l. ©Susan Van Etten/PhotoEdit; m.r. ©Natalie Fobes; bg. Zigy Caluzny. A13: t.r. Harry Cabluck/Associated Press, AP; bg. ©Daemmrich/The Image Works. A14: bg. ©Brown Brothers; b.r. ©Harvard College Library. A15: m.r. ©Dallas Theatre Center; bg. ©1998 Carol Rosegg; t.r.©Elizabeth Simpson/FPG. A16: bg. ©Grant Heilman/Grant Heilman Photography; t.l.©Steve Starr/Stock Boston.] H3: H4: b.r. The Bettman Archive; b. The Bettman Archive. H5: Frank Fisher/West Stock. H6: t.l. Matt Bradley/West Stock. H7: t.r. ©Dorling Kindersley; r. ©Rick Latoff/Photri-Microstock; b.r. Joseph H. Bailey; b.l. © Photri-Microstock; t.l. Richard T. Nowitz/Folio, Inc. H8: r. Jon Riley/Folio, Inc.; b.r. ©Dorling Kindersley; b.l. Pete Souza/Folio, Inc.; t.l. Ed Castle/Folio, Inc. H11: b. J.A. Kraulis/Master File. 8, 9:Kevin Fleming/Corbis. 10: David R. Frazier Photolibrary/Photo Researchers, Inc.. 11: Tom Bean/DRK Photo. 12: Bob Daemmrich Photos, Inc. 13: b. Bob Daemmrich/The Image Works; t. Alan Schein/The Stock Market. 14: Jeff Greenberg/PhotoEdit. 15: t. Gloria Ferniz/San Antonio Express/News; b. Tom Reel/San Antonio Express/News. 16: Bob Daemmrich/Stock • Boston. 19: John Doman/St. Paul Pioneer Press Photo. 20: J. Zimmerman/FPG International. 21: t. David Cavagnaro/Peter Arnold Inc.; b. Roxie Ricter. 22: l. David Weintraub/Stock • Boston; r. Morton Beebe, S.F./Corbis. 23: b. Joseph Sohm/ChromoSohm Inc/Corbis; t. Mark C. Burnett/Stock • Boston. 25: John Henley/The Stock Market. 26: Carl/Joan Vanderschuit/Index Stock Imagery/PictureQuest. 28: Al Keuning/Panoramic Images. 29: t. Ted Clutter/Photo Researchers, Inc.; b. Yoshie Nagao. 30: Amy C. Etra/PhotoEdit. 31: Kim Heacox/DRK Photo. 32: b. Phil Degginger/Bruce Coleman Inc.; t. Randy Brandon/AlaskaStock. 33: Jeff Greenberg– PhotoEdit. 34: r. Kent Dufault/Index Stock Imagery/PictureQuest; b. Michael Newman– PhotoEdit. 35: t. Everett Johnson/The Image Works; b. FPG International. 37: John Kieffer– Peter Arnold Inc.. 40: Tom & Pat Leeson/Photo Researchers, Inc.. 41: b. Lee Rentz/Bruce Coleman Inc.; t. John Neubauer/PhotoEdit. 42: t. Vince Streano/The Image Works; b. Jim Wark/Peter Arnold Inc.. 44: b. Bob Daemmrich/Stock • Boston; t. E.R. Degginger/Bruce Coleman Inc.. 45: FPG International. 46: Brian Smith/Matt Herald . 47: b. Jeff Greenberg/Peter Arnold Inc.; t. PhotoDisc. 48, 49: courtesy of Sean Carollo. 51: Paul McCormick/Image Bank. 52: Yoshie Nagao. 53: t.l. Steinhart Aquarium/Tom McHugh/Photo Researchers, Inc.; t.r. Michael Sacca/Earth Scenes. 54: b. Coastal Imagery; t. Mike Yamashita/Woodfin Camp and Associates. 55: r. The Granger Collection; l. Norman Myers-Bruce Coleman Inc.. 56: Photri-microstock. 57: c. SuperStock; b. SuperStock; t. SuperStock. 60: r. Joe Sohm/The Image Works. 70, 71: ART on FILE/Corbis. 72: Richard Sisk/Panoramic Images. 73: Richard T. Nowitz/Corbis. 74: John Elk III. 75: The Stock Market. 76: b. Nathan Benn/Corbis; t. Ron Sanford/International Stock. 78: b. Richard Sisk/Panoramic Images; t. Stephen Tremble. 79: t. David Muench; b. John Running. 80: r. Stephen Tremble; l. Stephen Tremble. 84: Richard T. Nowitz/Corbis. 85: t. Richard T. Nowitz/Corbis; b. Museo Navale, Genoa-Pegli/SuperStock. 86: t. The Granger Collection, New York; b. The Granger Collection, New York. 88: t. The Bettman Archive; b. The Granger Collection, New York. 89: b. Greig Cranna/Stock • Boston; t. Don Henley & Savage/Dominion Photosource. 90: The Granger Collection, New York. 94: t. The Granger Collection; b. The Granger Collection, New York. 95: Florida State Archives. 96: John Elk III/Stock • Boston. 97: The Granger Collection. 99: t. The Granger Collection; b. American Philosophical Society Library. 100: Oakland Museum of California. 101: b. David Muench; t. Gift of Mr. & Mrs. Lansell K. Christie/The Corcoran Gallery Of Art. 102: b. Chicago Historical Society; t. Denver Historical Society.. 103: Union Pacific Railroad Museum. 106: Larry Fisher. 107: t. Brown Brothers; b. Grace Davies/Omni-Photo Communications. 108: l. Brown Brothers; r. Brown Brothers. 109: t. Brown Brothers; b. Hazel Hankin/Stock • Boston. 110: Nancy A. Potter/Bruce Coleman Inc.. 111: Ellis Island Immigration Museum/ARAMARK. 114: Florida State Archives. 115: Brown Brothers. 116: t. Brown Brothers; c. Brown Brothers. 117: t. Corbis; b. The Phillips Collection, Washington D.C.. 118: Schomburg Center. 119: Bettmann/Corbis. 122: Mark Segal/Panoramic Images. 123: Michelle Bridwell/PhotoEdit/PictureQuest. 124: Mark Segal/Panoramic Images. 125: Scala/Art Resource. 126: t. Chicago Historical Society; b. Bettmann/Corbis. 127: Chicago Historical Society. 128: t.l. The Granger Collection, New York; b.l. The Granger Collection, New York; t.r. The Granger Collection, New York; b.r. Schenectady Museum; Hall of El. 129: Culver Pictures. 130: Mark Segal/Panoramic Images. 131: PhotoDisc. 132: The Granger Collection, New York. 133: t. Bettmann/Corbis; b. Bettmann/Corbis. 134: Bernardo Bucci/The Stock Market. 135: l. Photobition; r. Joseph Sohm/Chromosohm Inc./Corbis. 136: Michelle Bridwell/PhotoEdit/PictureQuest. 137: l. Bettmann/Corbis; r. Corbis. 138: t. David M. Phillips/Photo Researchers, Inc.. 139: t. Bettmann/Corbis; t.c. Bettmann/Corbis; b.c. National Portrait Gallery, Smithsonian Institution/Art Resource, NY; b. Bettmann/Corbis. 140: t. PhotoDisc; b.r. Mark Richards/PhotoEdit/PictureQuest; b.l. David Joel/Tony Stone/Getty Images. 141: Julie Houck/Corbis. 142: t. courtesy of Omar Khalid; 143: courtesy of Ross Dary. 144: Mark Segal/Panoramic Images. 146: r. Kim Blaxland/Tony Stone– Getty Images. 156: IFA/eStock Photography/PictureQuest. 158: Burke/Triolo Productions/Foodpix. 160: EyeWire/Getty Images. 161: Image Bank. 162: c. Paul Sakuma/Associated Press, AP; r. Michael Newman/PhotoEdit; l. James A. Sugar/Black Star Publishing/PictureQuest. 163: Darren Svan/Associated Press. 164: b. Bill Wilson; t. Ed Bock/The Stock Market. 165: Burke/Triolo Productions/Foodpix. 166: National Park Service. 167: t. National Park Service; b. National Park Service. 169: bg. PhotoDisc; b. PhotoDisc/Getty Images; t.r. PhotoDisc/Getty Images; t.c. PhotoDisc/Getty Images; b.l. PhotoDisc/Getty Images; b.c. PhotoDisc/Getty Images. 171: The Corcoran Gallery of Art/Corbis. 173: m.l. PhotoDisc; m.r. PhotoDisc. 175: Ron Edmonds/Associated Press. 176: courtesy of Deadra Brown. 177: courtesy of Robert Powell. 178: Index Stock Imagery. 180: t. Gary Irving/Tony Stone Images; b. Mark Richards/PhotoEdit. 181: Robert Fried/Stock • Boston. 182: Owen Franken/Corbis. 183: t. courtesy of the Mason family; b. Buddy Mays/Corbis. 184: courtesy of the Mason family. 185: t. courtesy of the Mason family; b. Hulton Getty/Liason Agency. 186: t. David Hiser–Photographers/Aspen/PictureQuest; b. Grant Heilman Photography. 187: Zefa Visual Media - Germany /Index Stock Imagery. 188: Anne-Marie Weber/FPG International. 192: FPG International/Getty Images. 193: Miles Ertman/Masterfile/TCL. 194: b.l. Ford Photomedia; b.c. Ford Photomedia; b.r. Ford Photomedia. 195: t. Bettmann/Corbis; b.l. Ford Photomedia; b.r. Ford Photomedia. 196: Index Stock Imagery. 199: Brian Haimer/PhotoEdit. 202: Gary Conner–Index Stock Imagery/PictureQuest. 203: t. George Hall/Corbis; b. Stephanie Maze–Corbis. 204: James Marshall/Corbis. 207: bg. Comstock Images; i. Henryk Kaiser/eStock Photography–PictureQuest. 209: Warren Morgan/Corbis. 210: r. Joseph Sohm/ChromoSohm Inc.. 216: Jim Pickerell/Stock Connection/PictureQuest. 218: David Young-Wolff/PhotoEdit. 219: t. Jeff Greenberg/PhotoEdit; b. Randy Faris/Corbis. 220: Chris Todd/The Clarion Ledger. 221: t. The Clarion Ledger; b. Joe Ellis/The Clarion Ledger. 222: Brian Albert Bloom/The Clarion Ledger. 223: t. Christopher D. Mims Public Affairs and Communications Office of the Mayor City of Jackson, Miss.; b. J. D. Schwalm/The Clarion Ledger. 224: b.c. Chris Todd/The Clarion Ledger; t. The Clarion Ledger; b.l. Joe Ellis/The Clarion Ledger; b.r. Joe Ellis/The Clarion Ledger. 225: t. Clarion Ledger; b.l. Melaine Duncan/Associated Press; b.c. The Clarion Ledger; b.r. Michael Pole/Corbis. 226: t. Wesley Ellis/Associated Press, AP; b. Philip Gould/Corbis. 227: The Clarion Ledger. 228: PhotoEdit. 229: Nancy Sheehan/PhotoEdit. 230: Sitki Tarlan/Panoramic Images. 231: r. Reuters NewMedia Inc./Corbis; b. Dennis Brack/Black Star. 232: b. Copyrighted by the White House Historical Association; Photograph by the National Geographic Society; t. Culver Pictures. 233: t. The Granger Collection; b. National Portrait Gallery, Smithsonian Institution/Art Resource, NY. 234: l. Doug Armand/Tony Stone/Getty Images; c. Joseph Sohm/Visions of America/Corbis; r. Lee Snider/Corbis. 236: l. Joseph Sohm/Chromosohm Inc./Corbis; r. Richard T. Nowitz; c. Michael Dick/Earth Scenes. 237: Brian K. Diggs/Associated Press; 240: Archivo Iconografico, S.A./Corbis. 241: Peter M. Wilson/Corbis. 242: Nik Wheeler/Corbis. 243: r. Carl & Ann Purcell/Corbis; l. Morry Gash/Associated Press; 244: b. Robert Frerck/Woodfin Camp and Associates; t. Nik Wheeler/Corbis. 245: Reuters NewMedia Inc./Corbis. 248: Bill Bachmann/Stock • Boston. 249: b. Dennis Brack/Black Star. 250: Richard Hutchings/PhotoEdit. 251: Andy Stacks/Stone/Getty Images; John Eastcott/Yva Momatiuk The Image Works. 252: b.l. The Western Reserve Historical Society; b.r. Robert Brenner–PhotoEdit. 253: Courtesy of Senator Liz Figueroa's Office. 254: Michael Newman–PhotoEdit/PictureQuest. 255: Tony Hopewell/FPG International. 256: Bettmann/Corbis. 257: b. Bettmann/Corbis; t. Corbis. 258: courtesy of Sinthia Franco. 259: courtesy of Jacob Matthews. 261: Jamey Penney/Associated Press, AP. 262: Elaine Thompson–Associated Press. 263: t. Diane L. Cohen/Sipa Press; b. Deborah Edwards - Oñoro. 264: t. Bettmann/Corbis; b.l. American Red Cross; b.r. American Red Cross. 265: b.l. American Red Cross; t. American Red Cross. 266: b. Radhika Chalasani/Sipa Press; t. James Rexroad 2001. 267: Jon Eeg/Associated Press. 268: David Young-Wolff/PhotoEdit/PictureQuest. 270: r. Wes Thompson/The Stock Market. 271: b. David Young-Wolff/PhotoEdit. 280: Bob Daemmrich Photos, Inc.. 282: Tom & Dee Ann McCarthy/The Stock Market. 283: t. Lawrence Migdale; b. Detroit Institute of Arts/Associated Press. 284: Bob Daemmrich Photos, Inc.. 285: t.l. Prakash Datwani; t.r. Bob Daemmrich Photos, Inc.; b. Lindsay Hebberd/Woodfin Camp and Associates. 286: Michael Newman/PhotoEdit. 288: b. Joseph Sohm/Corbis; t. Kenneth Garrett/Woodfin Camp and Associates. 289: Michael Krasowitz/FPG International/Getty Images. 292: Lawrence Migdale. 293: t. Araldo de Luca/Corbis; b. Pallas De Velletri/SuperStock. 294: t. Culver Pictures; b. Louis Psihoyos/Matrix. 295: t. Culver Pictures; c. Photo Assist–Woodfin Camp and Associates; b. Jeff Greenberg/Visuals Unlimited. 296: Jeff Greenberg/The Image Works. 297: Courtesy of Steven Kellogg/William Morrow and Company Inc. • New York. 298: b. The Granger Collection, New York; t. The Granger Collection. 302: Missouri Division of Tourism. 303: t. The Granger Collection, New York; c. The Granger Collection, New York; b. Missouri Division of Tourism. 304: t. The Granger Collection; b.l. Kay Simmon Blumberg–Museum of the City of New York; b.r. Museum of the City of New York/Berenice Abbott–Hulton|Archive by Getty Images. 305: t.l. Charles "Teenie" Harris/Corbis; t.r. Charles "Teenie" Harris/Corbis; b. David Young-Wolff/PhotoEdit. 306: b. Bettmann/Corbis; t. The Granger Collection. 307: Mug Shots/The Stock Market. 308: Gagosian Gallery, NY. 309: t. Chris Buck; b. Lawrence Migdale. 312: Stephen Morton/Associated Press, AP. 313: Les Riess; Panos Pictures. 314: Gary Conner/PhotoEdit. 315: Lawrence Migdale. 316: t. Culver Pictures; b. Polonia.net. 317: b.l. Bob Daemmrich Photos, Inc.; b.r. Bob Daemmrich Photos, Inc.. 318: t. Andy Cripe; b. Darrell Gulin/Corbis. 319: b.l. Damian Dovarganes/Associated Press; b.r. Tony Freeman/PhotoEdit. 320: t. Ariel Skelley/The Stock Market; b. Charlyn Zlotnik/Woodfin Camp and Associates. 321: Pete Saloutos/The Stock Market. 322: Bob Daemmrich Photos, Inc.. 323: Scott Barrow/International Stock. 324: The Stock Market. 325: b. The Stock Market; t. The Stock Market. 326: b. Bob Daemmrich/The Image Works; c. Photofest; t. "Back O' Town" by James Michalopoulos/New Orleans Jazz & Heritage Festival 2001 poster. 327: b. Philip Gould/Corbis; c. Philip Gould/Corbis; t. Robin May. 328: John Eastcott/Yva Momatiuk/The Image Works. 329: John Elk III; t. Phil Borden/PhotoEdit; c. Richard Cummins/Corbis; i. Jack Parsons/Omni-Photo Communications. 330: b.l. Les Riess; t. Lawrence Migdale; b.r. PhotoDisc. 331: Les Riess. 332: courtesy of Laua Zielinski. 333: courtesy of Lisa Trocchia. 334: Giacomo Pirozzi/Panos Pictures. 335: John Elk III/Bruce Coleman Inc.. 336: t. Liba Taylor/Panos Pictures; c. Jeremy Hartley/Panos Pictures; b. David Young-Wolff/PhotoEdit. 337: t. John Elk III/Bruce Coleman Inc.; b. John Elk III/Bruce Coleman Inc.. 338: t. Motherland Rhythm Art, Inc.; b.r. Bobo Burch/Bruce Coleman Inc.; b. John Elk III/Bruce Coleman Inc.. 339: Panos Pictures. 342: r. John Sohm/Stock • Boston. 348: Blair Seitz/Photo Researchers, Inc.. 350: Bob Daemmrich/Stock • Boston/PictureQuest. 351: r. Richard Hutchings/PhotoEdit; l. JonathanNourok/PhotoEdit. 352: Steve Jay Crise/Corbis. 353: SuperStock. 354: t. Flip Schulke/Corbis; b. Flip Schulke/Corbis. 355: l. National Portrait Gallery, Smithsonian Institution/Art Resource, NY; r. Bequest of Mrs. Benjamin Ogle Tayloe; Collection of The Corcoran Gallery of Art/Corbis. 356: Joseph Sohm/ChromoSohm Inc./Corbis. 358: AFP/Corbis. 359: t. Joseph Sohm/Visions of America/Corbis; b. Morton Beebe, S.F./Corbis. R52: Bernard Adnet.

Acknowledgments *(continued from page ii)*

From **The Everglades: River of Grass** by Marjory Stoneman Douglas, illustrated by Robert Fink. Copyright © 1947, (Renewed 1997), by Marjory Stoneman Douglas, Pineapple Press, Inc. Used by permission. From "Marjory Stoneman Douglas: 1890–1998: Florida's heroine; Pioneering writer, environmentalist and champion of the Everglades died this week at age 108," May 16, 1998, by Margaria Fichtner, copyright © 1998, *Knight Ridder Newspapers*. http://www.sunone.com/news/articles/05-16a.html. Used by permission. From "I Have Heard of a Land" by Joyce Carol Thomas, illustrated by Floyd Cooper. Copyright © 1998, by Joyce Carol Thomas and Floyd Cooper. Joanna Cotler Books, an imprint of HarperCollins Publishers. Used by permission. From **Between Earth and Sky, Legends of Native American Sacred Places** by Joseph Bruchac, illustrated by Thomas Locker. Copyright © 1996 by Bruchac, Locker. Harcourt Brace & Company. Used by permission. From **Communities, Adventures in Time and Place**. Copyright © 1997. Macmillan/McGraw-Hill. Used by permission. From the journal of William Clark. 26 September, 2001. http://www.pbs.org/weta/thewest/program/episodes/one/corpsof.htm Used by permission. From **Communities, Adventures in Time and Place**. Copyright © 1997. Macmillan/McGraw-Hill. Used by permission. From William A. Wieboldt letter. 26 September, 2001. http://www.chicagohs.org/fire/witnesses/wieboldt.html Used by permission. From Alexander Graham Bell quote, "Leave the beaten track…" 22 June, 2001. http://www.fitzgeraldstudio.com/html/bell/inventor.html Used by permission. From **The Babe and I** by David A. Adler, illustrated by Terry Widener. Copyright © 1999 by Adler and Widener. Gulliver Books, Harcourt Brace & Company. Used by permission. From Maggie Lena Walker. 30 October, 2001. http://www.nps.gov/malw/speech.htm Used by permission. From **Poor Richard's Almanack**. 27 September. 2001. http://library.thinkquest.org/22254/frquot.htm?tqskip=1 Used by permission. From **Working** by Studs Terkel. Copyright © 1972, 1974 by Studs Terkel. Pantheon Books, a division of Random House. Used by permission. From "The Model T Ford Club, Great Quotes by and About Henry Ford." 30 October, 2001. http://www.modelt.org/tquotes/html Used by permission. From "This Is My Country." Music by Al Jacobs, Words by Don Raye. Copyright © 1940 (Renewed). Shawnee Press, Inc., and Warock Corp. International. Copyright Secured. All Rights Reserved. Used by permission. From **Communities, Adventures in Time and Place**. Copyright © 1997. Macmillan/McGraw-Hill. Used by permission. From Helen Keller quotations on the web. 31 October, 2001. http://www.helen-keller.freeservers.com/quotes.htm Used by permission. From Doctors Without Borders Web site. 25 July, 2001. http://www.doctorswithoutborders.org/publications/voices/silvio 2001g.html Used by permission. From **My Very Own Room (Mi propio cuartito)** by Amada Irma Perez, illustrated by Maya Christina Gonzalez. Copyright © 2000 by Perez, Gonzalez. Children's Book Press, San Francisco, California. Used by permission. From **The Life of Washington** by Mason Locke Weems, 1809. 28 September, 2001. http://www.virginia.edu/gwpapers/documents/weems/Used by permission. From "Women to Watch, Maya Lin, Architect and Artists." 28 September, 2001. http://www.womenswire.com/watch/lin4/html Used by permission. From **Communities, Adventures in Time and Place**. Copyright © 1997. Macmillan/McGraw-Hill. Used by permission. From Abelardo de la Pena, Jr., "Cinco de Mayo!" 29 July, 2001. http://www.latinola.com/5demayo.html Used by permission. From "Jambalaya (On the Bayou)." Words and Music by Hank Williams. Copyright © 1952 (Renewed 1980) by Acuff-Rose Music, Inc., and Hiriam Music in the U.S.A. Used by permission.